BUSINESS MATHEMATICS AND STATISTICS

BUSINESS MATHEMATICS AND STATISTICS

G.R. Veena
Faculty-Mathematics
TISB, NAFL Valley, Bangalore

Seema Sambargi
Associate Professor
Adarsh Institute of Management and Information Technology, Bangalore

I.K. International Publishing House Pvt. Ltd.
NEW DELHI • BANGALORE

Published by

I.K. International Publishing House Pvt. Ltd.
S-25, Green Park Extension
Uphaar Cinema Market
New Delhi–110 016 (India)
E-mail: info@ikinternational.com

ISBN 978-93-82332-42-8

Published by Krishan Makhijani for I.K. International Publishing House Pvt. Ltd., S-25, Green Park Extension, Uphaar Cinema Market, New Delhi–110 016 and Printed by Rekha Printers Pvt. Ltd., Okhla Industrial Area, Phase II, New Delhi–110 020.

Preface

We wrote this book with an intention for providing a basic learning material in Mathematics and Statistics for students at the graduation level. This book could serve well to enhance the numerical and analytical skills of students pursuing B. Com and BBM of various universities across India. The concepts are presented in a simple and lucid style with ample illustrations and worked examples. Learning is reinforced by the use of thoughtful end-of-the-chapter summaries and stimulating exercises.

We would also like to place on records our acknowledgment of support and encouragement from our respective families, colleagues and friends.

We request the discerning readers to send their valuable suggestions and modifications to us at veena.gr@gmail.com or seemasambargi@gmail.com

G.R. Veena
Seema Sambargi

Contents

Part B Statistics

Part A

Mathematics

1

Number System

NUMBERS

Numbers we use for counting are called natural numbers. So $1, 2, 3 \ldots$ are natural numbers. If we add 2 natural numbers, we get again a natural number. Ex: 5 and 7 are natural numbers and $5+7=12$ is also a natural number. But if we subtract a smaller number from a bigger number or if we subtract a number from itself we won't get a natural number.

For example, $7-9=-2$ and $8-8=0$. Natural numbers including 0 and negative numbers are called integers. So $\cdots -2, -1, 0, 1, 2, \ldots$ are integers. If we add, subtract or multiply 2 integers we get again an integer. But if we divide we won't get an integer always.

For example, $5 \div 7 = \frac{5}{7}$ is not an integer.

The numbers which can be expressed in the form $\frac{p}{q}$ where p and q are integers and $q \neq 0$ are called rational numbers. In other words, a rational number is a number which can be written as a fraction with denominator not equal to zero.

EXAMPLE:

$$\frac{5}{3}, \frac{2}{8}, 9, 10 \left(\text{as } 9 = \frac{9}{1},\ 10 = \frac{10}{1}\right)$$

The rational numbers when they are expressed in decimal form are either terminating or non-terminating recurring decimals.

EXAMPLE:

$$\frac{5}{3} = 1.666\ldots$$
$$\frac{2}{8} = 0.25$$

If the decimal form is unending, non-repeating or non-terminating for a given fraction (number), then that number is irrational. Also, if there is no rational number b such that $a^x = b$ where x is a natural number. Then a is an irrational number, i.e., $a = \sqrt[x]{b}$ is irrational.

EXAMPLE:

$$\sqrt{2} = 1.41423\ldots$$
$$\pi = \frac{22}{7} = 3.1415\ldots$$
$$e = 2.718\ldots$$

In other words, irrational numbers are numbers which cannot be written as fractions, Such as π and $\sqrt{7}$ and in decimal form these numbers go on forever and the same pattern of digits is not repeated.

All the rational and irrational numbers come under the category real numbers.

$$\text{So } N = \{1, 2, 3, \ldots\} = \text{set of natural numbers}$$
$$I \text{ or } Z = \{0, \pm 1, \pm 2, \ldots\} = \text{set of integers}$$
$$Q = \{x | x = p/q \quad p, q \in z \text{ and } q \neq 0\} = \text{set of rational numbers}$$
$$R = \text{set of rational numbers union set of irrational numbers.}$$

Notice that a set of real numbers contains all rational numbers, irrational numbers, integers and natural numbers.

SOLVED EXAMPLES

1. Express $5.333\ldots$ as rational fraction

SOLUTION:
Let $x = 5.333\ldots$
Multiplying by 10,

$$10x = 53.333\ldots$$

Subtracting $10x - x = 53.333\cdots - 5.333\ldots$

$$9x = 48$$
$$x = \frac{48}{9}$$
$$\text{So} \quad 5.333\ldots = \frac{48}{9}$$

2. Express $6.131313\ldots$ as rational fraction
Let $6.131313\cdots = x$
Multiplying by 100

$$100x = 613.1313\ldots$$

Subtracting, $100x - x = 613.1313\cdots - 6.1313\ldots$

$$99x = 607$$

$$x = \frac{607}{99}$$

3. Prove that $\sqrt{2}$ is an irrational number.

Proof. If $\sqrt{2}$ is a rational number then it can be expressed as p/q where p and q are integers and $q \neq 0$.
So $\sqrt{2} = p/q$
Let p and q be so chosen that they have no common divisor, i.e., $\frac{p}{q}$ is in the simplest form
Squaring on both sides

$$2 = \frac{p^2}{q^2}$$

$$p^2 = 2q^2$$

$\Rightarrow$ p^2 is an even number
So p is an even number so it can be written as $2k$ where k is an integer.

So
$$p = 2k$$
$$(2k)^2 = 2q^2$$
$$4k^2 = 2q^2$$
$$q^2 = 2k^2 \Rightarrow q \text{ is an even number}$$

Hence, p and q are both even numbers. They have common factor 2, which contradicts the fact that p and q have no common divisors.
$\therefore$ $\sqrt{2}$ is an irrational number.

FACTOR OR DIVISOR

If a bigger natural number is divided by a smaller natural number, we get a quotient and a remainder. If the remainder = 0 in the division then the smaller number is called a factor or a divisor of the bigger number.

For example: 2 is a factor of 64.
8 is a factor of 16.

If x and y are 2 integers $x \neq 0$ is said to be a factor or divisor of y if there exists an integer k such that

$$y = kx.$$

EVEN AND ODD NUMBERS

The numbers which have 2 as their factor are called even numbers.

EXAMPLE:

$$2, 4, 6, 8, 10, 12, 14, \ldots$$

Clearly even numbers end with 0, 2, 4, 6, 8.

The numbers which are not divisible by 2 or the numbers which leave 1 as the remainder when divided by 2 are called odd numbers. Obviously odd numbers end with 1, 3, 5, 7 or 9.

Prime Numbers

A number $p > 1$ is called a prime number if its factors are ± 1 and $\pm$ itself only, i.e., it is divisible by ± 1 and itself only.

So 2, 3, 5, 7, 11, 13, 17... are prime numbers.

To test whether a given number is a prime number or not, take an integer larger than the approximate square root of the given number. Let it be x. Test the divisibility of every prime number less than x. If it is not divisible by any of them, then it is a prime number otherwise it is not.

EXAMPLE 1: 221

Consider $\sqrt{221} \simeq 15$

Prime numbers less than 15 are 2, 3, 5, 7, 11, 13.

Clearly 221 is not divisible by 2, 3, 5, 7 and 11, but it is divisible by 13, as $221 = 13 \times 17$

So 221 is not a prime number.

EXAMPLE 2: 97

$$\sqrt{97} \simeq 10$$

Prime numbers less than 10 are 2, 3, 5, 7.

Clearly 97 is not divisible by 2, 3, 5 or 7. So 97 is a prime number.

Composite Numbers

A number which has at least one divisor other than ± 1 and $\pm$ itself is a composite number. In other words, a number which is not a prime number is a composite number.

EXAMPLE:

4, 9, 10, 12, 14,... are composite numbers.

Cannonical Representation

Every composite number can be expressed as a product of prime factors. This representation is unique except for the different arrangement of factors.

For example:

(1) 75

$$75 = 3 \times 5 \times 5$$
$$= 3 \times 5^2$$

$$\begin{array}{r|l} 3 & 75 \\ \hline 5 & 25 \\ \hline 5 & 5 \\ \hline & 1 \end{array}$$

(2) 1220

$$1220 = 2 \times 5 \times 2 \times 61$$
$$= 5 \times 61 \times 2^2$$
$$= 2^2 \times 5 \times 61$$

$$\begin{array}{r|l} 2 & 1220 \\ \hline 5 & 60 \\ \hline 2 & 122 \\ \hline 61 & 61 \\ \hline & 1 \end{array}$$

The Number of Divisors and Sum of Divisors of a Composite Number

Let N be a composite number which can be expressed in the cannonical representation as

$$N = a^p b^q c^r \dots$$

where a, b, c are primes.

The number of divisors of N is given by the formula

$$(p+1)(q+1)(r+1)\dots$$

$$\text{Sum of divisors} = \frac{(a^{p+1}-1)(b^{q+1}-1)(c^{r+1}-1)\dots}{(a-1)(b-1)(c-1)\dots}$$

EXAMPLE: 24

Divisors of 24 = 1, 2, 3, 4, 6, 8, 12, 24

No. of divisors = 8.

Now let us apply the formula to verify :

$24 = 2^3 \times 3^1$

$$\begin{array}{r|l} 2 & 24 \\ \hline 2 & 12 \\ \hline 2 & 6 \\ \hline 3 & 3 \\ \hline & 1 \end{array}$$

$$\text{No. of divisors} = (3+1)(1+1)$$
$$= 4 \times 2$$
$$= 8$$

$$\text{Sum of divisors} = 1+2+3+4+6+8+12+24$$
$$= 60$$

Using the formula, we get

$$\frac{(2^{3+1}-1)(3^{1+1}-1)}{(2-1)(3-1)} = \frac{15 \times 8}{2} = 60$$

Finding the Unit Digit in a Given Number of the Form x^y

If x ends with 1, 5 or 6. Then unit digit is definitely 1, 5 or 6 itself as

$$1^2 = 1, \quad 1^3 = 1\ldots$$
$$5^2 = 25, \quad 5^3 = 125, \quad 5^4 = 625 \text{ and so on}$$
$$6^2 = 36, \quad 6^3 = 216, \quad 6^4 \text{ ends with 6 and so on.}$$

If x ends with 9 either the unit digit is 9 or 1. As $9^2 = 81$, $9^3 = 729$, $9^4 = 6561$ and so on the cycle repeats as 1, 9, 1, 9… same as the case of 4 in which cycle repeats as 6, 4, 6, 4…

If x ends with 2 the cycle repeats as 2, 4, 8, 6, 2, 4, 8, 6… i.e., unit digit is repeated after each 4 indices.

If x ends with 7 or 8 the corresponding cycles are 9, 3, 1, 7 and 4, 2, 6, 8 respectively and unit digit repeats after each 4 indices. Using these logic we can find the unit digit.

EXAMPLE: Find the unit digit in the following:

1. $(251)^{286}$

   251 ends with 1. So unit digit is 1.

2. $(257)^{63}$

   257 ends with 7

   Unit digit repeats after every 4 indices.

$$7^2 = 7 \times 7 \text{ end with 9}$$
$$7^3 = 49 \times 7 \text{ end with 3}$$
$$7^4 = \ldots 3 \times 7 \text{ end with 1}$$
$$7^5 = \ldots 1 \times 7 \text{ end with 7}$$
$$7^6 = \ldots 7 \times 7 \text{ end with 9}$$

Now,

$$4)\, 63\, (15$$
$$\underline{60}$$
$$03$$

$$63 = 15 \times 4 + 3$$
$$63 = 60 + 3$$

$$(257)^{63} = (257)^{60+3} = (257)^{60} \cdot (257)^3$$
$$\text{Unit digit of } (257)^{60} \cdot (257)^3$$
$$= \text{Unit digit of } (257)^3$$
$$= \text{Unit digit of } 7^3 = 3.$$

3. $(626)^{76}$

$$6^2 = 36$$
$6^3 = 36 \times 6 = 216$ unit digit in $(626)^{76}$ is same as $6^{76} = 6$.

4. $(252)^{54}$

Unit digit in $(252)^{54}$ is same as the unit digit in 2^{54}

Now, $2^2 = 4$
$$2^3 = 8$$
$$2^4 = 16$$
$$2^5 = 32$$
$$2^6 = 64$$

Unit digit is repeated after every 4 indices.

So

$$\begin{array}{r} 4)\ 54\ (13 \\ 4 \\ \hline 14 \\ 12 \\ \hline 2 \end{array}$$

$$2^{54} = 2^{52+2} = 2^{52} \cdot 2^2$$

Unit digit in 2^{54} is same as unit digit in 2^2

$= 4$.

5. $(679)^{780}$

Unit digit in $(679)^{780}$ is same as unit digit in 9^{780}

$$9^2 = 81$$
$$9^3 = \ldots 1 \times 9 = 9$$
$$9^4 = \ldots 9 \times 9 = \ldots 1$$

Unit digit repeats as 1, 9, 1, 9..., i.e., after every 2 indices, i.e., for odd index it is 9 and for even index it is 1.

$\therefore$ 9^{780} has the unit digit as 1.

$\therefore$ Unit digit in $(679)^{780}$ is 1.

Highest Common Factor (HCF) or Greatest Common Divisor

Consider the numbers 20 and 24

Positive divisors of 20 : 1, 2, 4, 5, 10, 20

Positive divisors of 24 : 1, 2, 3, 4, 6, 8, 12, 24.

Common divisors of 20 and 24 = 1, 2, 4.

Greatest common divisor = 4.

Incidentally we observe other common divisors of 20 and 24, i.e., 1 and 2 divides 4 divides 4, i.e., 1, 2 and 4 are factors of 4.

Definition

A positive integer d is called highest common factor or greatest common divisor of 2 integers a and b (atleast one of them being non-zero) if (i) d is a common factor of both a and b (ii) every other common factor of a and b divides d.

HCF of a and b is denoted by

$$(a,b) = d.$$

Note that 2 integers having their HCF or GCD = 1 are said to be relative prime or co-prime numbers.

i.e., a and b are relatively prime if and only if $(a,\ b) = 1$.

Methods of finding HCF

While defining HCF we listed the factors of 20 and 24 and then found HCF. This method becomes tedious when the numbers are big. So we use either factorisation or division method to find HCF.

Factorisation method: In this method, the given numbers are expressed in the cannonical form, i.e., as a product of prime factors. Then the product of common factors taken as many times as they appear gives the HCF. If there is no common factor, then HCF = 1.

Example 1: To find HCF of 224 and 460

$$224 = 2 \times 2 \times 2 \times 2 \times 2 \times 7$$

$$460 = 2 \times 2 \times 5 \times 23$$

$$\text{HCF} = 2 \times 2 = 4.$$

$$\begin{array}{r|l} 2 & 224 \\ \hline 2 & 112 \\ \hline 2 & 56 \\ \hline 2 & 28 \\ \hline 2 & 14 \\ \hline 7 & 7 \\ \hline & 1 \end{array} \qquad \begin{array}{r|l} 2 & 460 \\ \hline 2 & 230 \\ \hline 2 & 115 \\ \hline 23 & 23 \\ \hline & 1 \end{array}$$

EXAMPLE 2: To find HCF of 35, 46 and 81

$35 = 5 \times 7$

$46 = 2 \times 23$

$81 = 3 \times 3 \times 3 \times 3$

$$\begin{array}{r|l} 5 & 35 \\ \hline 7 & 7 \\ \hline & 1 \end{array} \qquad \begin{array}{r|l} 2 & 46 \\ \hline 23 & 23 \\ \hline & 1 \end{array} \qquad \begin{array}{r|l} 3 & 81 \\ \hline 3 & 27 \\ \hline 3 & 9 \\ \hline 3 & 3 \\ \hline & 1 \end{array}$$

There is no common factor in all the three.
So HCF = 1.

EXAMPLE 3:

$96 = 2^5 \times 3$

$64 = 2^6$

$81 = 3^4$

$$\begin{array}{r|l} 2 & 96 \\ \hline 2 & 48 \\ \hline 2 & 24 \\ \hline 2 & 12 \\ \hline 2 & 6 \\ \hline 3 & 3 \\ \hline & 1 \end{array} \qquad \begin{array}{r|l} 2 & 64 \\ \hline 2 & 32 \\ \hline 2 & 16 \\ \hline 2 & 8 \\ \hline 2 & 4 \\ \hline 2 & 2 \\ \hline & 1 \end{array} \qquad \begin{array}{r|l} 3 & 81 \\ \hline 3 & 27 \\ \hline 3 & 9 \\ \hline 3 & 3 \\ \hline & 1 \end{array}$$

There is no common factor in all the 3 prime factorisation
So HCF = 1.

Division method: In this method the bigger number is divided by the smaller one. If the remainder is zero, then the smaller number is the HCF. Otherwise divide the smaller number by the remainder. If the remainder in this division is zero then HCF is the first remainder. Otherwise continue the process till the zero remainder is obtained. The last non-zero remainder is HCF.

EXAMPLE 1: To find HCF of 224 and 460 by division method:

```
224) 460 (2
     448
     ---
      12) 224 (18
          12
          ---
          104
           96
          ---
            8) 12 (1
                8
              ---
               4) 8 (2
                  8
                 ---
                  0
```

Last non-zero remainder is 4.
So HCF = 4.

EXAMPLE 2: To find HCF of 35, 46 and 81.

To find HCF of 3 numbers by division method

First find the HCF of 2 numbers then find the HCF of the first HCF and the remaining number.

Now HCF of 35 and 46

```
35) 46 (1
    35
    --
    11) 35 (3
        33
        --
         2) 11 (5
            10
            --
             1) 2 (2
                2
                -
                0
```

Last non-zero remainder = 1. So HCF = 1

Clearly HCF of 1 and any number = 1.

So HCF of 1 and 81 = 1 as

```
1) 81 (81
   81
   --
   00
```

Last non-zero remainder = 1.

So HCF of 35, 46 and 81 = 1.

Least Common Multiple (LCM)

Consider the numbers 3 and 5

Multiples of 3 = 3, 6, 9, 12, 15, 18, 21, 24, 27, 30, 33,...

Multiples of 5 = 5, 10, 15, 20, 25, 30, 35, 40, 45, 50,...

Common multiples of 3 and 5 = 15, 30, 45,...

Least common multiple = 15.

Incidentally 15 divides other common multiples 30, 45,...

Definition

A positive number l is called the least common multiple of a and b if

(i) both a and b divide l

(ii) l divides every other common multiples of a and b.

Methods of finding LCM

While defining LCM, we found LCM of 3 and 5 by writing the multiples of 3 and 5. This method is tedious when the numbers are big. So we use either factorisation or division method to find LCM.

Factorisation method: The given numbers are expressed as a product of prime factors, i.e., in cannonical representation. LCM is the product of highest powers of each factor.

EXAMPLE:

(1) To find LCM of 48 and 72 :

$$48 = 2^4 \times 3$$
$$72 = 2^3 \times 3^2$$
$$\text{LCM} = 2^4 \times 3^2 = 16 \times 9 = 144$$

$$\begin{array}{r|l} 2 & 48 \\ 2 & 24 \\ 2 & 12 \\ 2 & 6 \\ 3 & 3 \\ & 1 \end{array} \qquad \begin{array}{r|l} 2 & 72 \\ 2 & 36 \\ 2 & 18 \\ 3 & 9 \\ 3 & 3 \\ & 1 \end{array}$$

(2) To find LCM of 86, 98 and 104

$$86 = 2 \times 43$$
$$98 = 2 \times 7^2$$
$$104 = 2^3 \times 13$$
$$\text{LCM} = 2^3 \times 43 \times 7^2 \times 13 = 219128$$

$$\begin{array}{r|l} 2 & 86 \\ 43 & 43 \\ & 1 \end{array} \qquad \begin{array}{r|l} 2 & 98 \\ 7 & 49 \\ 7 & 7 \\ & 1 \end{array} \qquad \begin{array}{r|l} 2 & 104 \\ 2 & 52 \\ 2 & 26 \\ 13 & 13 \\ & 1 \end{array}$$

Division method: The given numbers are written in a line and divided by any prime factor which divides at least 2 of them. The quotient and non-multiples are written and the process is repealed till relatively prime numbers (i.e., no common factor except 1) are obtained. The product of all these gives the LCM.

EXAMPLE: To find LCM of 86, 98 and 104

$$\begin{array}{r|l} 2 & 86, 98, 104 \\ \hline & 43, 49, 52 \end{array}$$

$$= 2 \times 43 \times 49 \times 52$$
$$= 219128$$

Relation between HCF and LCM

If l and d are LCM and HCF of 2 numbers a and b then

$$a \times b = l \times d$$

i.e., product of 2 numbers = Product of their LCM and HCF.

EXAMPLE: Let 35 and 40 be two numbers

$$\begin{aligned} 35 &= 5 \times 7 \\ 40 &= 2 \times 2 \times 2 \times 5 \\ \text{LCM} &= 5 \times 2^3 \times 7 = 280 \\ \text{HCF} &= 5 \end{aligned}$$

$$\begin{array}{r|l} 5 & 35 \\ \hline 7 & 7 \\ \hline & 1 \end{array} \qquad \begin{array}{r|l} 2 & 40 \\ \hline 2 & 20 \\ \hline 2 & 10 \\ \hline 5 & 5 \\ \hline & 1 \end{array}$$

$$\text{LCM} \times \text{HCF} = 280 \times 5 = 1400$$

$$\text{Product of numbers} = 35 \times 40 = 1400$$

LCM and HCF of Fractions

To find LCM and HCF of 2 or more fractions, we use the formula

$$\text{LCM} = \frac{\text{LCM of numerator}}{\text{HCF of denominator}}$$

$$\text{HCF} = \frac{\text{HCF of numerator}}{\text{LCM of denominator}}$$

EXAMPLE: To find LCM and HCF of

$$\frac{1}{5}, \frac{2}{3}, \frac{1}{2}$$

$$\text{Numerators}: 1, 2, 1$$

$$\text{LCM of numerators is } 2$$

$$\text{HCF of numerators} = 1$$

$$\text{Denominators}: 5, 3, 2$$

$$\text{LCM} = 5 \times 3 \times 2 = 30$$

$$\text{HCF} = 1$$

$$\begin{aligned} \text{Now LCM} &= \frac{\text{LCM of numerator}}{\text{HCF of denominator}} \\ &= \frac{2}{1} = 2 \end{aligned}$$

$$\text{HCF} = \frac{\text{HCF of numerator}}{\text{LCM of denominator}} = \frac{1}{30}$$

LCM and HCF of Decimals

To find LCM and HCF of decimals, eliminate decimals with appropriate multiplication either by 10 or 100 or 1000. Then find LCM or HCF. Divide the answer by the multiplied factor 10, 100 or 1000.

EXAMPLE: To find HCF & LCM of

3.2, 4.12, 1.3, and 7.

Multiplying the numbers by 100 to remove decimals, we get

320, 412, 130 and 700.

Now we find HCF:

```
320) 412 (1              130) 700 (5
     320                      650
     92) 320 (3                50) 130 (2
         276                       100
         44) 92 (2                  30) 50 (1
             88                         30
              4) 44 (1                  20) 30 (1
                 44                         20
                 00                         10) 20 (2
                                                20
                                                00
```

```
HCF of 320 and 412 is 4          4) 10 (2
                                     8
HCF of 130 and 700 is 10             2) 4 (2
                                        4
Now HCF of 4 and 10 is 2                0
```

So HCF of 320, 412, 130 and 700 is 2.

We multiplied all numbers by 100 earlier.

So dividing by 100 we get

HCF of 3.2, 4.12, 1.3 and 7 = 0.02.

Now to find LCM;

```
10 | 320,  412,  130,  700
 2 | 32,   412,  13,   70
 2 | 16,   206,  13,   35
   | 8,    103,  13,   35 → 8, 103, 13 and 35 are relatively prime
```

So LCM $= 10 \times 2 \times 2 \times 8 \times 103 \times 13 \times 35 = 14996800$

Dividing by 100 we get LCM of 3.2, 4.12, 1.3 and 7 as 1499.68

Note

1. HCF of fractions is always a fraction but LCM may be a fraction or a whole number.
2. The greatest number that will exactly divide x, y, z is HCF of x, y, z.
3. The greatest number that will divide x, y, z leaving remainder a, b, c respectively is the HCF of $x-a, y-b$ and $z-c$.
4. Least number which is exactly divisible by x, y and z is LCM x, y and z
5. Least number which when divided by x, y, z leaves the same remainder 'r' in each case would be [LCM of x, y, and z] $+r$

SOLVED EXAMPLES

1. Three strings of different lengths, 240 cm, 318 cm and 426 cm are to be cut into equal lengths. What is the greatest possible length of each piece?

SOLUTION:

We are trying to find what the 3 numbers have in common, i.e., a common factor. All 3 numbers must be able to be divided by the same number in order for all 3 strings to be cut into equal lengths. HCF is needed here because we are asked to find the greatest possible length.

Therefore,

$$\begin{array}{r|l} 2 & 240,\ \ 318,\ \ 426 \\ \hline 3 & 120,\ \ 159,\ \ 213 \\ \hline & \ \ 40,\ \ \ 53,\ \ \ 71 \end{array}$$

Divide by common factor 2
Divide by common factor 3

$$\text{HCF} = 2 \times 3 = 6$$

$\therefore$ The greatest possible length of each piece is 6 cm.

2. Two lighthouses flash their lights every 20 seconds and 30 seconds respectively. Given that they flashed together at 7 pm, when will they next flash together?

SOLUTION:

By trial and error we can find

First lighthouse flashes at 20, 40, 60 seconds
Second lighthouses flashes after 30, 60, 90 seconds

60 is a multiple common to 20 and 30, and thus the lighthouses will flash together in 60 seconds, i.e., at 7:01 pm.

This is same as finding the lowest common multiple, LCM of 20 and 30,

$$\begin{array}{r|l} 2 & 20,\ 30 \\ \hline 5 & 10,\ 15 \\ \hline & 2,\ 3 \end{array}$$

Divide by common factor 2

Divide by common factor 5

1 is the only common factor stop here.

$$\begin{aligned} \text{LCM} &= 5 \times 2 \times 2 \times 3 \\ &= 60\text{s} \\ &= 1 \text{ min} \end{aligned}$$

Both lighthouses flash together at every 1-min intervals.

∴ Time that they will next flash together = 7.01 pm

3. The HCF of 2 numbers is 11 and LCM is 693. If one of the numbers is 77, find the other.

SOLUTION:

$$\text{we have } l \times d = a \times b$$

$$\begin{aligned} b &= \frac{l \times d}{a} \\ &= \frac{11 \times 693}{77} \\ &= 99 \end{aligned}$$

So the other number is 99.

4. Find the largest number having 4 digits divisible by 12, 15, 18, 27

SOLUTION:

The largest number having 4 digits is 9999.

LCM of 12, 15, 18, 27 is 540

on dividing 9999 by 540 we get 279 as remainder,

Therefore the required number = 9999 – 279 = 9720.

5. Find least number which when divided by 20, 25, 35, 40 leaves remainders 14, 19, 29, 34 respectively.

SOLUTION:

$$\begin{aligned} 20 - 14 &= 6 \\ 25 - 19 &= 6 \\ 35 - 29 &= 6 \\ 40 - 34 &= 6 \end{aligned}$$

$$\begin{array}{r|llll} 5 & 20, & 25, & 35, & 40 \\ \hline 4 & 4, & 5, & 7, & 8 \\ \hline & 1, & 5, & 7, & 2 \end{array}$$

$$\begin{aligned} LCM &= 5 \times 4 \times 5 \times 7 \times 2 \\ &= 1400 \end{aligned}$$

Therefore, the required number = LCM of (20, 25, 35, 40) – 6

= 1400 – 6

= 1394.

6. Express $\frac{1095}{1168}$ in the simplest form:

$$\begin{array}{l} 1095)\ 1168\ (1 \\ \quad\ \ \underline{1095} \\ \qquad\ \ 73)\ 1095\ (15 \\ \qquad\qquad\ \ \underline{73} \\ \qquad\qquad\ 365 \\ \qquad\qquad\ \underline{365} \\ \qquad\qquad\quad 0 \end{array}$$

So, HCF is 73
Therefore,

$$\frac{1095/73}{1168/73} = 15/16$$

$$\frac{1095}{1168} = \frac{15}{16}$$

7. Find the GCD of 1.08, 0.36, 0.9

SOLUTION:
Multiplying by 100 and finding HCF of 108, 36, 90

$$\begin{array}{l} 36)\ 90\ (2 \\ \quad\ \ \underline{72} \\ \quad\ 18)\ 36\ (2 \\ \qquad\quad \underline{36} \\ \qquad\quad\ 0 \end{array}$$

HCF of 18 and 108 is 18

$$\begin{array}{l} 18)\ 108\ (6 \\ \quad\ \ \underline{108} \\ \qquad\ 0 \end{array}$$

Now, dividing by 100 to get HCF of 1.08, 0.36, 0.9 as 0.18.

8. Three numbers are in ratio 1 : 2 : 3 and HCF is 12. Find the numbers.

SOLUTION:
Let the three numbers be x, $2x$, $3x$. Therefore HCF is

$$\begin{array}{l} 2x)\ 3x\ (1 \\ \quad\ \ \underline{2x} \\ \qquad x)\ 2x\ (2 \\ \qquad\quad\ \underline{2x} \\ \qquad\qquad 0 \end{array}$$

HCF is x so, x is 12

Therefore, numbers are 12, 24, 36.

9. The sum of two numbers is 216 and their HCF is 27. Find the numbers.

SOLUTION:

Let the numbers be $27a$ and $27b$. Where a and b are co-prime numbers.

$$27a+27b=216$$
$$a+b=216/27=8$$

Since a and b are co-prime, a and b may be 1 and 7 or 3 and 5.

$$27(1)+27(7)=216$$

So the numbers are 27 and 89 or 27(3) and 27 (5) i.e., 81 and 135

10. The LCM of two numbers is 48. The numbers are in ratio 2 : 3. Find the sum of numbers:

SOLUTION:

Let the numbers be $2x$, $3x$

LCM of $2x$, $3x$ is $6x$

Therefore,

$$6x=48$$
$$x=8,$$

The numbers are 16 and 24

Their sum $=16+24=40$.

11. The HCF and LCM of two numbers are 84 and 21. If ratio of two numbers is 1 : 4. Then find the larger of two numbers

SOLUTION:

Let the numbers be x, $4x$

$$\text{Then } x\times 4x=84\times 21$$
$$x^2=84\times 21/4$$
$$x=21$$
$$\text{Larger number is } 4\times 21=84$$

12. Find the maximum number of students among them, 1001 chocolates and 910 biscuits can be distributed in such a way that each student gets same number of chocolates and same number of biscuits.

SOLUTION:

HCF of 1001 and 910

$$\begin{array}{r} 910)\ 1001\ (1 \\ 910 \\ \hline 91)\ 910\ (10 \\ 910 \\ \hline 0 \\ \hline \end{array}$$

Therefore, HCF = 91

Max number of students = 91.

13. Find the least number which should be added to 2497 so that the sum is divisible by 5, 6, 4, 3?

SOLUTION:

LCM of 5, 6, 4, 3 is 60.

On dividing 2497 by 60 we get 37 as remainder.

Therefore, number to be added is $60 - 37 = 23$.

So 23 should be added to 2497 to make it divisible by 5, 6, 4, 3.

14. Find the least number which is a perfect square and is divisible by each of numbers 16, 20, 24?

SOLUTION:

LCM of 16, 20, 24 is 240.

$$\begin{aligned} 240 &= 2 \times 2 \times 2 \times 2 \times 3 \times 5 \\ &= 2^2 \times 2^2 \times 3 \times 5 \end{aligned}$$

To make it a perfect square multiply by 3×5

Therefore, $240 \times 3 \times 5 = 3600$

So 3600 is the least perfect square number divisible by 16, 20 and 24.

IN A NUTSHELL

- Natural numbers: $\{1, 2, 3, \ldots\} = N$
- Integers $= \{0, \pm 1, \pm 2, \pm 3, \ldots\} = Z$ or I
- Rational numbers: $\left\{ \begin{array}{l} x | x = \dfrac{p}{q} \quad q \neq 0 \\ p \text{ and } q \text{ are integers} \end{array} \right\}$

- Irrational numbers: If decimal form of rational number is unending, non-repeating or non-terminating then it is an irrational number. Also if there is no rational number as such that $a^b = m$ when b is a whole number then a is irrational.
- Real numbers: Set containing both rational and irrational numbers $= R$
- Even numbers: Multiples of 2
- Odd numbers: The numbers which are not even
- Prime numbers: A number $p > 1$ which is divisible by 1 and itself only.
- Composite number: A number which is not a prime number
- Cannonical representation–Prime factorisation. Representing a composite number as a product of prime factors.
- HCF or GCD of 2 numbers a and b is d if d is a factor of both a and b and every other common factor of a and b divides 'd'.
- If HCF or GCD of 2 numbers a and $b = 1$. Then they are relatively prime or co-prime.
- LCM of 2 numbers a and b is l if both a and b divide l and l divides every other common multiple of a and b.
- Product of numbers = Product of their HCF and LCM i.e., $ab = l \times d$.
- HCF of fractions $= \dfrac{\text{HCF of numerators}}{\text{LCM of denominators}}$
- LCM of fractions $= \dfrac{\text{LCM of numerators}}{\text{HCF of denominators}}$
- To find LCM or HCF of decimals, multiply by appropriate number 100 or 1000 or 10,000 to make it a whole number. Then find the HCF or LCM finally divide the HCF of LCM by the number with which the numbers where multiplied.

CHECK YOUR PROGRESS

1. Factor into primes:
   a) 50 b) 34 c) 800 d) 72 e) 32 f) 67 g) 555 h) 79 i) 1440

   [**Ans.** $a) 2 \times 5^2$ $b) 2 \times 17$ $c) 2^5 \times 5^2$ $d) 2^3 \times 3^2$ $e) 2^5$ $f) 67$ $g) 3 \times 5 \times 37$ $h) 79$ $i) 2^5 \times 3^2 \times 5$]

2. List all the factors:
   a) 50 b) 34 c) 25 d) 72 e) 137 f) 51
   [a) 1, 2, 5, 10, 25, 50 b) 1, 2, 17, 34 c) 1, 5, 25
   d) 1, 2, 3, 4, 6, 8, 9, 12, 18, 24, 36, 72 e) 1, 137
   f) 1, 3, 17, 451]
3. Find the HCF of each pair of numbers:
   a) 10 and 16 b) 28 and 77 c) 36 and 48 d) 200 and 300
   [a) 2 b) 7 c) 12 d) 100]
4. Find the LCM of each pair of numbers:
   a) 4 and 6 b) 10 and 16 c) 20 and 30 d) 200 and 300
   [a) 12 b) 80 c) 60 d) 600]
5. Biscuits, instant noodles and water bottles are distributed to each refugee in a refugee camp. If a day's consumption is 284 packets of biscuits, 426 packets of instant noodles and 710 bottles of water, how many refugees are there in the camp? [142 refugees]
6. 294 blue balls, 252 pink balls and 210 yellow balls are distributed equally among some students with none left over. What is the biggest possible number of students? [42 students]
7. A group of girls bought 72 rainbow hairbands, 144 brown and black hairbands, and 216 bright coloured hairbands. What is the largest possible number of girls in the group? [72 girls]
8. A man has a garden measuring 84 m by 56 m. He wants to divide it equally into the minimum number of square plots. What is the length of each plot? [28 m]
9. Lakshmi wants to cut identical squares as big as she can from a piece of paper 168 mm by 196 mm. What is the length of each square? [28 cm]
10. 32 girls and 52 boys were on an overseas learning trip, and they were divided into as many groups as possible where the number of groups of girls and the number of groups of boys are the same. How many girls and how many boys are there in each group? [8 girls, 13 boys]
11. A small bus interchange has 2 feeder services that start simultaneously at 9 am. Bus number 201 leaves the interchange at 15-min intervals, while bus number 500 leaves at 20-min intervals. On a particular day, how many times did both services leave together from 9 am to 12 noon inclusive? [4 times]

12. Karuna, Geeta and Jaya were jumping up a flight of stairs. Karuna did 2 steps at a time, Geeta 3 steps at a time while Jaya 4 steps at a time. If they started on the same bottom step, on which step will all 3 land together the first time? [12th step]

13. Hema helps out at her mum's stall every 9 days while her sister every 3 days. When will they be together if they last helped on June 16, 2008? [June 25, 2008]

14. A group of students can be further separated into groups of 5,13 and 17. What is the smallest possible total number of students? [1105 students]

15. Jyothi goes to market every 64 days. Chirag goes to the same market every 72 days. They met each other one day. How many days later will they meet again? [576 days]

16. Mrs Girija and 3 of her friends went to a supermarket and found that a package of 6 dish cloths cost Rs.10. If they were to share the purchase such that each has the same number ofdish cloths, what is the minimum amount each has to pay? [Rs. 5]

17. Find the HCF of $\frac{4}{9}, \frac{10}{21}$ and $\frac{20}{63}$ [2/63]

18. Find the LCM of $\frac{2}{5}, \frac{81}{100}$ and $\frac{125}{302}$ [20250]

19. Find the LCM of 1.6, 0.28, 3.2, 4.9 [784]

20. Find the number of divisors and sum of divisors of 600 [24, 1110]

21. Find the unit digit in
    a. 551^{24} b. 626^{551} c. 679^{68} d. 9995^{99} [a. 1 b. 6 c. 1 d. 5]

22. Express 1.66666... as a rational fraction $\left[\frac{5}{3}\right]$

23. Check whether 331 is a prime or not? [331 is a prime number]

2

Theory of Equations

INTRODUCTION

Consider the algebraic expression

$$(x+y)^2 = x^2 + y^2 + 2xy$$

This expression holds good for all the values of x and y. Such an expression having '=' sign and holds for any values of unknowns involved is called an identity. Some of the algebraic identities are

$$(x-y)^2 = x^2 + y^2 - 2xy$$
$$x^2 - y^2 = (x+y)(x-y)$$
$$(x+y)^3 = x^3 + y^3 + 3xy(x+y)$$
$$(x-y)^3 = x^3 - y^3 - 3xy(x-y)$$
$$(x^3 + y^3) = (x+y)(x^2 - xy + y^2)$$

Now consider the expressions

$$x + 7 = 9.$$
$$x^2 - 2 = 7$$

In these expressions, the equality holds only for a particular value(s) of the unknowns involved it is called an equation.

So $x+7=9$ holds only when $x=2$

$x^2-2=7$ holds only when $x=+3$ or -3

The value(s) of unknown x that satisfies the equation is called a root(s) or solution of the equation.

An equation involving only one variable is called an ordinary equation.

EXAMPLE:

(i) $3x - 7 = 8$

(ii) $4x^2 + 8x + 1 = 0$

(iii) $x^3 - 6 = 2$

TYPES OF EQUATION

An ordinary equation involving only the first power of the unknown or an equation of the form $ax+b=0$ with $a \neq 0$ is called a linear equation.

EXAMPLE:

(i) $3x-7=8$

(ii) $\frac{x.}{2}+6=7$

An ordinary equation having highest power of unknown $=2$ or an equation of the form $ax^2+bx+c=0$ with $a \neq 0$ is called a quadratic equation.

EXAMPLE:

(i) $3x^2+8x-1=0$

(ii) $x^2+4=0$

(iii) $\frac{x^2}{4}-\frac{x}{2}=9$

An ordinary equation having highest power of unknown $=3$ or an equation of the form $ax^3+bx^2+cx+d=0$ with $a \neq 0$ is called a cubic equation.

EXAMPLE:

(i) $3x^3-4x^2+8x-1=0$

(ii) $x^3+x-1=0$

(iii) $4x^3+8=0$

If the highest power of unknown $=4$ in an ordinary equation then it is called biquadratic or quinic equation. If the highest power of unknown is n where $n \geq 5$, then it is called an equation of degree n.

In general, it is of the form

$$a_1x^n+a_2x^{n-1}+....+a_n=0$$

where $a_1 \neq 0$.

Linear Equations

An equation of the form $ax+b=0$ with $a \neq 0$ is called a linear equation.

Solution of linear equation: The value of unknown x which satisfies the linear equation is called solution or the root of the equation

Consider

$$ax + b = 0$$

$$ax = -b$$

$$x = -\frac{b}{a}$$

So linear equation has only one solution.

Note

The terms present to the lef' of the '=' sign are called left hand side (LHS). and that present to the right of the '=' sign are called right hand side (RHS). While shifting the terms from one side of the equation to the other side, reverse operation is taken.

EXAMPLE:

(i) If $x + 4 = 9$

Then shifting 4 to RHS, we get

$$x = 9 - 4$$

$$x = 5.$$

(ii) If $x - 4 = 9$

Shifting 4 to RHS, we get

$$x = 9 + 4$$

$$x = 13.$$

(iii) If $3x = 7$

Shifting 3 to other side, we get

$$x = \frac{7}{3}$$

(iv) If $\frac{x}{2} = 7$

Shifting 2 to other side, we get

$$x = 7 \times 2$$

$$x = 14.$$

So for addition reverse operation is subtraction and vice versa. For multiplication reverse operation is division and vice versa.

SOLVED EXAMPLES

1. Find the value of x if

$$4x+8=6(x-4)$$

SOLUTION:

$$4x+8=6(x-4)$$

$$4x+8=6x-24$$

Shifting $4x$ to RHS and 24 to LHS we get

$$8+24=6x-4x$$

$$32=2x$$

$$\Rightarrow \quad x=\frac{32}{2}=16$$

Verification: $4x+8=6(x-4)$

Put $x=16$

$$4(16)+8=6(16-4)$$

$$64+8=6(12)$$

$$72=72$$

2. Solve: $3(x-4)+26=9-8(x+2)$

Consider $3(x-4)+26=9-8(x+2)$

$$3x-12+26=9-8x-16$$

$$3x+14=-8x-7$$

$$3x+8x=-7-14$$

$$11x=-21$$

$$x=\frac{-21}{11}$$

3. Find the value of x if

$$4(x+2)-2(x-2)=6x-9$$

SOLUTION:

$$4x+8-2x+4=6x-9$$

$$2x+12=6x-9$$

$$12+9=6x-2x$$

$$21=4x$$

$$\Rightarrow \quad x=\frac{21}{4}.$$

4. Express x in terms of a and b if
$b(x-a) = a^2 - bx$

SOLUTION:

$$\text{Consider} \quad b(x-a) = a^2 - bx$$
$$bx - ab = a^2 - bx$$
$$bx + bx = a^2 + ab$$
$$2bx = a(a+b)$$
$$x = \frac{a(a+b)}{2b}$$

5. Find t if $\frac{t+1}{3} - \frac{t-1}{2} = t+7$

$$\text{Consider} \quad \frac{t+1}{3} - \frac{t-1}{2} = t+7$$
$$\frac{2(t+1) - 3(t-1)}{6} = t+7$$
$$\frac{2t+2-3t+3}{6} = \frac{t+7}{1}$$
$$\frac{-t+5}{6} = \frac{t+7}{1}$$

Cross-multiplying

$$1(-t+5) = 6(t+7)$$
$$-t+5 = 6t+42$$
$$5-42 = 6t+t = 7t$$
$$-37 = 7t \quad \Rightarrow \quad t = \frac{-37}{7}$$

6. Solve: $\frac{x+1}{-x-5} = \frac{2x-1}{3-2x}$

Consider $\frac{x+1}{-x-5} = \frac{2x-1}{3-2x}$

Cross-multiplying

$$(x+1)(3-2x) = (-x-5)(2x-1)$$
$$3x+3-2x^2-2x = -2x^2+x-10x+5$$
$$x+3-2x^2 = -2x^2-9x+5$$
$$x-2x^2+2x^2+9x = 5-3$$
$$10x = 2$$
$$x = \frac{2}{10} = \frac{1}{5}$$

7. Solve: $\dfrac{x+7}{x-2}+\dfrac{x+3}{x+4}=2$

Consider

$$\frac{x+7}{x-2}+\frac{x+3}{x+4}-2=0$$

$$\frac{x-2+2+7}{x-2}+\frac{x+3+1-1}{x+4}-2=0 \quad \text{(Note this step)}$$

$$\frac{x-2}{x-2}+\frac{9}{x-2}+\frac{x+4}{x+4}-\frac{1}{x+4}-2=0$$

$$1+\frac{9}{x-2}+1-\frac{1}{x+4}-2=0$$

$$\frac{9}{x-2}-\frac{1}{x+4}=0$$

$$\frac{9}{x-2}=\frac{1}{x+4}$$

$$9(x+4)=1(x-2)$$

$$9x+36=x-2$$

$$9x-x=-2-36$$

$$8x=-38$$

$$x=\frac{-38}{8}=\frac{-19}{4}$$

8. If the sum of 2 consecutive odd numbers is 104. Find the numbers.

Let one odd number be x, its consecutive odd number $= x+2$

Given:

$$\text{Their sum } = 104$$

$$x+x+2=104$$

$$2x+2=104$$

$$2x=102$$

$$x=51$$

So the consecutive odd numbers are 51 and 53.

9. A number decreased by 15 is same as 9 decreased by 2 times the number. Find the number.

Let the number be x

A number decreased by 15 is $x-15$

2 times the number $= 2x$

9 decreased by 2 times the number $9-2x$

Given:

$$x - 15 = 9 - 2x$$
$$x + 2x = 15 + 9$$
$$3x = 24$$
$$x = 8.$$

So the required number is 8.

10. Arun's age is twice of Raj's age. If their total age is 75 . Find their ages.
Let Arun's age be x
Raj's age $= 2x$
Given:

$$x + 2x = 75$$
$$3x = 75$$
$$x = 25$$

So Arun's age $= 25$ and Raj's age $= 50$.

Quadratic Equation

An equation of the form $ax^2 + bx + c = 0$ with $a \neq 0$ is called quadratic equation.

EXAMPLE:

(i) $3x^2 + x + 1 = 0$
(ii) $4x^2 - 1 = 0$
(iii) $x^2 + x - 1 = 0$

Solution of quadratic equation

1. **Factorisation method:** In this method, $ax^2 + bx + c = 0$ is factorised into 2 linear factors. Equating each of the linear factor to zero, we get the solution.

EXAMPLE: To solve $6x^2 + 5x - 1 = 0$

$$6x^2 + 6x - 1x - 1 = 0$$
$$6x(x+1) - 1(x+1) = 0$$
$$(6x-1)(x+1) = 0$$
$$6x - 1 = 0 \quad \text{or} \quad x + 1 = 0$$
$$6x = 1$$
$$x = \frac{1}{6} \quad \text{or} \quad x = -1$$

$$-6x^2 \left\langle \begin{array}{l} +6x \\ -1x \\ \hline +5x \end{array} \right.$$

2. **Formula method:** We can get the roots or solution of quadratic equation $ax^2+bx+c=0$ by using the formula

$$x=\frac{-b\pm\sqrt{b^2-4ac}}{2a}.$$

The formula is obtained by completing the square method, as follows :

Consider

$$ax^2+bx+c=0 \div \text{ by } a,$$

$$a\left[x^2+\frac{b}{a}+\frac{c}{a}\right]=0$$

$$x^2+\frac{b}{a}+\frac{c}{a}=0 \qquad \text{adding and subtracting } \left(\frac{b}{2a}\right)^2 \text{ to make it a perfect square}$$

$$x^2+\frac{b}{a}+\left(\frac{b}{2a}\right)^2-\left(\frac{b}{2a}\right)^2-\frac{c}{a}=0$$

$$\left(x+\frac{b}{2a}\right)^2=\left(\frac{b}{2a}\right)^2-\frac{c}{a}$$

$$x+\frac{b}{2a}=\pm\sqrt{\frac{b^2}{(2a)^2}-\frac{c}{a}}$$

$$x=-\frac{b}{2a}\pm\sqrt{\frac{b^2-4ac}{(2a)^2}}$$

$$x=-\frac{b}{2a}\pm\frac{\sqrt{b^2-4ac}}{\sqrt{4a^2}}$$

$$x=\frac{-b\pm\sqrt{b^2-4ac}}{2a}.$$

Example: To solve $6x^2+5x-1=0$ by formula method :

$a=6,\ b=5$ and $c=-1$

$$\text{formula }: x=\frac{-b\pm\sqrt{b^2-4ac}}{2a}$$

$$x=\frac{-5\pm\sqrt{5^2-4(6)(-1)}}{2(6)}$$

$$x=\frac{-5\pm\sqrt{25+24}}{12}$$

$$x=\frac{-5\pm 7}{12}=\frac{-5+7}{12} \quad \text{or} \quad \frac{-5-7}{12}$$

$$x = \frac{2}{12} \quad \text{or} \quad \frac{-12}{12}$$

$$x = \frac{1}{6} \quad \text{or} \quad -1$$

Note:

Quadratic equation has 2 and only 2 roots. These 2 roots may be equal or unequal. Above example has 2 unequal roots -1 and $\frac{1}{6}$ where as x^2+2x+1 has 2 equal roots as 1.

Solved Examples

1. Solve by factorisation method:

$$x^2 - 16x + 64 = 0 \qquad 64x^2 \left\langle \begin{array}{l} -8x \\ -8x \\ \hline -16x \end{array} \right.$$

$$x^2 - 8x - 8x + 64 = 0$$

$$x(x-8) - 8(x-8) = 0$$

$$(x-8)(x-8) = 0$$

$$x - 8 = 0$$

$$x = 8.$$

2. Solve by formula method:

$2x^2 + 4x - 11 = 0$

Solution:

Comparing with $ax^2 + bx + c = 0$

$a = 2,\ b = 4,\ c = -11$

$$x = \frac{-b \pm \sqrt{b^2 - 4ac}}{2a} \qquad \text{(formula)}$$

$$x = -\frac{4 \pm \sqrt{4^2 - 4(2)(-11)}}{2(2)}$$

$$x = -\frac{4 \pm \sqrt{16 + 88}}{4}$$

$$x = -1 \pm \frac{\sqrt{104}}{4}$$

3. Solve: $\sqrt{x+2}\,.\sqrt{x-1} = \sqrt{x+8}$

Consider $\sqrt{x+2}\,.\sqrt{x-1} = \sqrt{x+8}$

Squarring on both sides

$$(x+2)(x-1) = x+8$$

$$x^2 + 2x - x - 2 = x + 8$$

$$x^2 + x - 2 - x - 8 = 0$$
$$x^2 - 10 = 0$$
$$x^2 = 10$$
$$x = \pm\sqrt{10}.$$

4. Solve: $t^4 - 10t^2 + 9 = 0$.
Let $t^2 = x$.

$$(x^2) - 10x + 9 = 0$$
$$x^2 - 9x - 1x + 9 = 0$$
$$x(x-9) - 1(x-9) = 0$$
$$(x-9)(x-1) = 0$$
$$x = 9 \text{ or } x = 1$$

But $x = t^2$. So $t = \pm\sqrt{x}$

$$t = \pm\sqrt{x} = \pm\sqrt{9} = \pm 3$$
$$= \pm\sqrt{1} = \pm 1.$$

5. Solve: $2^{2x} - 6 \times 2^x + 5 = 0$.
Let

$$2^x = y$$
$$2^{2x} = y^2$$
$$y^2 - 5y + 4 = 0$$
$$y^2 - 4y - 1y + 4 = 0$$
$$y(y-4) - 1(y-4) = 0$$
$$(y-1)(y-4) = 0$$
$$y = 1 \text{ or } y = 4$$
$$\text{But } y = 2^x$$
$$2^x = 1 \quad \text{or} \quad 2^x = 4$$
$$2^x = 2^0 \qquad 2^x = 2^2$$
$$x = 0 \quad \text{or} \quad x = 2.$$

Nature of the roots in quadratic equation: The quadratic equation $ax^2 + bx + c = 0$ has 2 and only 2 roots. The roots can be found by using the formula.

$$x = \frac{-b \pm \sqrt{b^2 - 4ac}}{2a}.$$

$b^2 - 4ac$ is called discriminant.

if $b^2 - 4ac = 0$ then $x = \frac{-b}{2a}$. So the roots are equal.

if $b^2 - 4ac > 0$ and is a perfect square then the roots are rational and unequal.

if $b^2 - 4ac > 0$ then the roots are real.

If $b^2 - 4ac < 0$ then $\sqrt{b^2 - 4ac}$ is negative square root of a number. But $\sqrt{-1} = i$, imaginary number. So the roots are imaginary.

Relation between the roots and co-efficient: $ax^2 + bx + c = 0$ has 2 roots say α and β.

$$\alpha = \frac{-b + \sqrt{b^2 - 4ac}}{2a} \text{ and } \beta = \frac{-b - \sqrt{b^2 - 4ac}}{2a}.$$

Sum of the roots $= \alpha + \beta$

$$= \frac{-b + \sqrt{b^2 - 4ac}}{2a} + \frac{-b - \sqrt{b^2 - 4ac}}{2a}$$

$$\alpha + \beta = -\frac{2b}{2a} = -\frac{b}{a}.$$

Product of the roots $= \alpha\beta$

$$= \left(\frac{-b + \sqrt{b^2 - 4ac}}{2a}\right)\left(\frac{-b - \sqrt{b^2 - 4ac}}{2a}\right)$$

$$= \frac{(-b)^2 - \left(\sqrt{b^2 - 4ac}\right)^2}{(2a)^2} = \frac{b^2 - b^2 + 4ac}{4a^2}$$

$$\alpha\beta = \frac{c}{a}.$$

SOLVED EXAMPLES

1. Examine the nature of the roots in

(i) $x^2 + 2x + 5 = 0$ (ii) $x^2 - 4x - 1 = 0$ (iii) $x^2 + 14x + 49 = 0$
(iv) $x^2 - 2x - 15 = 0$

(i) Comparing with $ax^2 + bx + c = 0$, $a = 1$, $b = 2$, $c = 5$

$$b^2 - 4ac = 2^2 - 4(1)(5)$$

$$4 - 20 = -16 < 0$$

Since $b^2 - 4ac < 0$, the roots are imaginary.

(ii) Comparing with $ax^2 + bx + c = 0$, $a = 1$, $b = -4$ and $c = -1$

$$b^2 - 4ac = (-4)^2 - 4(-1)(1)$$

$$16 + 4 = 20 > 0$$

Since $b^2 - 4ac > 0$, the roots are real.

(iii) Comparing with $ax^2+bx+c=0$

$a=1,\ b=14,\ c=49$

$$b^2-4ac=(14)^2-4(49)(1)$$
$$=196-196$$
$$b^2-4ac=0$$

Since $b^2-4ac=0$, the roots are equal and real.

$$x=\frac{-b}{2a}=-\frac{14}{2}=-7.$$

(iv) Comparing with $ax^2+bx+c=0$, we get

$a=1,\ b=-2$ and $c=-15$

$$b^2-4ac=(-2)^2-4(1)(-15)$$
$$4+60=64>0$$

and 64 is a perfect square as $8^2=64$

$\therefore$ the roots are rational and unequal.

2. For what values of m is the roots of the equation $2x^2+mx+8=0$ are equal.

SOLUTION:

The roots of the quadratic equation $ax^2+bx+c=0$ are equal only when $b^2-4ac=0$

$$\text{i.e. } m^2-4(-8)(2)=0$$
$$m^2-64=0$$
$$m^2=64$$
$$m=\pm 8.$$

3. For what value of k is the roots of the equation $(k-1)x^2+2kx+k+2=0$ are equal.

SOLUTION:

For the roots of $ax^2+bx+c=0$ to be equal, $b^2-4ac=0$

Comparing with $ax^2+bx+c=0$, we get

$a=k-1, b=2k$ and $c=+k+2$

$$b^2-4ac=(2k)^2-4(k-1)(k+2)=0$$
$$4k^2-(4k^2-4k+8k-8)=0$$
$$4k^2-4k^2-4k+8=0$$
$$4k=8$$
$$k=2.$$

4. Form the quadratic equation whose roots are $3-\sqrt{2}$ and $3+\sqrt{2}$

Let $ax^2+bx+c=0$ be the quadratic equation.

Consider $ax^2+bx+c=0 \div$ by a

$$x^2+\frac{b}{a}x+\frac{c}{a}=0$$

$$x^2-\left(-\frac{b}{a}\right)x+\frac{c}{a}=0$$

$$x^2-(\text{sum of the roots})x+(\text{product of roots})=0$$

$$x^2-\left(3-\sqrt{2}+3+\sqrt{2}\right)x+(3-\sqrt{2})(3+\sqrt{2})=0$$

$$x^2-6x+3^2-(\sqrt{2})^2=0$$

$$x^2-6x+9-2=0$$

$$x^2-6x+7=0.$$

5. Find the sum and product of the roots of the equation $x^2+8x-1=0$. Also find $\frac{1}{\alpha}+\frac{1}{\beta}$ where α and β are roots.

SOLUTION:

For the quadratic equation $ax^2+bx+c=0$.

Sum of roots $=\alpha+\beta=\dfrac{-b}{a}$

Product of the roots $=\alpha\beta=\dfrac{c}{a}$

For the equation x^2+8x-1, $a=1$, $b=8$, $c=-1$

So

$$\alpha+\beta=\frac{-8}{1}=-8$$

$$\alpha\beta=\frac{c}{a}=\frac{-1}{1}=-1$$

$$\text{Now } \frac{1}{\alpha}+\frac{1}{\beta}=\frac{\alpha+\beta}{\alpha\beta}=\frac{-8}{-1}=8.$$

6. The sum of a number and its reciprocal is 8.125. Find the number.

Let the number be x its reciprocal $=\frac{1}{x}$. Their sum = 8.125

$$x+\frac{1}{x}=8.125$$

$$\frac{x^2+1}{x}=8.125$$

$$\frac{x^2+1}{x}=\frac{8125}{1000}=\frac{65}{8}$$

$$8x^2+8=65x$$

$$8x^2 - 65x + 8 = 0$$
$$8x^2 - 64x - 1x + 8 = 0$$
$$8x(x-8) - 1(x-8) = 0$$
$$(x-8)(8x-1) = 0$$
$$x = 8 \text{ or } x = \frac{1}{8}$$

So the required number is 8.

Simultaneous linear equation in 2 variables: Linear equation in 2 variables is of the form $ax + by = c$ where a and b are constants and x and y are variables.

EXAMPLE: (i) $3x + 4y = 8$ (ii) $8x - 9y = 3$.

The graph of linear equation is a straight line. Hence, called linear equation.

The value of x and y which satisfy 2 linear equations in 2 variables say $a_1x + b_1y = c_1$ and $a_2x + b_2y = c_2$ simultaneously is called the solution of $a_1x + b_1y = c_1$ and $a_2x + b_2y = c_2$.

There are a number of methods to solve simultaneous linear equations.

1. **Substitution method:** In this method, one of the variables is expressed in terms of the other from one of the given equations. By substituting this in the remaining equation we get a linear equation which can be solved. Again by plugging in this value in any one of the equation, we get the value of other variable.

   EXAMPLE: To solve $2x - y = 8$ and $x + 2y = 9$ by substitution method:

   $$\text{Consider } 2x - y = 8$$
   $$2x - 8 = y$$

   Consider $x + 2y = 9$, substituting $y = 2x - 8$

   $$x + 2(2x-8) = 9$$
   $$x + 4x - 16 = 9$$
   $$5x = 9 + 16$$
   $$x = \frac{25}{5} = 5$$
   $$\text{Again } y = 2x - 8$$
   $$y = 2(5) - 8$$
   $$y = 10 - 8 = 2.$$

   So $x = 5$ and $y = 2$.

2. **Elimination method:** In this method, the given equations are multiplied with suitable constants so that the co-efficient of one of the variables in both the equations become equal. Then by adding/subtracting the multiplied equations, we get a linear equation in one variable, which can be solved. By substituting this value of one variable in one of the given equations, we get the value of another variable.

EXAMPLE: To solve $x+4y=14$ and $7x-3y=5$.

SOLUTION:

$$x+4y=14 \quad (1)$$

$$7x-3y=5 \quad (2)$$

$$(1)\times 7 \quad = \quad 7x + 28y = 98$$

$$(2)\times 1 \quad = \quad 7x - 3y = 5$$

$$(-)\ (+)\quad (-)$$

Subtracting ,

$$31y = 93$$

$$y=\frac{93}{31}=3$$

Substituting $y=3$ in (1)

$$x+4y=14$$

$$x+4(3)=14$$

$$x=14-12$$

$$x=2.$$

So solution is $x=2$ and $y=3$.

SOLVED EXAMPLES

1. Solve: $\dfrac{x+1}{y+1}=\dfrac{4}{5}$ and $\dfrac{x-1}{y-1}=\dfrac{2}{3}$

Consider

$$\frac{x+1}{y+1}=\frac{4}{5}$$

$$(x+1)5=4(y+1)$$

$$5x+5=4y+4$$

$$5x-4y=4-5$$

$$5x-4y=-1 \quad (1)$$

Consider

$$\frac{x-1}{y-1}=\frac{2}{3}$$

$$(x-1)3 = 2(y-1)$$
$$3x-3 = 2y-2$$
$$3x-2y = 3-2$$
$$3x-2y = 1 \qquad (2)$$

$$(1)\times 3 \quad = \quad 15x-12y = -3$$
$$(2)\times 5 \quad = \quad 15x-10y = 5$$
$$(-)\ (+) \qquad (-)$$

Subtracting $\quad -2y = -8$

$$y = 4$$

Substituting $y = 4$ in (1)

$$5x-4y = -1$$
$$5x-4(4) = -1$$
$$5x = -1+16 \Rightarrow x = \frac{15}{5} = 3$$

2. Solve: $\dfrac{2}{x} - \dfrac{6}{y} = -1$ and $\dfrac{6}{x} + \dfrac{3}{y} = 4$

$$\frac{2}{x} - \frac{6}{y} = -1 \qquad (1)$$
$$\frac{6}{x} + \frac{3}{y} = 4 \qquad (2)$$

$$(1)\times 3 \quad = \quad \frac{6}{x} - \frac{18}{y} = -3$$
$$(2)\times 1 \quad = \quad \frac{6}{x} + \frac{3}{y} = 4$$
$$(-)\ (-) \qquad (-)$$

Subtracting $\quad \dfrac{-21}{y} = -7$

$$-7y = -21$$
$$y = 3.$$

Substituting $y = 3$ in (1)

$$\frac{2}{x} - \frac{6}{3} = -1$$
$$\frac{2}{x} - 2 = -1$$

$$\frac{2}{x} = -1+2 = 1$$
$$x = 2.$$

Miscellaneous Problems

1. In a fraction, the denominator exceeds the numerator by 2. If from the numerator 4 is subtracted or if the denominator 12 is added the fraction obtained in both the cases is same. Find the fraction.

SOLUTION:

Let $\frac{x}{y}$ be the required fraction.

Given:

$$\text{Denominator} = \text{Numerator } +2$$
$$y = x+2.$$

4 subtracted from the numerator is $x-4$

12 is added to the denominator is $y+12$.

$$\frac{x-4}{y} = \frac{x}{y+12}$$
$$\text{But } y = x+2$$
$$\frac{x-4}{x+2} = \frac{x}{x+2+12}$$
$$\frac{x-4}{x+2} = \frac{x}{x+14}$$
$$(x-4)(x+14) = x(x+2)$$
$$x^2-4x+14x-56 = x^2+2x$$
$$x^2-4x+14x-56-x^2-24 = 0$$
$$8x-56 = 0$$
$$8x = 56$$
$$x = \frac{56}{8} = 7$$

$\therefore$ Required fraction $= \dfrac{x}{x+2} = \dfrac{7}{9}$.

2. The sum of two numbers is 45 and their difference is 5. Find the numbers.

Let the 2 numbers be x and y

Given:

$$x+y = 45$$
$$x-y = 5$$

$$\text{Adding we get } 2x = 50$$
$$x = 25$$
$$x + y = 45$$
$$25 + y = 45$$
$$y = 45 - 25 = 20.$$

So the numbers are 20 and 25.

3. The length of a room is twice its breadth. If the length is reduced by 5 ft and breadth is increased by 3ft, the area remains the same as before. Find the length and breadth of the room.

SOLUTION:

Let l and b be the length and breadth of a room.

Given:

$$l = 2b$$

we know, area of room = length$\times$ breadth

$$A = l \times b$$
$$A = 2b \times b = 2b^2$$
$$\text{also given } (l - 5)(b + 5) = A$$
$$(2b - 5)(b + 5) = 2b^2$$
$$2b^2 - 5b + 10b - 25 = 2b^2$$
$$2b^2 + 5b - 25 - 2b^2 = 0$$
$$5b = 25$$
$$b = 5.$$

So $l = 2 \times 5 = 10$ and $b = 5$.

4. The sum of the digits of a number consisting of 2 digits is 9. If the digits are reversed, the resulting number will be greater than the original number by 45. Find the number.

SOLUTION:

Let the 2 digits of number be XY with x in 10's place and y in unit's place.

So the number is $10x + y$ (1)

Given:

$$\text{Sum of digits} = 9$$
$$x + y = 9$$
$$y = 9 - x \qquad (2)$$

If the digits are reversed, it becomes yx

$$\text{But } yx = 10y + x \qquad \left[\begin{array}{l}\text{Example: } 64 = 60+4 \\ \qquad\qquad\quad 6\times 10+4\end{array}\right]$$

$$10y + x = (10x + y) + 45$$

But from (2) $y = 9 - x$

$$10(9-x) + x = (10x + 9 - x) + 45$$

$$90 - 10x + x = 10x + 9 - x + 45$$

$$90 - 9x = 9x + 54$$

$$90 - 54 = 9x + 9x$$

$$36 = 18x$$

$$\Rightarrow x = 2.$$

But $y = 9 - x = 9 - 2 = 7$

$\therefore$ The required number $= xy = 27$.

5. A commodity was produced by using 3 units of labour and 2 units of capital. The total cost comes to 62. If the commodity is produced by using 4 units of labour and one unit of capital, the cost comes out to 56. What is the cost per unit of the labour and capital?

SOLUTION:

Let the cost per unit of labour be x and that for capital be y.

Given:

$$3x + 2y = 62 \qquad (1)$$

and

$$4x + y = 56 \qquad (2)$$

$$4x + y = 56$$

$$y = 56 - 4x$$

Substituting in (1) we get

$$3x + 2y = 62$$

$$3x + 2(56 - 4x) = 62$$

$$3x + 112 - 8x - 62 = 0$$

$$-5x + 50 = 0$$

$$x = \frac{50}{5} = 10$$

$$y = 56 - 4(10) = 16.$$

$\therefore$ Cost of labour = Rs 10 and capital = Rs 16.

6. 5 years ago the father was 5 times as old as his son and in 3 years he will be 3 times as old as his son. Find their present ages.

Let the present age of father and son be x and y respectively.

5 years ago, Father's age $= x - 5$

Son's age $= y - 5$

$$\text{Given:} \quad x - 5 = 5(y - 5)$$
$$x - 5 = 5y - 25$$
$$x = 5y - 25 + 5$$
$$x = 5y - 20 \qquad (1)$$

After 3 years,

$$\text{Father's age } = x + 3$$
$$\text{Son's age } = y + 3$$
$$\text{Given} \quad x + 3 = 3(y + 3)$$
$$x + 3 = 3y + 9$$
$$5y - 20 + 3 = 3y + 9$$
$$5y - 17 = 3y + 9$$
$$5y - 3y = 17 + 9$$
$$2y = 26$$
$$y = 13$$

$\therefore \quad x = 5y - 20 = 5(13) - 20 = 65 - 20 = 45$

$\therefore$ Father's age = 45 years and son's age = 13 years.

7. A man invested Rs. 30,000 in two types of bonds. On one he earns 5% and on the other he gets 7%. If his total earning is Rs. 2000. Find his investment in each type of bonds.

Let the money invested on 5% bond be x and that on 7% be y.

Given:

$$x + y = 30,000$$
$$y = 30,000 - x \qquad (1)$$
$$\text{Also} \quad 5\% \text{ of } x + 7\% \text{ of } y = 2000$$
$$\frac{5x}{100} + \frac{7y}{100} = 2000$$
$$5x + 7y = 2,00,000$$

But $y = 30,000 - x$ from (1)

$$5x + 7 = (30,000 - x) = 2,00,000$$
$$5x + 2,10,000 - 7x = 2,00,000$$
$$2,10,000 - 2x = 2,00,000$$
$$2,10,000 - 2,00,000 = 2x$$
$$10,000 = 2x$$
$$\Rightarrow x = 5000$$
$$\therefore \quad y = 30,000 - 5000$$
$$y = 25,000$$

So he invested Rs. 5,000/- on 5% bond and Rs. 25,000/- on 7% bond.

8. Taxi fare consists of a constant charge together with the charge for the distance covered. A person pays Rs. 82 for a journey of 15 km and Rs. 142 for a journey of 27 km. Find the charges one will have to pay for a journey of 50 km.

Let the constant charge be x and charge per kilometre be y.

Given:

$$x + 15y = 82 \Rightarrow x = 82 - 15y$$
$$x + 27y = 142$$
$$82 - 15y + 27y = 142$$
$$82 + 12y = 142$$
$$12y = 142 - 82$$
$$y = \frac{60}{12} = 5$$
$$x = 82 - 15(5) = 82 - 75 = 7$$

So for a journey of 50 km it would be

$$x + 50y = 7 + 50(5)$$
$$= 7 + 250 = \text{Rs } 257$$

9. Students of a class are to stand in rows. If one student is extra in a row, there would be 2 rows less. If one student is less in a row, there would be 3 rows more. Find the number of students in the class.

Let x be the number of students in each row and y be the number of rows.

Total number of students $= xy$

Given:

$$(x+1)(y-2) = xy \quad \text{(As there are same number of students)}$$
$$xy + y - 2x - 2 = xy$$
$$y - 2x = 2 \qquad (1)$$

Also given $\quad (x-1)(y+3) = xy$

$$xy - y + 3x - 3 = xy$$
$$-y + 3x = 3 \qquad (2)$$

Solving (1) & (2)

$$y - 2x = 2$$
$$-y + 3x = 3$$
$$\text{Adding,} \quad x = 5$$

Substituting $x = 5$ in (1)

$$y - 2(5) = 2$$
$$y = 2 + 10$$
$$y = 12$$

∴ Total number of students $= 12 \times 5 = 60$.

10. The difference of the ages of Sunil and his father is 30 years. If their difference of the squares of their ages is 1560. Find their ages.

SOLUTION:

Let Sunil's age be y and his father's age be x.

Given:

$$x - y = 30$$
$$\Rightarrow x = 30 + y \qquad (1)$$

Also $\quad x^2 - y^2 = 1560$

But $\quad x^2 - y^2 = (x+y)(x-y)$

$$(x+y)(x-y) = 1560$$
$$(x+y)30 = 1560$$
$$x + y = \frac{1560}{30} = 52$$
$$x + y = 52$$

From (1) $\quad x = 30 + y$

$$30 + y + y = 52$$

$$2y = 52 - 30 = 22$$
$$y = 11$$

So Sunil's age is 11 and his father's age is $30 + 11 = 41$ years.

11. A shopkeeper buys a number of books for Rs. 1200. If he had bought 10 more books for the same amount, each book would have cost Rs. 20 less. How many books did he buy?

Let x be the number of books and y be the price of each book.

Given:

$$xy = 1200 \Rightarrow y = \frac{1200}{x}$$
$$(x+10)(y-20) = 1200$$
$$xy + 10y - 20x - 200 = 1200$$
$$x\left(\frac{1200}{x}\right) + 10\left(\frac{1200}{x}\right) - 20x = 1200 + 200$$
$$\frac{1200x}{x} + \frac{12000}{x} - 20x = 1400$$
$$\frac{1200x + 12000 - 20x^2}{x} = 1400$$
$$1200x + 12000 - 20x^2 = 1400x$$
$$-20x^2 + 1200x - 1400x + 12000 = 0$$
$$-20x^2 - 200x + 12000 = 0$$
$$\div \text{ by } -20$$
$$x^2 + 10x - 600 = 0$$
$$x^2 + 30x - 20x - 600 = 0$$
$$x(x+30) - 20(x+30) = 0$$
$$(x+30)(x-20) = 0$$
$$x = -30 \text{ or } x = 20.$$

$\therefore$ No. of books = 20.

Price of each book $= \frac{1200}{20} = 60$

12. A plane left 30 min. later than the scheduled time and in order to reach the destination 1500 km away in time, it has to increase the speed by 250 km/hr from the usual speed. Find its usual speed.

We know, Speed $= \frac{\text{Distance}}{\text{Time}}$

Distance = 1500 km

Let the usual speed be x and usual time be y

Speed $= x = \dfrac{1500}{y}$ (1)

Given: 30 min later the time, $\dfrac{1}{2}$ hr. later, i.e., 0.5 hr later $= y - 0.5$ and Speed $= x + 250$.
Distance = 1500 km

$$x + 250 = \frac{1500}{y - 30}$$

But $x = \dfrac{1500}{y}$ from (1) so

$$\frac{1500}{y} + 250 = \frac{1500}{y - 0.5}$$

$$\frac{1500 + 250y}{y} = \frac{1500}{y - 0.5}$$

Cross-multiplying,

$$\frac{1500 + 250y}{y} = \frac{1500}{y - 0.5}$$

$$(1500 + 250y)(y - 0.5) = 1500y$$

$$1500y - 750 + 250y^2 - 125y = 1500y$$

$$250y^2 - 125y - 750 = 0$$

$\div$ by 25

$$10y^2 - 5y - 30 = 0$$

$\div 5$

$$2y^2 - y - 6 = 0 \qquad -12\langle\begin{matrix}-4\\+3\end{matrix} \;\; \underline{}\; -1$$

$$2y^2 - 4y + 3y - 6 = 0$$

$$2y(y - 2) + 3(y - 2) = 0$$

$$y = \frac{-3}{2} \text{ or } y = 2.$$

$$\text{Speed } = \frac{1500}{y} = \frac{1500}{2} = 750 \text{ km/hr.}$$

IN A NUTSHELL

- An equation of the form $ax + b = 0$ with $a \neq 0$ is called linear equation.
- Linear equation has one and only one solution.
- An equation of the form $ax^2 + bx + c = 0$ with $a \neq 0$ is called quadratic equation.
- Quadratic equation has 2 only 2 solutions or roots.

- The roots of $ax^2+bx+c=0$ may be found by factorisation method or by using the formula,

$$x=\frac{-b+\sqrt{b^2-4ac}}{2a}$$

- b^2-4ac for quadratic equation, $ax^2+bx+c=0$ is called discriminant (D)
- If $D>0$, then 2 real and distinct roots. If $D=0$, 2 roots are real and equal. If $D<0$, the roots are not real or they are imaginary.
- Sum of the roots $=-\frac{b}{2a}$ and product of roots $=\frac{c}{a}$ for the quadratic equation $ax^2+bx+c=0$ with $a\neq 0$.
- Simultaneous linear equations in 2 variables may be solved by substitution method, where one variable is expressed in terms of another from one equation and that value is substituted in another equation to get the linear equation which is solved to get the value of the unknowns.
- Simultaneous linear equations in 2 variable may be solved by elimination method, where co-efficient of one of the variables is made equal by multiplying both the equations by appropriate constants. Then by adding/subtracting value of one unknown is obtained. Then by substituting these values in any of the given equation gives the value of the other variable.

CHECK YOUR PROGRESS

I. Solve:

1. $\frac{x+2}{5}=\frac{x-1}{2}$ $[x=3]$
2. $\frac{1}{x+1}+\frac{1}{x+4}=\frac{1}{x+2}+\frac{1}{x+3}$ $[x=-2\frac{1}{2}]$
3. $2-\frac{x+2}{3}=\frac{x+8}{5}-\frac{2x+4}{3}$ $[x=-8]$
4. $b(a+x)=b^2+ax$ $[x=b]$
5. $3(x+5)-25=9+2(x-7)$ $[x=5]$

II. Solve the following quadratic equations:

1. $15x^2-7x-36=0$ $\left[\frac{9}{5},\frac{-4}{3}\right]$
2. $\sqrt{5}x^2+9x+4\sqrt{5}=0$ $\left[-\sqrt{5},\frac{-4}{\sqrt{5}}\right]$

3. $\dfrac{x+1}{x-1} - \dfrac{x-1}{x+1} = \dfrac{5}{6}$ $[x=5]$

$x \neq 1$ and $x \neq -1$

4. $2x + \dfrac{1}{2x} = \dfrac{13}{6}$ $\left[\dfrac{1}{3}, \dfrac{3}{4}\right]$

5. $\sqrt{2x^2 - 2x + 1} = 2x - 3$ $[x=4]$

III. Solve:

1. $3^{x-2} + 3^{3-x} = 4$ $[2, 3]$

2. $2^{2x+3} - 9 \times 2^x + 1 = 0$ $[0, -3]$

3. $9^{x+2} - 6 \times 3^{x+1} + 1 = 0$ $[-2]$

4. $9x^4 - 30x^2 + 25 = 0$ $[\pm\sqrt{\frac{5}{3}}]$

IV. Find the discriminant of

1. $x^2 - 5x + 1 = 0$ $[21]$

2. $\sqrt{3}x^2 - 2\sqrt{3}x - \sqrt{3} = 0$ $[24]$

3. $9y^2 - 30y + 25 = 0$ $[0]$

4. $ax^2 + bx + c = 0$ $[b^2 - 4ac]$

V. 1. Find the value of k so that the equation $2x^2 + kx + 8 = 0$ will have real roots $[k \geq 8,\ k \leq -8]$

2. Find k so that $(4-k)x^2 + (2k+4)x + 8k + 1 = 0$ will have equal roots $[k = 0 \text{ or } 3]$

3. Find the sum and product of the roots of the equation $x^2 - 3\sqrt{2} + 4 = 0$ $[3\sqrt{2}, 4]$

4. Comment on the nature of roots of the equation $2x^2 - 3x + 5 = 0$ [No real roots or roots are imaginary]

VI. Solve the following equations by substitution method:

1. $2x - y = 8,\ x + 2y = 9$ $(\lambda = 5 \quad y = 2)$

2. $4x + y = 24,\ 3x - 5y = 18$ $(x = 6 \quad y = 0)$

3. $6x - 5y + 2 = 0,\ 5x - 6y + 9 = 0$ $(x = 3,\ y = 4)$

4. $\dfrac{4}{x} + 5y = 7,\ \dfrac{3}{x} + 4y = 5,\ x \neq 0$ $(x = \dfrac{1}{3},\ y = -1)$

VII. Solve each of the following:

1. $4x - 3y - 7 = 0, \quad 3x + 4y + 1 = 0$ $\quad (x = 1, y = -1)$
2. $\frac{2}{x} + \frac{3}{y} = 2, \quad \frac{1}{x} - \frac{4}{y} = 6$ $\quad (x = \frac{11}{26}, y = -\frac{11}{10})$
3. $\frac{x+1}{2} + \frac{y-1}{3} = 8, \quad \frac{x-1}{3} + \frac{y+1}{2} = 9$ $\quad (x = 7, y = 13)$
4. $\frac{5}{x+y} - \frac{2}{x-y} = -1, \quad \frac{15}{x+y} + \frac{8}{x-y} = 11$ $\quad (x = 3, y = 2)$
5. $ax + by = 1, \quad bx + ay = \frac{2ab}{a^2+b^2}$ $\quad (x = \frac{a}{a^2+b^2}, y = \frac{b}{a^2+b^2})$

VIII.

1. The sum of 3 consecutive numbers is 162. Find them. [53, 54, 55]
2. The sum of 3 consecutive odd numbers is 189. Find the least number among them. [61]
3. If the sum of 2 numbers is 112 and four times of one equal to three times the other. Find them.

   [48, 64]
4. A number consists of 2 digits, whose sum is 9. If 27 is added to the number, its digits are reversed. Find the number.

   [36]
5. A fraction becomes $\frac{1}{2}$ when 1 is subtracted from the numerator and 2 is added to the denominator. It becomes $\frac{1}{3}$ when 7 is subtracted from the numerator and 2 is subtracted from the denominator. Find the fraction.

   $\left[\frac{15}{26}\right]$
6. If the denominator of a fraction is added to its numerator and numerator is subtracted from the denominator, the fraction becomes $\frac{11}{3}$. If the denominator exceeds the numerator by 3. Find the fraction.

   $\left[\frac{4}{7}\right]$
7. 3 years ago the age of the mother was 5 times the age of her daughter and 2 years hence, she will be thrice as old as her daughter will be. Find their present ages.

   [28 years, 8 years]

8. A father's age is thrice the sum of ages of his 2 sons. After 5 years, his age will be twice the sum of their ages. How old is the father?

[45 years]

9. 9 oranges and 5 apples cost Rs. 154 and 13 oranges and 7 apples cost Rs. 222. Find the cost of one orange and one apple separately.

[Orange: Rs. 15, apple: Rs. 2]

10. A man wanted to exchange Rs. 1000 in 2 types of notes of Rs. 5 and Rs. 10 denominations. If he got Rs. 180 notes in all find the notes of each kind.

[Rs. 5: 160, Rs. 10: 20]

11. A man walks a certain distance at a certain speed. Had he walked 1/2 km/hr faster, he would have taken 1 hr less. But if he had gone 1 km/hr slower, he would have taken 3 hours more. Find the distance

[36 km]

12. A man starts his job with a certain monthly salary and earns a fixed increment, every year. If his salary was 15,000 after 4 years of service and Rs. 18,000 after 10 years of service, what was his salary and what is the annual increment?

[Rs. 13,000, Rs. 500]

13. The area of floor of a rectangular room remains the same if its length is increased by 7 m and breadth is decreased by 3 m. Also it remains unaffected if the length is decreased by 7 m and breadth is increased by 5 m. Find the dimension of the floor.

[Length: 28 m breadth 15 m]

14. There are two examination rooms A and B. If 10 candidates are sent from A to B, the number of students in each room is same. If 20 students are sent from B to A, the number of students in A is double the number of students in B. Find the number of students in each room.

[A : 100, B : 80]

15. Divide 51 into 2 parts whose product is 378.

[9, 42]

16. The sum of reciprocals of 2 consecutive numbers is $\frac{23}{132}$. Find the numbers.

[11, 12]

17. A shopkeeper buys a number of books for Rs. 80. If he had bought 4 more books for the same amount, each book would have cost him Re. 1 less. How many books should he buy?

[16]

18. In a flight of 2800 km, an aircraft was slowed down due to bad weather. Its average speed was reduced by 100 km/hr and time increased by 30 min. Find the original duration of the flight.

[$3\frac{1}{2}$ hrs]

19. The sum of the squares of 2 consecutive natural numbers is 313. Find the numbers.

[12, 13]

20. The time taken by a person to cover 150 km was $2\frac{1}{2}$ hrs more than the time taken in return journey. If he had returned at a speed 10 km/hr more than the speed of going, what was the speed per hour in each direction?

[20 km/hr, 30 km/hr]

3

Progression

INTRODUCTION

A manager of an enterprise spends Rs. 10 lakh for production every year. He proposes to spend Rs. 0.75 lakh more every year to meet the increasing demand of the market. If he wants to find how much he has to spend after 10 years or the sum of all expenses during 10 years, he can use arithmetic progression.

In this chapter, we will discuss arithmetic and geometric progression.

Sequence

A sequence is an ordered arrangement of numbers according to a specific rule. The individual numbers that form a sequence are called terms of a sequence.

EXAMPLE: 1, 2, 4, 8, ... form a sequence

1, 2, 4, 8 are 1st, 2nd, 3rd, and 4th are terms of a sequence. They are represented by T_1 T_2 T_3 T_4.

ARITHMETIC SEQUENCE OR ARITHMETIC PROGRESSION

A sequence in which the difference between the consecutive terms is constant is called arithmetic sequence. In other words, if any term minus the previous term is constant in a sequence then it is arithmetic sequence or arithmetic progression (A.P). The constant is called common difference.

EXAMPLE: 7, 10, 13, 16 ... is an arithmetic sequence as

any term-previous term = constant

i.e., $10-7=13-10=16-13=3$.

General Term or n^{th} Term of an Arithmetic Progression

If we know the first term and common difference or any 2 terms in an arithmetic progression, we can find the whole sequence or a particular term of a sequence by using general term or n^{th} term.

Let a be the first term and d be common difference. Then by definition,

$$\text{First term} = a$$

$$\text{Second term} = a+d \quad (\text{second term-first term} = d \text{ as } a+d-a=d)$$

$$3^{\text{rd}} \text{ term} = a+d+d = a+2d$$

$$4^{\text{th}} \text{ term} = a+2d+d = a+3d$$

$$5^{\text{th}} \text{ term} = a+4d = a+(5-1)d$$

$$\vdots$$

$$n^{\text{th}} \text{ term} = a+(n-1)d$$

So $\qquad T_n = a+(n-1)d.$

SOLVED EXAMPLES

1. Find the 30th term in the A.P.

6, 3, 0, −3...

Given: $\quad a = 6$

$$d = 3-6 = -3$$

$$n^{\text{th}} \text{ term} = a+(n-1)d$$

$$T_{30} = 6+(30-1)(-3)$$

$$= 6+(29)(-3) = 6-87$$

$$T_{30} = -81$$

2. An arithmetic sequence has −20 as its 2nd term and common difference 3. Find its 10th term.

Given: $\quad 2^{\text{nd}} \text{ term} = -20 = T_2 = a+d$

$$d = 3$$

$$a+d = -20$$

$$a = -20-3 = -23$$

To find: T_{10}

$$T_n = a+(n-1)d$$

$$T_{10} = -23+(10-1)(3)$$

$$= -23+9(3) = 4$$

$$T_{10} = 4.$$

3. If $x+5$, $2x+5$ and $4x-5$ are 3 consecutive terms of A.P. Find x.

SOLUTION:

In A.P. any term − previous term = Constant

$$\text{So } T_2 - T_1 = T_3 - T_2$$

$$(2x+5)-(x+5)=(4x-5)-(2x+5)$$
$$2x+5-x-5=4x-5-2x-5$$
$$x=2x-10$$
$$10=x.$$

4. The 14th term of an A.P. is 100 and 2nd term is 4. Find the common difference.

Given: $T_{14}=100=a+(14-1)d$

i.e., $a+13d=100 \quad (1)$

$T_2=9=a+d$

$a+d=4 \quad (2)$

Solving (1) & (2)

$$a+13d=100$$
$$a+d=4$$
$$(-)\,(-)\qquad(-)$$
$$12d=96$$
$$d=8.$$

$\therefore$ Common difference $=8$.

5. In the arithmetic sequence, if the mth term is n and n^{th} term is m. Find the common difference. Also find the $(m+n)^{\text{th}}$ term.

SOLUTION:

Given: $T_m=n$

$a+(m-1)d=n \quad (1)$

n^{th} term is m

$a+(n-1)d=m \quad (2)$

Solving (1) & (2), we get

$$a+(m-1)d=n$$
$$a+(n-1)d=m$$
$$(-)(-)\qquad(-)$$
$$(m-1-n+1)d=n-m$$
$$(m-n)d=n-m$$
$$d=\frac{n-m}{m-n}=-\frac{(m-n)}{m-n}=-1$$
$$\therefore\quad d=-1$$

Consider (1)

$$a+(n-1)d=m$$
$$a+(n-1)(-1)=m$$
$$a-n+1=m$$
$$a=m+n-1$$

To find $(m+n)^{\text{th}}$ term:

$$T_{m+n}=a+(m+n-1)d$$
$$T_{m+n}=(m+n-1)+(m+n-1)(-1)$$
$$m+n-1-m-n+1$$
$$T_{m+n}=0.$$

6. The third and fifth terms of A.P. are $x+y$ and $x-y$ respectively. Find the 12th term

Given: $T_3=x+y$

$$a+(3-1)d=x+y$$
$$a+2d=x+y \qquad (1)$$
$$T_5=x-y$$
$$a+4d=x-y \qquad (2)$$

Solving (1) & (2)

$$a+2d=x+y$$
$$a+4d=x-y$$
$$(-)\ (-)\ (-)\ (+)$$
$$-2d=2y$$
$$d=-y$$

Substituting $d=-y$ in (1), we get

$$a+2d=x+y$$
$$a+2(-y)=x+y$$
$$a-2y=x+y$$
$$a=x+y+2y$$
$$a=x+3y.$$

To find 12th term:

$$T_{12} = a + 11d = x + 3y + 11(-y)$$
$$= x + 3y - 11y$$
$$T_{12} = x - 8y$$

ARITHMETIC SERIES

If the terms of an arithmetic sequence are added it becomes an arithmetic series.

Sum of the First *n* Terms of an Arithmetic Progression

Let a be the first term, d be the common difference and S_n be the sum of the first n terms of an arithmetic sequence

Then

$$S_n = a + a + d + a + 2d + \cdots + a + (n-1)d$$

Let $\quad l = a + (n-1)d$

$$S_n = a + a + d + a + 2d + \cdots + l$$

Since the proceeding term to $a + d$ is a,

proceeding term to l is $l - d$

proceeding term to $l - d$ is $l - d - d = l - 2d$

So

$$S_n = a + a + d + a + 2d + \cdots + l - 2d + l - d + l \quad (1)$$

Writing in reverse order,

$$S_n = l + l - d + l - 2d + \cdots + a + 2d + a + d + a \quad (2)$$

Adding (1) and (2), we get

$$2S_n = a + l + a + l + \cdots + a + l \qquad (n \text{ times})$$

$$\therefore \quad 2S_n = n(a + l)$$

$$S_n = \frac{n}{2}(a + l) \qquad \text{but } l = a + (n-1)d$$

$$S_n = \frac{n}{2}[a + a + (n-1)d]$$

$$S_n = \frac{n}{2}[2a + (n-1)d]$$

SOLVED EXAMPLES

1. Find the sum first 10 terms in the sequence 10, 4, −2...

SOLUTION:

$$a = 10, \quad d = 4 - 10 = -6 \quad n = 10$$

$$S_n = \frac{n}{2}[2a + (n-1)d]$$

$$S_{10} = \frac{10}{2}[2(10) + (10-1)(-6)]$$

$$= 5[20 + 9(-6)]$$

$$5(20 - 54) = 5(-34)$$

$$S_{10} = -170$$

2. For the following arithmetic sequence. Find the sum:

$$3, 5, 7, 9 \ldots 29.$$

Given: $a = 3,\ l = 29 = T_n,\ d = 5 - 3 = 2$

$$T_n = a + (n-1)d$$

$$29 = 3 + (n-1)^2$$

$$29 - 3 = (n-1)^2$$

$$\frac{26}{2} = n - 1$$

$$\Rightarrow \quad n = 13 + 1 = 14$$

$$S_n = \frac{n}{2}[a + T_n]$$

$$S_{14} = \frac{14}{2}[3 + 29]$$

$$S_{14} = 7(32)$$

$$S_{14} = 224$$

3. Find the sum of first 10 terms if

$$T_n = -2 + 8n$$

$$T_1 = -2 + 8(1) = 6 = a$$

$$T_2 = -2 + 8(2) = 14$$

$$T_2 - T_1 = d = 14 - 6 = 8$$

$$n = 10 \text{ (Given)}$$

$$S_n = \frac{n}{2}[2a + (n-1)d]$$

$$S_{10} = \frac{10}{2}[2(6)+(10-1)8]$$
$$S_{10} = 5(12+9(8))$$
$$S_{10} = 5(84)$$
$$S_{10} = 420$$

4. The 4th term of an A.P. is 5 while the sum of 6 terms is 10. Find the sum of first 19 terms.

Given: 4th term $= T_4 = 5$

$$a+(4-1)d = 5$$
$$a+3d = 5 \qquad (1)$$

Sum of 6 terms = 10

$$S_6 = 10$$
$$S_n = \frac{n}{2}[2a+(n-1)d]$$

So $\frac{6}{2}[2a+(6-1)d] = 10$

$$3(2a+5d) = 10$$
$$.6a+15d = 10 \qquad (2)$$

Solving (1) & (2), we get

$$(1)\times 6 = 6a+18d = 30$$
$$6a+15d = 10$$
$$(-)(-)\quad(-)$$
$$3d = 20$$
$$d = \frac{20}{3}$$

Substituting $d = \frac{20}{3}$ in (1)

$$a+3\left(\frac{20}{3}\right) = 5$$
$$a = 5-20$$
$$a = -15$$

To find S_{19}:

$$S_n = \frac{n}{2}[2a+(n-1)d]$$
$$S_{19} = \frac{19}{2}\left[2(-15)+(19-1)\frac{20}{3}\right]$$

$$= \frac{19}{2}\left[-30 + 18 \times \frac{20}{3}\right]$$

$$\frac{19}{2}[90] = 19 \times 45$$

$$= 855$$

5. Find the sum of all integers between 300 and 500 which are divisible by 8.

SOLUTION:

First number above 300 divisible by 8 is 304 and last number below 500 is 496.

So required sum $= S_n = 304,\ 312,\ 320, \ldots, 496.$

This is an A.P. with $a = 304$ and $T_n = 496,\ d = 8.$

$$T_n = a + (n-1)d = 304 + (n-1)8$$

$$496 - 304 = (n-1)8$$

$$\frac{192}{8} = n - 1 \Rightarrow n = 25$$

$$\text{Now } S_n = \frac{n}{2}[a + T_n] = \frac{25}{2}[304 + 496]$$

$$S_n = \frac{25 \times 800}{2} = 10{,}000$$

$$\therefore \quad 304 + 312 + \cdots + 496 = 10{,}000.$$

ARITHMETIC MEANS

If $a,\ A_1,\ A_2,\ A_3,\ A_4, \ldots A_n,\ b$ are in arithmetic progression then $A_1,\ A_2,\ A_3, \ldots A_n$ are the n arithmetic means between a and b. To find arithmetic means, we notice

$a,\ A_1,\ A_2, \ldots A_n,\ b$ are in A.P.

So n^{th} term $T_n = a + (n-1)d$

a is the first term and b is $(n+2)^{\text{nd}}$ term

$$T_{n+2} = a + (n+2-1)d$$

$$b = a + (n+1)d$$

$$\Rightarrow \quad d = \frac{b-a}{n+1}$$

by using this we can write,

$$A_1 = a + d = a + \frac{b-a}{n+1}$$

$$A_2 = A_1 + d \quad \text{or} \quad a + 2d = a + 2\left(\frac{b-a}{n+1}\right)$$

$$\text{and so on} \quad A_n = a + n\left(\frac{b-a}{n+1}\right)$$

ARITHMETIC MEAN

If a, x, b are in arithmetic progression then x is called arithmetic mean between a and b.

Since a, x, b are in A.P.

$$\text{any term} - \text{previous term} = \text{constant}$$
$$x - a = b - x$$
$$x + x = b + a$$
$$2x = a + b$$
$$x = \frac{a+b}{2}$$
$$\therefore \quad \text{Arithmetic mean} = \frac{a+b}{2}$$

SOLVED EXAMPLES

1. Find 5 arithmetic means between 13 and -23.

Let 13, $A_1\ A_2\ A_3\ A_4\ A_5\ -23$ be the arithmetic sequence.

-23 is the 7th term and 13 is first term.

$$\text{We have } T_n = a + (n-1)d$$
$$T_7 = 13 + (7-1)d$$
$$-23 = 13 + 6d$$
$$\frac{-23 - 13}{6} = d$$
$$-6 = d$$
$$\text{So} \quad A_1 = 13 + (-6) = 13 - 6 = +7$$
$$A_2 = 7 - 6 = +1$$
$$A_3 = +1 - 6 = -5$$
$$A_4 = -5 - 6 = -11$$
$$A_5 = -11 - 6 = -17$$

2. There are n arithmetic means between 3 and 35. So that the ratio of 4th mean to the nth mean is 1:3. Find n.

Let 3, $A_1\ A_2 \ldots A_n$ 35 be the arithmetic sequence.

$$a = 3, (n+2)^{\text{nd}} \text{ term} = 35$$
$$\text{Given } A_4 : A_n = 1 : 3$$
$$\frac{A_4}{A_n} = \frac{1}{3}$$
$$\frac{3+4d}{3+nd} = \frac{1}{3}$$

But n^{th} mean is the last but 2nd term, so it is $35 - d$.

$$\frac{3+4d}{35-d} = \frac{1}{3}$$
$$3(3+4d) = 35-d$$
$$9+12d = 35-d$$
$$13d = 35-9$$
$$d = \frac{26}{13}$$
$$d = 2$$

$(n+2)^{\text{nd}}$ term is 35. So

$$a+(n+2-1)d = 35$$
$$3+(n+1)2 = 35$$
$$(n+1)2 = 32$$
$$n+1 = \frac{32}{2} = 16$$
$$n = 16-1 = 15$$

GEOMETRIC PROGRESSION

A geometric progression is a sequence in which the ratio between any two consecutive terms is constant. In other words, in a geometric progression (G.P.),

$$\frac{\text{any term}}{\text{previous term}} = \text{constant.}$$

This constant is called common ratio (r).

EXAMPLE: 1, 2, 4, 8... is a G.P.

n th Term or General Term of a G.P.

Let a be the first term and r be the common ratio. Then

$$\text{First term} = a$$
$$2^{\text{nd}} \text{ term} = ar \quad \left[\text{as } \frac{ar}{a} = r\right]$$
$$3^{\text{rd}} \text{ term} = ar^2$$
$$\vdots \qquad \vdots$$
$$n^{\text{th}} \text{ term} = ar^{n-1}$$

So n^{th} term or general term of a geometric progression is $ar^{(n-1)}$. It is denoted by T_n.

$$\therefore \quad T_n = ar^{n-1}.$$

SOLVED EXAMPLES

1. Find the common ratio, the fifth term of the geometric progression $-1, 4, -16, 64\ldots$

Given:

$$a = -1$$

$$r = \frac{\text{any term}}{\text{previous term}} = \frac{4}{-1} = -4$$

$$\therefore \quad \text{Common ratio} = -4$$

$$T_n = ar^{n-1}$$

$$T_5 = -1(-4)^{5-1} = -1(-4)^4$$

$$= -256$$

2. The 3rd and 7th terms of G.P. are $\frac{3}{4}$ and 12 respectively. Find the 10th term and what term is equal to 3072?

Given: $T_3 = \frac{3}{4}$ and $T_7 = 12$

$$ar^{3-1} = \frac{3}{4} \quad \text{and} \quad ar^{7-1} = 12$$

$$ar^2 = \frac{3}{4} \quad \text{and} \quad ar^6 = 12$$

Dividing we get

$$\frac{ar^6}{ar^2} = \frac{12}{3}$$

$$r^4 = \frac{48}{3} = 16$$

$$r = 2$$

$$ar^2 = \frac{3}{4}$$

$$a(2)^2 = \frac{3}{4}$$

$$a = \frac{3}{4 \times 4} = \frac{3}{16}$$

To find 10th term :

$$T_n = ar^{n-1}$$

$$T_{10} = \frac{3}{16}(2)^{10-1}$$

$$\frac{3}{16}(2)^9 = 3 \times 2^5 = 32 \times 3$$

$$= 96$$

3. The sum of the first and 3rd terms of a G.P. is 40 whereas the sum of its 2nd and 4th term is 96. Find the 6th term of the sequence.

$$n^{\text{th}} \text{ term} = T_n = ar^{n-1} \text{ for a G.P.}$$

$$\text{Given } T_1 + T_3 = 40$$

$$ar^0 + ar^{3-1} = 40$$

$$a + ar^2 = 40$$

$$a(1+r^2) = 40 \qquad (1)$$

Also given $T_2 + T_4 = 96$

$$ar^{2-1} + ar^{4-1} = 96$$

$$ar + ar^3 = 96$$

$$ar(1+r^2) = 96 \qquad (2)$$

Dividing (2) by (1), we get

$$\frac{ar\,(1+r^2)}{a\,(1+r^2)} = \frac{96}{40}$$

$$r = \frac{24}{10} = \frac{12}{15}$$

Substituting $r = \dfrac{12}{5}$ in (1), we get

$$a\left(1+\left(\frac{12}{5}\right)^2\right) = 40$$

$$a\left(\frac{25+144}{25}\right) = 40$$

$$a = \frac{40 \times 25}{169}$$

$$a = \frac{1000}{169}$$

$$\text{Now } T_6 = ar^{6-1} = ar^5 = \frac{1000}{169}\left(\frac{12}{5}\right)^5$$

GEOMETRIC SERIES

If the terms of an geometric sequence are added it becomes a geometric series.
Sum of the first n terms of a G.P:

Let a be the first term, r be the common ratio and S_n be the sum of the first n terms. Then

$$S_n = a + ar + ar^2 + \cdots + ar^{n-1} \qquad (1)$$

Multiplying by r we get

$$rS_n = ar + ar^2 + ar^3 + \ldots ar^n \qquad (2)$$

Subtracting (2) from (1) (if r is < 1)

$$S_n - rS_n = a - ar^n$$
$$S_n(1-r) = a(1-r^n)$$
$$S_n = \frac{a(1-r^n)}{1-r} \qquad r \neq 1$$

If $r = 1$. Then,

$$S_n = a + a.1 + a(1)^2 + \cdots + a(1)^{n-1} = a + a + \cdots + a(n \text{ times})$$
$$S_n = na.$$

Subtracting (1) from (2) if r is > 1, we get

$$S_n = \frac{a(r^n-1)}{r-1}$$

$\therefore$ Sum to n terms in a G.P.

$$\text{if } r < 1 \text{ is } S_n = \frac{a(1-r^n)}{1-r}, \text{ if } r > 1\ S_n = \frac{a(r^n-1)}{r-1}$$

and if $r = 1$, $S_n = na$.

Solved Examples

1. Find the number of terms and the sum of the numbers in the sequence

$$100,\ -10,\ 1, \ldots, -10^{-5}$$

Solution:

Clearly $100,\ -10,\ 1, \ldots, -10^{-5}$ is a G.P, with $a = 100$, $r = \frac{-10}{100} = \frac{-1}{10}$

$$T_n = -10^{-5}$$

To find, n and S_n

we have

$$T_n = ar^{n-1}$$
$$-10^{-5} = 100\left(-\frac{1}{10}\right)^{n-1}$$
$$\frac{-10^{-5}}{100} = (-10^{-1})^{n-1}$$
$$\frac{-10^{-5}}{(-10)^2} = (-10)^{-n+1}$$
$$(-10)^{-5+2} = (-10)^{-n+1}$$

$\because$ the bases are equal, index must be same

$$\therefore \quad -3 = -n + 1$$

$$-3 - 1 = -n \Rightarrow \quad n = 4.$$

Now

$$S_n = \frac{a(1-r^n)}{1-r} = 100\frac{\left(1-\left(\frac{-1}{10}\right)^4\right)}{1-\left(-\frac{1}{10}\right)}$$

$$S_4 = \frac{100\left(1-\frac{1}{10000}\right)}{1+\frac{1}{10}}$$

$$= \frac{100\left(\frac{9999}{10000}\right)}{\frac{11}{10}} = \frac{9999}{100} \times \frac{10}{11}$$

$$S_4 = \frac{909}{10}$$

2. The 3rd term of a geometric sequence is 36 and the 10th term is 78,732. Find the 1st term in the sequence and the sum of these terms.

Given: $T_3 = 36$ and $T_{10} = 78,732$

To find : a and S_n

$$T_n = ar^{n-1}$$

$$ar^{3-1} = 36 \quad \text{and} \quad ar^9 = 78,732$$

$$ar^2 = 36.$$

By dividing, we get

$$\frac{ar^9}{ar^2} = \frac{78732}{36} = \frac{13122}{6} = 2187$$

$$r^7 = 2187 = 3^7$$

$$\Rightarrow \quad r = 3$$

$$\begin{array}{r|l} 3 & 2187 \\ 3 & 729 \\ 3 & 243 \\ 3 & 81 \\ 3 & 27 \\ 3 & 9 \\ 3 & 3 \\ & 1 \end{array}$$

$$ar^2 = 36$$
$$a(3)^2 = 36$$
$$a = \frac{36}{6} = 6$$
$$S_n = \frac{a(r^n - 1)}{r - 1} \qquad \text{Since } r = 3 > 1$$
$$S_{10} = \frac{6(3^{10} - 1)}{3 - 1} = 3(3^{10} - 1)$$

3. A geometric series has nine terms, a common ratio of 2 and a sum of 3577. Find the first term.

Given: $n = 9,\ r = 2$ and $S_n = 3577$

To find a

$$S_n = \frac{a(r^n - 1)}{r - 1} \qquad \because \quad r = 2 > 1$$

$$S_g = \frac{a(2^9 - 1)}{2 - 1} = 3577$$

$$(2^3)^2 = 8^2$$
$$2^6 = 64$$
$$2^6.2^3 = \frac{64 \times 8}{512}$$

$$a(512 - 1) = 3577$$
$$a = \frac{3577}{511} = 7$$
$$\therefore \quad a = 7.$$

SUM TO INFINITY OF AN INFINITE GEOMETRIC PROGRESSION

We have $S_n = \dfrac{a(1 - r^n)}{1 - r}$ if $r < 1$ If r is a fraction between -1 and $+1$, then r^n becomes smaller and smaller as n becomes larger and larger. So r^n may be neglected if $-1 < r < 1$. This value of S_n for large value of n i.e., ∞ is

$$S_\infty = \frac{a}{1 - r}$$

EXAMPLE: Find the sum of $1 + \frac{1}{2} + \frac{1}{4} + \frac{1}{8} + \ldots$

$1 + \frac{1}{2} + \frac{1}{4} + \ldots$ is a geometric series

with $a = 1,\ r = \dfrac{\frac{1}{2}}{1} = \dfrac{1}{2} < 1$

So $S_\infty = \dfrac{a}{1 - r} = \dfrac{1}{1 - \frac{1}{2}} = \dfrac{1}{\frac{2 - 1}{2}} = 2$

Geometric Means

If $a, g_1, g_2, g_3, \ldots, g_n$ b are in geometric progression, Then $g_1, g_2, \ldots, g_n$ are said to be n geometric means between a and b.

To find geometric means we notice b is the $(n+2)^{\text{nd}}$ term of the G.P. and a is first term.

$$\text{So} \quad T_n = ar^{n-1}$$

$$T_{n+2} = ar^{n+2-1} = ar^{n+1}$$

$$b = ar^{n+1} \quad \Rightarrow \quad r^{n+1} = \frac{b}{a}$$

$$r = \sqrt[n+1]{\frac{b}{a}}$$

After getting the value of r, we get

$g_1 = ar,\ g_2 = g_1,\ r,\ g_3 = g_2 r = ar^3$ and so on and $g_n = ar^n$.

Geometric mean

If a, G, b are in geometric progression then G is the geometric mean between a and b.

In G.P. any term – previous term = constant

$$\text{So} \quad \frac{G}{a} = \frac{b}{G}$$

$$G^2 = ab$$

$$G = \sqrt{ab}$$

$\therefore$ geometric mean between a and b is $\sqrt{ab}$.

Solved Examples

1. Find 3 geometric means between 7 and 4375.

Let $7, g_1, g_2, g_3, 4375$ be the geometric progression.

$$a = 7 \quad 5^{\text{th}} \text{ term} = 4375$$

$$T_n = ar^{n-1}$$

$$T_5 = 7r^{5-1}$$

$$4375 = 7r^4$$

$$\frac{4375}{7} = r^4$$

$$625 = r^4 \quad \Rightarrow \quad r = 5$$

$$\text{So} \quad g_1 = ar = 7 \times 5 = 35$$

$$g_2 = g_1 r = 35 \times 5 = 175$$

$$g_3 = g_2 \times r = 175 \times 5 = 875$$

Miscellaneous Problems

1. Find the sum of $6+66+666+\ldots$ n terms

SOLUTION:

$$\text{Let } S = 6+66+666+\ldots n \text{ terms}$$
$$S = 6(1+11+111+\ldots)$$

Multiplying by 9

$$9S = 6(9+99+999+\ldots)$$
$$9S = 6(10-1+100-1+1000-1+\ldots)$$
$$9S = 6\{(10+100+1000+\ldots n \text{ terms}) - 1 - 1\ldots n \text{ terms}\}$$
$$9S = 6\left\{\frac{10(10^n-1)}{10-1} - n\right\} \quad \text{as } 10+100+\ldots \text{ is a G.P. with } a=10,\ r=10.$$
$$S = \frac{6}{9}\left\{\frac{10(10^n-1)}{9} - n\right\}$$
$$S = \frac{60(10^n-1)}{81} - \frac{6n}{9}.$$

2. Find 3 numbers in arithmetic progression, whose sum is 30 and their product is 840.

SOLUTION:
Let the 3 numbers in A.P. be $a-d$, a and $a+d$.

$$\text{Given their sum} = 30$$
$$= \quad a-d+a+a+d = 30 \Rightarrow$$
$$3a = 30 \Rightarrow a = 10$$
$$\text{Their product} = 840$$
$$(a-d)(a)(a+d) = 840$$
$$(10^2-d^2)10 = 840$$
$$100-d^2 = \frac{840}{10}$$
$$100-d^2 = 84$$
$$100-84 = d^2$$
$$\Rightarrow \quad d^2 = 16$$
$$d = \pm 4.$$

So the numbers are $10-4$, 10 and $10+4$, i.e., 6, 10 and 14.

3. Find 3 numbers in G.P. whose sum is 56 and product is 4096.

Let the 3 numbers in G.P. be $\frac{x}{r}$, x and xr.

Given their product = 4096

$$\frac{x}{r} \times x \times xr = 4096$$
$$x^3 = 4096$$
$$x = \sqrt[3]{4096} = 16$$
$$\text{Their sum} = 56$$
$$\therefore \quad \frac{x}{r} + x + xr = 56$$
$$\frac{16}{r} + 16 + 16r = 56$$
$$\frac{16 + 16r + 16r^2}{r} = 56$$
$$16 + 16r + 16r^2 = 56r$$
$$16r^2 - 40r + 16 = 0$$
$$\div \text{ by } 8$$
$$2r^2 - 5r + 2 = 0$$
$$2r^2 - 4r - 1r + 2 = 0$$
$$2r(r-2) - 1(r-2) = 0$$
$$r = 2 \text{ or } r = \frac{1}{2}.$$

So the numbers are $\frac{16}{2}$, 16, 16×2

8, 16 and 32.

4. Three numbers whose sum is 18 are in A.P. If 2, 4 and 11 are added to them respectively then the resulting numbers are in G.P. Find the numbers.

SOLUTION:

Let the 3 numbers in A.P. be $x-d$, x and $x+d$.

$$\text{Given their sum} = 18$$
$$x - d + x + x + d = 18 \quad \Rightarrow \quad x = 6.$$

If 2, 4 and 11 is added to $x-d$, x and $x+d$ respectively then,

$x-d+2$, $4+x$ and $x+d+11$ are in G.P.

$6-d+2$, $4+6$ and $6+d+11$ are in G.P.

$8-d$, 10 and $17+d$ are in G.P.

So common ratio

$$= \frac{10}{8-d} = \frac{17+d}{10}$$

$$100 = (17+d)(8-d)$$

$$100 = 136 + 8d - 17d - d^2$$

$$d^2 + 9d - 36 = 0$$

$$d^2 + 12d - 3d - 36 = 0$$

$$d(d+12) - 3(d+12) = 0$$

$$d = 3 \quad \text{or} \quad d = -12.$$

When $d = 3$, the numbers are $6-3,\ 6,\ 6+3$

$$= 3,\ 6,\ 9$$

When $d = -12$, the numbers are $6+12,\ 6,\ 6-12$

$$18,\ 6,\ -6.$$

So we get 2 set of numbers satisfying the conditions of the given problem.

5. The distance passed over by a certain pendulum bob in a clock in succeeding swings form a G.P. 16 cm, 12 cm, 9 cm, ... cm. Calculate the distance traversed by the bob before it comes to rest.

SOLUTION:

The distance traversed

$$= 16 + 12 + 9 + \cdots \infty$$

$$a = 16,\ r = \frac{12}{16} = \frac{3}{4} < 1$$

$$\therefore \quad S_\infty = \frac{a}{1-r} = \frac{16}{1-\frac{3}{4}} = \frac{16 \times 4}{1} = 64$$

$$\therefore \quad \text{Distance traversed } = 64 \text{ cm.}$$

6. Ajith saved Rs. 82,500 in 10 months. In each month after the first month he saved Rs. 500 more than he did in the previous month. How much did he save in the first month?

SOLUTION:

Given:

$$S_{10} = 82{,}500$$

$$n = 10$$

$$d = 500.$$

$$\text{We have } S_n = \frac{n}{2}[2a+(n-1)d]$$
$$82,500 = \frac{10}{2}[2a+(10-1)500]$$
$$82,500 = 5(2a+4500)$$
$$\frac{82,500}{5} = 2a+4500$$
$$16,500-4500 = 2a \Rightarrow 2a = 12,000$$
$$a = 6000.$$

So Ajith saved Rs 6000 in the first month.

7. A company manufactures 26,000 bikes in the first year. If the production capacity increases every year by 2000, find in how many years the production will be doubled?

Given:

$$T_1 = 26,000$$
$$d = 2000$$

To find n when $T_n = 2T_1$

But $T_n = a+(n-1)d$

$$2T_1 = 26,000+(n-1)2000$$
$$2(26,000) = 26,000+(n-1)2000$$
$$26,000 = (n-1)2000$$
$$\frac{26000}{2000} = n-1$$
$$13 = n-1$$
$$\Rightarrow n = 14.$$

The production will be doubled during the 14th year, i.e., after 13 years.

8. Firm XYZ begins production with 10,000 soft toys per year and decreases production by 1000 toys per year. Firm ABC starts production with 5000 toys and raises production by 250 toys per year. (i) When will the production of two firms equal? (ii) What will be the production in that year?

Production of toys by XYZ in the consecutive years $= 10,000, 9000, 8000, \ldots$
Production of toys by ABC is $5000, 5250, 5500, \ldots$

Let in the nth year, production is same

$$T_n = a + (n-1)d$$
$$10{,}000 + (n-1)(-1000) = 5000 + (n-1)250$$
$$10{,}000 - 5000 = (n-1)(250 + 1000)$$
$$5000 = (n-1)(+1250)$$
$$n - 1 = \frac{5000}{1250} = 4$$
$$n = 4 + 1 = 5$$

$\therefore$ During 5th year of production, the production of firms will be same.
Now $T_5 = 5000 + (5-1)250 = 6000$.

9. If the value of TV is depreciated by 20% annually, what will be its estimated value at the end of 5 years, if its present value is 15,000.

20% depreciation means, for Rs. 100, value after 1year is 100-20=Rs. 80

$\therefore$ 20% depreciation for 15,000 means

$$\text{value after 1 year} = 15{,}000 \times \frac{80}{100}$$
$$\text{value after 2 years} = \left(15{,}000 \times \frac{80}{100}\right) \times \frac{80}{100}$$
$$= 15{,}000 \times \left(\frac{80}{100}\right)^2$$

$\therefore$ value after each year forms a G.P. $15{,}000\left(\frac{80}{100}\right), 15{,}000\left(\frac{80}{100}\right)^2 \ldots$

with $a = 15{,}000\left(\frac{50}{100}\right)$ $r = \frac{80}{100}$.

Value after 5 years in T_5

$$T_5 = ar^{n-1} = 15{,}000\left(\frac{80}{100}\right)^{5-1}$$
$$T_5 = 15{,}000\left(\frac{4}{5}\right)^5$$
$$= 15{,}000 \times 0.32768$$
$$= 4915.2$$

10. Abhay is entitled to receive an annual payment which for each year is less by one tenth of what it was for the year before. If the first payment is

Rs. 10,000. What is the total amount he receives assuming he lives forever.

$$\text{First instalment} = 10{,}000$$

$$2^{\text{nd}} \text{ instalment} = 10{,}000 - \left(\frac{1}{10} \times 10{,}000\right)$$

$$= 9000$$

$$3^{\text{rd}} \text{ instalment} = 90 - \left(\frac{1}{10} \times 9000\right)$$

$$= \text{Rs } 8100$$

So 10,000, 9000, 8100,... is a G.P.

$$a = 10{,}000, \quad r = \frac{9000}{10{,}000} = \frac{9}{10}$$

If he lives forever, then

$$S_\infty = \frac{a}{1-r} = \frac{10{,}000}{1 - \frac{9}{10}}$$

$$= \frac{10{,}000 \times 10}{1} = 1{,}00{,}000$$

The maximum total amount would be Rs. 1,00,000.

IN A NUTSHELL

- Arrangement of numbers according to a particular rule is a sequence.
- If any term $-$ previous term $=$ constant. Then it is an arithmetic sequence or A.P.
- If a is the first term and d is common difference then T_n, n^{th} term of A.P is $T_n = a + (n-1)d$.
- Sum of the first n terms $= S_n = \frac{n}{2}[2a + (n-1)d]$

  $$S_n = \frac{n}{2}[a + T_n]$$
- If $a, x_1, x_2, x_3, \ldots, x_n$ b are in A.P. then $x_1, x_2, \ldots, x_n$ are arithmetic means between a and b.

  $$x_1 = a + d \quad x_2 = a + 2d \text{ or } x_1 + d$$

  $$x_3 = a + 3d \text{ or } x_2 + d \text{ and so on.}$$
- If a, x, b are in A.P. then x is arithmetic mean between a and b

  $$\therefore \quad x = \frac{a+b}{2}.$$

- If $\dfrac{\text{any term}}{\text{previous term}} = \text{constant}$ in a sequence, then it is geometric sequence or geometric progression or G.P.
- If a is the first term, r is common ratio and T_n and S_n are n^{th} term sum to n terms of a G.P. then

$$T_n = ar^{n-1}$$

$$S_n = \frac{a(1-r^n)}{1-r} \text{ if } r < 1$$

$$S_n = \frac{a(r^n-1)}{r-1} \text{ if } r > 1$$

$$S_n = na \qquad \text{if } r = 1$$

- If r is between -1 and 1, the sum of infinite terms in a geometric progression is
$S_\infty = \dfrac{a}{1-r}$.

- If $a,\ x_1,\ x_2,\ x_3,\ldots,x_n b$ are in G.P. then $x_1,\ x_2,\ldots,x_n$ are n geometric means between a and b. $x_1 = ar, \quad x_2 = x_1 r \quad \text{or} \quad ar^2\ldots$
- If $a_1,\ x_1,\ b$ are in G.P. then x is a geometric mean between a and b. $x = \sqrt{ab}$.

CHECK YOUR PROGRESS

1. Find the specified term in the following arithmetic progression

   a) 6, 17, 28, 39,...50th term

   [545]

   b) 87, 83, 79, 75,...40th term

   [−69]

2. In an arithmetic sequence if 3rd term is 8 and 8th term is -17. Find the 20th term

   [−77]

3. Find k so that the terms $3k+1$, k and -3 are in the arithmetic progression

   [$k = 2$]

4. Which term of the sequence 2, 9, 16, 23,... is 828.

   [119th term]

5. Find the sum of:

   a) $4+7+10+13+\ldots$ to 50 terms

   [3875]

   b) $-6+1+8+15+\cdots+141$

   [1485]

6. Find 3 numbers in A.P. So that their sum is 12 and their product is -80.

   [10, 14, -2]

7. Amith borrowed Rs. 4500 without interest and promises to pay back in 30 instalments, each of value Rs. 10 more than the previous one. Find the first and the last instalments.

   [5295]

8. Find the number of boys in a class whose ages are in A.P. with the common difference of 4 months. The youngest boy is just 8 years old and the sum of ages is 168 years.

   [16]

9. Find the 12th term of the sequence $8, 4, 2, 1, \frac{1}{2}, \ldots$

   $\left[\frac{1}{256}\right]$

10. If $k-1$, $2k$ and $21-k$ are in G.P. Find k.

    $\left[k=\frac{7}{5} \text{ or } 3\right]$

11. Find the general term of a geometric sequence whose 2nd term is -6 and 5th term is 162.

    $[2(-3)^{n-1}]$

12. Find 3 numbers in G.P. whose sum is $\frac{7}{3}$ and sum of their squares is $\frac{91}{9}$

    $-\left[3, -1\frac{1}{3}\right]$

13. If a ball has elasticity such that it bounces up 80% of its previous height. Find the total vertical distance travelled down and up by this ball when it dropped from an attitude of 3 meters. Ignore friction and air resistance.

    [27 m]

14. As a prize for inventing the game of chess, its originator is said to have asked for one grain of wheat to be placed on the first square of the board, 2 on the 2nd, 4 on the 3rd, 8 on the 4th and so on until each of the 64 squares had been covered. How much wheat would have been the prize?

    [1.8×10^{19} or about 200 billion tonnes]

15. Find the sum to n terms:

    $5+55+555+\ldots$

    $\left[50\frac{(10^n-1)}{81}-\frac{5n}{9}\right]$

16. Insert 4 geometric means between 3 and 96

[6, 12, 24, 48]

17. Find 5 arithmetic means between 15 and -21

[$9, 3, -3, -9, -15$]

18. The price fixed for laying a cable is Rs. 2.50 per metre for the first 100 metres and an additional Rs. 0.25 for every subsequent metre. Find the cost of last metre and total cost of laying 220 m cable.

[Total: Rs. 2365. Last one: Rs. 32.50]

19. The arithmetic mean of 2 numbers is $\frac{25}{2}$ and their geometric mean is 12. Find the numbers

[16 & 9]

20. A machine is brought for Rs. 20,000. Depreciation is calculated at 10% p.a. for the 1st five years, on the basis of diminishing value. Find the book value of the machine after 5 years.

[11,809.8]

MULTIPLE CHOICE QUESTIONS

1. The HCF of 36 and 84 is
   a) 16 b) 6 c) 12 d) 18
2. The LCM of 24, 36 and 40 is
   a) 120 b) 240 c) 360 d) 480
3. The HCF of $\frac{9}{10}, \frac{12}{25}, \frac{18}{35}$ and $\frac{21}{40}$ is
   a) $\frac{3}{5}$ b) $\frac{252}{5}$ c) $\frac{3}{1400}$ d) $\frac{63}{700}$
4. The product of 2 numbers is 4107. If the HCF of these numbers is 37 then the greater number is
   a) 101 b) 107 c) 111 d) 185
5. Three numbers which are co-prime to each other are such that the product of the first two is 551 and that of last two is 1073. The sum of 3 numbers is
   a) 75 b) 81 c) 85 d) 89
6. The greatest number which on dividing 1657, 2037 leaves remainder 6 and 5 respectively, is
   a) 123 b) 127 c) 235 d) 305
7. The least number which when divided by 5, 6, 7 and 8 leaves a remainder 3 but when divided by 9 leaves no remainder is
   a) 1677 b) 1683 c) 2523 d) 3363

8. How many different factors are there for the number 48 excluding 1 and 48
   a) 12 b) 4 c) 8 d) none
9. What is the remainder when $9+9^2+9^3+9^8$ is divided by 6
   a) 3 b) 2 c) 0 d) 5
10. Six bells commence tolling together and foll at intervals of 2, 4, 6, 8, 10 and 12 seconds respectively. In 30 minutes how many times do they toll together?
    a) 4 b) 10 c) 15 d) 16
11. Which of the following are prime numbers? (i) 101 (ii) 127 (iii) 199 (iv) 221
    a) (i) & (iv) b) (ii) & (iii) c) (i) (ii) & (iii) d) (i) (iii) & (iv)
12. The greatest possible length which can be used to measure exactly the lengths 7 m, 3 m, 85 cm, 12 m, 95 cm is
    a) 15 cm b) 25 cm c) 35 cm d) 42 cm
13. The least multiple of 7 which leaves a remainder of 4 when divided by 6, 9, 15 and 18 is
    a) 74 b) 94 c) 184 d) 364
14. The least number which should be added to 2494 so that the sum is exactly divisible by 5, 6, 4 and 3 is
    a) 3 b) 13 c) 23 d) 33
15. If the sum of two numbers is 55 and HCF and LCM of these numbers are 5 and 120 respectively, then the sum of the reciprocals of numbers is
    a) $\frac{55}{601}$ b) $\frac{601}{55}$ c) $\frac{11}{120}$ d) $\frac{120}{11}$
16. The roots of the equation $x^2-11x+30=0$ are
    a) 5, −6 b) 6, −5 c) 5, 6 d) −5, −6
17. The roots of the equation $2+6x-x^2$ are
    a) $-3+\sqrt{11}$ b) $-3\pm\sqrt{11}$ c) $\pm3+\sqrt{11}$ d) $3\pm\sqrt{11}$
18. $5x-(-2x)-x=$
    a) $2x$ b) $4x$ c) $6x$ d) $8x$
19. If $x=-2$ $y=-1$ and $z=0$ then $(x-y)^{z-x}=$
    a) 9 b) 1 c) −1 d) $\frac{1}{9}$
20. A runs $\frac{13}{5}$ times as fast as *B*. If *A* gives a start of 240 m. How far must the post be so that *A* and *B* might reach at the same time
    a) 390 m b) 330 m c) 600 m d) 720
21. If x, y, z are consecutive negative integers and if $x>y>z$, which of the following must be a positive odd integer?
    a) $x\,y\,z$ b) $(x-y)(y-z)$ c) $x-yz$ d) $x(y+z)$

22. 5 years ago, B's age was three times that of A. Ten years ago B's age was $\frac{1}{2}$ of C. If C represents C's current age which of the following represent A's current age?
   a) $\frac{c}{6}+5$ b) $2C$ c) $\frac{C-10}{3}$ d) $\frac{5C}{3}-10$
23. The range of real values of x satisfying the inequalities $3x-2>7$ and $4x-13>15$ is
   a) $x>3$ b) $x>7$ c) $x<7$ d) $x<3$
24. A portion of Rs. 7200 is inverted at a 4% annual return while the remainder is invested at a 5% annual return. If the annual income from both portions is the same then the total income from the two investments is
   a) Rs. 160 b) Rs. 320 c) Rs. 400 d) Rs. 720
25. A railway half ticket costs half the full fare and the reservation change is the same on half ticket as on full ticket. One reserved first class ticket from Bangalore to Mangalore cost Rs. 216 and one full and one half reserved first class tickets costs Rs. 327. What is the basic first class full fare and what is the reservation charge?
   a) Rs. 105 and Rs. 6 b) Rs. 216 and Rs. 12 c) Rs. 210 and Rs. 12
   d) Rs. 210 and Rs. 6
26. What must be added to $3x^2-6x\,a$ to make it a perfect square?
   a) a^2 b) $3a^2$ c) $6a^2$ d) $12a^2$
27. If $x=2$ then value of $(x^x)^{(x^x)}+\frac{1}{x}=$
   a) $16\frac{1}{2}$ b) $64\frac{1}{2}$ c) $256\frac{1}{2}$ d) $1024\frac{1}{2}$
28. 1, 3, 4, 7, 11, —, 29, 47...
   a) 15 b) 16 c) 17 d) 18
29. Pick the numbers which do not belong to sequence 2, 4, 8, 16, 20
   a) 2 b) 4 c) 8 d) 20
30. The sum of all positive integers upto 1000 which are divisible by 5 and not divisible by 2 is
   a) 10050 b) 5050 c) 5000 d) 50,000
31. The sum of the 3 numbers in A.P. is 21 and the product of their extremes is 45. The numbers are
   a) 5, 7, 9 b) 9, 7, 5 c) both (a) and (b) d) none
32. The sum of the first 50 terms common to series 15, 19, 23... and 14, 19, 24... is
   a) 25,450 b) 24,550 c) 50,900 d) cannot be determines
33. The sum of all the integers which are multiples of 7 and lie between 200 and 400 are
   a) 8729 b) 8700 c) 8428 d) None

34. The sum of the first and the 9th term of an A.P. is 24. What is the sum of first 9 terms of the progression?
    a) 216 b) 108 c) 54 d) None
35. The sum of 20 terms of the series $12+22,\ 32+42,\ 52+62$ is
    a) 210 b) 519 c) 190 d) None
36. An equipment costs Rs. 6,00,000. If it depreciates 15% in the 1st year 13.5% in the next year 12% in the 3rd year and so on what will be its value at the end of 10 years, (all percentage applying to original cost)
    a) 2,00,000 b) 1,05,000 c) 4,05,000 d) 6,50,000
37. Which of the following has the most number of divisors
    a) 99 b) 101 c) 176 d) 182
38. The G.C.D of 1.08, 0.36, 0.9 is
    a) 0.03 b) 0.9 c) 0.18 d) 0.108
39. Three numbers are in the ratio 3:4:5 and their LCM is 2400. Their HCF is
    a) 40 b) 80 c) 120 d) 200
40. The ratio of 2 numbers is 3:4 and their HCF is 4 their LCM is
    a) 12 b) 16 c) 24 d) 48
41. The difference between the square of 7 and the sum of the first 7 odd numbers is
    a) 2 b) 3 c) 4 d) 0
42. Express 5175 as product of primes
    a) $15^2 \times 23$ b) $115 \times 3^2 \times 5$ c) $5^2 \times 3^2 \times 2^3$ d) $5 \times 3 \times 2^3$
43. The smallest number which when diminished by 7 is divisible by 12, 16, 18, 21 and 28 is
    a) 1008 b) 1015 c) 1022 d) 1032
44. Let N be the greatest number that will divide 1305, 4665 and 6905 leaving the same remainder in each case. The sum of digits in N is
    a) 4 b) 5 c) 6 d) 8
45. A father is 3 times as old as his son. After 15 years the father will be twice as old as his son's age at that time. Hence, the father's present age is
    a) 36 b) 42 c) 45 d) 48
46. 4, 12, 36, 108, —, 972, 2916
    a) 144 b) 216 c) 324 d) 432
47. Ram had to do a multiplication. Instead of taking 35 as one of the multiplies, he took 53. As a result the product went up by 540. What is the new product?
    a) 1050 b) 540 c) 1440 d) 1590
48. If $(x+2)^2 = 9$ and $(y+3)^2 = 25$ then the maximum value of $\frac{x}{y}$ is
    a) $\frac{1}{2}$ b) $\frac{5}{2}$ c) $\frac{5}{8}$ d) $\frac{1}{8}$

49. Solution for inequality $33x - 2 > 1$ is

    a) $x > 1$ b) $x > 3$ c) $x > 2/3$ d) $x > \frac{1}{3}$

50. The total number of different divisors of 7200 is

    a) 20 b) 4 c) 54 d) 32

ANSWERS

1 (c)	2 (c)	3 (c)	4 (c)	5 (c)
6 (b)	7 (b)	8 (c)	9 (c)	10 (d)
11 (c)	12 (c)	13 (d)	14 (c)	15 (c)
16 (c)	17 (d)	18 (c)	19 (b)	20 (a)
21 (b)	22 (a)	23 (b)	24 (b)	25 (d)
26 (b)	27 (c)	28 (d)	29 (d)	30 (d)
31 (c)	32 (a)	33 (a)	34 (b)	35 (a)
36 (b)	37 (c)	38 (c)	39 (a)	40 (d)
41 (d)	42 (c)	43 (b)	44 (a)	45 (c)
46 (c)	47 (d)	48 (c)	49 (c)	50 (c)

4

Matrices and Determinants

INTRODUCTION

Information can often be conveniently presented as an array of rows and columns. But timetable, football league results, etc., often use this form of presentation. Such an arrangement of information is called a matrix. Uses of matrices span several areas from simply solving system of simultaneous equations to designing computer games graphics, analysing relationships, coding and operations research, to mention a few.

MATRIX

A matrix is a rectangular array of elements. The elements can be symbols, expressions or numbers. The arrangement is usually enclosed between square brackets [ ].

$$\text{Order of a matrix} = \text{Number of rows} \times \text{Number of columns}$$

If a matrix has m rows and n columns then

$$\text{Order} = m \times n.$$

EXAMPLE: If $A = \begin{bmatrix} 1 & 2 & 3 \\ 2 & 3 & 4 \end{bmatrix}$. Then A has order 2×3.

TYPES OF MATRICES

1. Rectangular Matrix

If in a matrix the number of rows is not equal to the number of columns then that matrix is called a rectangular matrix.

EXAMPLE:

$$X = \begin{bmatrix} 1 & 1 & 7 \\ 2 & 3 & 5 \end{bmatrix}_{2\times 3}$$

(a) Row matrix or row vector: If a matrix has only one row then it is called row matrix.

EXAMPLE: $A = \begin{bmatrix} a_1 & a_2 & a_3 \end{bmatrix}_{1\times 3}$

(b) Column matrix or column vector: If a matrix has only one column then it is called column matrix.

EXAMPLE: $B = \begin{bmatrix} b_1 \\ b_2 \\ b_3 \end{bmatrix}_{3\times 1}$

2. Square Matrix

If in a matrix, the number of rows is equal to the number of columns then it is called a square matrix.

EXAMPLE: $M = \begin{bmatrix} 1 & 2 & 3 \\ 4 & 5 & 6 \\ 7 & 8 & 9 \end{bmatrix}_{3\times 3}$ $\quad N = \begin{bmatrix} a & b \\ c & d \end{bmatrix}$

In a square matrix the entries from the left top corner to the right bottom corner are called principal diagonal elements. So in the above examples $1, 5, 9$ and a, d are principal diagonal elements.

(a) Diagonal matrix: If in a square matrix all the non-diagonal elements are zeros then it is called diagonal matrix.

EXAMPLE: $\begin{bmatrix} 1 & 0 & 0 \\ 0 & 2 & 0 \\ 0 & 0 & 3 \end{bmatrix}$ $\quad \begin{bmatrix} 4 & 0 \\ 0 & 5 \end{bmatrix}$

Scalar matrix: If in a diagonal matrix, all the diagonal elements are equal then it is called scalar matrix.

EXAMPLE: $\begin{bmatrix} 5 & 0 & 0 \\ 0 & 5 & 0 \\ 0 & 0 & 5 \end{bmatrix}$ $\quad \begin{bmatrix} a & 0 \\ 0 & a \end{bmatrix}$

Identity matrix: If in a scalar matrix, all the diagonal elements are equal to 1 then it is called identity matrix or unit matrix.

EXAMPLE: $\begin{bmatrix} 1 & 0 \\ 0 & 1 \end{bmatrix}$ $\quad \begin{bmatrix} 1 & 0 & 0 \\ 0 & 1 & 0 \\ 0 & 0 & 1 \end{bmatrix}$

Upper triangular matrix: A square matrix is called upper triangular matrix if all the non-diagonal elements below the principal diagonals are zeros.

EXAMPLE: $\begin{bmatrix} 1 & 2 & 3 \\ 0 & 4 & 5 \\ 0 & 0 & 6 \end{bmatrix}$ $\begin{bmatrix} a & b \\ 0 & c \end{bmatrix}$

Lower triangular matrix: A Square matrix is called lower triangular matrix if all the non-diagonal elements above the principal diagonal are zeros.

EXAMPLE: $\begin{bmatrix} 1 & 0 & 0 \\ 2 & 3 & 0 \\ 4 & 5 & 6 \end{bmatrix}$ $\begin{bmatrix} a & 0 \\ b & c \end{bmatrix}$

Null matrix or zero matrix: If each element of a matrix is zero then it is called zero matrix or null matrix.

EXAMPLE: $\begin{bmatrix} 0 & 0 & 0 & 0 \\ 0 & 0 & 0 & 0 \end{bmatrix}$, $\begin{bmatrix} 0 & 0 \\ 0 & 0 \end{bmatrix}$

Transpose of a matrix: If the rows and columns of a given matrix say A, are interchanged then it is transpose of a matrix A. It is denoted by A' or A^T.

EXAMPLE: If $A = \begin{bmatrix} 1 & 2 & 3 \\ 4 & 5 & 6 \\ 7 & 8 & 9 \end{bmatrix}$. Then

$$A^T \text{ or } A' = \begin{bmatrix} 1 & 4 & 7 \\ 2 & 5 & 8 \\ 3 & 6 & 9 \end{bmatrix}$$

Symmetric matrix: If $A = A^T$ for a matrix A. Then A is called a symmetric matrix.

EXAMPLE: $\begin{bmatrix} a & b & c \\ b & d & e \\ c & e & f \end{bmatrix}$, $\begin{bmatrix} 1 & 2 \\ 2 & 3 \end{bmatrix}$

Algebra of Matrices

1. Equality: Two matrices of the same order are said to be equal if the corresponding elements are equal.

i.e., $\begin{bmatrix} a & b \\ c & d \end{bmatrix} = \begin{bmatrix} 1 & 2 \\ 3 & 4 \end{bmatrix}$ if and only if $a = 1$, $b = 2$, $c = 3$ and $d = 4$.

2. Addition and subtraction: Two or more matrices of the same order can be added or subtracted. It is the matrix obtained by adding or subtracting the corresponding elements.

$$\text{i.e., if } A=\begin{bmatrix} a_1 & a_2 \\ a_3 & a_4 \end{bmatrix} \quad B=\begin{bmatrix} b_1 & b_2 \\ b_3 & b_4 \end{bmatrix}. \text{ Then}$$

$$A+B=\begin{bmatrix} a_1+b_1 & a_2+b_2 \\ a_3+b_3 & a_4+b_4 \end{bmatrix}$$

$$A-B=\begin{bmatrix} a_1-b_1 & a_2-b_2 \\ a_3-b_3 & a_4-b_4 \end{bmatrix}$$

EXAMPLE: If $A=\begin{bmatrix} 1 & 2 \\ 3 & 4 \end{bmatrix}$ and $B=\begin{bmatrix} 5 & 6 \\ 7 & 8 \end{bmatrix}$. Then

$$A+B=\begin{bmatrix} 1+5 & 2+6 \\ 3+7 & 4+8 \end{bmatrix}=\begin{bmatrix} 6 & 8 \\ 10 & 12 \end{bmatrix}$$

$$A-B=\begin{bmatrix} 1-5 & 2-6 \\ 3-7 & 4-8 \end{bmatrix}=\begin{bmatrix} -4 & -4 \\ -4 & -4 \end{bmatrix}.$$

Scalar multiplication: If A is any matrix and K is any non-zero scalar or constant then KA is a matrix obtained by multiplying each and every element of A by K.

$$\text{i.e., if } A=\begin{bmatrix} a_1 & a_2 \\ a_3 & a_4 \end{bmatrix}. \text{ Then } KA=K\begin{bmatrix} a_1 & a_2 \\ a_3 & a_4 \end{bmatrix}$$

$$KA=\begin{bmatrix} Ka_1 & Ka_2 \\ Ka_3 & Ka_4 \end{bmatrix}$$

EXAMPLE: If $A=\begin{bmatrix} 3 & 5 & 6 \\ 1 & 0 & 2 \end{bmatrix}$. Then

$$5A=5\begin{bmatrix} 3 & 5 & 6 \\ 1 & 0 & 2 \end{bmatrix}=\begin{bmatrix} 15 & 25 & 30 \\ 5 & 0 & 10 \end{bmatrix}$$

Matrix Multiplication: The product of 2 matrices is possible only when the number of columns in the first matrix is equal to the number of rows in the 2nd matrix.

If A is a matrix of order $m \times n$

and B is a matrix of order $n \times p$

Then AB is possible and it is of order $m \times p$. To get elements of AB, the elements of 1st row of A are multiplied by the elements of 1st column of B and the products

are added. The sum corresponds to 1st row, 1st column element. Similarly, other elements are obtained.
i.e., if

$$A = \begin{bmatrix} a_{11} & a_{12} & a_{13} \\ a_{21} & a_{22} & a_{23} \end{bmatrix}_{2\times 3} \qquad B = \begin{bmatrix} b_{11} & b_{21} \\ b_{12} & b_{22} \\ b_{13} & b_{23} \end{bmatrix}_{3\times 2}$$

$$2 \times \boxed{3 \quad 3} \times 2$$

AB is possible and is of order 2×2.

$$AB = \begin{bmatrix} a_{11}b_{11} + a_{12}b_{12} + a_{13}b_{13} & a_{11}b_{21} + a_{12}b_{22} + a_{13}b_{23} \\ a_{21}b_{11} + a_{22}b_{12} + a_{23}b_{13} & a_{21}b_{21} + a_{22}b_{22} + a_{23}b_{23} \end{bmatrix}$$

Notice that BA is also possible.

$$\begin{matrix} B & A \\ 3 \times \boxed{2 \quad 2} \times 3 \end{matrix}$$

BA is of order 3×3.

$$BA = \begin{bmatrix} b_{11} & b_{21} \\ b_{12} & b_{22} \\ b_{13} & b_{23} \end{bmatrix} \begin{bmatrix} a_{11} & a_{12} & a_{13} \\ a_{21} & a_{22} & a_{23} \end{bmatrix}$$

$$\begin{bmatrix} b_{11}a_{11} + b_{21}a_{21} & b_{11}a_{12} + b_{21}a_{22} & b_{11}a_{13} + b_{21}a_{23} \\ b_{12}a_{11} + b_{22}a_{21} & b_{12}a_{12} + b_{22}a_{22} & b_{12}a_{13} + b_{22}a_{23} \\ b_{13}a_{11} + b_{23}a_{21} & b_{13}a_{12} + b_{23}a_{22} & b_{13}a_{13} + b_{23}a_{23} \end{bmatrix}$$

EXAMPLE: If $A = \begin{bmatrix} 1 & 2 \\ 3 & 4 \end{bmatrix}$ $B = \begin{bmatrix} 5 & 6 \\ 7 & 8 \end{bmatrix}$. Then

$$AB = \begin{bmatrix} 1\times 5 + 2\times 7 & 1\times 6 + 2\times 8 \\ 3\times 5 + 4\times 7 & 3\times 6 + 4\times 8 \end{bmatrix} = \begin{bmatrix} 19 & 22 \\ 43 & 50 \end{bmatrix}$$

$$BA = \begin{bmatrix} 5 & 6 \\ 7 & 8 \end{bmatrix} \begin{bmatrix} 1 & 2 \\ 3 & 4 \end{bmatrix}$$

$$= \begin{bmatrix} 5\times 1 + 6\times 3 & 5\times 2 + 6\times 4 \\ 7\times 1 + 8\times 3 & 7\times 2 + 8\times 4 \end{bmatrix} = \begin{bmatrix} 23 & 34 \\ 31 & 46 \end{bmatrix}$$

Note that $AB \neq BA$ in general.

SOLVED EXAMPLES

1. If $A = \begin{bmatrix} 2 & -1 \\ 0 & 2 \end{bmatrix}$ $B = \begin{bmatrix} 1 & -1 \\ 2 & 3 \end{bmatrix}$. Then find (i) $A + B$ (ii) $3A + 4B$ (iii) $A' - 3B'$

SOLUTION:

(i) $A+B=\begin{bmatrix} 2 & -1 \\ 0 & 2 \end{bmatrix}+\begin{bmatrix} 1 & -1 \\ 2 & 3 \end{bmatrix}=\begin{bmatrix} 3 & -2 \\ 2 & 5 \end{bmatrix}$

(ii) $3A+4B = 3\begin{bmatrix} 2 & -1 \\ 0 & 2 \end{bmatrix}+4\begin{bmatrix} 1 & -1 \\ 2 & 3 \end{bmatrix}=\begin{bmatrix} 6 & -3 \\ 0 & 6 \end{bmatrix}+\begin{bmatrix} 4 & -4 \\ 8 & 12 \end{bmatrix}$

$=\begin{bmatrix} 10 & -7 \\ 8 & 18 \end{bmatrix}$

(ii) $A'-3B' = \begin{bmatrix} 2 & 0 \\ -1 & 2 \end{bmatrix}-3\begin{bmatrix} 1 & 2 \\ -1 & 3 \end{bmatrix}$

$=\begin{bmatrix} 2-3 & 0-2 \\ -1+3 & 2-9 \end{bmatrix}=\begin{bmatrix} -1 & -2 \\ 2 & -7 \end{bmatrix}$

2. If $A=\begin{bmatrix} 1 & -1 & 0 \\ 2 & -1 & 2 \\ 1 & 3 & 2 \end{bmatrix}$ and $B=\begin{bmatrix} 5 & -1 & 3 \\ 1 & 1 & 2 \\ 1 & 0 & 1 \end{bmatrix}$ Then find AB andBA. Is $AB=BA$?

SOLUTION:

$$AB=\begin{bmatrix} 1 & -1 & 0 \\ 2 & -1 & 2 \\ 1 & 3 & 2 \end{bmatrix}\begin{bmatrix} 5 & -1 & 3 \\ 1 & 1 & 2 \\ 1 & 0 & 1 \end{bmatrix}$$

$$=\begin{bmatrix} 1\times 5+(-1)(1)+0(1) & 1(-1)+(-1)(1)+0\times 0 & 1(3)+(-1)(2)+(0)(1) \\ 2\times 5-1\times 1+2(1) & 2(-1)+(-1)(1)+2(0) & 2(3)+(-1)(2)+2(1) \\ 1\times 5+3(1)+2(1) & 1(-1)+3(1)+2(0) & 1(3)+3(2)+2(1) \end{bmatrix}$$

$$=\begin{bmatrix} 4 & -2 & 1 \\ 11 & -3 & 6 \\ 10 & 2 & 11 \end{bmatrix}$$

$$BA=\begin{bmatrix} 5 & -1 & 3 \\ 1 & 1 & 2 \\ 1 & 0 & 1 \end{bmatrix}\begin{bmatrix} 1 & -1 & 0 \\ 2 & -1 & 2 \\ 1 & 3 & 2 \end{bmatrix}$$

$$=\begin{bmatrix} 5-2+3 & -5+1+9 & 0-2+6 \\ 1+2+2 & -1-1+6 & 0+2+4 \\ 1+0+1 & -1+0+3 & 0+0+2 \end{bmatrix}$$

$$= \begin{bmatrix} 6 & 5 & 4 \\ 5 & 4 & 6 \\ 2 & 2 & 2 \end{bmatrix}$$

$AB \neq BA$.

3. If $A = \begin{bmatrix} 1 & 0 \\ 2 & 1 \end{bmatrix}$ $B = \begin{bmatrix} 1 & 2 & 3 \\ 2 & -1 & 1 \end{bmatrix}$ and $c = \begin{bmatrix} 2 & -1 \\ -3 & 2 \\ 1 & 1 \end{bmatrix}$. Then prove that $A(BC) = (AB)C$

Proof.

$$\text{Consider} BC = \overrightarrow{\begin{bmatrix} 1 & 2 & 3 \\ 2 & -1 & 1 \end{bmatrix}} \begin{bmatrix} 2 & -1 \\ -3 & 2 \\ 1 & 1 \end{bmatrix}\Bigg\downarrow = \begin{bmatrix} 2-6+3 & -1+4+3 \\ 4+3+1 & -2-2+1 \end{bmatrix}$$

$$BC = \begin{bmatrix} -1 & 6 \\ 8 & -3 \end{bmatrix}$$

$$A(BC) = \overrightarrow{\begin{bmatrix} 1 & 0 \\ 2 & 1 \end{bmatrix}} \begin{bmatrix} -1 & 6 \\ 8 & -3 \end{bmatrix}\Bigg\downarrow$$

$$= \begin{bmatrix} -1+0 & 6+0 \\ -2+8 & 12-3 \end{bmatrix} = \begin{bmatrix} -1 & 6 \\ 6 & 9 \end{bmatrix} \qquad (1)$$

Now

$$AB = \overrightarrow{\begin{bmatrix} 1 & 0 \\ 2 & 1 \end{bmatrix}} \begin{bmatrix} 1 & 2 & 3 \\ 2 & -1 & 1 \end{bmatrix}\Bigg\downarrow = \begin{bmatrix} 1+0 & 2+0 & 3+0 \\ 2+2 & 4-1 & 6+1 \end{bmatrix}$$

$$= \begin{bmatrix} 1 & 2 & 3 \\ 4 & 3 & 7 \end{bmatrix}$$

$$(AB)C = \overrightarrow{\begin{bmatrix} 1 & 2 & 3 \\ 4 & 3 & 7 \end{bmatrix}} \begin{bmatrix} 2 & -1 \\ -3 & 2 \\ 1 & 1 \end{bmatrix}\Bigg\downarrow$$

$$= \begin{bmatrix} 2-6+3 & -1+4+3 \\ 8-9+7 & -4+6+7 \end{bmatrix}$$

$$= \begin{bmatrix} -1 & 6 \\ 6 & 9 \end{bmatrix} \qquad (2)$$

From (1) & (2) $A(BC) = (AB)C$.

4. A matrix is defined by $M = \begin{bmatrix} -1 & 0 \\ 0 & -1 \end{bmatrix}$. Find $M^2, M^3, M^4 \ldots M^n$.

SOLUTION:

$$M^2 = \begin{bmatrix} -1 & 0 \\ 0 & -1 \end{bmatrix}\begin{bmatrix} -1 & 0 \\ 0 & -1 \end{bmatrix} = \begin{bmatrix} 1 & 0 \\ 0 & 1 \end{bmatrix}$$

$$M^3 = M^2 \cdot M = \begin{bmatrix} 1 & 0 \\ 0 & 1 \end{bmatrix}\begin{bmatrix} -1 & 0 \\ 0 & -1 \end{bmatrix} = \begin{bmatrix} -1 & 0 \\ 0 & -1 \end{bmatrix}$$

$$M^4 = M^3 \cdot M = \begin{bmatrix} -1 & 0 \\ 0 & -1 \end{bmatrix}\begin{bmatrix} -1 & 0 \\ 0 & -1 \end{bmatrix} = \begin{bmatrix} 1 & 0 \\ 0 & 1 \end{bmatrix}$$

$$M^n = \begin{bmatrix} (-1)^n & 0 \\ 0 & (-1)^n \end{bmatrix} \quad \text{as} \quad M^2 = \begin{bmatrix} (-1)^2 & 0 \\ 0 & (-1)^2 \end{bmatrix},$$

$$M^3 = \begin{bmatrix} (-1)^3 & 0 \\ 0 & (-1)^3 \end{bmatrix} \quad \text{and} \quad M^4 = \begin{bmatrix} (-1)^4 & 0 \\ 0 & (-1)^4 \end{bmatrix}.$$

5. Find a and b if $aA + B = A$ where $A = \begin{bmatrix} 2 & 5 \\ -3 & 4 \end{bmatrix}$ and $B = \begin{bmatrix} -b & -10 \\ 6 & -2b \end{bmatrix}$

SOLUTION:

Consider $aA + b = A$

$$a\begin{bmatrix} 2 & 5 \\ -3 & 4 \end{bmatrix} + \begin{bmatrix} -b & -10 \\ 6 & -2b \end{bmatrix} = \begin{bmatrix} 2 & 5 \\ -3 & 4 \end{bmatrix}$$

$$\Rightarrow \begin{bmatrix} 2a & 5a \\ -3a & 4a \end{bmatrix} + \begin{bmatrix} -b & -10 \\ 6 & -2b \end{bmatrix} = \begin{bmatrix} 2 & 5 \\ -3 & 4 \end{bmatrix}$$

$$\Rightarrow 2a - b = 2, \quad 5a - 10 = 5, \quad -3a + 6 = -3 \quad \text{and} \quad 4a - 2b = 4$$

$5a = 15 \Rightarrow a = 3.$

$2a - b = 2$

$2(3) - b = 2$

$6 - 2 = b \Rightarrow b = 4.$

Hence, $a = 3$ and $b = 4$.

6. Find x if $x^2\begin{bmatrix} 1 & -1 \\ 2 & 1 \end{bmatrix} + x\begin{bmatrix} 2 & 4 \\ 1 & -6 \end{bmatrix} + \begin{bmatrix} 3 & 1 \\ 4 & 5 \end{bmatrix} = \begin{bmatrix} 6 & 4 \\ 7 & 0 \end{bmatrix}$

SOLUTION:
From the matrix equation, we get

$$x^2 + 2x + 3 = 6$$

$$-x^2+4x+1=4$$
$$2x^2+x+4=7$$
$$x^2-6x+5=0$$

Solving,

$$x^2-5x-1x+5=0$$
$$x(x-5)-1(x-5)=0$$
$$(x-5)(x-1)=0$$
$$x=5 \quad \text{or} \quad x=1$$

$x=5$ is not satisfied by the equation $x^2+2x+3=6$

$$\text{as} \quad 5^2+2(5)+3=6$$
$$25+10+3=6$$
$$38=6 \quad \rightarrow \quad \text{impossible}$$

So $x=1$ is the solution as it is satisfied by all the above equations.

7. Find 2 matrices A and B if $A+B=\begin{bmatrix} 2 & 7 \\ 5 & 6 \end{bmatrix}$ and $A-B=\begin{bmatrix} 6 & 3 \\ -1 & 2 \end{bmatrix}$

SOLUTION:

Adding we get

$$A+B+A-B=\begin{bmatrix} 2+6 & 7+3 \\ -1+5 & 6+2 \end{bmatrix}$$
$$2A=\begin{bmatrix} 8 & 10 \\ 4 & 8 \end{bmatrix}$$
$$A=\frac{1}{2}\begin{bmatrix} 8 & 10 \\ 4 & 8 \end{bmatrix}=\begin{bmatrix} 4 & 5 \\ 2 & 4 \end{bmatrix}$$

Subtracting

$$A+B-(A-B)=\begin{bmatrix} 2-6 & 7-3 \\ 5-(-1) & 6-2 \end{bmatrix}$$
$$A+B-A+B=\begin{bmatrix} -4 & 4 \\ 6 & 4 \end{bmatrix}$$
$$2B=\begin{bmatrix} -4 & 4 \\ 6 & 4 \end{bmatrix} \Rightarrow B=\begin{bmatrix} -2 & 2 \\ 3 & 2 \end{bmatrix}$$

Verification: $A+B=\begin{bmatrix} 4 & 5 \\ 2 & 4 \end{bmatrix}+\begin{bmatrix} -2 & 2 \\ 3 & 2 \end{bmatrix}=\begin{bmatrix} 2 & 7 \\ 5 & 6 \end{bmatrix}$

8. If $A = \begin{bmatrix} 1 & 7 \\ -2 & 1 \end{bmatrix}$ $B = \begin{bmatrix} 2 & 3 \\ -1 & 6 \end{bmatrix}$ and $C = \begin{bmatrix} 5 & 1 \\ 1 & 2 \end{bmatrix}$. Then prove that $A(B+C) = AB + AC$.

Proof.

$$B+C = \begin{bmatrix} 2 & 3 \\ -1 & 6 \end{bmatrix} + \begin{bmatrix} 5 & 1 \\ 1 & 2 \end{bmatrix} = \begin{bmatrix} 7 & 4 \\ 0 & 8 \end{bmatrix}$$

$$A(BC) = \begin{bmatrix} 1 & 7 \\ -2 & 1 \end{bmatrix} \begin{bmatrix} 7 & 4 \\ 0 & 8 \end{bmatrix}$$

$$= \begin{bmatrix} 7+0 & 4+56 \\ -14+0 & -8+8 \end{bmatrix} = \begin{bmatrix} 7 & 60 \\ -14 & 0 \end{bmatrix} \qquad (1)$$

Now

$$AB = \begin{bmatrix} 1 & 7 \\ -2 & 1 \end{bmatrix} \begin{bmatrix} 2 & 3 \\ -1 & 6 \end{bmatrix} = \begin{bmatrix} 2-7 & 3+42 \\ -4-1 & -6+6 \end{bmatrix}$$

$$= \begin{bmatrix} -5 & 45 \\ -5 & 0 \end{bmatrix}$$

$$AC = \begin{bmatrix} 1 & 7 \\ -2 & 1 \end{bmatrix} \begin{bmatrix} 5 & 1 \\ 1 & 2 \end{bmatrix} = \begin{bmatrix} 5+7 & 1+14 \\ -10+1 & -2+2 \end{bmatrix}$$

$$= \begin{bmatrix} 12 & 15 \\ -9 & 0 \end{bmatrix}$$

$$AB + AC = \begin{bmatrix} -5 & 45 \\ -5 & 0 \end{bmatrix} + \begin{bmatrix} 12 & 15 \\ -9 & 0 \end{bmatrix}$$

$$= \begin{bmatrix} +7 & 60 \\ -14 & 0 \end{bmatrix} \qquad (2)$$

From (1) & (2) $A(B+C) = AB + AC$.

9. If $A = \begin{bmatrix} 4 & 2 \\ 3 & 0 \end{bmatrix}$ Find a matrix X such that $AX = 6I$ where $I = \begin{bmatrix} 1 & 0 \\ 0 & 1 \end{bmatrix}$

SOLUTION:

Let $X = \begin{bmatrix} a & b \\ c & d \end{bmatrix}$. Then $AX = \begin{bmatrix} 4 & 2 \\ 3 & 0 \end{bmatrix} \begin{bmatrix} a & b \\ c & d \end{bmatrix}$

$$\begin{bmatrix} 4a+2c & 4b+2d \\ 3a+0 & 3b+0 \end{bmatrix} = 6 \begin{bmatrix} 1 & 0 \\ 0 & 1 \end{bmatrix}$$

$$\begin{bmatrix} 4a+2c & 4b+2d \\ 3a & 3b \end{bmatrix} = \begin{bmatrix} 6 & 0 \\ 0 & 6 \end{bmatrix}$$

$$4a + 2c = 6 \quad 4b + 2d = 0$$

$$3a = 0 \quad 3b = 6$$

$$\Rightarrow \quad a = 0, \quad b = 2, \quad c = 3, \quad d = -4$$

$$\therefore \quad X = \begin{bmatrix} a & b \\ c & d \end{bmatrix} = \begin{bmatrix} 0 & 2 \\ 3 & -4 \end{bmatrix}$$

10. If $A = \begin{bmatrix} 2 & 3 & 4 \\ 1 & 0 & -1 \\ 1 & 1 & 2 \end{bmatrix}$ $B = \begin{bmatrix} 1 & 7 & 3 \\ 2 & 7 & 1 \\ 1 & 2 & -1 \end{bmatrix}$. Then prove that $(A+B)' = A' + B'$

Proof.

$$A + B = \begin{bmatrix} 2+1 & 3+7 & 4+3 \\ 1+2 & 0+7 & -1+1 \\ 1+1 & 1+2 & 2-1 \end{bmatrix} = \begin{bmatrix} 3 & 10 & 7 \\ 3 & 7 & 0 \\ 2 & 3 & 1 \end{bmatrix}$$

$$(A+B)' = \begin{bmatrix} 3 & 3 & 2 \\ 10 & 7 & 3 \\ 7 & 0 & 1 \end{bmatrix} \qquad (1)$$

$$A' + B' = \begin{bmatrix} 2 & 1 & 1 \\ 3 & 0 & 1 \\ 4 & -1 & 2 \end{bmatrix} + \begin{bmatrix} 1 & 2 & 1 \\ 7 & 7 & 2 \\ 3 & 1 & -1 \end{bmatrix} = \begin{bmatrix} 2+1 & 1+2 & 1+1 \\ 3+7 & 0+7 & 1+2 \\ 4+3 & -1+1 & 2-1 \end{bmatrix}$$

$$A' + B' = \begin{bmatrix} 3 & 3 & 2 \\ 10 & 7 & 3 \\ 7 & 0 & 1 \end{bmatrix} \qquad (2)$$

From (1) and (2) $(A+B)' = A' + B'$. **Proved**

DETERMINANTS

Every square matrix is associated with a unique real number called its determinant value.

If $A = \begin{bmatrix} a & b \\ c & d \end{bmatrix}$. Then determinant of A is denoted by det A or $|A|$ and its value is $\begin{vmatrix} a & b \\ c & d \end{vmatrix} = ad - bc.$

EXAMPLE: If $A = \begin{bmatrix} 1 & 2 \\ 4 & -3 \end{bmatrix}$. Then $|A| = \begin{vmatrix} 1 & 2 \\ 4 & -3 \end{vmatrix}$

$$= 1 \times (-3) + 2 \times (4)$$

$$-3 + 8 = 5$$

If $A = \begin{bmatrix} a & b & c \\ d & e & f \\ g & h & i \end{bmatrix}$. Then det A is given by

$$|A| = \begin{vmatrix} a & b & c \\ d & e & f \\ g & h & i \end{vmatrix} = a\begin{vmatrix} e & f \\ h & i \end{vmatrix} - b\begin{vmatrix} d & f \\ g & i \end{vmatrix} + c\begin{vmatrix} d & e \\ g & h \end{vmatrix}$$

$$= a(ei - fh) - b(di - gf) + c(dh - ge)$$

For example, if $A = \begin{bmatrix} 1 & 2 & 3 \\ 4 & 0 & 5 \\ 2 & 3 & 1 \end{bmatrix}$. Then

$$\det A = \begin{vmatrix} 1 & 2 & 3 \\ 4 & 0 & 5 \\ 2 & 3 & 1 \end{vmatrix} = 1\begin{vmatrix} 0 & 5 \\ 3 & 1 \end{vmatrix} - 2\begin{vmatrix} 4 & 5 \\ 2 & 1 \end{vmatrix} + 3\begin{vmatrix} 4 & 0 \\ 2 & 3 \end{vmatrix}$$

$$= 1(0 - 15) - 2(4 - 10) + 3(12 - 0)$$

$$- 15 + 16 + 36$$

$$37$$

Singular and non-singular matrices: If for a given matrix A, det $A = 0$, then it is called singular matrix. Otherwise it is non-singular, i.e., if det $A \neq 0$ then matrix A is non-singular.

Note: For 2 matrices A and B,

$$\det AB = \det A \cdot \det B$$

$$\text{i.e.,} \quad |AB| = |A| \cdot |B|$$

SOLVED EXAMPLES

1. If $A = \begin{bmatrix} 1 & 7 \\ 2 & 6 \end{bmatrix}$, $B = \begin{bmatrix} 1 & 5 \\ 1 & 6 \end{bmatrix}$. Then find det A, $|B|$, AB, $|AB|$ and hence prove that det AB = det $A \cdot$ det B.

SOLUTION:

$$\det A = \begin{vmatrix} 1 & 7 \\ 2 & 6 \end{vmatrix} = 1(6) - 7(2) = 6 - 14 = -8$$

$$|B| = \begin{vmatrix} 1 & 5 \\ 1 & 6 \end{vmatrix} = 1(6) - 5(1) = 6 - 5 = 1$$

$$AB = \begin{bmatrix} 1 & 7 \\ 2 & 6 \end{bmatrix}\begin{bmatrix} 1 & 5 \\ 1 & 6 \end{bmatrix} = \begin{bmatrix} 1+7 & 5+42 \\ 2+6 & 10+36 \end{bmatrix} = \begin{bmatrix} 8 & 47 \\ 8 & 46 \end{bmatrix}$$

$$\det AB = \begin{vmatrix} 8 & 47 \\ 8 & 46 \end{vmatrix} = 8(46) - 8(47)$$

$$= 8(46 - 47) = 8(-1) = -8$$

Now $\det A \cdot \det B = -8 \times 1 = -8$

Hence, $\det AB = \det A \cdot \det B$.

2. Find x if the matrix $\begin{bmatrix} 1 & 4 \\ 8 & x \end{bmatrix}$ is singular.

SOLUTION:

Given: Matrix $\begin{bmatrix} 1 & 4 \\ 8 & x \end{bmatrix}$ is singular

So $\begin{vmatrix} 1 & 4 \\ 8 & x \end{vmatrix} = 0$

$$x - 32 = 0$$

$$x = 32$$

3. Find x if $\begin{vmatrix} 1 & 3 & x \\ 1 & 2 & 1 \\ 2 & 1 & -1 \end{vmatrix} = 20$

SOLUTION:

$$1\begin{vmatrix} 2 & 1 \\ 1 & -1 \end{vmatrix} - 3\begin{vmatrix} 1 & 1 \\ 2 & -1 \end{vmatrix} + x\begin{vmatrix} 1 & 2 \\ 2 & 1 \end{vmatrix} = 20$$

$$1(-2-1) - 3(-1-2) + x(1-4) = 20$$

$$-3 + 9 - 3x = 20$$

$$6 - 3x = 20$$

$$3x = 6 - 20$$

$$x = -\frac{14}{3}$$

4. Express the determinant $\begin{vmatrix} x^2 & 2 \\ 3x & 5 \end{vmatrix}$ in terms of the matrix $A = \begin{bmatrix} 5x & 2 \\ 3 & 1 \end{bmatrix}$

SOLUTION:

$$\begin{vmatrix} x^2 & 2 \\ 3x & 5 \end{vmatrix} = 5x^2 - 6x = x(5x - 6)$$

$$= x\begin{vmatrix} 5x & 2 \\ 3 & 1 \end{vmatrix}$$

$$= x|A|$$

5. For what value(s) of K will the matrix $\begin{bmatrix} (1-K) & 1 & 1 \\ 1 & (1-K) & 1 \\ 1 & 1 & K \end{bmatrix}$ be singular.

SOLUTION:

For the matrix to be singular, $\begin{vmatrix} 1-K & 1 & 1 \\ 1 & 1-K & 1 \\ 1 & 1 & K \end{vmatrix} = 0$

$$(1-K)\begin{vmatrix} 1-K & 1 \\ 1 & K \end{vmatrix} - 1\begin{vmatrix} 1 & 1 \\ 1 & K \end{vmatrix} + 1\begin{vmatrix} 1 & 1-K \\ 1 & 1 \end{vmatrix} = 0$$

$$(1-K)\left[(1-K)K-1\right] - 1(K-1) + 1(1-(1-K)) = 0$$

$$(1-K)\left(K-K^2-1\right) - K+1+1-1+K = 0$$

$$(1-K)(K-K^2-1)+1 = 0$$

$$K^3 - 2K^2 - 2K = 0$$

$$K\left(K^2-2K-2\right) = 0$$

$$K = 0 \quad \text{or} \quad K^2 - 2K - 2 = 0$$

$$K = \frac{+2 \pm \sqrt{4-4(+1)(-2)}}{2}$$

$$K = \frac{2 \pm 2\sqrt{3}}{2} = 1 \pm \sqrt{3}$$

$$\therefore \quad K = 0 \text{ or } k = 1 \pm \sqrt{3}$$

Minor, Cofactor and Adjoint of a Square Matrix

Let $A = \begin{bmatrix} a_{11} & a_{12} & \dots & a_{1n} \\ a_{21} & a_{22} & \dots & a_{2n} \\ a_{n1} & a_{n2} & \dots & a_{nn} \end{bmatrix}$ be a square matrix of order $n \times n$. Then minor of an element a_{ij} is the determinant obtained by deleting the row and the column containing it (i.e., i^{th} row and j^{th} column). If the minors are multiplied with $(-1)^{i+j}$ i.e., with proper sign + or − we get cofactors. If we take the transpose of the cofactors' matrix we get the adjoint of a matrix.

Illustration:

1. If $A = \begin{bmatrix} 0 & 1 \\ 2 & 3 \end{bmatrix}$

$$\text{Minor of } 0 = 3 \quad \text{Cofactor } = (-1)^{1+1} \cdot 3 = 3$$

$$\text{Minor of } 1 = 2 \quad \text{Cofactor } = (-1)^{1+2} \cdot 2 = -2$$

$$\text{Minor of } 2 = 1 \quad \text{Cofactor } = (-1)^{2+1} \cdot 1 = -1$$

$$\text{Minor of } 3 = 0 \quad \text{Cofactor } = (-1)^{2+2} \cdot 0 = 0$$

Cofactor matrix $= \begin{bmatrix} 3 & -2 \\ -1 & 0 \end{bmatrix}$. Taking transpose we get

adjoint of $A = \begin{bmatrix} 3 & -1 \\ -2 & 0 \end{bmatrix}$

2. If $A = \begin{bmatrix} 1 & 2 & 3 \\ 4 & 5 & 6 \\ 7 & 8 & 9 \end{bmatrix}$

$$\text{Minor of } 1 = \begin{vmatrix} 5 & 6 \\ 8 & 9 \end{vmatrix} = 45 - 48 = -3$$

$$\text{Minor of } 2 = \begin{vmatrix} 4 & 6 \\ 7 & 9 \end{vmatrix} = 36 - 42 = -6$$

$$\text{Minor of } 3 = \begin{vmatrix} 4 & 5 \\ 7 & 8 \end{vmatrix} = 32 - 35 = -3$$

$$\text{Minor of } 4 = \begin{vmatrix} 2 & 3 \\ 8 & 9 \end{vmatrix} = 18 - 24 = -6$$

$$\text{Minor of } 5 = \begin{vmatrix} 1 & 3 \\ 7 & 9 \end{vmatrix} = 9 - 21 = -12$$

$$\text{Minor of } 6 = \begin{vmatrix} 1 & 2 \\ 7 & 8 \end{vmatrix} = 8 - 14 = -6$$

$$\text{Minor of } 7 = \begin{vmatrix} 2 & 3 \\ 5 & 6 \end{vmatrix} = 12 - 15 = -3$$

$$\text{Minor of } 8 = \begin{vmatrix} 1 & 3 \\ 4 & 6 \end{vmatrix} = 6 - 12 = -6$$

$$\text{Minor of } 9 = \begin{vmatrix} 1 & 2 \\ 4 & 5 \end{vmatrix} = 5 - 8 = -3$$

Hence,

Matrix of minors $= \begin{bmatrix} -3 & -6 & -3 \\ -6 & -12 & -6 \\ -3 & -6 & -3 \end{bmatrix}$ multiplying with $\begin{bmatrix} + & - & + \\ - & + & - \\ + & - & + \end{bmatrix}$

We get the cofactor matrix $= \begin{bmatrix} -3 & 6 & -3 \\ 6 & -12 & 6 \\ -3 & 6 & -3 \end{bmatrix}$

Taking transpose we get

Adjoint of $A = \begin{bmatrix} -3 & 6 & -3 \\ 6 & -12 & 6 \\ -3 & 6 & -3 \end{bmatrix}$

Inverse of a Square Matrix

If A is a non-singular matrix of order $n \times n$ then there exists a matrix B such that $AB = BA = I$ where I is the identity matrix of order $n \times n$. The matrix B is called inverse of A and it is denoted by $B = A^{-1}$.

$$\therefore \quad A \cdot A^{-1} = A^{-1} \cdot A = I.$$

Inverse of a matrix can be obtained by using the formula, $A^{-1} = \frac{1}{|A|}$ adjoint of A.

Example: To find the inverse of $\begin{bmatrix} 1 & 2 \\ 5 & 11 \end{bmatrix}$

Let $A = \begin{bmatrix} 1 & 2 \\ 5 & 11 \end{bmatrix}$

$$|A| = \begin{bmatrix} 1 & 2 \\ 5 & 11 \end{bmatrix} = 11 - 10 = 1 \neq 0 \quad \text{so } A^{-1} \text{ exists.}$$

$$A^{-1} = \frac{\text{adjoint of } A}{|A|}$$

Now

Minor of 1 = 11,

Minor of 2 = 5,

Minor of 5 = 2 and

Minor of 11 = 1

Matrix of minors $= \begin{bmatrix} 11 & 5 \\ 2 & 1 \end{bmatrix}$

Multiplying with $\begin{bmatrix} + & - \\ - & + \end{bmatrix}$ we get cofactor matrix $= \begin{bmatrix} 11 & -5 \\ -2 & 1 \end{bmatrix}$

Taking transpose we get

$$\text{adj } A = \begin{bmatrix} 11 & -2 \\ -5 & 1 \end{bmatrix}$$

$$A^{-1} = \frac{1}{|A|}\begin{bmatrix} 11 & -2 \\ -5 & 1 \end{bmatrix} = \frac{1}{1}\begin{bmatrix} 11 & -2 \\ -5 & 1 \end{bmatrix}$$

$$\therefore \quad A^{-1} = \begin{bmatrix} 11 & -2 \\ -5 & 1 \end{bmatrix}$$

Note: Adjoint of a square matrix of order 2×2 can be written directly by interchanging principal diagonal elements and changing the signs of the remaining elements.

EXAMPLE: (i) If $A = \begin{bmatrix} 1 & 2 \\ 3 & 4 \end{bmatrix}$ Adj $A = \begin{bmatrix} 4 & -2 \\ -3 & 1 \end{bmatrix}$

(ii) $A = \begin{bmatrix} 1 & -2 \\ 3 & 4 \end{bmatrix} \Rightarrow$ Adj $A = \begin{bmatrix} 4 & 2 \\ -3 & 1 \end{bmatrix}$

To find inverse of a square matrix of order 3:

Let $A = \begin{bmatrix} 1 & 2 & 3 \\ 0 & 1 & 2 \\ 1 & 5 & -3 \end{bmatrix}$

$$|A| = 1\begin{vmatrix} 1 & 2 \\ 5 & -3 \end{vmatrix} - 2\begin{vmatrix} 0 & 2 \\ 1 & -3 \end{vmatrix} + 3\begin{vmatrix} 0 & 1 \\ 1 & 5 \end{vmatrix}$$

$$= 1(-3-10) - 2(0-2) + 3(0-1)$$

$$-13 + 4 - 3 = -14 \neq 0$$

So A^{-1} exists

$$A^{-1} = \frac{1}{|A|} \cdot \text{adj } A$$

Now

$$\text{Minor of } 1 = \begin{vmatrix} 1 & 2 \\ 5 & -3 \end{vmatrix} = -3 - 10 = -13$$

$$2 = \begin{vmatrix} 0 & 2 \\ 1 & -3 \end{vmatrix} = 0 - 2 = -2$$

$$3 = \begin{vmatrix} 0 & 1 \\ 1 & 5 \end{vmatrix} = 0 - 1 = -1$$

$$0 = \begin{vmatrix} 2 & 3 \\ 5 & -3 \end{vmatrix} = -6 - 15 = -21$$

$$1 = \begin{vmatrix} 1 & 3 \\ 1 & -3 \end{vmatrix} = -3 - 3 = -6$$

$$2 = \begin{vmatrix} 1 & 2 \\ 1 & 5 \end{vmatrix} = 5 - 2 = 3$$

$$1 = \begin{vmatrix} 2 & 3 \\ 1 & 2 \end{vmatrix} = 4 - 3 = 1$$

$$5 = \begin{vmatrix} 1 & 3 \\ 0 & 2 \end{vmatrix} = 2 - 0 = 2 \quad \text{and minor of } -3 = \begin{bmatrix} 1 & 2 \\ 0 & 1 \end{bmatrix} = 1$$

Matrix of minors $= \begin{bmatrix} -13 & -2 & -1 \\ -21 & -6 & -3 \\ 1 & 2 & 1 \end{bmatrix}$. Multiplying with $= \begin{bmatrix} + & - & + \\ - & + & - \\ + & - & + \end{bmatrix}$ we get

$$\text{Cofactor matrix} = \begin{bmatrix} -13 & 2 & -1 \\ 21 & -6 & -3 \\ 1 & -2 & 1 \end{bmatrix}$$

Taking transpose, we get

$$\text{Adj } A = \begin{bmatrix} -13 & 21 & 1 \\ 2 & -6 & -2 \\ -1 & -3 & 1 \end{bmatrix}$$

$$A^{-1} = \frac{1}{|A|} \text{Adj } A = \frac{1}{-14} \begin{bmatrix} -13 & 21 & 1 \\ 2 & -6 & -2 \\ -1 & -3 & 1 \end{bmatrix}$$

Note: We can write the adjoint of a square matrix directly by writing the minors multiplied by proper signs (+ or –) column wise,

$$\text{i.e., if } A = \begin{bmatrix} \boxed{1 \quad 2 \quad 3} \\ 0 \quad 1 \quad 2 \\ 1 \quad 5 \quad -3 \end{bmatrix}$$

$$\text{Adj } A = \begin{bmatrix} +\begin{vmatrix} 1 & 2 \\ 5 & -3 \end{vmatrix} & -\begin{vmatrix} 2 & 3 \\ 5 & -3 \end{vmatrix} & +\begin{vmatrix} 2 & 3 \\ 1 & 2 \end{vmatrix} \\ -\begin{vmatrix} 0 & 2 \\ 1 & -3 \end{vmatrix} & +\begin{vmatrix} 1 & 3 \\ 1 & -3 \end{vmatrix} & -\begin{vmatrix} 1 & 3 \\ 0 & 2 \end{vmatrix} \\ +\begin{vmatrix} 0 & 1 \\ 1 & 5 \end{vmatrix} & -\begin{vmatrix} 1 & 2 \\ 1 & 5 \end{vmatrix} & +\begin{vmatrix} 1 & 2 \\ 0 & 1 \end{vmatrix} \end{bmatrix}$$

$$\text{Adj } A = \begin{bmatrix} -13 & 21 & 1 \\ 2 & -6 & -2 \\ -1 & -3 & 1 \end{bmatrix}$$

SOLVED EXAMPLES

1. Find A^{-1} and hence prove that

$$A \cdot \text{adj } A = |A|.I \quad \text{if} \quad A = \begin{bmatrix} 1 & 2 \\ 0 & 4 \end{bmatrix}$$

SOLUTION:

$$A = \begin{bmatrix} 1 & 2 \\ 0 & 4 \end{bmatrix} \qquad |A| = 1(4) - 2(0) = 4 \neq 0$$

A^{-1} exists

$$\text{adj } A = \begin{bmatrix} 4 & -2 \\ 0 & 1 \end{bmatrix}$$ (interchanging 1 and 4 changing signs of 2 and 0)

$$A^{-1} = \frac{1}{|A|} \cdot \text{adj } A = \frac{1}{4}\begin{bmatrix} 4 & -2 \\ 0 & 1 \end{bmatrix}$$

$$A^{-1} = \begin{bmatrix} 1 & -\frac{1}{2} \\ 0 & \frac{1}{4} \end{bmatrix}$$

Now to prove $A \cdot \text{adj } A = |A|I$,

$$A \cdot \text{adj } A = \begin{bmatrix} 1 & 2 \\ 0 & 4 \end{bmatrix} \begin{bmatrix} 4 & -2 \\ 0 & 1 \end{bmatrix}$$

$$= \begin{bmatrix} 4+0 & -2+2 \\ 0+0 & 0+4 \end{bmatrix} = \begin{bmatrix} 4 & 0 \\ 0 & 4 \end{bmatrix} = 4\begin{bmatrix} 1 & 0 \\ 0 & 1 \end{bmatrix} = |A|I. \quad \textbf{Proved.}$$

2. Find A^{-1} and hence verify that $A \cdot A^{-1} = A^{-1} \cdot A = I$ for the matrix

$$\begin{bmatrix} 2 & 3 \\ -1 & -2 \end{bmatrix}$$

SOLUTION:

$$A = \begin{bmatrix} 2 & 3 \\ -1 & -2 \end{bmatrix} \quad |A| = \begin{vmatrix} 2 & 3 \\ -1 & -2 \end{vmatrix} = -4-(-3)$$

$$-4+3 = -1 \neq 0$$

So A^{-1} exists.

$$\text{adj } A = \begin{bmatrix} -2 & -3 \\ 1 & 2 \end{bmatrix}$$

$$A^{-1} = \frac{1}{|A|} \cdot \text{adj } A = \frac{1}{-1}\begin{bmatrix} -2 & -3 \\ 1 & 2 \end{bmatrix} = \begin{bmatrix} 2 & 3 \\ -1 & -2 \end{bmatrix}$$

Now consider

$$A \cdot A^{-1} = \begin{bmatrix} 2 & 3 \\ -1 & -2 \end{bmatrix}\begin{bmatrix} 2 & 3 \\ -1 & -2 \end{bmatrix} = \begin{bmatrix} 4-3 & 6-6 \\ -2+2 & -3+4 \end{bmatrix}$$

$$= \begin{bmatrix} 1 & 0 \\ 0 & 1 \end{bmatrix} = I$$

Similarly, $A^{-1} \cdot A = \begin{bmatrix} 2 & 3 \\ -1 & -2 \end{bmatrix}\begin{bmatrix} 2 & 3 \\ -1 & -2 \end{bmatrix} = \begin{bmatrix} 1 & 0 \\ 0 & 1 \end{bmatrix} = I$

So $A \cdot A^{-1} = A^{-1} \cdot A = I$ **Hence, proved.**

3. If $A = \begin{bmatrix} 5 & -8 & -1 \\ 2 & -3 & -1 \\ -3 & 5 & 1 \end{bmatrix}$ and $B = \begin{bmatrix} 2 & 3 & 5 \\ 1 & 2 & 3 \\ 1 & -1 & 1 \end{bmatrix}$

Find AB and hence, find A^{-1}.

SOLUTION:

$$AB = \begin{bmatrix} 5 & -8 & -1 \\ 2 & -3 & -1 \\ -3 & 5 & 1 \end{bmatrix}\begin{bmatrix} 2 & 3 & 5 \\ 1 & 2 & 3 \\ 1 & -1 & 1 \end{bmatrix}$$

$$= \begin{bmatrix} 10-8-1 & 15-16+1 & 25-24-1 \\ 4-3-1 & 6-6+1 & 10-9-1 \\ -6+5+1 & -9+10-1 & -15+15+1 \end{bmatrix}$$

$$= \begin{bmatrix} 1 & 0 & 0 \\ 0 & 1 & 0 \\ 0 & 0 & 1 \end{bmatrix} = I$$

$$AB = I \quad \text{so} \quad A^{-1} = B$$

$$A^{-1} = \begin{bmatrix} 2 & 3 & 5 \\ 1 & 2 & 3 \\ 1 & -1 & 1 \end{bmatrix}$$

4. Find A^{-1} if $A = \begin{bmatrix} 1 & 0 & 1 \\ 2 & 1 & 0 \\ 1 & 0 & -1 \end{bmatrix}$

SOLUTION:

$$A^{-1} = \frac{\text{adj } A}{|A|}$$

$$|A| = \begin{vmatrix} 1 & 0 & 1 \\ 2 & 1 & 0 \\ 1 & 0 & -1 \end{vmatrix} = 1(-1-0) - 0 + 1(0-1)$$

$$-1-1 = -2 \neq 0 \quad \text{So } A^{-1} \text{ exist.}$$

$$\text{adj } A = \begin{bmatrix} \begin{vmatrix} 1 & 0 \\ 0 & -1 \end{vmatrix} & -\begin{vmatrix} 0 & 1 \\ 0 & -1 \end{vmatrix} & \begin{vmatrix} 0 & 1 \\ 1 & 0 \end{vmatrix} \\ -\begin{vmatrix} 2 & 0 \\ 1 & -1 \end{vmatrix} & +\begin{vmatrix} 1 & 1 \\ 1 & -1 \end{vmatrix} & -\begin{vmatrix} 1 & 1 \\ 2 & 0 \end{vmatrix} \\ \begin{vmatrix} 2 & 1 \\ 1 & 0 \end{vmatrix} & -\begin{vmatrix} 1 & 0 \\ 1 & 0 \end{vmatrix} & +\begin{vmatrix} 1 & 0 \\ 2 & 1 \end{vmatrix} \end{bmatrix}$$

$$\text{adj } A = \begin{bmatrix} -1 & 0 & -1 \\ 2 & -2 & 2 \\ -1 & 0 & 1 \end{bmatrix}$$

$$A^{-1} = \frac{\text{adj } A}{|A|} = \frac{1}{-2}\begin{bmatrix} -1 & 0 & -1 \\ 2 & -2 & 2 \\ -1 & 0 & 1 \end{bmatrix}$$

$$A^{-1} = \begin{bmatrix} \frac{1}{2} & 0 & \frac{1}{2} \\ -1 & +1 & -1 \\ \frac{1}{2} & 0 & -\frac{1}{2} \end{bmatrix}$$

5. If $A = \begin{bmatrix} 8 & -1 & -3 \\ 2 & -1 & 0 \\ -7 & 2 & 3 \end{bmatrix}$ and $B = \begin{bmatrix} 1 & 1 & 1 \\ 2 & -1 & 2 \\ 1 & 3 & 2 \end{bmatrix}$. Find AB and hence, find B^{-1}.

SOLUTION:

$$AB = \begin{bmatrix} 8-2-3 & 8+1-9 & 8-2-6 \\ 2-2+0 & 2+1+0 & 2-2+0 \\ -7+4+3 & -7-2+9 & -7+4+6 \end{bmatrix} = \begin{bmatrix} 3 & 0 & 0 \\ 0 & 3 & 0 \\ 0 & 0 & 3 \end{bmatrix}$$

$$AB = 3\begin{bmatrix} 1 & 0 & 0 \\ 0 & 1 & 0 \\ 0 & 0 & 1 \end{bmatrix}$$

$$AB = 3I$$

$$\frac{1}{3}AB = I$$

$$\therefore \quad B^{-1} = \frac{1}{3}A$$

$$B^{-1} = \frac{1}{3}\begin{bmatrix} 8 & -1 & -3 \\ 2 & -1 & 0 \\ -7 & 2 & 3 \end{bmatrix}$$

Solution of System of Linear Equations

Consider 2 equations in 2 variables

$$a_1x + b_1y = d_1$$
$$a_2x + b_2y = d_2$$

The solution is the value of x and y which simultaneously satisfy the above equations. The solution can be obtained by various methods. Cramer's rule and matrix method are two such methods.

1. Cramer's Rule

Let $A = \begin{vmatrix} a_1 & b_1 \\ a_2 & b_2 \end{vmatrix} = a_1b_2 - a_2b_1$

$$A_x = \begin{vmatrix} d_1 & b_1 \\ d_2 & b_2 \end{vmatrix} = d_1b_2 - d_2b_1$$

$$A_y = \begin{vmatrix} a_1 & d_1 \\ a_2 & d_2 \end{vmatrix} = a_1d_2 - a_2d_1$$

Then by Cramer's rule,

$$x = \frac{A_x}{A} \quad \text{and} \quad y = \frac{A_y}{A}$$

2. Matrix Method

Let $A = \begin{bmatrix} a_1 & b_1 \\ a_2 & b_2 \end{bmatrix}$ $X = \begin{bmatrix} x \\ y \end{bmatrix}$ and $D = \begin{bmatrix} d_1 \\ d_2 \end{bmatrix}$

Matrix equation

$$AX = D$$
$$\Rightarrow \quad X = A^{-1}D$$
$$\text{i.e.,} \quad \begin{bmatrix} x \\ y \end{bmatrix} = A^{-1}D$$

Note: If there are 3 equations in 3 variables say

$$a_1x + b_1y + c_1z = d_1$$
$$a_2x + b_2y + c_2z = d_2$$
$$a_3x + b_3y + c_3z = d_3$$

Then

Cramer's rule

$$A = \begin{vmatrix} a_1 & b_1 & c_1 \\ a_2 & b_2 & c_2 \\ a_3 & b_3 & c_3 \end{vmatrix}$$

$$A_x = \begin{vmatrix} d_1 & b_1 & c_1 \\ d_2 & b_2 & c_2 \\ d_3 & b_3 & c_3 \end{vmatrix}$$

$$A_y = \begin{vmatrix} a_1 & d_1 & c_1 \\ a_2 & d_2 & c_2 \\ a_3 & d_3 & c_3 \end{vmatrix}$$

$$A_z = \begin{vmatrix} a_1 & b_1 & d_1 \\ a_2 & b_2 & d_2 \\ a_3 & b_3 & d_3 \end{vmatrix}$$

$$x = \frac{A_x}{A}, \quad y = \frac{A_x}{A} \quad \text{and } z = \frac{A_z}{A}$$

Matrix method:

$$A = \begin{bmatrix} a_1 & b_1 & c_1 \\ a_2 & b_2 & c_2 \\ a_3 & b_3 & c_3 \end{bmatrix} \quad X = \begin{bmatrix} x \\ y \\ z \end{bmatrix} \quad D = \begin{bmatrix} d_1 \\ d_2 \\ d_3 \end{bmatrix}$$

$$AX = D$$
$$X = A^{-1}D$$

SOLVED EXAMPLES

Solve the following by Cramer's rule:

1.
$$2x - 3y = 8$$
$$x + 5y = 3$$

SOLUTION:

$$Let \quad A = \begin{bmatrix} 2 & -3 \\ 1 & 5 \end{bmatrix}$$

$$|A| = 2(5) - (-3)1$$
$$10 + 3 = 13$$

$$|A_x| = \begin{vmatrix} 8 & -3 \\ 3 & 5 \end{vmatrix} = 8(5) - (-3)(3) = 40 + 9 = 49$$

$$|A_y| = \begin{vmatrix} 2 & 8 \\ 1 & 3 \end{vmatrix} = 2(3) - 8(1) = 6 - 8 = -2$$

$$\therefore \quad x = \frac{A_x}{A} = \frac{49}{13} \quad \text{and} \quad y = \frac{A_y}{A} = \frac{-2}{13}$$

2.
$$x + y + z = 3$$
$$x + 2y + 3y = 4$$
$$x + 4y + 9z = 6$$

SOLUTION:

$$\text{Let } |A| = \begin{vmatrix} 1 & 1 & 1 \\ 1 & 2 & 3 \\ 1 & 4 & 9 \end{vmatrix} \quad |A_x| = \begin{vmatrix} 3 & 1 & 1 \\ 4 & 2 & 3 \\ 6 & 4 & 9 \end{vmatrix} \quad |A_y| = \begin{vmatrix} 1 & 3 & 1 \\ 1 & 4 & 3 \\ 1 & 6 & 9 \end{vmatrix} \quad \text{and}$$

$$|A_z| = \begin{vmatrix} 1 & 1 & 3 \\ 1 & 2 & 4 \\ 1 & 4 & 6 \end{vmatrix}$$

$$|A| = 1\begin{vmatrix} 2 & 3 \\ 4 & 9 \end{vmatrix} - 1\begin{vmatrix} 1 & 3 \\ 1 & 9 \end{vmatrix} + 1\begin{vmatrix} 1 & 2 \\ 1 & 4 \end{vmatrix}$$
$$= 1(18 - 12) - 1(9 - 3) + 1(4 - 2)$$
$$6 - 6 + 2 = 2$$

$$|A_x| = 3\begin{vmatrix} 2 & 3 \\ 4 & 9 \end{vmatrix} - 1\begin{vmatrix} 4 & 3 \\ 6 & 9 \end{vmatrix} + 1\begin{vmatrix} 4 & 2 \\ 6 & 4 \end{vmatrix}$$
$$3(18 - 12) - 1(36 - 18) + 1(16 - 12)$$

$$3(6)-1(18)+1(4)$$

$$18-18+4=4$$

$$|A_y| = 1\begin{vmatrix} 4 & 3 \\ 6 & 9 \end{vmatrix} - 3\begin{vmatrix} 1 & 3 \\ 1 & 9 \end{vmatrix} + 1\begin{vmatrix} 1 & 4 \\ 1 & 6 \end{vmatrix}$$

$$1(36-18)-3(9-3)+1(6-4)$$

$$18-3(6)+2=2$$

$$|A_z| = 1\begin{vmatrix} 2 & 4 \\ 4 & 6 \end{vmatrix} - 1\begin{vmatrix} 1 & 4 \\ 1 & 6 \end{vmatrix} + 3\begin{vmatrix} 1 & 2 \\ 1 & 4 \end{vmatrix}$$

$$1(12-16)-1(6-4)+3(4-2)$$

$$-4-2+6=0$$

$$x = \frac{A_x}{A} = \frac{4}{2} = 2, \quad y = \frac{A_y}{A} = \frac{2}{2} = 1, \quad \text{and} \quad z = \frac{A_z}{A} = \frac{0}{2} = 0$$

3. Solve the following system of equations using matrix method:

1. $2x + y = 3$

   $x - 3y = 4$

SOLUTION:

Let $A = \begin{bmatrix} 2 & 1 \\ 1 & -3 \end{bmatrix} \quad X = \begin{bmatrix} x \\ y \end{bmatrix} \quad D = \begin{bmatrix} 3 \\ 4 \end{bmatrix}$

Matrix equation: $AX = D$

$$X = A^{-1}D$$

Now $A^{-1} = \dfrac{\text{adj}A}{|A|}$

$$|A| = \begin{vmatrix} 2 & 1 \\ 1 & -3 \end{vmatrix} = -6-1 = -7 \neq 0 \quad \text{So } A^{-1} \text{ exists}$$

$$\text{adj } A = \begin{bmatrix} -3 & -1 \\ -1 & 2 \end{bmatrix}$$

$$A^{-1} = \frac{1}{-7}\begin{bmatrix} -3 & -1 \\ 3 & 1 \end{bmatrix} = \frac{1}{7}\begin{bmatrix} 3 & 1 \\ 1 & -2 \end{bmatrix}$$

Now

$$A^{-1}D = \frac{1}{7}\begin{bmatrix} 3 & 1 \\ 1 & -2 \end{bmatrix}\begin{bmatrix} 3 \\ 4 \end{bmatrix} = \frac{1}{7}\begin{bmatrix} 9+4 \\ 3-8 \end{bmatrix}$$

$$\begin{bmatrix} x \\ y \end{bmatrix} = \frac{1}{7}\begin{bmatrix} 13 \\ -5 \end{bmatrix} = \begin{bmatrix} \frac{13}{7} \\ -\frac{5}{7} \end{bmatrix}$$

$$x = \frac{13}{7} \quad \text{and} \quad y = -\frac{5}{7}$$

4.

$$\begin{aligned} x+y &= 1 \\ z+x &= 2 \\ y+z &= 7 \end{aligned}$$

SOLUTION:

$$\begin{aligned} x+y+0z &= 1 \\ x+0y+1z &= 2 \\ 0x+1y+1z &= 7 \end{aligned}$$

Let $A = \begin{bmatrix} 1 & 1 & 0 \\ 1 & 0 & 1 \\ 0 & 1 & 1 \end{bmatrix} \quad X = \begin{bmatrix} x \\ y \\ z \end{bmatrix} \quad D = \begin{bmatrix} 1 \\ 2 \\ 7 \end{bmatrix}$

Matrix equation:

$$AX = D$$
$$X = A^{-1}D$$

Now

$$A^{-1} = \frac{\text{adj}A}{|A|}$$

$$|A| = \begin{vmatrix} 1 & 1 & 0 \\ 1 & 0 & 1 \\ 0 & 1 & 1 \end{vmatrix} = 1\begin{vmatrix} 0 & 1 \\ 1 & 1 \end{vmatrix} - 1\begin{vmatrix} 1 & 1 \\ 0 & 1 \end{vmatrix} + 0$$

$$1(-1) - 1(1) = -2 \neq 0$$

So A^{-1} exits

$$\text{adj } A = \begin{bmatrix} +\begin{vmatrix} 0 & 1 \\ 1 & 1 \end{vmatrix} & -\begin{vmatrix} 1 & 0 \\ 1 & 1 \end{vmatrix} & \begin{vmatrix} 1 & 0 \\ 0 & 1 \end{vmatrix} \\ -\begin{vmatrix} 1 & 1 \\ 0 & 1 \end{vmatrix} & +\begin{vmatrix} 1 & 0 \\ 0 & 1 \end{vmatrix} & -\begin{vmatrix} 1 & 0 \\ 1 & 1 \end{vmatrix} \\ \begin{vmatrix} 1 & 0 \\ 0 & 1 \end{vmatrix} & -\begin{vmatrix} 1 & 1 \\ 0 & 1 \end{vmatrix} & \begin{vmatrix} 1 & 1 \\ 1 & 0 \end{vmatrix} \end{bmatrix}$$

$$\text{Adj } A = \begin{bmatrix} -1 & -1 & 1 \\ -1 & 1 & -1 \\ 1 & -1 & -1 \end{bmatrix}$$

$$A^{-1} = \frac{\text{adj } A}{|A|}$$

$$= \frac{1}{-2} \begin{bmatrix} -1 & -1 & 1 \\ -1 & 1 & -1 \\ 1 & -1 & -1 \end{bmatrix}$$

$$X = A^{-1}D = \frac{1}{2} \begin{bmatrix} 1 & 1 & -1 \\ 1 & -1 & 1 \\ -1 & 1 & 1 \end{bmatrix} \begin{bmatrix} 1 \\ 2 \\ 7 \end{bmatrix}$$

$$= \frac{1}{2} \begin{bmatrix} 1+2-7 \\ 1-2+7 \\ -1+2+7 \end{bmatrix} = \frac{1}{2} \begin{bmatrix} -4 \\ 6 \\ 8 \end{bmatrix}$$

$$X = \begin{bmatrix} -2 \\ 3 \\ 4 \end{bmatrix} = \begin{bmatrix} x \\ y \\ z \end{bmatrix} \quad \text{so} \quad \begin{matrix} x = -2 \\ y = 3 \quad \& \\ z = 4 \end{matrix}$$

APPLICATION OF MATRICES IN BUSINESS PROBLEMS

1. Autoservice sold 15 mopeds, 23 bikes and 60 scooters in 2010 and 20 mopeds, 48 bikes and 25 scooters in 2011. Represent the data in matrix form.

SOLUTION:

	mopeds	bikes	scooters
2010	15	23	60
2011	20	48	25

So corresponding matrix is $\begin{bmatrix} 15 & 23 & 60 \\ 20 & 48 & 25 \end{bmatrix}$

2. Suppose the matrices X and Y represents the number of items of different kinds produced by 2 manufacturing units in one day $X = \begin{bmatrix} 2 \\ 1 \\ 3 \end{bmatrix}$ and $Y = \begin{bmatrix} 5 \\ 3 \\ 2 \end{bmatrix}$. Compute $3X + 5Y$, what does $3X + 5Y$ represent?

SOLUTION:

$$3X+5Y = 3\begin{bmatrix}2\\1\\3\end{bmatrix}+5\begin{bmatrix}5\\3\\2\end{bmatrix}$$

$$=\begin{bmatrix}6\\3\\9\end{bmatrix}+\begin{bmatrix}25\\15\\10\end{bmatrix}=\begin{bmatrix}31\\18\\19\end{bmatrix}$$

$3X+5Y$ represents the total number of units produced by one unit in 3 days and another unit in 5 days.

3. Ajith buys 5 kg of sugar, 15 kg of wheat, 20 kg of rice and 10 kg of ragi. If the cost of each kg is Rs. 30, Rs. 35 and Rs. 12 respectively. Then find the total cost by matrix method.

SOLUTION:

Matrix representing Commodities

$$= \begin{bmatrix}5 & 15 & 20 & 10\end{bmatrix}$$

$$\text{Matrix representing the cost} = \begin{bmatrix}30\\25\\35\\12\end{bmatrix}$$

$$\text{Total cost} = \begin{bmatrix}5 & 15 & 20 & 10\end{bmatrix}\begin{bmatrix}30\\25\\35\\12\end{bmatrix}$$

$$= [150+325+700+120]$$

$$= [1395]$$

$\therefore$ Total cost = Rs. 1395.

4. Supreme Company sold 20 metal chairs, 40 wooden chairs and 35 plastic chairs, in the month of October, and 15 metal chairs, 35 wooden chairs and 30 plastic in the month of November. The selling price of metal chair is Rs. 200, wooden chair is Rs. 400 and plastic chair is Rs. 300. Find the total revenue in the month of October and November.

SOLUTION:

Matrix representing no. of chairs of different variables with different months

$$\begin{bmatrix}20 & 40 & 35\\15 & 35 & 30\end{bmatrix}$$

$$\text{Matrix representing the price} = \begin{bmatrix} 200 \\ 400 \\ 300 \end{bmatrix}$$

$$\text{Total revenue} = \overrightarrow{\begin{bmatrix} 20 & 40 & 35 \\ 15 & 35 & 30 \end{bmatrix}} \begin{bmatrix} 200 \\ 400 \\ 300 \end{bmatrix}\downarrow$$

$$= \begin{bmatrix} 4000+16000+10500 \\ 3000+14000+9000 \end{bmatrix}$$

$$= \begin{bmatrix} 30500 \\ 26000 \end{bmatrix}$$

Revenue in October = Rs.30500

Revenue in November = Rs.26000

Total revenue = Rs.56500

5. In Chikmagalore town there are 7 colleges and 15 schools. Each school has 8 peons, 6 clerks and 2 cashiers. Each college has 15 peons, 9 clerks and 3 cashiers. In addition, each college has 1 section officer and 2 librarians. The monthly salary of each of them is as follows:

Peons: Rs. 6000 Clerk: Rs. 8500 Cashier: Rs. 10000 Rs. Section Officer: 11000 and Librarian: Rs. 12000 using matrices.

Find: (1) total number of posts of each kind in schools and colleges taken together, (2) monthly salary bill of all the school and colleges taken together.

SOLUTION:

Let $A = [7 \quad 15]$ represents the number of colleges and schools in that order

$$B = \begin{matrix} \\ \text{College} \\ \text{School} \end{matrix} \begin{bmatrix} \text{Peon} & \text{Clerk} & \text{Cashier} & \text{S.off} & \text{Lib.} \\ 15 & 9 & 3 & 1 & 2 \\ 8 & 6 & 2 & 0 & 0 \end{bmatrix} = \text{No. of employees}$$

$$C = \begin{matrix} \text{Peon} \\ \text{Clerk} \\ \text{Cashier} \\ \text{S.off} \\ \text{Librarian} \end{matrix} \begin{bmatrix} 6000 \\ 8500 \\ 10000 \\ 11000 \\ 12000 \end{bmatrix} = \text{Salaries}$$

No.of employees = AB

$$\begin{bmatrix} 7 & 15 \end{bmatrix}\begin{bmatrix} 15 & 9 & 3 & 12 \\ 8 & 6 & 2 & 00 \end{bmatrix}$$

$$= \begin{bmatrix} 105+120 & 63+90 & 21+30 & 7+0 & 14+0 \end{bmatrix}$$

$$= \begin{bmatrix} 225 & 153 & 51 & 7 & 14 \end{bmatrix}$$

1st element, i.e., 225 = No. of peons

153 = No. of clerks and so on.

Total monthly salaries of schools and colleges $= BC$

$$= \overrightarrow{\begin{bmatrix} 15 & 9 & 3 & 1 & 2 \\ 8 & 6 & 2 & 0 & 0 \end{bmatrix}} \begin{bmatrix} 6000 \\ 8500 \\ 10000 \\ 11000 \\ 12000 \end{bmatrix}\Big\downarrow$$

$$= \begin{bmatrix} 90000+76500+30000+11000+24000 \\ 48000+51000+20000+0+0 \end{bmatrix}$$

$$= \begin{bmatrix} 231500 \\ 119000 \end{bmatrix}$$

Total monthly salary bill of all colleges and schools together $= A(BC)$

$$= \begin{bmatrix} 7 & 15 \end{bmatrix}\begin{bmatrix} 2 & 3 & 1 & 5 & 0 & 0 \\ 1 & 1 & 9 & 0 & 0 & 0 \end{bmatrix}$$

$$= \begin{bmatrix} 16,20,500+17,85,000 \end{bmatrix}$$

$$= \begin{bmatrix} 34,05,500 \end{bmatrix}$$

Total salary = Rs.34,05,500

Aliter: Total Salary = Total no. of employers × Salary

$$\begin{bmatrix} 225 \; 153 \; 51 \; 7 \; 14 \end{bmatrix} \begin{bmatrix} 6000 \\ 8500 \\ 10000 \\ 11000 \\ 12000 \end{bmatrix}$$

$$= [13,50,000+13,00,500+5,10,000+77,000+1,68,000]$$

$$= \begin{bmatrix} 34,05,500 \end{bmatrix}$$

$\therefore$ Total salary = Rs. 34,05,500

6. Raghu has the following record of sales during 2 months for 2 items A and B which have different rates of commission.

Month	Sales of units		Total commission
	A	*B*	in Rs.
Jan	400	700	900
Feb	500	600	1000

Find out the rates of commissions on items *A* & *B*.

SOLUTION:

Let x and y denote the rates of commission in rupees per unit for A and B respectively. Then data can be expressed as a system of linear equations

$$400x+700y = 900$$
$$500x+600y = 1000$$

or

$$4x+7y = 9$$
$$5x+6y = 10$$

Solving these equations by Cramer's rule.

$$A = \begin{vmatrix} 4 & 7 \\ 5 & 6 \end{vmatrix} = 24-35 = -11 \neq 0. \text{ So solution exists}$$

$$A_x = \begin{vmatrix} 9 & 7 \\ 10 & 6 \end{vmatrix} = 54-70 = -16$$

$$A_y = \begin{vmatrix} 4 & 9 \\ 5 & 10 \end{vmatrix} = 40-45 = -5$$

$$x = \frac{A_x}{A} = \frac{-16}{-11} = \frac{16}{11}$$

$$y = \frac{A_y}{A} = \frac{-5}{-11} = \frac{5}{11}$$

$\therefore$ Rate of commissions for A and B are respectively Rs. $\frac{16}{11}$ and Rs. $\frac{5}{11}$

7. The prices of 3 commodities A, B, C are a, b and c respectively X sells 1 unit of A, 1 unit of B and 1 unit of C. Y sells 3 units of A 1 unit of B and purchases 1 unit of C. Z sell 1 unit of A 3 units of B and purchases 1 unit of C. In the process X, Y, Z earns Rs. 9000, Rs. 1000, Rs. 5000 respectively. Using matrices find the prices units of the commodities. Note that selling the units is positive earning and buying the units negative.

SOLUTION:

The above data can be written in the form of equation as

$$\begin{aligned} X &: a+b+c &= 9000 \\ Y &: 3a+b-c &= 1000 \\ Z &: a+3b-C &= 5000 \end{aligned}$$

Solving these equations by matrix method:

$$\text{Let } A = \begin{bmatrix} 1 & 1 & 1 \\ 3 & 1 & -1 \\ 1 & 3 & -1 \end{bmatrix} \quad X = \begin{bmatrix} a \\ b \\ c \end{bmatrix} \quad D = \begin{bmatrix} 9000 \\ 1000 \\ 5000 \end{bmatrix}$$

$$\text{Matrix equation: } \begin{aligned} AX &= D \\ X &= A^{-1}D \end{aligned}$$

Now

$$|A| = \begin{vmatrix} 1 & 1 & 1 \\ 3 & 1 & -1 \\ 1 & 3 & -1 \end{vmatrix} = 1(-1+3) - 1(-3+1) + 1(9-1)2+2+8 = 12 \neq 0$$

A^{-1} exists

$$\text{adj } A = \begin{bmatrix} \begin{vmatrix} 1 & -1 \\ 3 & -1 \end{vmatrix} & -\begin{vmatrix} 1 & 1 \\ 3 & -1 \end{vmatrix} & \begin{vmatrix} 1 & 1 \\ 1 & -1 \end{vmatrix} \\ -\begin{vmatrix} 3 & -1 \\ 1 & -1 \end{vmatrix} & +\begin{vmatrix} 1 & 1 \\ 1 & -1 \end{vmatrix} & -\begin{vmatrix} 1 & 1 \\ 3 & -1 \end{vmatrix} \\ \begin{vmatrix} 3 & 1 \\ 1 & 3 \end{vmatrix} & -\begin{vmatrix} 1 & 1 \\ 1 & 3 \end{vmatrix} & \begin{vmatrix} 1 & 1 \\ 3 & 1 \end{vmatrix} \end{bmatrix}$$

$$\text{adj } A = \begin{bmatrix} 2 & 4 & -2 \\ 2 & -2 & 4 \\ 8 & -2 & -2 \end{bmatrix}$$

$$A^{-1} = \frac{1}{12}\begin{bmatrix} 2 & 4 & -2 \\ 2 & -2 & 4 \\ 8 & -2 & -2 \end{bmatrix} = \frac{1}{6}\begin{bmatrix} 1 & 2 & -1 \\ 1 & -1 & 2 \\ 4 & -1 & -1 \end{bmatrix}$$

$$X = A^{-1}D = \frac{1}{6}\begin{bmatrix} 1 & 2 & -1 \\ 1 & -1 & 2 \\ 4 & -1 & -1 \end{bmatrix}\begin{bmatrix} 9000 \\ 1000 \\ 5000 \end{bmatrix}$$

$$\frac{1}{6}\begin{bmatrix} 9000 & +2000 & -5000 \\ 9000 & -1000 & +10000 \\ 36000 & -1000 & -5000 \end{bmatrix}$$

$$\frac{1}{6}\begin{bmatrix} 6000 \\ 18000 \\ 30000 \end{bmatrix}$$

$$\begin{bmatrix} a \\ b \\ c \end{bmatrix} = \begin{bmatrix} 1000 \\ 3000 \\ 5000 \end{bmatrix}$$

$\Rightarrow \quad a = \text{Rs. } 1000; \quad b = \text{Rs. } 3000 \quad \text{and} \quad c = \text{Rs. } 5000$

IN A NUTSHELL

- Matrix is an arrangement of elements in horizontal rows and vertical columns.
- Order of the matrix = No. of rows × No. of columns
- Two matrices of the same order are said to be equal if and only if the corresponding elements are equal.
- Two or more matrices of the same order can be be added/subtracted. It is obtained by adding/subtracting corresponding terms.
- Scalar multiple of a matrix is a matrix obtained by multiplying each and every element by a scalar.
- Matrix multiplication is possible only when number of columns in the first matrix = No. of rows in the 2nd matrix. If A is order $m \times n$ and B is of order $n \times p$, AB is of order $n \times p$ and BA is not possible unless $p = m$. So in general $AB \neq BA$.
- By writing rows as columns and columns as rows in matrix A, we get the transpose of a matrix A. It is denoted by A' or A^T.
- A unique value associated with every square matrix is called its determinant value.
- If $|A| = 0$ for a matrix A. Then A is called singular matrix.
- For non-singular matrix, i.e., for matrix with $|A| \neq 0$, there exists a unique matrix A^{-1} such that $A.A^{-1} = A^{-1}.A = I$.
- $A^{-1} = \dfrac{\text{adj A}}{|A|}$
- The determinant obtained by deleting the row and column containing the element is called minor of that element. If the minors are multiplied with $(-1)^{i+j}$ [i = row number, j = column number] we get cofactors. The transpose of the cofactor matrix is called adjoint of the matrix.
- If $A = \begin{bmatrix} a & b \\ c & d \end{bmatrix}$ then $|A| = ad - bc$
- If A= $\begin{bmatrix} a_1 & b_1 & c_1 \\ a_2 & b_2 & c_2 \\ a_3 & b_3 & c_3 \end{bmatrix}$ $\quad |A| = a_1 \begin{vmatrix} b_2 & c_2 \\ b_3 & c_3 \end{vmatrix} - b_1 \begin{vmatrix} a_2 & c_2 \\ a_3 & c_3 \end{vmatrix} + c_1 \begin{vmatrix} a_2 & b_2 \\ a_3 & b_3 \end{vmatrix}$

- The solution of system of equations

$$\begin{aligned} a_1x+b_1y+c_1z &= d_1 \\ a_2x+b_2y+c_2z &= d_2 \\ a_3x+b_2y+c_2z &= d_2 \end{aligned}$$

By Cramer's rule:

$$A = \begin{vmatrix} a_1 & b_1 & c_1 \\ a_2 & b_2 & c_2 \\ a_3 & b_3 & c_3 \end{vmatrix} \quad A_x = \begin{vmatrix} b_1 & b_1 & c_1 \\ d_2 & b_2 & c_2 \\ d_3 & b_3 & c_3 \end{vmatrix}$$

$$A_y = \begin{vmatrix} a_1 & d_1 & c_1 \\ a_2 & d_2 & c_2 \\ a_3 & d_3 & c_3 \end{vmatrix} \quad A_z = \begin{vmatrix} a_1 & d_1 & d_1 \\ a_2 & b_2 & d_2 \\ a_3 & b_3 & d_3 \end{vmatrix}$$

$$x = \frac{A_x}{A}, \quad y = \frac{A_y}{A} \quad z = \frac{A_z}{A}$$

By matrix method:

$$\text{Let } A = \begin{bmatrix} a_1 & b_1 & c_1 \\ a_2 & b_2 & c_2 \\ a_3 & b_3 & c_3 \end{bmatrix} \quad X = \begin{bmatrix} x \\ y \\ z \end{bmatrix} \quad \text{and} \quad D = \begin{bmatrix} d_1 \\ d_2 \\ d_3 \end{bmatrix}$$

Then matrix equation $\begin{aligned} AX &= D \\ X &= A^{-1}D \end{aligned}$

CHECK YOUR PROGRESS

1. If $A = \begin{bmatrix} 2 & -3 \\ 1 & 6 \end{bmatrix}$ $B = \begin{bmatrix} 1 & 1 \\ 2 & -3 \end{bmatrix}$ then find: (a) $A+B$ (b) $2A-3B$ (c) $A+A'$

$$\left[\textbf{Ans.} \quad (a) = \begin{bmatrix} 3 & -2 \\ 3 & 3 \end{bmatrix} \; (b) = \begin{bmatrix} 1 & -9 \\ -4 & 21 \end{bmatrix} \; (c) = \begin{bmatrix} 4 & -2 \\ -2 & 12 \end{bmatrix}\right]$$

2. If $A = \begin{bmatrix} 2 & 3 & 4 \\ 1 & -1 & 0 \\ 6 & 2 & -1 \end{bmatrix}$ and $B = \begin{bmatrix} 1 & 3 & 2 \\ 1 & -2 & 1 \\ 0 & 0 & 1 \end{bmatrix}$ then find (a) $A+B$ (b) $3B-2A'$

$$\left[\textbf{Ans.} \quad (a) = \begin{bmatrix} 3 & 6 & 6 \\ 2 & -3 & 1 \\ 6 & 2 & 0 \end{bmatrix} \quad (b) = \begin{bmatrix} -1 & 7 & -6 \\ -3 & -4 & -1 \\ -8 & 0 & 5 \end{bmatrix}\right]$$

3. If $X = \begin{bmatrix} 2 \\ 0 \\ 1 \end{bmatrix}$ and $Y = \begin{bmatrix} 5 & 4 & 3 \end{bmatrix}$ then find AB and BA is $AB = BA$?

$$\left[\textbf{Ans.} \quad (a) = \begin{bmatrix} 10 & 8 & 6 \\ 0 & 0 & 0 \\ 5 & 4 & 3 \end{bmatrix} \quad (b) = \begin{bmatrix} 13 \end{bmatrix} \quad (c) \begin{bmatrix} \text{No} \end{bmatrix}\right]$$

4. If $A = \begin{bmatrix} 1 & 1 & 1 \\ 1 & 1 & 1 \\ 1 & 1 & 1 \end{bmatrix}$ Then prove that $A^2 = 3A$.

5. Find x and y if $= \begin{bmatrix} 1 & 2 \\ 4 & x \end{bmatrix} + \begin{bmatrix} y & 3 \\ -2 & 3 \end{bmatrix} = \begin{bmatrix} 3 & 5 \\ 2 & 6 \end{bmatrix}$

[**Ans.** $x = 3,\ y = 2$]

6. Solve for x and y:

$\begin{bmatrix} 3 & -4 \\ 9 & 2 \end{bmatrix} \begin{bmatrix} x \\ y \end{bmatrix} = \begin{bmatrix} 10 \\ 2 \end{bmatrix}$ [**Ans.** $x = \frac{2}{3}\ \ y = -2$]

7. If $A = \begin{bmatrix} 1 & -3 \\ 1 & 0 \end{bmatrix}$ Then prove that $A^2 - A - 3I = 0$

8. If $A = \begin{bmatrix} 1 & 2 \\ 4 & 7 \end{bmatrix}$ Find a matrix X such that $AX = I$

$$\left[\textbf{Ans.} \quad \begin{bmatrix} -7 & 2 \\ 4 & -1 \end{bmatrix}\right]$$

9. If $A = \begin{bmatrix} 2 & 3 \\ -4 & 0 \end{bmatrix}$ $B = \begin{bmatrix} -1 & 2 \\ 2 & 1 \end{bmatrix}$ and $C = \begin{bmatrix} 1 & 2 \\ 3 & -2 \end{bmatrix}$ Then prove that $(A+B)\,C = AC + BC$.

10. Find det A if $A = \begin{bmatrix} 1 & 2 & 3 \\ 2 & -1 & 3 \\ -1 & 2 & 3 \end{bmatrix}$

[**Ans.** $|A| = 18$]

11. If the matrix $\begin{bmatrix} 2 & x & 3 \\ 4 & 1 & 6 \\ 1 & 2 & 7 \end{bmatrix}$ is singular find x

$$\left[\textbf{Ans.} \quad x = \frac{8}{11}\right]$$

12. If $A = \begin{bmatrix} 1 & 2 \\ -3 & 4 \end{bmatrix}$ and $B = \begin{bmatrix} 2 & 0 \\ 6 & 7 \end{bmatrix}$ find $|AB|$

[**Ans.** $|AB| = 28$]

13. If $A = \begin{bmatrix} 1 & 2 \\ 3 & -1 \end{bmatrix}$ and $B = \begin{bmatrix} 2 & -1 \\ 3 & 2 \end{bmatrix}$ Then prove that $(AB)' = B'A'$

14. If $2A+B=\begin{bmatrix}-7 & 11\\ 7 & 4\end{bmatrix}$ and $A+2B=\begin{bmatrix}-8 & 13\\ 14 & 5\end{bmatrix}$ Find A.

$$\left[\textbf{Ans.}\quad \begin{bmatrix}-2 & 3\\ 0 & 1\end{bmatrix}\right]$$

15. Find AB if $A=\begin{bmatrix}3 & 2\\ 5 & 1\\ 1 & 1\end{bmatrix}$ and $B=\begin{bmatrix}1\\ 3\end{bmatrix}$ Is it possible to compute BA? Why?

$$\left[\textbf{Ans.}\quad = \begin{bmatrix}9\\ 8\\ 4\end{bmatrix}\ \text{No.of column in B} \neq \text{No. of rows in A}\right]$$

16. Prove that $=\begin{bmatrix}2 & -1 & -6\\ -3 & 1 & 9\\ 4 & 3 & -12\end{bmatrix}$ is singular

17. Find the inverse of A $\begin{bmatrix}4 & 3\\ 2 & 5\end{bmatrix}$

$$\left[\textbf{Ans.}\quad = \frac{1}{14}\begin{bmatrix}5 & -3\\ -2 & 4\end{bmatrix}\right]$$

18. Find the inverse of the matrix $A=\begin{bmatrix}1 & 1 & 2\\ 0 & -2 & 2\\ -1 & 1 & 3\end{bmatrix}$

$$\left[\textbf{Ans.}\quad \frac{1}{6} = \begin{bmatrix}-8 & -1 & -2\\ -2 & 5 & -2\\ 2 & -2 & 2\end{bmatrix}\right]$$

19. If $A=\begin{bmatrix}2 & 3\\ 1 & 6\end{bmatrix}$ $B=\begin{bmatrix}1 & 2\\ 4 & 1\end{bmatrix}$ then verify that $(AB)^{-1}=B^{-1}A^{-1}$

20. If $A=\begin{bmatrix}1 & 2 & 3\\ 0 & 4 & 1\\ 4 & 0 & 2\end{bmatrix}$ and $B=\begin{bmatrix}1 & 1 & 3\\ 1 & 3 & -3\\ -2 & 4 & -4\end{bmatrix}$ Verify that $(AB)^{-1}=B^{-1}A^{-1}$.

21. Using Cramer's rule, solve the following system of equations:

(a) $5x+6y=9$
$6x-5y=23$

(b) $3x+4y=10$
$4x-5y=3$

(c) $x-4y-3z=9$
$5x+y=19$
$2x-5z=3$

(d) $x-y-2z=3$
$2x+y+z=5$
$4x-y-2z=11$

Ans. (a) $x=3, y=-1$ (b) $x=2, y=1$
(c) $x=4, y=-1, z=1$ (d) $x=\frac{8}{3}, y=-\frac{1}{3}, z=0$

22. Using matrix method solve the following system of equations:

(a) $7x - y = 16$, $2x + 3y = -2$ (b) $2x - 3y = 4$, $3x + 2y = 5$ (c) $x + y + 2z = 9$, $3x + 2y + z = 10$, $x + 2y + 3z = 14$

(d) $x + y = 1$, $y + z = 7$, $z + x = 2$ (e) $x - y - z = -1$, $y + 3z = 3$, $x + 4z = 2$

Ans.
(a) $x = 2 \quad y = -2$
(b) $x = \frac{23}{13} \quad y = -\frac{2}{3}$
(c) $x = 1,\ y = 2,\ z3 = 3$
(d) $x = -2,\ y = 3,\ z = 4$
(e) $x = 2,\ y = 3,\ z = 0$

23. The price of tickets to a musical concert is as follows:
Front row Rs. 85, Centre Row Rs. 65, Back row: Rs. 35 Circle seat Rs. 40
The number of tickets sold for 3 concerts are as follows:

	Front row	Centre row	Back row	Circle seat
Friday	220	430	555	355
Saturday	245	485	520	310
Sunday	280	430	515	375

Write down 2 matrices so that the elements of their product will give the total amount of ticket sales for the three performances. Hence, calculate the total amount collected for performances.

[Rs. 2,48,000]

24. A company is considering which of the 3 methods of production it should use in producing 3 goods A, B, C. The amount of each good produced by each method is shown by the matrix.

$$\begin{array}{c} \\ \text{I} \\ \text{II} \\ \text{III} \end{array} \begin{array}{c} A\ B\ C \\ \begin{bmatrix} 4 & 8 & 2 \\ 5 & 7 & 1 \\ 5 & 3 & 9 \end{bmatrix} \end{array}$$

The vector [10 4 6] represents the profit per unit for the goods A, B, C in that order. Find which method maximises profit?

[Method III profit 116]

25. The prices of the 3 commodities A, B, C are a, b, and c per unit respectively. Ajith purchases 4 units of c, 3 units of a and 5 units of b. Bala purchases 3 units of b and sells 2 units of a and 1 unit of c. Chetan purchases 1 unit of a, sells 4 units of b and 6 units of c. In the process Ajith, Bala and Chetan earns Rs. 6000, Rs. 5000 and Rs. 13000 respectively. Using matrices, find the prices per unit of the 3 commodities. Note that selling the unit is positive earning and buying the unit is negative.

$$\begin{bmatrix} \text{Price per unit} \\ \text{a} = \text{Rs. 3000, b} = \text{Rs. 1000 and c} = \text{Rs. 2000} \end{bmatrix}$$

5

Commercial Arithmetic

INTEREST

Interest is the compensation which the lender of sum of money receives from the borrower for the use of money lent. The money lent is called 'principal'. The time for which money is lent is called the 'period or term'. The interest per year (per annum) for Rs. 100 is called 'rate of interest'. The sum of principal and interest is called the 'amount'.

Simple Interest

Simple interest is the amount that is calculated on the original principal alone for the time during which money lent is being used. For the sum of Rs. P at $R\%$ simple interest per annum for T years, the simple interest (SI) is given by the formula, $\text{SI} = \frac{PRT}{100}$.

EXAMPLE: Ravi needed capital for his bakery. He borrowed Rs. 60,000 for 4 years at a simple interest rate of 8% per annum.

(a) How much interest must be paid?

(b) How much money will Ravi pay at the end of 4 years?

(a)

$$P = \text{Rs. } 60{,}000$$

$$R = 8\%$$

$$T = 4 \text{ years}$$

$$I = \frac{PRT}{100}$$

$$= \frac{60{,}000 \times 8 \times 4}{100}$$

$$I = \text{Rs. } 19{,}200$$

(b)

$$\text{Amount} = \text{Principal} + \text{Interest}$$

$$= \text{Rs. } 60{,}000 + 19{,}200$$

$$= \text{Rs. } 79{,}200$$

Compound Interest

When the interest produced after each prefixed period is added to the principal and whole amount is considered the principal for the calculation of interest for the next period, then the sum by which the original principal is increased at the end of all prefixed period (often called conversion period or interest period) is called the compound interest.

EXAMPLE: Find the compound interest on Rs. 2000 for 3 years at 5% per annum compounded annually

$$\text{First year: } P = 2000$$
$$R = 5\%$$
$$T = 1$$
$$I = \frac{PRT}{100} = \frac{2000 \times 5 \times 1}{100} = 100$$

By the end of 1st year

$$\text{Principal} = \text{Rs. } 2000 + \text{Rs. } 100 = \text{Rs. } 2100$$
$$R = 5\%$$
$$T = 1 \text{ year}$$
$$I = \frac{2100 \times 5 \times 1}{100} = 105$$

By the end of 2nd year

$$\text{Principal} = \text{Rs. } 2100 + 105 = 2205$$
$$R = 5\%$$
$$T = 1 \text{ year}$$
$$I = \frac{2205 \times 5 \times 1}{100} = 110.25$$

$\therefore$ By the end of 3rd year,

$$\text{Compound interest} = 100 + 105 + 110.25$$
$$= \text{Rs. } 315.25$$

If P is the principal, R is the rate of interest and n is the number of conversion periods and A is the amount received at the end of n conversion periods then

$$A = P\left(1 + \frac{R}{100}\right)^n$$
$$\text{Compound interest} = A - P$$

So in the above example,

$$A = 2000\left(1+\frac{5}{100}\right)^3 = \text{Rs. } 2315.25$$

$$\text{CI} = \text{Rs. } 2315.25 - 2000 = \text{Rs. } 315.25$$

Note:

1. If the rates of interest $R_1, R_2 \ldots$ are different for each conversion period $n_1, n_2 \ldots$ Then

$$A = \left(1+\frac{R_1}{100}\right)^{n_1}\left(1+\frac{R_2}{100}\right)^{n_2} \ldots$$

2. If the conversion period n contains fractional part say $n = n_1 + \frac{p}{q}(p < q)$. Interest for the integral part n_1 years accumulates at compound interest and for the fractional part $\frac{p}{q}$ simple interest is calculated on the amount due at the end of the nth year.
3. Compound interest formula is used to find the growth rate. R in the compound interest formula is taken as growth rate, which is usually expressed as a percentage.
4. Compound interest formula is used to find the depreciation under decline balance method. Since depreciation reduces the value of the asset progressively R in such a case is taken with negative sign.

SOLVED EXAMPLES

1. Find the simple interest on:

(i) Rs. 5000 for 2 years at 6% p.a.

(ii) Rs. 10,000 for 2 months at 15% p.a.

(iii) Rs. 1500 for 73 days at 10% p.a.

(iv) Rs. 6,000 for 3 years 2 months 15 days at 4% p.a.

SOLUTION:

(i) $SI = \frac{PRT}{100} = \frac{5000 \times 5 \times 2}{100} = \text{Rs. } 500$

(ii) $SI = \frac{PRT}{100} = \frac{10,000 \times \frac{2}{12} \times 6}{100} = \text{Rs. } 100$

(iii) $SI = \frac{PRT}{100} = \frac{1500 \times 10}{100} \times \frac{73}{365} = \text{Rs. } 30$

(iv) $SI = \frac{PRT}{100} = \frac{6000 \times 4}{100} \times \frac{77}{24} = \text{Rs. } 770$

$$\left(\text{As } T = 3 \text{ years } + 2\frac{1}{2} \text{ months}\right.$$

$$3 \text{ years } + \frac{5}{2} \text{ months}$$

$$3 \text{ years } + \frac{5}{2 \times 12} \text{ years}$$

$$\left.\frac{77}{24} \text{ years}\right)$$

2. At what rate per cent per annum will simple interest on Rs. 1,00,000 for 73 days be Rs. 400

Given: $P = \text{Rs. } 1,00,000$

$R = ?$

$T = 73 \text{ days} = \frac{73}{365} \text{ years}$

$I = 400$

SOLUTION:

$$I = \frac{PRT}{100}$$

$$400 = \frac{1,00,000 \times R \times 73}{100 \times 365}$$

$$\frac{400 \times 100 \times 365}{1,00,000 \times 73} = R$$

$$2 = R$$

$\therefore$ Rate of interest $= 2\%$

3. A certain sum at certain rate of interest per annum simple interest becomes Rs. 11,500 in 3 years and Rs. 12,500 in 5 years. Find the rate of per cent per annum.

SOLUTION:

Let P be the principal, R be the rate of interest.

We know $I = \frac{PRT}{100}$

Given: amount after 3 years = Rs. 11,500

$$P + \frac{PR(3)}{100} = \text{Rs. } 11,500 \qquad (1)$$

Amount after 5 years = Rs. 12,500

$$P + \frac{PR(5)}{100} = \text{Rs. } 12,500 \qquad (2)$$

Dividing equation (2) by (1)

$$\frac{P + \frac{PR(5)}{100}}{P + \frac{PR(3)}{100}} = \frac{12,500}{11,500}$$

$$\frac{P\left(\frac{100+5R}{100}\right)}{P\left(\frac{100+3R}{100}\right)} = \frac{125}{115}$$

$$\frac{100+5R}{100+3R} = \frac{\cancel{125}^{25}}{\cancel{115}_{23}}$$

Cross-multiplying

$$2300 + 115R = 2500 + 75R$$

$$115R - 75R = 2500 - 2300$$

$$40R = 200$$

$$R = \frac{200}{40} = 5$$

∴ Rate of interest = 5%

4. Find the compound interest on Rs. 5000 for 2 years at 10% per annum interest being payable half yearly.

SOLUTION:

Given: $P = \text{Rs. } 5000$

$R = 10\%$ per annum so $R = \frac{10}{2} = 5\%$ for $\frac{1}{2}$ years

$n = 2 \times 2 = 4$ (As interest is payable $\frac{1}{2}$ yearly)

$$A = P\left(1 + \frac{R}{100}\right)^n$$

$$= 5000\left(1 + \frac{5}{100}\right)^4$$

$$= 5000(1.05)^4$$

$$\text{Compound interest} = 5000(1.05)^4 - 5000$$

$$= 6077.53 - 5000$$

$$= \text{Rs. } 1077.53$$

5. A sum of money invested at compound interest amounts to Rs. 2916 at the end of 2 years and to Rs. 3148.28 at the end of 3 years. Find the rate of interest. Also find the sum of money invested.

SOLUTION:

Let R be the rate of interest and P be the principal.

Given: $A_2 = 3148.28,\ n = 3$

$A_1 = 2916,\ n = 2$

$$A = P\left(1+\frac{R}{100}\right)^n$$

$$3148.28 = P\left(1+\frac{R}{100}\right)^3$$

$$3148.28 = P\frac{(100+R)^3}{100^3} \qquad (1)$$

$$2916 = P\frac{(100+R)^2}{100^2} \qquad (2)$$

Divide equation (2) by equation (1)

$$\frac{3148.28}{2916} = \frac{\frac{P(100+R)^3}{100^3}}{\frac{P(100+R)^2}{100^2}}$$

$$\frac{3148.28}{2916} = \frac{100+R}{100}$$

$$314828 = 291600 + 2916R$$

$$\frac{314828 - 291600}{2916} = R$$

$$R = 8\%$$

$\therefore$ From (2)

$$2916 = \frac{P(100+R)^2}{100^2}$$

$$\frac{2916 \times 100^2}{(100+5)^2} = P \quad \Rightarrow \quad P = \text{Rs. } 2500.$$

6. The population of a country becomes double in 30 years. If the growth is compounded annually. Calculate the growth rate.

Given: $n = 30$

Let P be the population of a country and after 30 years it would be $2P$.

Using compound interest formula,

$$A = P\left(1+\frac{R}{100}\right)^n$$

$$2P = P\left[1+\frac{R}{100}\right]^{30}$$

$$2 = (1+0.0R)^{30}$$

Consider log on both sides

$$\log 2 = 30\ \log\ (1\times 0.0R)$$

$$\frac{\log 2}{30} = \log\ (1+0.0R)$$

$$\frac{0.3010}{30} = \log\ (1+0.0R)$$

$$0.01003 = \log\ (1+0.0R)$$

$$1.02336 = 1+0.0R$$

$$0.02336 = 0.0R$$

$$\Rightarrow \quad R = \frac{0.02336}{0.01}$$

$$R = 2.336\%$$

7. The cost of a machine is Rs. 40,000. It depreciates 20% annually. What is its value four years hence?

Given: $P = \text{Rs. } 40,000$

$R = -20\%$ as it is depreciation

$n = 4$ years

$$A = P\left(1+\frac{R}{100}\right)^n$$

Value of the machine after 4 years

$$A = 40,000\left(1+\left(\frac{-20}{100}\right)\right)^4$$

$$40,000(1-0.2)^4$$

$$40,000\times\frac{8}{10}\times\frac{8}{10}\times\frac{8}{10}\times\frac{8}{10}$$

$$\text{Rs. } 16,384$$

$\therefore$ Value of the machine after 4 years = Rs. 16,384

ANNUITIES

Definition

Annuity: An annuity is a sequence of equal payments made at equal intervals of time.

EXAMPLE: LIC premium, bank loan repayment EMI's, etc.

Payment Period: The time between two successive payment dates of annuity is called its payment period or payment interval.

Term: The total time from the beginning of the first payment period to the end of the last period is called the term of an annuity.

Types

Annuities are classified on the basis of their term or on the basis of payment interval.

1. **On the basis of their terms**

   (a) **Annuity certain:** An annuity certain is an annuity which begins and ends on certain fixed dates.

   EXAMPLE: Bank recurring deposits.

   (b) **Contingent annuity:** A contingent annuity is one whose payment continues for a period of time which depends on the happening of an event the date of which cannot be accurately foretold.

   EXAMPLE: Life insurance premiums are paid annually and stop when the insured person dies.

   (c) **Perpetual annuity or perpetuity:** A perpetual annuity is an annuity whose payments continues forever.

   EXAMPLE: In endowment funds of trusts the principal amount is not touched and the interest earned is used for welfare activities. So they are perpetual annuities.

2. **On the basis of payment interval and time of payment**

   Ordinary annuity: An ordinary annuity is an annuity in which the first payment is made at the end of the first payment period.

   EXAMPLE: A personal loan from a bank.

   Note: Ordinary annuity is certain but the converse may not be true.

   Annuity due: An annuity in which the payments are made at the beginning of each payment period is called annuity due.

   EXAMPLE: A saving scheme for 10 years in which equal deposits are made at the beginning of each year.

   Deferred annuity: Deferred means postponed. A deferred annuity is an annuity in which the first payment is postponed for a period of time equivalent to certain number of payment periods. This period is called deferment period.

EXAMPLE: When a housing loan is sanctioned, EMI generally starts after sometime say 6 months after the loan is sanctioned.

Note: Deferred annuity can be an ordinary annuity or it can be annuity due.

Formulae

1. The amount or future value S of an ordinary annuity of Rs. R per period for n periods at the rate i per period is given by

$$S = R\left[\frac{(1+i)^n - 1}{i}\right]$$

2. (a) Present value P of an ordinary annuity of Rs. R per payment period for n periods at the rate of i per period is given by

$$P = R\left[\frac{1-(1+i)^{-n}}{i}\right]$$

(b) Present value P of deferred annuity for n periods of Rs. R each deferred for m periods at the rate i per period is

$$P = (1+i)^{-m} R\left[\frac{1-(1+i)^{-n}}{i}\right]$$

Perpetuity $p_\infty = \frac{R}{i}$

SOLVED EXAMPLES

1. Find the amount of an ordinary annuity of Rs. 10,000 payable at the end of each year for 3 years at 10% per annum compounded annually.

SOLUTION:

Given: $R = \text{Rs. } 10000$

$$i = \frac{10}{100} = 0.1$$

$$n = 3$$

$$S = R\left(\frac{(1+i)^n - 1}{i}\right)$$

$$S = 10{,}000\left(\frac{(1+0.1)^3 - 1}{0.1}\right) = 10{,}000 \times 3.31$$

$$= \text{Rs. } 33100$$

2. To save for a child's education, a family decides to invest Rs. 20,000 at the end of each 6 month period in a fund paying 8% per year compounded biannually. Find the amount of the investment at the end of 18 years.
Given:

$$R = \text{Investment per period} = \text{Rs. } 20,000$$

$$n = \text{No. of periodic payments} = 18 \times 2 = 36$$

$$i = \text{interest rate per period} = \frac{8}{2 \times 100} = 0.04$$

$$S = R\left\{\frac{(1 \times i)^n - 1}{i}\right\}$$

$$S = 20,000\left[\frac{(1 \times 0.04)^{36} - 1}{0.04}\right]$$

$$S = 5,00,000\,[(1.04)^{36} - 1]$$

Let $x = (1.04)^{36}$
Consider log on both sides

$$\log x = \log\,(1.04)^{36}$$

$$\log x = 36\,\log\,(1.04)$$

$$\log x = 0.612$$

$$x = \text{antilog } 0.612 = 4.093$$

$$\therefore \quad S = 5,00,000(4.093 - 1)$$

$$5,00,000(3.093) = 15,46,500$$

$\therefore$ Amount of the annuity = Rs. 15,46,500

3. A machine costs Rs. 98,000 and its effective life is estimated to be of 12 years. If the scrap value is Rs. 3000 only, what should be retained out of profits at the end of each year to accumulate at compound interest at 5% per annum for depreciation so that a new machine can be purchased at the same price after 12 years.

SOLUTION:
Total cost = Rs. 98,000
Amount realised from Rs. 3000
Remaining amount Rs. 98,000 – Rs. 3000 = Rs. 95,000

$$S = \text{Rs. } 95,000$$

$$n = 12 \quad i = \frac{5}{100} = 0.05$$

$$S = R\left\{\frac{(1+i)^n - 1}{i}\right\}$$

$$95,000 = R\left[\frac{(1+0.05)^{12} - 1}{0.05}\right]$$

$$R = \frac{95000 \times 0.05}{1.797 - 1}$$

$$R = \text{Rs. } 5959.84$$

Let

$$x = (1.05)^{12}$$
$$\log x = \log (1.05)^1$$
$$= 12\log 1.05$$
$$= 12 \times 0.0212$$
$$\log x = 0.2544$$
$$x = 1.797$$

So, Rs. 5959.84 should be retained every year.

4. Find the present value of an annuity of Rs. 9000 payable at the end of each 6 months for 5 years if money is worth 6% converted biannually:

SOLUTION:

The present value P of an ordinary annuity of Rs. R per payment period for n periods at the rate i per period is given by

$$P = R\left[\frac{1-(1+i)^{-n}}{i}\right]$$

Here $R = \text{Rs. } 9000, \quad n = 5 \times 2 = 10 \quad i = \frac{6}{2 \times 100} = 0.03$

$$P = 9000\left[\frac{1-(1+0.03)^{-10}}{0.03}\right]$$
$$= \frac{9000}{0.03}(1-(1.03)^{-10})$$
$$3,00,000(1-0.7447)$$
$$= 3,00,000(0.2553) = \text{Rs. } 76,590$$

Let $x = (1.03)^{-10}$

$$\log x = -10\log(1.03)$$
$$x = \text{antilog}(-0.12)$$
$$\text{antilog}(\bar{1}.872)$$
$$x = 0.7447$$

5. An annuity consists of 5 annual payments of Rs. 10,000 each first being made at the end of 4 years. Find the amount of this annuity if money is worth 8% effective.

SOLUTION:

Clearly, the given annuity is a deferred annuity consisting of 5 payments, the first being deferred for 3 years. The amount

$$S = R\left[\frac{(1+i)^n - 1}{i}\right]$$

where $R = 10,000 \quad n = 5, \quad i = \dfrac{8}{100} = 0.08$

$$S = 10,000\left[\frac{(1+0.08)^5 - 1}{0.08}\right] = \frac{10,000}{0.08}(1.49 - 1)$$

$$= \text{Rs. } 58,625$$

6. A man repaid his house building advance in equal instalments of Rs. 40,000 per annum for 5 years. If the money is worth 8% per annum compounded annually and repayment starts after initial gap of 2 years. Find the sum borrowed.

SOLUTION:

It is deferred annuity consisting of 5 payments of Rs. 40,000 each and it is deferred for one period as first payment is made at the end of the 2nd year from the date of sanction of the loan.

$$R = 40,000$$

$$n = 5, \quad m = 1, \quad i = \frac{8}{100} = 0.08$$

$$P = (1+i)^{-m} R\left[\frac{1-(1+i)^{-n}}{i}\right]$$

$$P = (1.08)^{-1}\, 40000\left[\frac{1-(1.08)^{-5}}{0.08}\right]$$

$$\frac{40,000}{1.08 \times 0.08} \times 1 - 0.6805 \quad \text{(using log)}$$

$$= 1,47,916.66$$

$\therefore$ Sum borrowed = Rs. 1,47,916.66.

7. Assuming the rate of interest to be 7% p.a. Calculate the amount to be deposited today in order to earn an annual income of Rs. 21,000 in perpetuity beginning from the end of 15 years from now.

Given: Rate of interest = 7% $\Rightarrow$ $i = 0.07$

$$R = 21,000$$

$$P_\infty = \frac{R}{i} = \frac{21,000}{0.07} = 3,00,000$$

$$\text{Present value of } 3,00,000 = \frac{3,00,000}{(1+0.07)^{14}}$$

$$= \text{Rs. } 47,915.66$$

Hence, he must deposit Rs. 4,79,112.66 today.

BILL DISCOUNTING

Every producer wants to sell his goods in cash, but due to competition in the market he is bound to sell his goods on credit also and give some time to the buyer to pay the amount before the expiry of some specified time period. Suppose a merchant *A* purchase goods worth say Rs. 1,00,000 from another merchant *B* at a credit for a certain period say 1 year. Then *B* prepares a special bill called 'bill of exchange'. On the receipt of the goods, *A* gives an agreement duly signed on the bill stating that he has accepted the bill and the money can be withdrawn from his band account after 1 year of the date of bill. On this bill, there is an order from *A* to his bank asking to pay Rs. 1,00,000 to *B* after 1 year.

If *B* needs the money earlier than one year. He can sell the bill to a banker or a broker who pays him the money against the bill but somewhat less than the face value. Bill discounting is ess ntially lending by the banker's charges interest for doing this service.

Definitions

Bill: The document which required an individual to pay a fixed amount after a fixed later date.

Discount: When a bill is cashed in advance, an amount is deducted by the money lender from the amount of the bill due. This amount deducted is called discount.

Banker's discount: The interest on the face value of the bill is called banker's discount.

True discount: The present value of a sum of money (A) is that principal which is placed on stipulated rate for a specified period will amount to that sum of money (A) at the end of specified period. The interest on the present value of the bill is true discount. Banker's gain = Banker's discount - True discount

Banker's gain = Banker's discount-True discount

Illustration: Bill of exchange:

Stamp

No.5, Ashok Nagar
Bangalore
3/3/2012

To

XYZ
Jayanagar
Bangalore

One year later pay me or my order the sum of Rs. 1,00,000 (rupees one lakh) for value received.

ABC

In the above bill of exchange

Drawer is ABC so payee is ABC

Drawee or acceptor is XYZ

Drawing date = 3/3/2012

Face value or bill amount = Rs. 1,00,000

= Normal value of the bill

Legally due date = Drawing date + Bill period + Grace period of 3 days

(It is customary to give 3 days grace period)

So, in the above bill, legally due date is

$$\begin{aligned} \text{Date of drawing} &= 3/3/2012 \\ \text{Bill period} &= 0.0.1 \\ \text{Grace period} &= 3.0.0 \\ \hline \text{Legally due date} &= 6/3/2013 \end{aligned}$$

Note that if the legally due date is a holiday then the previous day is taken as legally due date.

Formulae

If F is the face value of the bill, P is the present value of the bill, R = Rate of interest, t is the time in years, BD is banker's discount, TD is true discount, BG is banker's gain. Then

$$BG = BD - TD$$

$$BD = \frac{FtR}{100}$$

$$TD = \frac{PtR}{100}$$

Banker's present worth or the discounted value of bill = $F - BD$

$$F - \frac{FtR}{100}$$

$$F\left(1 - \frac{tR}{100}\right)$$

True present worth: P_w

$$\text{As } F = P_w + \frac{P_w tR}{100}$$

$$F = P_w\left(1 + \frac{tR}{100}\right)$$

$$P_w = \frac{F}{1 + \frac{tR}{100}}$$

$$F = \frac{BD \times TD}{BG}$$

$$BG = TD \times \frac{tR}{100}$$

$$BG = \frac{(TD)^2}{P_w}; \quad TD = \sqrt{P_w \times BG}$$

SOLVED EXAMPLES

1. A bill of Rs. 25,000 dated 7th Jan 2008 is payable 3 months after date. Calculate the due date of the bill if the central government has declared a holiday on the date of maturity.

SOLUTION:

Date of bill = 7.1.2008

Bill period = 0.3.0

Grace period = 3.0.0

10/4/2008

Since date of maturity is declared a public holiday, due date = 9/4/2008.

2. Find the present value, true discount, banker's discount and banker's gain on a bill of Rs. 10,450 due in 9 months at 6% p.a.

SOLUTION:

Given: $F = \text{Rs.}10,450$

$$t = 9 \text{ months} = \frac{9}{12} = \frac{3}{4} \text{ years}$$

$$R = 6$$

$$\text{Banker's discount} = \frac{FtR}{100} = 10,045 \times \frac{3}{4} \times \frac{6}{100}$$

$$= \text{Rs. } 470.25$$

$$\text{True present worth} = \frac{F}{1 + \frac{tR}{100}} = \frac{10,450}{1 + \left(\frac{3}{4} \times \frac{6}{100}\right)} = 10,000$$

$$\therefore P = 10{,}000$$

$$\text{True discount} = \frac{PtR}{100}$$

$$= 10000 \times \frac{3}{4} \times \frac{6}{100}$$

$$= \text{Rs. } 450$$

$$\text{Banker's gain} = BD - TD = 470.25 - 450$$

$$= \text{Rs. } 20.25.$$

3. A purchases good from B for Rs. 20,000 on 1st Aug. 2000. He pays Rs. 10,000 in cash immediately and sends his acceptance for 3 months for the balance B gets the bill discounted with his bank on the same date at 5% per annum. Calculate the discount and net amount received by B.

SOLUTION:

Given:

$$R = 5\%$$

$$F = 20{,}000 - 10{,}000 = 10{,}000$$

$$t = 3 \text{ months} = \frac{3}{12} = \frac{1}{4} \text{ year}$$

$$BD = \frac{FtR}{100} 10{,}000 \times \frac{1}{4} \times \frac{5}{100} = \text{Rs. } 125$$

$$\text{Net amount received by } B = 10{,}000 - 125$$

$$= \text{Rs. } 9875$$

4. X draws a bill for Rs. 8800 on 1st Jan. 2010 payable after 4 months. Y accepts it and returns it to X. The bill is discounted by X from the bank for Rs. 8360 on the same day. Find the rate at which the bank discounted the bill.

SOLUTION:

Given: $F = 8800$

$$BD = 8800 - 8360 = \text{Rs. } 440$$

$$t = \text{period} = 4 \text{ months} = \frac{4}{12} = \frac{1}{3} \text{ year}$$

$$BD = \frac{FtR}{100}$$

$$440 = 8800 \times \frac{1}{3} \times \frac{R}{100}$$

$$\frac{440 \times 3}{88} = R \Longrightarrow R = 15\%$$

5. The banker's gain on a bill is $\frac{1}{2}$ of banker's discount and the rate of interest is 20% p.a. Find the unexpired period of the bill.

SOLUTION:

Given: $BG = \frac{1}{2}BD, \quad R = 20\%$

$$\text{But } BG = BD - TD$$

$$\frac{1}{2}BD = BD - TD$$

$$\Longrightarrow TD = BD - \frac{1}{2}BD$$

$$TD = \frac{1}{2}BD$$

$$\frac{PtR}{100} = \frac{1}{2}\frac{FtR}{100}$$

$$\text{But } P = \frac{F}{1 + \frac{tR}{100}}$$

$$\left(\frac{F}{1 + \frac{tR}{100}}\right)\frac{tR}{100} = \frac{1}{2}\frac{FtR}{100}$$

$$\frac{1}{100 + tR} = \frac{1}{200}$$

$$\frac{1}{100 + 2t} = \frac{1}{200}$$

$$200 = 100 + 20t$$

$$\frac{100}{200} = t$$

$$t = 5 \text{ years.}$$

6. The difference between the banker's discount and true discount on a certain sum of money due in 3 months is Rs. 99. Find the amount of the bill if the rate of interest is 12% p.a.

SOLUTION:

Given:

$$BD - TD = 99$$

$$t = 3 \text{ months} = \frac{3}{12}\text{year}\frac{1}{4}\text{year}$$

$$R = 12\%$$

$$\frac{FtR}{100} - \left(\frac{F}{1+\frac{tR}{100}}\right)\frac{tR}{100} = 99$$

$$\frac{F \times 12}{4 \times 100} = \left(\frac{F}{1+\frac{1}{4}\times\frac{12}{100}}\right)\frac{1}{4}\times\frac{12}{100} = 99$$

$$0.03F = \frac{\overset{3}{\cancel{21}}F}{\underset{103}{4\cancel{12}}} = 99$$

$$\frac{3.09\,F - 3F}{103} = 99$$

$$0.09\,F = 103 \times 99$$

$$F = \frac{103 \times 99}{0.09} = 1,13,300$$

7. A bill for Rs. 2,92,000 drawn at 6 months was discounted on 10/4/2010 for Rs. 2,91,600. If the discount rate is 5% p.a. On what date was the bill drawn?

SOLUTION:

Given: $F = 2,92,000$

$$R = 5\%,$$

$$F - \frac{FtR}{100} = 2,91,600$$

$$292000\left(1 - \frac{t(5)}{100}\right) = 2,91,600$$

$$1 - 0.05t = \frac{2,91,600}{2,92,000} \quad \Rightarrow \quad 0.0,27,398 = t$$

$$\Rightarrow \quad t = 10 \text{ days} \qquad t = 0.0273 \times 365 \text{ days}$$

Number of days from legally due date to discounted days = 10 days

$$\text{Bill was discounted on} = 10/4/2010$$
$$\text{Legally due date} = 10/4/2010 + 10 \text{ days}$$
$$= 20/4/2010$$
$$\text{Bill period} = 6 \text{ months}$$
$$\text{Grace period} = 3 \text{ days}$$

So bill drawing date

$$= 20/4/2010$$
$$= 3/6/0$$
$$17/10/2009$$

∴ Bill was drawn on 17/10/2009

8. If the banker's gain is Rs. 3 on a bill which was drawn on April 8th at 6 months period and was discounted on may 18th at 5%. Find the true discount, banker's discount and the sum of the bill.

SOLUTION:

$$\text{Date on which bill was drawn} = 8-4$$
$$\text{Period + grace period} = 3-6$$
$$\text{Legally due date} = 11^{\text{th}} \text{ Oct.}$$
$$\text{Date on which it was discounted} = \text{may } 10^{\text{th}}$$

Time for which bill has yet to run, 18th May to 11th Oct.

May	+June	+July	+Aug	+Sept	+Oct	
13	+30	+31	+31	+30	+11	= 146days

$$t = \frac{146}{365} = \frac{2}{5}\text{yrs.}$$

Banker's gain = Simple interest on true discount

$$\text{i.e.,} \quad 3 = \frac{P \times 5 \times \frac{2}{5}}{100}$$
$$P = 150$$

$$\text{Banker's discount} = TD + SI \text{ on } TD$$
$$150 + \frac{150 \times \frac{2}{5} \times 5}{100}$$

$$150 + 3 = 153.$$

$$\text{Sum} = \frac{BD \times TD}{BD - TD} = \frac{153 \times 150}{153 - 150} = 7650$$

$\therefore$ Sum of the bill = Rs. 7650.

9. The true discount on a bill of Rs. 3060 due after 8 months is Rs. 60. Find the rate of interest per annum, banker's discount and the banker's gain.

SOLUTION:

$$F = \text{Rs. } 3060$$

$$TD = \text{Rs. } 60$$

$$t = 8\text{months} = \frac{8}{12} = \frac{2}{3} \text{ years}$$

$$R = ? \quad BD = ? \quad BG = ?$$

$$\text{Present worth} = P = 3060 - 60 = 3000$$

$$TD = \frac{PtR}{100}$$

$$60 = 3000 \times \frac{2}{3} \times \frac{R}{100}$$

$$\frac{60 \times 300}{2 \times 3000} = R$$

$$R = 3\%$$

$$BD = FtR = 3060 \times \frac{2}{3} \times \frac{3}{100}$$

$$BD = 61.2$$

$$\text{Banker's gain} = BD - TD$$

$$= 61.2 - 60$$

$$= \text{Rs. } 1.20$$

(OR)

$$BG = \frac{(TD)^2}{P_w} = \frac{(60)^2}{3000} = \frac{3600}{3000} = 1.20$$

$$BD = TD + BG = 60 + 1.2 = 61.2$$

10. A bill of exchange was drawn on 1st July for 20,000 for 3 months was dishonoured on due date and a sum of Rs. 200 was incurred as noting charges. The bill was renewed for another 3 months with 12% per annum. Find the amount of the renewed bill and the new due date.

SOLUTION:

$$\text{Date of writing the bill} = 1^{\text{st}} \text{ July}$$

$$\text{Bill period} = 3 \text{ months}$$

$$\text{Legally due date} = 1^{\text{st}} \text{ July} + 3 \text{ month} + 3 \text{ days (grace period)}$$

$$= 4^{\text{th}} \text{ Oct.}$$

$$\text{Amount of bill} = \text{Rs. } 20,000$$

$$\text{Nothing charges Rs. } 200$$

$$\text{Amount payable by drawee} = \text{Rs. } 20,200$$

$$\text{Term of new bill} = 3 \text{ months} = \frac{3}{12} = \frac{1}{4} \text{ year}$$

$$\text{Rate of interest} = 12\%$$

$$\text{Interest} = \frac{20,200 \times 12 \times \frac{1}{4}}{100} = \text{Rs. } 606$$

$$\therefore \quad \text{Amount of new bill} = \text{Rs. } 20,200 + 606$$

$$= 20,806$$

$$\text{Date of new bill} = 4^{\text{th}} \text{ Oct} + 3 \text{ months} + 3 \text{ days}$$

$$= 7^{\text{th}} \text{ Jan.}$$

IN A NUTSHELL

- Simple interest = $\dfrac{\text{PRT}}{100}$

- Amount = $P\left(1+\dfrac{R}{100}\right)^n$

- Compound interest = Amount−Principal

- $A = \left(1+\dfrac{R_1}{100}\right)^{n_1}\left(1+\dfrac{R_2}{100}\right)^{n_2}\ldots$

- $S = R\left[\dfrac{(1+i)^n-1}{i}\right]$

- $P = R\left[\dfrac{1-(1+i)^{-n}}{i}\right]$
- For deferred annuities, $P = (1+i)^{-m} \cdot R\left[\dfrac{1-(1+i)^{-n}}{i}\right]$
- Perpetuity $P_\infty = \dfrac{R}{i}$
- $BG = BD - TD$
- $BD = \dfrac{FtR}{100}$
- $TD = \dfrac{PtR}{100}$
- Banker's present worth: $F\left(1 - \dfrac{tR}{100}\right)$
- True present worth: $= P_w = \dfrac{F}{1+\dfrac{tR}{100}}$

$$F = \frac{BD \times TD}{BG}$$

$$BG = TD \times \frac{tR}{100}$$

$$BG = \frac{(TD)^2}{P_w};\ TD = \sqrt{p_w \times BG}$$

CHECK YOUR PROGRESS

1. Find the simple interest on Rs. 30,000 at 18% per annum for the period from 5th Feb 88 to 18th Apr. 88.

   [Rs. 900]

2. A certain sum of money amount to Rs. 756 in 2 years and Rs. 873 in $3\frac{1}{2}$ years. Find the sum and rate interest.

   [Rs. 600 and 13% p.a]

3. Find the compound interest on Rs. 51,200 at 15% p.a for 9 months compounded quartely.

   [Rs. 5978.70]

4. A sum of money amounts to Rs. 10,648 in 3 years and Rs. 9680 in 2 years at compound interest. What is the rate of interest?

   [10% p.a]

5. A sum of money placed at compound interest doubles itself in 5 years. In how many years it will amount to eight times itself?

[15 years]

6. The value of a machine depreciated at 25% p.a. If its present value is Rs. 14,400. Find the value of machine 2 years ago.

[Rs. 25,600]

7. Present population of a colony is 12,000. Increasing at a certain rate, the population becomes 27,000 after 6 years. What will be the size of population after 3 years from now?
8. When Amit was born, Rs. 1000 was placed in an account, that pays at the rate of 6% p.a. compounded quarterly. If the account was not disturbed what will be there in Amit's credit on his 20th birthday?

[Rs. 3,206]

9. The population of a country becomes double in 40 years. If the growth is compounded annually calculate the growth rate.

[1.7%]

10. Find the amount of an ordinary annuity of 12 monthly payment of Rs. 1500 that earns interest at 12% per year compounded monthly.

[Rs. 18,915]

11. What sum must be invested at the end of each year to provide for the replacement at the end of 10 years of a machine costing Rs. 10,000 if money is worth 5% effective?

[Rs. 795.05]

12. What is the present value of an annuity that pays Rs. 200 per month for 5 years if money is worth 6% compounded monthly?

[Rs. 10345]

13. Find the monthly payment necessary to pay off a house loan of Rs. 1,50,000 at 12% per annum in 10 years.

[Rs. 2152.08]

14. An annuity consists of a 5 annual payment of Rs. 1500 each, the first being made at the end of 14 years. Find the amount of this annuity money is worth 7% effective.

[Rs. 8625]

15. Find the present value of a sequence of annual payment of Rs. 1500 each, the first being made at the end of 7 years and the last at the end of 16 years if money is worth 7% effective.

[Rs. 7018.99]

16. To save for a child's education, a family decides to invest Rs. 3000 at the end of each six month period in a fund paying 8% per annum compounded biannually. Find the amount of the investment at the end of 18 years.

[Rs. 231975]

17. A bill has been drawn on June 12th for 2 months. Find its due date.

[14th Aug]

18. Rama draws a bill for Rs. 10,000 on 10th July payable after 4 months. Rakesh accepts it and returns it to Rama. Rama discounts the same on 10th Sept, and got Rs. 9800. Calculate the rate at which the bank discounted the bill.

[12%]

19. The banker's gain on a certain bill due 6 months hence is Rs. 10, the rate of interest being 10% p.a. Find the face value of the bill.

[Rs. 4200]

20. A bill for Rs. 1460 drawn at 3 months was discounted at 4% p.a. on 9th Nov. for 1454.40, on what date the bill was drawn.

[Sept. 11]

21. The present worth of a sum due sometimes hence is Rs. 576 and banker's gain is Re. 1. Find the true discount.

[Rs. 24]

22. If the difference of simple interest and true discount of a sum due one year 6 months hence 8% p.a. is Rs. 81.45. Find the sum.

[Rs. 6335]

23. A bill for Rs. 2920 drawn at 6 months was discounted on 10/4/10 for Rs. 2916. If the discount rate is 5% per annum, on what date was the bill drawn?

[17/10/10]

24. The banker's gain on a sum due 3 years hence at 5% is Rs. 90. Find the banker's discount.

[Rs. 690]

25. The banker's gain of a certain sum due 2 years hence at 5% per annum is Rs. 8. Find the present worth.

[Rs. 800]

6

Ratio and Proportion

INTRODUCTION

Two quantities of the same kind can be compared either by subtraction method or by division method. Example: If I have Rs. 1000 and you have Rs. 6000. Then we can compare the money by subtraction method and say 'you have Rs. 5000 more than what I have'. Or we can compare by division method and say you have 6 times the money what I have. In subtraction method we find how much more (or less) is one quantity than the other, and in division method, we find how many times (or what fractional part) is one quantity of the other.

Ratio analysis is one of the powerful tools of the financial analysis. It is a way by which financial stability and health of a concern can be judged.

RATIO

A relationship or comparison between two quantities of the same kind is called ratio. The comparison is made by considering what multiple part or parts of the first quantity is the second. The ratio of 2 quantities a and b is denoted by $a : b$ or $\frac{a}{b}$. The first term or the numerator is called antecedent and the second term or the denominator b is called consequent.

Note that when the terms of the ratio are multiplied or divided by the same quantity the ratio does not alter.

For instance: $1 : 4 = 2 : 8 = 100 : 400 = \frac{1}{4} : 1$. Also note that a ratio is a pure number. Hence, it has no units.

Compound Ratio

If $a : b$ and $c : d$ are 2 ratios then the ratio $ac : bd$ is called their compound ratio.

Ex: Compound ratio of $5 : 2$ and $3 : 7$ is $5 \times 3 : 2 \times 7$ i.e., $15 : 14$.

Duplicate and Subduplicate Ratios

If $a : b$ is the given ratio then the ratio $a^2 : b^2$ is called duplicate ratio and the ratio $\sqrt{a} : \sqrt{b}$ is called subduplicate ratio.

Ex: For the ratio 1 : 9, duplicate ratio is 1 : 81 and subduplicate ratio is 1 : 3.

Triplicate and Subtriplicate Ratio

If $a : b$ is the given ratio then $a^3 : b^3$ is the triplicate ratio and $\sqrt[3]{a} : \sqrt[3]{b}$ is its subtriplicate ratio.

EXAMPLE: For the ratio 8 : 1 triplicate ratio is $8^3 : 1^3 = 512 : 1$. Subtriplicate ratio is 2 : 1.

SOLVED EXAMPLES

1. Find the ratio between:

(a) 1 hr 10 min and 210 min.

$$1 \text{ hr } 10 \text{ min} = 60 + 10 \text{ min} = 70 \text{ min}$$

$$\therefore \quad \text{Ratio} = \frac{70}{210} = \frac{1}{3} = 1 : 3$$

(b) 6 Rs. 50 ps and 2 Rs. 25 ps

$$\frac{6.50}{2.25} = \frac{650}{225} = \frac{26}{9} = 26 : 9$$

(c) 3 kg 30 gm and 1 kg 260 gm

$$\frac{3.030}{1.260} = \frac{101}{42} = 101 : 42$$

2. Ajith's monthly salary is Rs. 5000 and Arun's annual income is Rs. 1,20,000. What is the ratio of their incomes?

SOLUTION:

Ajith's annual income = $5000 \times 12 = 60{,}000$

Arun's annual income = 1,20,000

So ratio = $\dfrac{60{,}000}{1{,}20{,}000} = \dfrac{1}{2} = 1 : 2$

(OR)

Ajith's monthly salary = Rs. 5000

Arun's monthly salary = $\dfrac{1{,}20{,}000}{12} = 10{,}000$

Ratio = $\dfrac{5000}{10{,}000} = \dfrac{1}{2} = 1 : 2$

3. Compare 2 : 5 and 3 : 7

$$2 : 5 = \frac{2}{5}$$

$$3 : 7 = \frac{3}{7}$$

To compare 2 fractions first we make the denominators same.

$$\frac{2}{5} \times \frac{7}{7} = \frac{14}{35} \text{ and } \frac{3}{7} \times \frac{5}{5} = \frac{15}{35}$$

$$\text{Clearly } \frac{15}{35} \text{ is more than } \frac{14}{35}$$

So 3 : 7 is greater than 2 : 5.

4. A number is divided into 3 parts in the ratio. 1 : 3 : 6. If the 3rd part is 36. Find the other 2 parts.

SOLUTION:

Let x, $3x$ and $6x$ be the parts of the number.

$$3^{\text{rd}} \text{ part} = 36$$

$$6x = 36 \Rightarrow x = 6$$

$$1^{\text{st}} \text{ part} = 6$$

$$2^{\text{nd}} \text{ part} = 3x = 3 \times 6 = 18$$

5. In a mixture of 35 litres, the ratio of milk and water is 6:1. If 1 litre of water is added to the mixture, find the ratio of milk and water in the new mixture.

SOLUTION:

$$\text{Given: milk: water } = 6 : 1$$

$$\text{Sum} = 6 + 1 = 7$$

$$\text{Milk in 35 litres} = \frac{6}{7} \times 35 = 30$$

$$\text{Water in 35 litres} = \frac{1}{7} \times 35 = 5 \text{ litres}$$

Now if 1 litre of water is added, quantity of water in new mixture = $5 + 1 = 6$ litres

$$\text{Milk in new mixture} = 30 \text{ litres}$$

$$\text{So their ratio} = 30 : 6 = 5 : 1$$

$$\text{So milk: water} = 5 : 1.$$

6. A mixture contains nuts and screws in the ratio 4:3. If 7 screws are added to the mixture the ratio becomes 3: 4. Find the number of nuts in the mixture.

SOLUTION:

Let the number of nuts and screws be $4x$ and $3x$

If 7 screws are added then

$$4x : 3x+7 = 3:4$$

$$\text{i.e.,} \quad \frac{4x}{3x+7} = \frac{3}{4}$$

$$16x = 3(3x+7)$$

$$16x - 9x = 21$$

$$7x = 21$$

$$x = 3$$

So number of nuts $= 4x = 4 \times 3 = 12$.

7. 5 years ago, mother's age was 5 times her daughter's age. After 2 years she will be 3 times her daughter's age. Find the ratio of their present ages.

SOLUTION:

Let daughter's age 5 years ago be x and her mother's age $= 5x$

After 2 years,

$$\text{Daughter's age} = x+5+2 = x+7$$

$$\text{Mother's age} = 5x+5+2 = 5x+7$$

$$\text{Given } x+7 = 3(5x+7)$$

$$5x+7 = 3(x+7)$$

$$5x+7 = 3x+21$$

$$2x = 14$$

$$x = 7$$

$$\text{Mother's age} = 5x+5 = 35+5 = 40$$

$$\text{Daughter's age} = x+5 = 7+5 = 12$$

$$\text{Ratio of their ages} = 40:12 = 10:3.$$

8. If 4 shares of T is worth 3 shares of S, 5 shares of S is worth 16 shares of F and 7 shares of F is worth 2 shares of C. How many shares of T is worth 24 shares of C?

SOLUTION:

$$\text{Given: } T:S = 4:3$$

$$S:F = 5:16$$

$$F:C = 7:2$$

$$\text{Let } T:C = x:24$$

$$\text{Now } \frac{T}{C} = \frac{T}{S} \times \frac{S}{F} \times \frac{F}{C}$$

$$\frac{x}{24} = \frac{4}{3} \times \frac{5}{16} \times \frac{7}{2}$$

$$x = \frac{24 \times 4 \times 5 \times 7}{3 \times 16 \times 2} = 35$$

$$\therefore \quad T : C = 35 : 24$$

$\therefore$ 35 shares of T is worth 24 shares of C.

9. X, Y, Z start a business with a capital of Rs. 1,05,000 of this Rs. 44,000 are contributed by X, Rs. 37,000 by Y and the rest by Z. After 5 months Z withdraws Rs. 8000 capital while X and Y each adds Rs. 4000. At the end of the year, 12% of the original capital is the profit and is shared in the ratio of capitals. Find to the nearest amount to be received by each.

SOLUTION:

$$\text{Total capital} : 1,05,000$$

$$X\text{'s contribution} : 44,000$$

$$Y\text{'s contribution} : 37,000$$

$$Z\text{'s contribution} = 1,05,000 - (44,000 + 37,000)$$

$$= 1,05,000 - 81,000$$

$$= 24,000$$

A's share in capital = Rs. 44,000 used for 12 months and Rs. 4000 used for $(12 - 5) = 7$ months

$$44000 \times 12 + 4000 \times 7$$

$$528000 + 28000$$

$$556000$$

Similarly B's share = Rs. 37,000 used for 12 months and 4000 used for 7 months

$$37,000 \times 12 + 4000 \times 7$$

$$4,44,000 + 28,000 = 4,72,000$$

C's share in capital = Rs. 24,000 used for 5 months and Rs. $24,000 - 8000$ used for $(12 - 5)$ months

$$24,000 \times 5 + 16,000 \times 7$$

$$1,20,000 + 1,12,000 = 2,32,000$$

Now ratio of capital of A, B and C

$$= 556000 : 472000 : 232000$$

$$= 139 : 118 : 58$$

Total : $139 + 118 + 58 = 315$

$$\text{Now profit} = 12\% \text{ of capital}$$

$$\frac{12}{100} \times 105000 = 12,600$$

$$A\text{'s share in profit} = \frac{139}{315} \times 12600 = 5560$$

$$B\text{'s share in profit} = \frac{118}{315} \times 12600 = 4720$$

$$C\text{'s share in profit} = \frac{58}{315} \times 12600 = 2320$$

10. Three containers have milk and water in the ratio 6 : 1, 5 : 2 and 3 : 1 respectively. If all the contents are mixed together. Find the ratio of milk and water in the final mixture.

$$\text{Quantity of milk in 1}^{\text{st}} \text{ container} = \frac{6}{7}$$

$$2^{\text{nd}} \text{ container} = \frac{5}{7}$$

$$3^{\text{rd}} \text{ container} = \frac{3}{4}$$

Quantity of milk if all are mixed, $\frac{6}{7} + \frac{5}{7} + \frac{3}{4} = \frac{65}{28}$

$$\text{Quantity of water} = \frac{1}{7} + \frac{2}{7} + \frac{1}{4} = \frac{19}{28}$$

$$\text{Milk: water} = \frac{65}{28} : \frac{19}{28}$$

$$= 65 : 19$$

Proportions: If two ratios are equal then the four quantities comprising them form a proportion.

i.e., if $a : b = c : d$ then a, b, c, d are said to be in proportion.

In a proportion $a : b = c : d$ the 2nd and 3rd term b and c are called means and 1st and 4th terms are called extremes. In every proportion product of the means = product of the extremes.

$$a : b = c : d$$

$\Rightarrow$ $bc = ad$. This is also known as rule of 3.

Ex: If $2:3 = 8:x$. Then

$$2x = 8 \times 3$$
$$x = \frac{8 \times 3}{2}$$
$$x = 12$$

Invertendo: If $a:b = c:d$ then $b:a = d:c$
Alternendo: If $a:b = c:d$ then $a:c = b:d$
Componendo: If $a:b = c:d$ then $a+b:b = c+d:d$
Dividendo: If $a:b = c:d$ then $a-b:b = c-d:d$
Componendo and dividendo: If $a:b = c:d$ then

$$a+b:a-b = c+d:c-d$$

All the above proportions follow from the definition.

Continued Proportion: Quantities $a, b, c, d, e\ldots$ are said to be in continued proportion if

$$\frac{a}{b} = \frac{b}{c} = \frac{c}{d} = \frac{d}{e} = \ldots \quad \text{i.e.,}$$
$$a:b = b:c = c:d = d:e\ldots$$

Three quantities a, b, c are in continued proportion if $a:b = b:c$. Here b is called mean proportional and c is called third proportional.

Direct and Inverse Proportion: Quantities are said to be in direct proportion when an increase (or decrease) in one kind is accompanied by an increase (or decrease) in the other.

EXAMPLE:

No. of pencils:	1	2	3	4	5
Price of pencils:	5	10	15	20	25

As the number of pencils increases, price of pencils also increases and vice versa.

Quantities are said to be in inverse proportion when an increases (or decrease) in one kind is accompanied by decrease (or increase) in the other.

Ex:

No. of workers	1	2	3	4
No. of days	12	6	4	3

As the number of workers increases, number of days required to finish the work decreases and vice versa.

Solved Examples

1. Find the missing term:

(a) $4 : x = 12 : 27$

(b) $10 : 50 = 500 : ?$

Solution:

(a) $4 : x = 12 : 27$

$$12x = 4 \times 27$$

$$x = \frac{4 \times 27}{12} = 9$$

(b) $10 : 50 = 500 : ?$

$$10x = 50 \times 500$$

$$x = \frac{50 \times 500}{10} = 2500$$

2. Find the 3rd proportional to 2 : 70.

Let the 3rd proportional be x

Then $2 : 70 = 70 : x$

$$2x = 70 \times 70$$

$$x = \frac{70 \times 70}{2} = 2450$$

3. Find the 4th proportional to 9 : 2 : 81

Solution:

Let the fourth proportional be x

$$9 : 2 = 81 : x$$

$$9x = 2 \times 81$$

$$x = \frac{2 \times 81}{9} = 18$$

4. Find the mean proportional to 5 : 45

Solution:

Let the mean proportional be x

Then $5 : x = x : 45$

$$x^2 = 5 \times 45$$

$$x = \sqrt{225} = 15$$

5. If $3x+y:4x-7y=3:2$. Find $x:y$

SOLUTION:

Given: $3x+y:4x-7y=3:2$

$$
\begin{aligned}
3(4x-7y) &= 2(3x+y)\\
12x-21y &= 6x+2y\\
12x-6x &= 21y+2y\\
6x &= 23y\\
\frac{x}{y} &= \frac{23}{6}\\
x:y &= 23:6
\end{aligned}
$$

6. If $a:b=3:5$ then find $4a+3b:3a+4b$

Consider $4a+3b:3a+4b$

$$= \frac{4a+3b}{3a+4b}$$

$$= \frac{a\left(4\left(\frac{a}{b}\right)-3\right)}{b\left(3\left(\frac{a}{b}\right)+4\right)}$$

$$\frac{4\left(\frac{3}{5}\right)+3}{3\left(\frac{3}{5}\right)+4} \qquad \text{as} \quad a:b=3:5, \quad \frac{a}{b}=\frac{3}{5}$$

$$\frac{\frac{12+15}{5}}{\frac{9+4}{5}} = \frac{27}{13}$$

$\therefore \quad 4a+3b:3a+4b=27:13$

7. What must be added to 9, 42, 3 and 18, so that the sums will be in proportion.

SOLUTION:

Let x be added to 9, 42, 3 and 18

$9+x:42+x=3+x:18+x$

$$
\begin{aligned}
(9+x)(18+x) &= (42+x)(3+x)\\
162+18x+9x+x^2 &= 126+3x+42x+x^2\\
162+27x+x^2 &= 126+45x+x^2\\
36-18x &= 0\\
x &= \frac{36}{18}=2
\end{aligned}
$$

8. If $x:y=1:2$, $y:z=3:1$ and $z:w=2:3$, then find $x:y:z:w$

$$x:y = 1:2$$
$$y:3 = 3:1$$

To make y same, multiply first ratio by 3 and 2nd by 2

$$x:y=3:6$$
$$y:z=6:2$$

Now $x:y:z=3:6:2$

$$z:w=2:3$$

Z in both the ratios are same

So $x:y:z:w=3:6:2:3.$

9. Divide \$ 590 among x,y,z so that $x:y=3:4$ and $y:z=5:6$

$$x:y=3:4$$
$$y:z=5:6$$

Multiply 1st ratio by 5 and 2nd ratio by 4

$$x:y=15:20$$
$$y:z=20:24$$

Hence $x:y:z=15:20:24$

Their sum $=15+20+24=59$

Out of \$ 590, x's share $=\frac{15}{59}\times 590=\$\ 150$

y's share $=\frac{20}{59}\times 590=\$\ 200$

z's share $=\frac{24}{59}\times 590=\$\ 240$

10. Divide Rs. 4150 into 3 parts such that 4 times the 1st part, 5 times the 2nd part and 7 times the 3rd part are equal.

SOLUTION:

Given: Let 1st, 2nd and 3rd part be a,b,c.

Given $4a=5b=7c=x$

Then $a=\frac{x}{4},\ b=\frac{x}{5}$ and $c=\frac{x}{7}$

$a:b:c=\frac{x}{4}:\frac{x}{5}:\frac{x}{7}$ Multiplying with $\frac{4\times 5\times 7}{x}$

i.e., $a:b:c=35:28:20$

$$\text{Their sum } = 35+28+20=83$$

$$1^{\text{st}} \text{ part } = \frac{35}{83} \times 4150 = 1750$$

$$2^{\text{nd}} \text{ part } = \frac{28}{83} \times 4150 = 1400$$

$$3^{\text{rd}} \text{ part } = \frac{20}{83} \times 4150 = 1000$$

11. If 10 carpenters can earn Rs. 1050 in 7 days. In how many days will 15 carpenters earn Rs. 2250?

SOLUTION:

carpenters	money	days
↓ 10	Rs. 1050 ↑	7 ↑
15	Rs. 2250	x

Here no. of days is unknown.

Leaving money or keeping money constant, consider no. of carpenters and no. of days. As the number of carpenters increases no. of days, required to complete the task decreases. So it is inverse proportion. We denote this by 2 arrows in opposite direction.

Now leaving no. of carpenters or keeping the no. of carpenters fixed. Let us consider money and days. As the number of days increase, money earned also increases. So it is direct proportion. So draw an arrow with the same direction as days.

Now writing compound proportion

$$\left.\begin{array}{c}10:15\\2250:1050\end{array}\right\} = x:7$$

$$15 \times 1050 \times x = 7 \times 10 \times 2250$$

$$x = \frac{7 \times 10 \times 2250}{15 \times 1050} = 10$$

$\therefore$ 15 carpenters earn Rs. 2250 in 10 days.

12. Five men can earn Rs. 3600 in 6 days working 9 hours a day. How much will 8 men earn in 12 days working 6 hours a day?

men	days	hours	money
↓ 5	6 ↓	9 ↓	3600 ↓
8	12	6	x

Here money is unknown.

Taking men and money, as the number of men increases money earned also increases. So it is direct proportion.

Taking days and money, as no. of days increases money earned also increases. So it is direct proportion.

Taking hours and money and keeping no. of men and days fixed. As the no. of hours increases, money earned also increases. So it is direct proportion.

Corresponding compound proportion is

$$\begin{array}{l} 5:8 \\ 6:12 \\ 9:6 \end{array} = 3600 : x$$

$$5 \times 6 \times 9 \times x = 8 \times 12 \times 6 \times 3600$$

$$x = \frac{8 \times 12 \times 6 \times 3600}{5 \times 6 \times 9} = 7680$$

∴ 8 carpenters earn Rs. 7680 in 12 days working 6 hours a day.

Accounting Ratios

The term accounting ratios is used to describe significant relationships which exists between figures shown in a balance sheet, in a profit and loss account, in a budgetary control system or in any other part of the accounting organisation.

Nature of Ratio Analysis

Ratios by themselves are not an end but only one of the means of understanding the financial health of a business entity. Ratio analysis is a technique of:

(i) Establishing meaningful relationship between significant variables of financial statements.

(ii) Interpreting the relationships to form judgement regarding the financial affairs of the unit.

Advantages of Ratio Analysis

Ratios as a tool of financial analysis provide symptoms with the help of which any analyst is in a position to diagnose the financial health of the unit. Financial analysis may be compared with the biopsy conducted by the doctor on the patient in order to diagnose the causes of illness, so that treatment may be prescribed to the patient to help him recover.

CLASSIFICATION OF RATIOS

Ratios may be classified in a number of ways keeping in view the particular purpose. Ratios indicating profitability are calculated on the basis of profit and loss account, those indicating financial position are computed on the basis of the balance sheet and those which show operating efficiency or productivity or effective use of resources are calculated on the basis of figures in the profit and loss account and the balance sheet.

I. (1) Profitability Ratio

Profitability is the overall measure of the company with regard to efficient and effective utilisation of resources at its command. It indicates in a nutshell the effectiveness of the decisions taken by the management from time to time. These ratios are calculated to enlighten the end results of business activity which is the sole criterion of the overall efficiency of a business concern. The following are important profitability ratios.

Gross profit ratio: This ratio tells gross margin on trading and is calculated by using the formula, Gross profit ratio $= \dfrac{\text{Gross profit}}{\text{Net Sales}} \times 100$

Example: If gross profit is 40,000 and net sales is 5,00,000 the

$$\text{GPR} = \frac{40,000}{5,00,000} \times 100 = 8\%.$$

Higher the ratio, the better it is. A low ratio indicates unfavourable trends in the form of reduction in selling prices not accompanied by proportionate decrease in cost of goods or increase in the cost of production.

(2) Operating Ratio

This ratio indicates the proportion that the cost of sales bears to sales. Cost of sales include direct cost of goods sold as well as other operating expenses, administration, selling and distribution expenses which have matching relationship with sales. It excludes income and expenses which have no bearing on production and sales, i.e., non-operating incomes and expenses as interest and dividend received on investment interest paid on long term loans and debentures, profit or loss on sale of fixed assets or long term investments. It is calculated by using

$$\frac{\text{Cost of goods sold operating expenses}}{\text{Net sales}} \times 100$$

Here

Cost of goods sold = Opening stock + Purchases + Direct expenses + Manufacturing expenses – Closing stock or sales – Gross profit.

Operating expenses = Administrative expenses + Selling and distribution expenses.

EXAMPLE:

Particulars	Rs.	Particulars	Rs.
Sales less returns	4,00,000	Selling expenses	25,000
Gross profit	1,40,000	Income from investment	1,000
Administration expenses	35,000	Loss on account of fire	2,000

Find the operating profit ratio.

SOLUTION:

$$\text{Operating profit} = \text{Gross profit} - \text{Administration} + \text{Selling expenses}$$
$$= 1,40,000 - (35,000 + 25,000)$$
$$= \text{Rs } 80,000$$
$$\text{Operating profit ratio} = \frac{80,000}{4,00,000} \times 100$$
$$= 20\%$$

Lower the ratio, the better it is. Higher the ratio, the less favourable it is because it would have smaller margin of operating profit for the payment of dividends and the creation of reserves.

Operating Profit Ratio

This ratio establishes the relationship between operating profit and sales and is calculated as follows:

$$\text{Operating profit ratio} = \frac{\text{Operating profit}}{\text{Net sales}} \times 100$$

$$\text{Where operating profit} = \text{Net profit} + \text{Non-operating expenses}$$
$$- \text{non-operating income}$$

Or

$$\text{Gross profit} - \text{operating expenses}$$

Operating profit ratio can also be calculated with the help of operating ratio by using

$$\text{Operating profit ratio} = 100 - \text{Operating ratio.}$$

Higher the operating profit ratio, the better it is.

Net Profit Ratio

It expresses the relationship between the net profit after taxes and sales. This ratio is a measure of the overall profitability. Net profit is arrived at after taking into account both the operating and non-operating items of incomes and expenses.

The ratio indicates what portion of the net sales is left for the owners after all expenses have been met. It is calculated by using the formula,

$$\text{Net profit ratio} = \frac{\text{Net profit after tax}}{\text{Net sales}} \times 100$$

The ratio differs from the operating profit ratio inasmuch as it is calculated after deducting non-operating expenses, such as loss on sale of fixed assets, etc., from operating profit and adding non-operating income like interest dividends on investments profit on sale of investments or fixed assets, etc., to such profit. Higher the ratio, the better it is because it gives an idea of improved efficiency of the concern.

II. Turnover or Performance or Activity Ratio

Turnover ratios indicate position of assets usage. These are usually calculated on the basis of sales and are expressed in integers rather than as percentage. The greater the ratio, more will be the efficiency of assets usage.

1. Sales to fixed assets (or fixed assets turnover ratio)

It is calculated by using

$$\frac{\text{Sales}}{\text{Net fixed assets}} \quad \text{(i.e., fixed assets less depreciation)}$$

This ratio shows how well the fixed assets are being used in the business.

Total assets turnover ratio: This ratio is calculated by dividing the net sales by the value of total assets.

$$\text{i.e.,} \quad \frac{\text{Net sales}}{\text{Total assets}}$$

A high ratio is an indicator of over-trading of total assets while a low ratio reveals idle capacity.

Receivable or debtors turnover ratio: It indicates the number of times on the average the receivable are turnover in each year. The higher the value of ratio, the more is the efficient management of debtors. It measures the accounts receivable in terms of number of days of credit sales during a particular period. This ratio is calculated by using $\frac{\text{Net credit sales}}{\text{Average debtors}}$

This ratio is a measure of the collectivity of accounts receivables and tells about how the credit policy of the company is being enforced. Higher the ratio, more the chances of bad debts and lower the ratio, less the chances of bad debts. Suppose in 2011, debtors in the beginning Rs. 4,00,000. Debtors at the end

Rs. 5, 00,000 credit sales during the year is Rs. 22,50,000. The debtors turnover ratio and collection period will be calculated by using

$$\text{Debtors turnover ratio} = \frac{\text{Credit sales}}{\text{Average Debtors}}$$

$$= \frac{2250000}{4,50,000} = 5$$

$$\text{Collection period} = \frac{365}{\text{Debtors turnover ratio}}$$

$$= \frac{365}{5} = 73 \text{ days.}$$

Creditors or accounts payable turnover ratio

It is calculated by using $\dfrac{\text{Credit purchases}}{\text{Average accounts payable}}$

For example, if credit purchases during 2010 are 2,00,000 and accounts payable on 1.1.2010 and 31.12.2010 are Rs. 46,000 and Rs. 34,000 respectively then Creditors turnover ratio= $2,00,000 \div \frac{1}{2}(46,000 + 34,000) = 5$

A high ratio indicates that creditors are not paid in time while a low ratio gives an idea that the business is not taking full advantages of credit period allowed by the creditors.

III. Financial Ratios

These ratios are calculated to judge the financial position of the concern from long term as well as short term solvency point of view. Financial ratios can be broadly divided into: (i) liquidity ratio and (ii) stability ratio.

Liquidity ratios are used to measure the terms ability to meet short term obligations. They compare short term obligations to short term (or current) resources available to meet these obligations. The important liquidity ratios are discussed below.

(a) Current ratio (or working capital ratio)

It is calculated by using the formula:

$$\text{Current ratio} = \frac{\text{Current assets}}{\text{Current liabilities}}$$

Generally 2 : 1 is considered ideal for a concern. If the ratio is less than 2, difficulty may be experienced in the payment of current liabilities and day-to-day operations of the business may suffer. If the ratio is higher than 2 it it is very comfortable for the creditors but for the concern it is an indicator of ideal funds and a lack of enthusiasm for work.

For the calculation of this ratio current assets include cash, bank balance, short term investment, bills receivable, trade debtors, short term loans and advances, inventories and pre-paid payments and current liabilities includes bank overdrafts, bills payable, trade creditors, provision for taxation, proposed dividends, unclaimed dividends, advanced payments and unexpired discounts, accrued interest on loans and debentures, outstanding expenses and the portion of long term debt to mature within one year.

(b) Liquid ratio: (Acid test or quick ratio)

This is the ratio of liquid assets to liquid liabilities. It shows a firm's ability to meet current liabilities with its most liquid (quick) assets. 1 : 1 is considered ideal ratio for a concern because it is wise to keep the liquid assets at least equal to the liquid liabilities at all times. Liquid assets are those assets which are readily converted into cash and will include cash balances, bills receivable, sundry debitors and short term investments. This ratio is the 'acid test' of a concern's financial so soundness. It is calculated by using liquid ratio $= \dfrac{\text{Liquid assets}}{\text{Current(or liquid) liabilities}}$

Suppose liquid liabilities Rs. 3,00,000. Current ratio 2, liquid ratio 1.5. Quick assets and stock in trade are calculated as

$$\text{Current ratio} = \frac{\text{Current assets}}{\text{Current liabilities}}$$

$$\begin{aligned}\text{Current assets} &= \text{Current liabilities} \times \text{Current ratio}\\ &= \text{Rs. } 3,00,000 \times 2 = \text{Rs. } 6,00,000\end{aligned}$$

$$\text{Quick ratio} = \frac{\text{Quick assets}}{\text{Current liabilites}}$$

$$\begin{aligned}\text{Quick assets} &= \text{Current liabilities} \times \text{Quick ratio}\\ &= \text{Rs. } 3,00,000 \times 1.5 = \text{Rs. } 4,50,000\end{aligned}$$

$$\begin{aligned}\therefore \quad \text{Stock in trade} &= \text{Current assets} - \text{Quick assets}\\ &= \text{Rs. } 6,00,000 - 4,50,000\\ &= \text{Rs. } 1,50,000\end{aligned}$$

SOLVED EXAMPLES

1. The following is the extracts of financial information related to *XYZ* Ltd.

Balance sheet as on 31st Dec

(Rs. in Lakhs)

Liabilities	**2010**	**2011**	**Assets**	**2010**	**2011**
Share capital	10	10	Fixed assets	30	30
Reserve & surplus	30	10	Current assets		
Loan funds	60	70	Stocks	30	20
Current liabilities	30	20	Debtors	30	30
			Cash/Bank balances	10	20
			Prepaid expenses	30	10
	130	110		130	110

Sales (Rs. Lakhs): 2010 – 270 2011 – 300

(i) Calculate for the 2 years debit equity ratio, quick ratio, working capital turnover ratio.

(ii) Find the sales volume that should have been generated in 2010 if the company were to have maintained its working capital turnover ratio.

SOLUTION:

(i)
$$\text{Debt equity ratio} = \frac{\text{Long term debts}}{\text{Share holders fund}}$$

$$\text{In 2010} = \frac{60}{40} = 1.5 : 1$$

$$\text{In 2011} = \frac{70}{20} = 3.5 : 1$$

$$\text{Quick ratio} = \frac{\text{Liquid assets}}{\text{Liquid liabilities}}$$

$$\text{In 2010} = \frac{40}{30} = 1.33 : 1 \quad \text{or} \quad 4 : 3$$

$$\text{In 2011} : \frac{50}{20} = 2.5 : 1$$

$$\text{Working capital turnover ratio} = \frac{\text{Sales}}{\text{Working capital}}$$

$$\text{In 2010} : \frac{270}{70} = 3.86 \text{ times}$$

$$\text{In 2011} : \frac{300}{60} = 5 \text{ times}$$

(ii)
$$\text{Working capital turnover} = \frac{\text{Sales}}{\text{Working captial}}$$
$$5 = \frac{\text{sales}}{70}$$
$$\text{or sales} = 5 \times 70 = 350$$
i.e., Sales = Rs. 350 lakh.

2. Calculate the following for the year 2007 and 2008 using figures made available:
   (a) Current ratio
   (b) Debt/Equity ratio
   (c) Fixed assets turnover ratio
   (d) Inventory turnover ratio
   (e) Earning per share.

Balance sheet as on 31st Dec

(Rs. in lakhs)

Liabilities	2006	2007	2008	Assets	2006	2007	2008
Share capital of Rs. 10 each	800	1000	1000	Fixed assets Gross block	2800	3000	4000
Reserves & surplus	700	800	1000	Less: Depreciation	920 1880	1400 1600	2000 2000
Secured turn loan	800	2000	2400	Stocks	1520	2400	2800
Sundry creditors	1200	900	1100	Debtors	480	500	900
				Other current assets	420	1200	1300
	4300	5700	7000		4300	5700	7000

Extracts from profit and loss account for the year ended 31st Dec

(Rs. in lakhs)

	2007	2008
Sales	4,800	7200
Profit before depreciation & interest on term loans	1500	2400
Depreciation	480	600
Interest on term loans	420	600
Tax	300	600
Dividents	100	150

SOLUTION:

	2007	2008
(a) Current ratio $= \dfrac{\text{Current assets}}{\text{Current liabilities}}$	$\dfrac{4100}{1900} = 2.16:1$	$\dfrac{5000}{2600} = 1.92:1$
(b) $\dfrac{\text{Debt (secured term loans)}}{\text{Equity}}$	$\dfrac{2000}{1800} = 1.11:1$	$\dfrac{2400}{2000} = 1.20:1$
(c) $\dfrac{\text{Sales}}{\text{Average fixed assets (Net)}}$	$\dfrac{4800}{1740} = 2.76$	$\dfrac{7200}{1800} = 4.00$
(d) $\dfrac{\text{Cost of goods sold (sales-profit before dep. interest)}}{\text{Average inventory}}$	$\dfrac{3300}{1960} = 1.68$ times	$\dfrac{4800}{2600} = 1.85$
(e) $\dfrac{\text{Earning available to equity shareholders}}{\text{No. of equity shares}}$	$\dfrac{300}{100} = 3$	$\dfrac{600}{100} = 6$

3. From the following information, make out a statement of proprietor's fund with as many details as possible:
   (i) Current ratio = 2.5
   (ii) Liquid ratio = 1.5
   (iii) Proprietary ratio (fixed assets/proprietor's fund) = 0.75
   (iv) Working capital Rs. 60,000
   (v) Reserve and surplus Rs. 40,000
   (vi) Bank overdraft Rs. 10,000
   (vii) There is no long term loan or fictitious assets.

SOLUTION:

Calculation of the amount of current assets and current liabilities:

$$\text{Current assets} - \text{Current liabilities} = \text{Working capital}$$

$$2.5x - x = \text{Rs. } 60{,}000$$

$$1.5x = \text{Rs. } 60{,}000$$

$$x = \frac{60000}{1.5} = \text{Rs. } 40{,}000$$

$\therefore$ Current liabilities = Rs. 40,000.

$\therefore$ Current assets $= 2.5x = 2.5 \times 40{,}000 = 1{,}00{,}000$

Given that bank overdraft = Rs. 10,000

Liquid liabilities = Rs. 40,000 – Rs. 10,000

= Rs. 30,000

$$\text{Liquid ratio} = \frac{\text{Liquid assets}}{\text{Liquid liabilities}}$$

$$1.5 = \frac{\text{Liquid assets}}{\text{Rs. } 30,000}$$

$$\Rightarrow \quad \text{Liquid assets} = \text{Rs. } 45,000$$

$$\text{Stock} = \text{Current assets} - \text{Liquid assets}$$

$$\text{Rs. } 1,00,000 - \text{Rs. } 45,000 = \text{Rs. } 55,000$$

Calculation of the amount of proprietor's fund:

$$\text{Proprietor's fund} = \text{Fixed assets} + \text{Current assets} - \text{Outsider's liabilities}$$

If proprietors fund $= x$, fixed assets $= 0.75\,x$

Since proprietor's ratio = 0.75.

$$\therefore \quad x - 0.75\,x = \text{Rs. } 1,00,000 - \text{Rs. } 40,000$$

$$\Rightarrow x = 2,40,000$$

So proprietor's funds are Rs. 2,40,000. Reserves and surplus are given to us as Rs. 40,000. So capital Rs. $2,40,000 - 40,000 = 2,00,000$.

$$\text{Fixed assets} = 0.75 \times \text{proprietor's fund}$$

$$\text{So fixed assets} = 2,40,000 \times 0.75$$

$$= \text{Rs. } 1,80,000.$$

Statement of Proprietor's Fund

Proprietor's fund:		**Rs.**	**Rs.**	**Rs.**
Capital			2,00,000	
Reserves and surplus			40,000	
Represented by				2,40,000
Fixed assets:		–	1,80,000	
Current assets:				
Stock	Rs. 55,000			
Liquid assets	Rs. 45,000			
		1,00,000		
Less: Current liabilities:				
Bank overdrafts	Rs. 10,000			
Liquid liabilities	Rs. 30,000			
		40,000	60,000	2,40,000

IN A NUTSHELL

- For the ratio $a:b$, duplicate ratio is $a^2:b^2$ sub-duplicate ratio is $\sqrt{a}:\sqrt{b}$, triplicate ratio is $a^3:b^3$ and subtriplicate ratio is $\sqrt[3]{a}:\sqrt[3]{b}$
- If $a:b=c:d$ then a, b, c, d are said to be in proportion d is called fourth proportional and $ad=bc$
- If $a:b=b:c$. Then b is called mean proportional and c is called 3rd proportional
- If $a:b=c:d$. Then

  Invertendo: $b:a=d:c$

  Alternendo: $a:c=b:d$

  Componendo: $a+b:b=c+d:d$

  Dividendo: $a-b:b=c-d:d$

  Componendo & Dividendo: $a+b:a-b=c+d:c-d$

- If $a:b=c:d$ is a direct proportion then $a:b=d:c$ or $b:a=c:d$ represents an inverse proportion and vice versa.
- Gross profit ratio $= \dfrac{\text{Gross profit}}{\text{Net sales}} \times 100$
- Operating ratio $= \dfrac{\text{Cost of goods sold + Operating expenses}}{\text{Net sales}} \times 100$
- Operating profit ratio $= \dfrac{\text{Operating profit}}{\text{Net sales}} \times 100$
- Net profit ratio $= \dfrac{\text{Net profit after tax}}{\text{Net sales}} \times 100$
- Fixed assets turnover ratio $= \dfrac{\text{Sales}}{\text{Net fixed assets}}$
- Total assets turnover ratio $= \dfrac{\text{Net sales}}{\text{Total assets}}$
- Debtor's turnover ratio $= \dfrac{\text{Net credit sales}}{\text{Average debtors}}$
- Creditor's turnover ratio $= \dfrac{\text{Credit purchases}}{\text{Average accounts payable}}$
- Current ratio $= \dfrac{\text{Current assets}}{\text{Current liabilities}}$
- Acid test or quick ratio $= \dfrac{\text{Liquid assets}}{\text{Current liabilities}}$

CHECK YOUR PROGRESS

1. Find the ratio between: (a) 3 kg 50 gm and 4 kg 500 gm. (b) 1 hr 15 min & 105 min

   [61 : 90, 5 : 7]

2. Which is greater ! 3 : 2 or 2 : 7

   [3 : 2]

3. Express 24 : 88 in the simplest form

   [3 : 11]

4. Find: (i) 3rd proportional to 2 : 6

   (ii) 4th proportional to 4, 5 and 12

   [(i) 18 (ii) 15]

5. If $x : y = 2 : 3$, $y : z = 4 : 5$, $z : w = 6 : 7$ then find $x : y : z : w$

   [16 : 24 : 30 : 35]

6. The ratio between *A*'s and *B*'s age at present is 2 : 3. *A* is 6 years younger to *B*. Find the ratio of *A*'s age to *B*'s age after 6 years

   [3:4]

7. *X*,*Y*,*Z*, start a business with investments of Rs. 25,000 Rs. 16,000 and Rs. 12,000 respectively. If the profit for the year amounts to Rs. 6,850. Find the share of each partner

   [Rs. 2650, Rs. 2200, Rs. 2000]

8. 8 men can build a wall in 6 days. In how many days 12 men can do the same work?

   [4 days]

9. 6 carpenters working 7 hours a day can complete 24 chairs in 20 days. How many days will 12 carpenter working 6 hours a day take to complete 36 chairs?

   [105 days]

10. 8 men can dig a pit in 20 days. If a man works half as much again as a boy then in how many days 4 men and 9 boys can dig a similar pit?

    [16 days]

11. *XYZ* company has drawn up the following profit and loss account for the year ended 31st march 2010:

	Rs.		Rs.
To opening stock	26,000	By sales	1,60,000
To purchases	80,000	By closing stock	38,000
To wages	24,000		
To manufacturing expenses	16,000		
To gross profit c/d	52,000		
	1,98,000		1,98,000
To selling & dist.expenses	4,000	By gross profit b/d	52,000
To administrator expenses	22,800	By compensation for acquisition of land	4,800
To general expenses	1200		
To value of furniture (loss by fire)	800		
To net profit	28,000		
	56,800		56,800

Find:

(i) Gross profit ratio

(ii) Net profit ratio

(iii) Operating ratio

(iv) Operating profit ratio

[**Ans.** (i) 32.5% (ii) 17.5% (iii) 85% (iv) 15%
(i) 0.325 (ii) 0.175 (iii) 0.85 (iv) 0.15]

12. The following are summarised profit and loss account for the year ending 31.12.2011 and the balance sheet as at the date:

Trading and profit & loss account

	Rs		Rs
To opening stock	10,000	By sales	1,00,000
To purchases	55,000	By closing stock	15,000
To gross profit	50,000		
	1,15,000		1,15,000
To administrative expenses	15,000	By gross profit	50,000
To interest	3,000		
To selling expenses	12,000		
To net profit	20,000		
	50,000		50,000

Balance Sheet

	Rs.		Rs.
Capital	1,00,000	Land & building	50,000
Profit & loss account	20,000	Plant & machinery	30,000
Creditors	25,000	Stock	15,000
Bills payable	15,000	Sundry debtors	15,000
		Bills receivable	12,500
		Cash in hand and at bank	17,500
		furniture	20,000
	1,60,000		1,60,000

Additional Information

1. Average debtors Rs. 12,500
2. Average credit purchases Rs. 40,000

   Calculate:

   (i) Stock turnover ratio

   (ii) Debtor's turnover ratio

   (iii) Creditor's turnover ratio

   (iv) Sales to working capital

   (v) Sales to fixed assets

   (vi) Sales to capital employed

   (vii) Return on shareholders investment

   (viii) Current ratio

   (ix) Acid test ratio

   (x) Gross profit ratio

   (xi) Net profit ratio

   (xii) Operating ratio.

[**Ans**. (i) 4 (ii) 8 (iii) 1 : 1 (iv) 5 : 1 (v) 1 : 1 (vi) 0.83 : 1 (vii) $16\frac{2}{3}\%$ (viii) 1.5 : 1 (ix) 1 : 125 (x) 20% (xi) 20% (xii) 77%]

13. The following information relates to Sri Ram in respect of the year ended 31st march 2000.

    (i) Gross profit ratio – 25%

    (ii) Net profit / sales : (a) 20%

(b) Stock turnover ratio – 10

(c) Net profit / capital – $1/5$

(d) Capital / Total liabilities – $1/2$

(e) Fixed assets / Capital – $5/4$

(f) Fixed assets / Total current assets – $5/7$

(g) Fixed assets – Rs. $10,000,00$

(h) Closing stock – Rs. $1,00,000$.

Prepare a trading and profit and loss account for the year ended 31st march 2000 and balance sheet on that date.

[**Ans.** G.P. Rs. 3,33,333 N.P. Rs. 2,66,667 B/S total Rs. 24,00,000]

Hint: Administrative, selling & distribution expenses Rs. 66,666.

14. With the help of the following information, complete the balance sheet of ABC Ltd.

Equity Rs. 1,00,000

The relevant ratios of the firm are as follows:

$$\text{Current dept to total debt} = 0.40$$
$$\text{Total debt to owners equity} = 0.60$$
$$\text{Fixed assets to owner's equity} = 0.60$$
$$\text{Total assets turnover} = 2 \text{ times}$$
$$\text{Inventory turnover} = 8 \text{ times}$$

[**Ans.** Balance sheet total: Rs. 1,60,000]

Hints: Current debts Rs. 24,000, Long term debt: Rs. 36,000, Fixed assets Rs. 60,000, Cash Rs. 60,000 and Inventory Rs. 40,000.

From the following particulars prepare a summarised balance sheet in detail as on 31st march 10

Fixed assets to net worth	0.8 : 1
Current ratio	3 : 1
Reserves included in proprietor's fund	25%
Acid test ratio	3 : 2
Fixed assets	Rs. 8,00,000
Cash & bank balance	Rs. 15,000
Current liabilities	Rs. 1,50,000

[**Ans.** B/S Total Rs. 12,50,000]

15. You are given the following information about 2 companies

	Company A Rs.	Company B Rs.
Cash	180	140
Debentures	1,520	3200
Inventory	1,800	3200
Bills payable	270	1000
Creditors	500	4000
Accrued expenses	150	125
Tax payable	750	1000

(i) Calculate the liquid ratios for 2 companies.

(ii) Give your interpretation of the liquidity position of the two companies as revealed by the ratios.

[**Ans.** (i) $CR = A - 2.0958 \quad B - 1.43, \quad LR - A - 1.02, \quad B = 0.545$
$ALR\ A - 0.107\ B - 0.022$
Company A is better than company B.]

Part B

Statistics

7

Introduction to Statistics

Statistics has been defined in innumerable ways. While some of them correspond to the historical development of the subject, others correspond to its ever expanding areas of application. But, no single definition has been able to encompass the various concepts, methods and methodologies used in most scientific and business enquiries that we collectively call 'Statistics'. Curiously, the word 'Statistics' can be used in two senses, i.e., plural and singular. In its plural sense, the word means statistical data. Thus, we have statistics pertaining to population, employment, production, exports, imports, income, etc., of a particular state during a specified time period. Some definitions of statistics in its plural sense are given below.

Statistics as Numerical Data—Some Definitions

1. "Statistics are the classified facts representing the conditions of the people in a state... especially those facts which can be stated in numbers or in tables of numbers or any tabular or classified arrangement."
   —Webster.
2. "Statistics are numerical statement of facts in any department placed in relation to each other." —Bowley
3. "By Statistics we mean quantitative data affected to a marked extent by multiplicity of causes." —Yule and Kendall
4. "Statistics are measurements, enumerations or estimates of natural phenomenon, usually systematically arranged, analysed and presented as to exhibit important interrelationships among them."
   —A.M. Tuttle

But, the most comprehensive and exhaustive definition of statistics in its plural sense given by Prof. Horace Secrist is as follows.

"By statistics we mean an aggregate of facts affected to a marked extent by multiplicity of causes, numerically expressed, enumerated or estimated according to reasonable standards of accuracy, collected in a systematic manner for a pre-determined purpose and placed in relation to each other."

In the singular sense Statistics refers to the whole body of analytical tools that are used to collect, organise and interpret data and, finally draw conclusions. A precise and comprehensive definition in this sense is given by F.E. Croxten and D.J. Cowden which is as follows— *"Statistics is the science of collection, presentation, analysis and interpretation of numerical data."*

Some other definitions for Statistics as statistical methods, i.e., in its singular sense are given below:

Statistics as Statistical Methods—Some Definitions

1. (i) Statistics may be called the science of counting.

   (ii) Statistics may rightly be called the science of averages.

   (iii) Statistics is the science of the measurement of social organism, regarded as a whole in all its manifestations. —Bowley

2. "Statistics is the science of estimates and probabilities." —Boddington

3. "Statistics is the science and art of handling aggregate of facts observing, enumerating, recording, classifying and otherwise systematically treating them." —Harlow

4. "……Statistical method include all those devices of analysis and synthesis by means of which statistics (data) are scientifically collected and used to explain or describe phenomena either in their individual or related capacities." —Secrist

5. "Statistics is the branch of scientific method which deals with the data obtained by counting or measuring the properties of population of natural phenomena." —Kendall

6. "Statistics is the science which deals with the method of collecting, classifying, presenting, comparing and interpreting numerical data collected to throw some light on any sphere of inquiry." —Seligman

7. "Statistics refers to the body of technique or methodology which has been developed for the collection, presentation and analysis of quantitative data and for the use of such data in decision-making."
—Netter & Wasserman

8. "Modern statistics refers to a body of methods and principles that have been developed to handle the collection, description, summarisation and analysis of numerical data. Its primary objective is to assist the researcher in making decisions or generalisations about the nature and characteristics of all the potential observations under consideration of which the collected data form only a small part." —Lincon L. Chao

9. "Statistics is a method of decision making in the face of uncertainty on the basis of numerical data and calculated risks."
—Prof. Ya-Lun-Chou

10. "The science of statistics is the method of judging collective, natural or social phenomenon from the results obtained from the analysis or enumeration or collection of estimates." —King

11. "Statistics may be regarded as a body of methods for making wise decisions in the face of uncertainty." —Wallis and Roberts

IMPORTANCE AND SCOPE OF STATISTICS

The scope and application of Statistics has assumed unprecedented dimensions these days. No field of human endeavour has been left untouched by statistical methods. In fact all fields, i.e., from Anthropology to Zoology have found applications of Statistics. The application of Statistics in any field gives rise to a new discipline which generally ends with the word '*metrics*'. For example 'Econometrics' is the application of Statistics in Economics while 'Biometrics' is the application of Statistics to Biology.

While there is no denying that statistical methods find application in fields as diverse as politics, biology, trade, etc., as students and practitioners of Business and Management it is important to familiarize ourselves to its scope in Economics, Business Management, Commerce, etc.

STATISTICS AND THE STATE

The origin and initial stages of development of statistics was for the purpose of administration. In fact, the origin of the word statistics itself can be traced back to the Latin word 'status' the French word 'statistique' and the German word 'statistik' all meaning 'state—a political state'. For efficient administration, the government requires facts and figures regarding defence force population, food production, imports, exports, prices, consumption, investments, etc. Popular statistical methods such as time series analysis, index numbers, forecasting and demand analysis are extensively practised in formulating economic policies. The governments also collect data on population dynamics in order to initiate and implement various welfare policies and programmes.

In addition to the statistical bureaus in all ministries and government departments in the central and state governments there are other important agencies in the field like the Central Statistical Organisation (CSO), Registrar General of India (RGI), National Sample Survey Organisation etc.

Statistics in Biology, Medicine, Agriculture, etc.

The knowledge of statistical techniques in all natural sciences—botany, zoology, microbiology, medicine, agriculture, etc., is of great importance. For example, they are applied in the study of growth of plant, migration of birds, movement of fish schools in the oceans, efficacy of new drugs or treatments, theories of heredity, spread of disease among trees in a forest, estimation of number of tigers in a forest, weather forecast, estimation of rainfall, estimation of yield of crop, effect of fertilizer on yield, growth of bacteria, birth rate, death rate, population growth, etc. In particular, the branch of statistics which deals with problems relating to population growth is called Demography. Another branch that deals with insurance, risk, premiums, etc. is Acturial Science.

Statistics in Economics

All branches of Economics make extensive use of statistical methods. For example:

(i) Forecasting techniques are used for curve fitting by the principle of least squares and exponential smoothing to predict inflation rate, unemployment, manufacturing, capacity utilization, GDP, etc.

(ii) Index numbers are useful in economic planning as they indicate the changes over a specified period of time in: (a) cost of living, (b) whole sale prices of commodity, (c) imports, (d) exports, (e) industrial production, (f) agricultural production, etc.

(iii) Time series analysis is used for studying the behaviour of prices, production and consumption of commodities, money in circulation, bank deposits and clearings, etc.

(iv) Demand analysis is used to study the relationship between the price of a commodity and its output (supply).

Statistics in Business Management

Business Management is all about decision making in the face of uncertainties. According to Ya-Lin-Chou, "Statistics is a method of decision making in the face of uncertainty on the basis of numerical data and calculated risks". Statistical reports provide a summary of business activities which improves the capabilities of making better and more effective decisions regarding future activities.

An offshoot of statistics, Operations Research (or Management Science) is the body of knowledge involving quantitative approaches to decision making.

Let us consider a few activities of a typical business organisation where statistics plays an important role.

Marketing: Before a product is launched the market research team of the organisation will undertake a pilot survey. This pilot survey will make use of various statistical techniques to analyse data on population, purchasing power, habits of consumers, pricing, competition and many other aspects. Such studies will reveal the possible market potential for the new product. Analysis of data on sales volume, purchasing power, demographics, etc., would be helpful in establishing sales territories, routing of salesmen, advertising strategies, etc.

Production: Statistical methods are used extensively to carry out programmes for improvement in the quality of the existing products and setting. Decisions about inventory, make or buy, job sequencing, etc., are all based on statistically analysed data.

Finance: Statistical analysis of data on assets and liabilities, income and expenditure, etc., help to ascertain the financial results of various operation. Financial forecasts, break-even analysis, investment decisions under uncertainty—all involve the application of statistics.

Human Resource: In the process of manpower planning the Human Resource Department of an organisation typically makes statistical studies of wage rates, incentive plans, cost of living, attrition rates, employment trends, performance appraisals, training and development programmes, etc.

STATISTICS AND COMPUTERS

Developments in the field of computer and information technology and the advent of personal computers have revolutionised the areas to which statistical techniques are applied. Many statistical techniques are available as 'statistical software packages'.

A statistical package is a suite of computer programs that are specialised for statistical analysis. It enables us to obtain the results of standard statistical procedures and statistical significance tests, without requiring low level numerical programming. Most statistical packages also provide facilities for data management. Popular statistical packages include SPSS, SAS, MINITAB, R, Analyse it-add on to Microsoft EXCEL, etc. While most of them are commercial software, R is a open source free software and hence can easily be downloaded and used. Also, since EXCEL is available almost on all windows based personal computers it is easily accessible.

Use of computers and software, however, presupposes that the user is able to interpret the computer output that are generated.

FUNCTIONS OF STATISTICS

The important functions fulfilled by Statistics are:

(1) *It simplifies complexity of the data.*

Complex numerical data are simplified by the use of statistical methods. For example, complex data regarding varying daily prices of stocks and shares can be reduced to the form of an index, say SENSEX or BSE index.

(2) *It reduces the bulk of the data.*

Voluminous data can be reduced to just a few descriptive figures such as averages, co-efficients, rates, etc.

(3) *It adds precision to thinking.*

Statistics sharpens a researcher's thinking process. It sieves away unwanted and distracting information.

(4) *It helps in comparing different sets of data.*

The sales of a company may be compared among the company's different products or they may be compared with those of another company.

(5) *It guides in the formulation of policies and helps in planning.*

Planning and policy making by governments and organisations are all based on the past data and future trends.

(6) *It indicates trends, tendencies or positions.*

Based on available data, future prediction or forecasting can be done for any number of situations. For example, population of a city in the next 20 years can be estimated based on its population for the past two years.

(7) *It helps in studying relationship between different factors.*

Statistical methods can be used to find the extent and nature of relationship between factors affecting a phenomenon.

LIMITATIONS OF STATISTICS

Although the scope of Statistics is very wide and applications innumerable, it does suffer from a few limitations. The major limitations are:

1. *Statistics does not deal with qualitative data. It deals only with quantitative data.*

   Statistical methods can be applied to numerically expressed data. But there are several phenomenon or concepts that are not amenable to measurement. For example, beauty, courage, intelligence, taste, etc., cannot be numerically expressed. Statistics has no role in all such cases where information is not quantified. (But, this problem can be circumvented by assigning notional numbers in terms of say, ranks or grades, and statistics can be used.)

2. *Statistics does not deal with individual facts.*

   Statistical methods can be applied only to aggregate of facts. Single fact cannot be statistically studied. For example, the marks of a student in an individual subject is meaningless, unless to facilitate comparing similar marks of other students or of the same student for different subjects or different years.

3. *Statistical inferences are not exact.*

   Unlike the laws of physics or other natural sciences statistical laws are true only on an average: Statistical inferences are only in terms of probability or chance and not in terms of certainty.

   For example, consider the statement:

   "It has been found that 90% of patients respond to a particular treatment". This does not imply that if nine patients have been successfully treated so far, the tenth one is bound to fail. It only means that in a large number of patients 90% respond successfully to the treatment.

4. *Statistics is liable to be misused.*

   Probably, the most important limitation of statistics is that it must be used by experts. Also, the use of statistical tools by inept and untrained people might lead to fallacious conclusions. Often statistics are deliberately misused by politicians, businessmen and administrators.

   For example, a detergent manufacturing company might claim in its advertisements that 80% of detergent users prefer its brand to the competitor's brand. This statement does not mention the number of people surveyed, how they were surveyed, who the people were, etc. Obviously the statement looks doctored and is deliberately misleading.

MISUSE AND DISTRUST IN STATISTICS

As discussed earlier, one of the major drawbacks of Statistics is that it can be misused. Generally, Statistics lends credibility to an arguement. And so, people tend to manipulate figures in support of their arguments and theories. This obviously is an unscientific application and an attempt to misuse Statistics. Some of the common ways through which Statistics can be misused include:

(1) Quoting figures without proper context.

(2) Comparing totally unrelated sets of figures.

(3) Generalising from part to whole.

(4) Quoting favourable figures or results only. Growing misuse of statistics by people has created distrust in statistics. The extent of distrust in statistics best exemplified by the following statements.

(i) If figures say so, it can't be otherwise!

(ii) Statistics can prove anything!

(iii) An ounce of truth will produce tons of Statistics!

(iv) Figures do not lie. Liars figure!

(v) There are three types of lies—lies, damned lies, and Statistics—wicked in the order of naming.

(The last statement is attributed to Mark Twain)

At this juncture, it must be pointed out that statistics by itself neither proves nor disproves anything. It is only a tool which if rightly used may prove extremely useful and if misused, might be disastrous. According to King "Science of statistics is the most useful servant, but only of value to those who understand its proper use."

IN A NUTSHELL

- Statistics in its singular sense refers to the statistical methods and principles used for classification and analysis of quantitative data so as to arrive at valid conclusions. In its plural sense it refers to numerical facts pertaining to a particular phenomenon.
- *Functions of Statistics* : (i) It simplifies complexity of data, (ii) reduces the bulk of data, (iii) adds precision to thinking, (iv) helps in comparing different sets of data, (v) guides formulation of policies and helps in planning and (vi) indicates trends and tendencies.

- *Scope of Statistics*: Statistics finds applications in almost all the fields but of interest to us its scope in state, business management, economics, biology, medicine and agriculture.
- *Limitations of Statistics*: (a) Statistics ignores qualitative aspects; (b) does not study individual items, (c) laws are not exact and (d) is liable to be misused.
- Since Statistics is liable to be misused, there is widespread mistrust about statistics.
- Developments in information technology has facilitated sophisticated software packages that aid statistical analysis.

CHECK YOUR PROGRESS

1. Give the definition of Statistics.
2. What do you mean by Statistics.
3. Give Prof. Horace Secrist's definition of Statistics.
4. Mention three functions of Statistics.
5. State any four limitations of Statistics.
6. Explain the scope of Statistics.
7. Explain the functions of Statistics.
8. What are the limitations of Statistics?
9. What is the scope of Statistics in
   (i) Economics and Business
   (ii) Biology, Medicine and Agriculture
10. Write a note on the scope of Statistics in the administration of a state.
11. Write a note on distrust for Statistics.
12. Write a note on the use of computers in Statistics.

8

Descriptive Statistics: Basic Concepts and Presentation of Data

In this chapter, we discuss a few important basic concepts and learn how to present data for further analysis.

BASIC CONCEPTS

Data are collections of any number of related observations. For example, we can collect the number of telephone connections that several workers from the telephone department install on a given day or that a worker installs per day over a period of several days. We call the results our data. A collection of data is called a *data set* and a single observation a *data point*.

In a statistical survey, the objects whose characteristics are studied are called *units* or *individuals*. The totality of (collection of all) units under consideration is called *population* or *universe*. For example, in the study of financial condition of families of a particular village, the set of all families belonging to the village is the population. The families are the units of the statistical survey.

A population which contains finite number of units is a *finite population*, while the one with infinite number of units is an infinite population.

Quantitative and Qualitative Data

The information on observed units and phenomenon can be broadly classified as:

(i) Qualitative

(ii) Quantitative

If the information about a characteristic of interest in an unit or phenomenon can be *measured* and *expressed numerically* we get the **quantitative data**. Data relating to height, weight, temperature, size, etc., are all examples of quantitative data. The quantitative characteristic of interest that varies from unit to unit is called a *variable*.

On the other hand, if units are classified into various groups based on the information about the *degree* of *presence or absence* of a characteristic of interest we have with us *qualitative data*. For example, the items manufactured by a machine may be classified as *'conforming'* or *'not conforming'* to a set of specifications, the persons in a community as *'dark'*, *'fair'*, or *'very fair'* by the colour of skin, the students of a class as *'genius'*, *'intelligent'*, *'average'*, *'dumb'* according to their intelligence. The qualitative characteristic of interest that varies from unit to unit in such cases is called an *'attribute'*.

Quantitative data is usually expressed using either:

1. Interval scale
2. Ratio scale

In an interval scale, numbers used to rank the objects also represent equal increments of the variable being measured. For example, consider the temperature readings 0°, 35°, 48°, 70°, 76° and 82°. Here we may write $48° < 70°$, which simply means 48° is colder than 70°. Also we can write $76° - 70° = 82° - 76°$, since equal temperature differences imply that the same amount of heat is needed to raise the temperature of an object from 70° to 76° or 76° to 82°. However, we cannot say that 70° is twice as hot as 35° even though $\frac{70°}{35°} = 2$. Also 0° does not imply the absence of temperature. In other words, the interval scale does not have a meaningful zero point.

On the other hand, **ratio scales** have a fixed and meaningful zero point. With such a scale, it is possible to say how many times greater or smaller one observation is than another. Variables measured on a ratio scale include height, weight, income, savings, etc.

Qualitative data are expressed using either

1. Nominal scale or
2. Ordinal scale

Though an attribute cannot strictly be measured, qualitative data can be made numerical for the sake of convenience, in an artificial manner. For instance, all non-conforming items may be denoted by '0' and all conforming items may be denoted by '1'. These are, then, said to be in a *nominal scale*, as they are numerical in name only. They do not share any of the properties of numbers.

On the other hand, *ordinal scale* permits ordering or ranking of observations. Teaching ability, (good, average, bad) social status (high, middle or low), grades of students (A, B, C or D) are all examples of attributes measured in an ordinal scale.

It is very important to distinguish between the various types of data, since the nature of data set may suggest the use of specific statistical techniques for further analysis.

PRESENTATION OF DATA

Recall that we defined Statistics as the science of collection, **presentation**, analysis and interpretation of numerical data. Quantitative data collected from surveys, reports, interviews, etc., are often summarized and presented using the following tools.

1. Frequency tables or frequency distributions
2. Graphs and diagrams.

1. Frequency Distribution

A systematic presentation of the values taken by a variable and the corresponding frequencies is called the *frequency distribution* of that variable. A tabular presentation of the frequency distribution is called the *frequency table*.

Frequency distribution is of two types: (a) discrete frequency distribution and (b) continuous frequency distribution.

If the variable can assume only a few values, a classification with respect to each and every value can be made and we have with us a **discrete frequency distribution.** For example, consider the following data regarding the number of children in a survey of 20 families.

2, 1, 0, 3, 1, 2, 2, 0, 3, 4, 2, 0, 1, 3, 2, 5, 2, 1, 1, 2.

The above data can be represented as a discrete frequency distribution as follows.

No. of children in the family (*variable*)	Tally marks	No. of families (*frequencies*)
0	111	3
1	~~1111~~	5
2	~~1111~~ 11	7
3	111	3
4	1	1
5	1	1
		20

On the other hand, if the range of values assumed by the variable is vast, we have with us a **continuous frequency distribution**. The vast range is divided into mutually exclusive sub-ranges called **class intervals** as shown in the following examples.

Consider the following data regarding the marks scored by 40 students of a class.

50,	40,	69,	73,	80,	79,	90,	99,	52,	70,
61,	71,	41,	53,	66,	63,	84,	74,	74,	87,
77,	55,	59,	64,	49,	75,	46,	75,	52,	96,
62,	78,	79,	45,	85,	66,	65,	71,	58,	89.

Marks (*Class Interval*)	**Tally marks**	**No. of students** (*Frequency*)
40 - 50	~~1111~~	5
50 - 60	~~1111~~ 11	7
60 - 70	~~1111~~ 111	8
70 - 80	~~1111~~ ~~1111~~ 11	12
80 - 90	~~1111~~	5
90 - 100	111	3
		40

2. Graphical Representation of Quantitative Data

Presenting data in the form of pictures makes them easier for comprehension. Pictures make the unwieldy data intelligible and convey the general pattern of the observations. They also facilitate comparisons of two or more data sets.

We now consider the following important types of graphical representations.

(i) Histogram

(ii) Frequency polygon

(iii) Frequency curve

(iv) Cumulative frequency curves or ogives

(i) Histogram

Here the frequency distribution is represented by a set of adjacent rectangles with the area of the rectangles proportional to class frequency. The variable being measured is presented on the horizontal X-axis and the class frequencies along the vertical Y-axis in a graph paper. Rectangles are then erected on the X-axis with the bases equal to the class interval and heights determined by the corresponding class frequency. Note that, if the class intervals are of unequal width, the rectangles are drawn with height proportional to frequency density (= frequency/width). This is to make the area proportional to class frequency.

Solved Examples

1. Construct histogram for the following hypothetical data regarding annual rainfall at a place for the past 85 years.

Annual Rainfall (in mm)	No. of years
80 – 85	4
85 – 90	8
90 – 95	17
95 – 100	26
100 – 105	15
105 – 110	10
110 – 115	5
	Total = 85

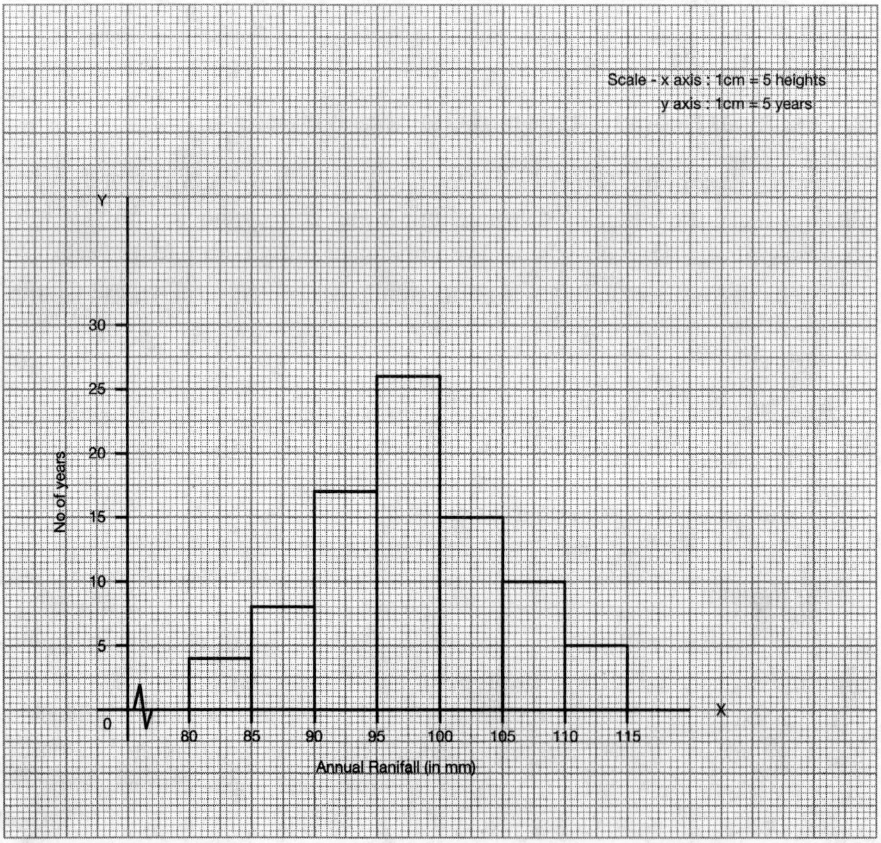

Fig. 8.1. Histogram showing the distribution of rainfall

2. Draw a histogram for the following frequency distribution regarding height of students in a college.

Height (in cm.)	No. of students
140 – 145	40
145 – 150	80
150 – 152	70
152 – 154	180
154 – 156	240
156 – 160	140
160 – 165	50
	800

SOLUTION:

Note that here the class intervals are of unequal width. Hence, we use the following table.

C.I	f	Width	Frequency density $= \dfrac{\text{Frequency}}{\text{Width}}$
140 - 145	40	$145 - 140 = 5$	8
145 - 150	80	5	16
150 - 152	70	2	35
152 - 154	180	2	90
154 - 156	240	2	120
156 - 160	140	4	35
160 - 165	50	5	10
	$\Sigma f = 800$		

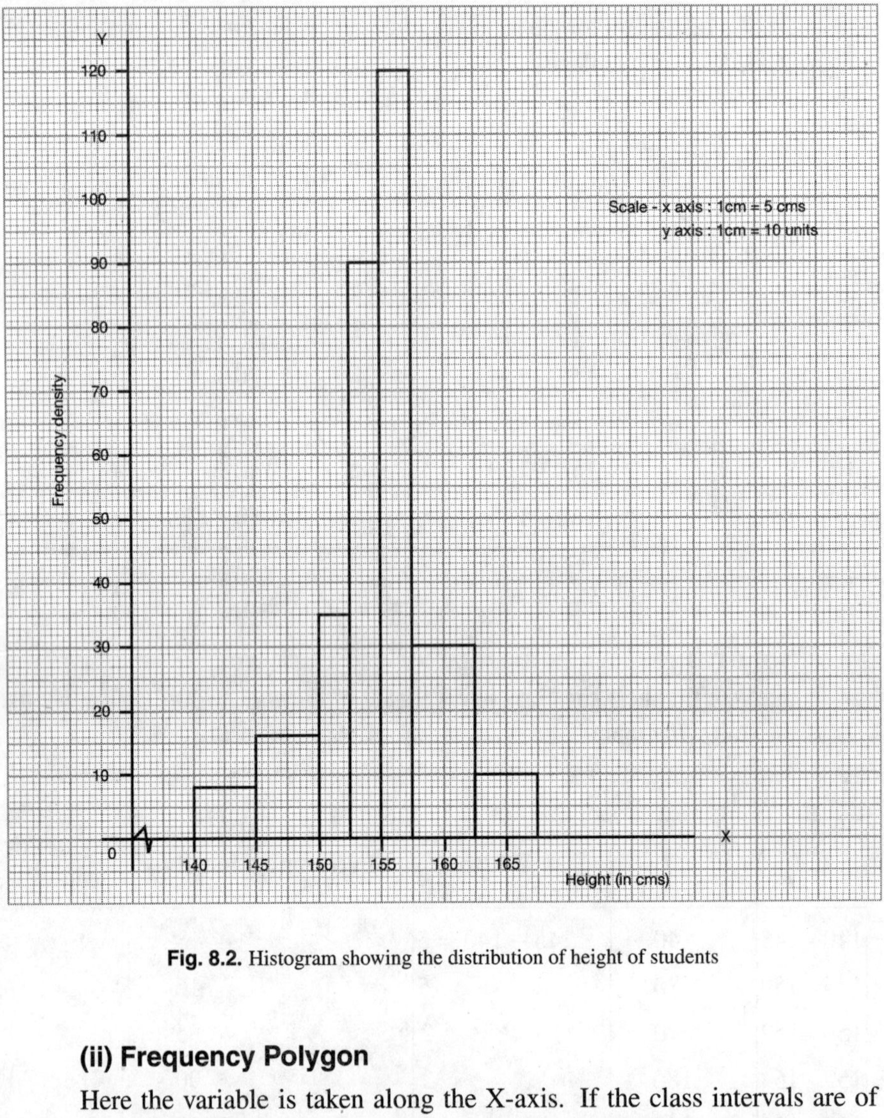

Fig. 8.2. Histogram showing the distribution of height of students

(ii) Frequency Polygon

Here the variable is taken along the X-axis. If the class intervals are of equal width, the class frequencies are plotted against the class mid values. If the class intervals are of unequal width, the class *frequency densities* are plotted against the class mid values. The points are then joined by straight line segments to get the frequency polygon.

3. Draw a frequency polygon for the following data regarding the monthly income of families.

Monthly income (in Rs.)	No. of families
3000 – 4000	15
4000 – 5000	20
5000 – 6000	27
6000 – 7000	34
7000 – 8000	25
8000 – 9000	12
9000 – 10,000	5

SOLUTION:

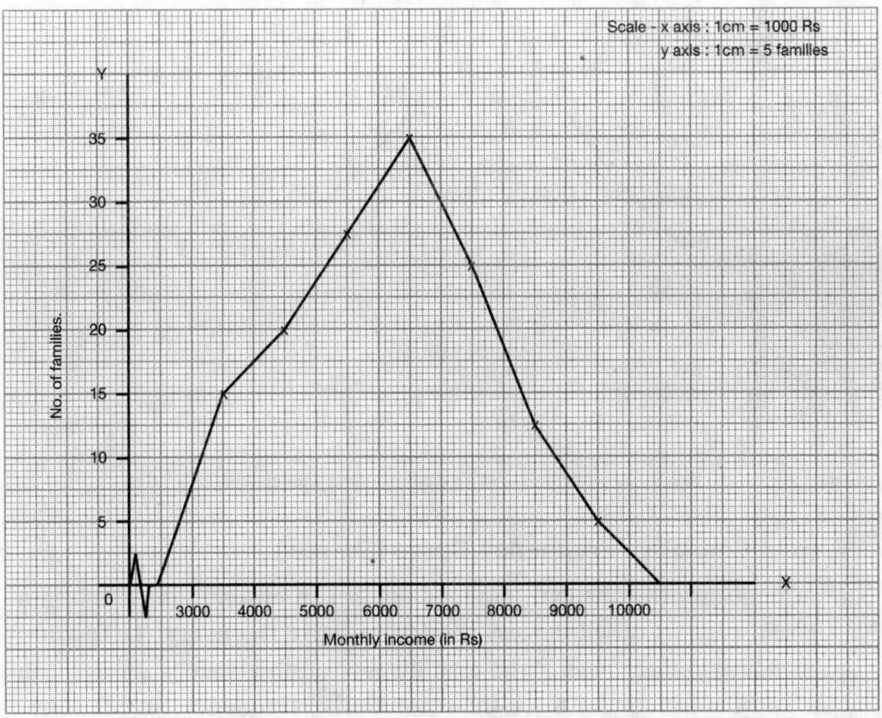

Fig. 8.3. Frequency polygon showing the distribution of monthly income

(iii) Frequency Curve

In the frequency polygon we joined the points, got by plotting the class mid values against class frequencies or frequency densities, by straight line segments. But in the **frequency curve** we join the points by a smooth curve. In practice, a frequency curve is drawn as an approximating smooth curve superimposed on a histogram.

4. Draw a frequency curve for the data regarding annual rainfall over 85 years given in illustration 1.1

SOLUTION:

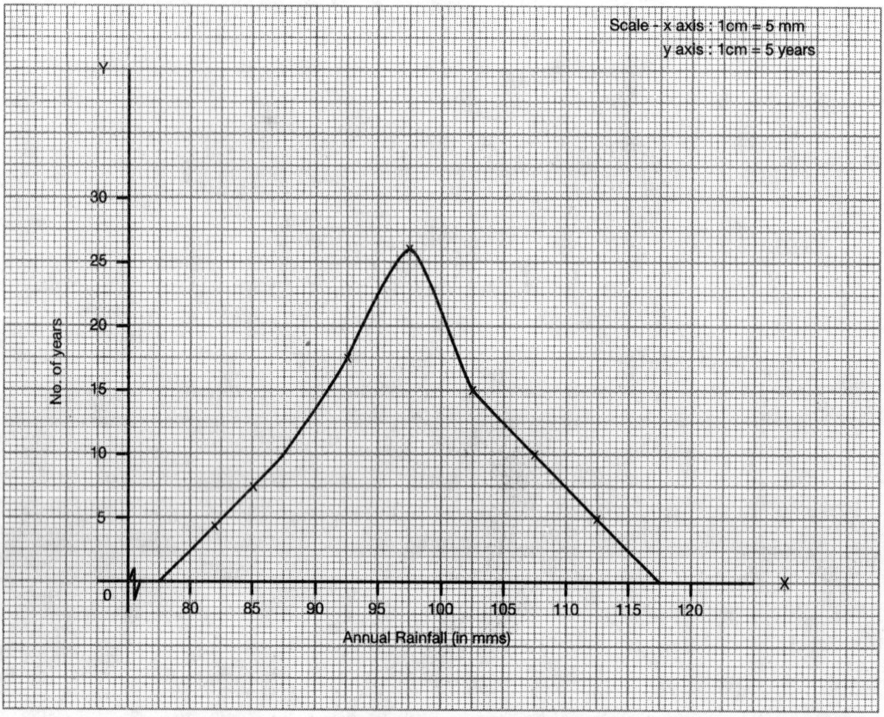

Fig. 8.4. Frequency curve for data regarding annual rainfall

(iv) Cumulative Frequency Curve (Ogives)

In frequency distribution, 'the total number of observations less than a given value' is called the **less than-cumulative frequency (l.c.f)** corresponding to that value. 'The total number of observations greater than a given value' is the **more-than-cumulative frequency (m.c.f)** corresponding to that value (unless otherwise mentioned cumulative frequency means **l.c.f**).

Ogives or cumulative frequency curves are smooth curves obtained by plotting the cumulative frequencies against variate values. There are two types of ogives.

(a) the less-than ogive (less-than cumulative frequency curve)

(b) the more-than ogive (more-than cumulative frequency curve)

Less-than Ogive: Here the variable is represented along the X-axis and the cumulative frequency is represented along the Y-axis. **The upper class limits of each class interval are plotted against the corresponding less-than cumulative frequencies.** The so obtained points are then joined by a smooth curve to get the less-than ogive.

The More-than Ogive: Here the *lower class limits of each class interval are plotted against the corresponding more-than cumulative frequency.* The points are joined by a smooth curve to get the more than ogive.

The two ogives are, usually, drawn together with common axis. The point of intersection of the two ogives corresponds to the **median** of the distribution. Ogives are also used to locate the various **partition values** (the concepts of median and other partition values are dealt with in detail in the next chapter).

5. Draw the two ogives and thus locate the median for the following data regarding the temperature observed for 2 months in a city.

Temperature (Celcius)	No. of days
28 – 32	7
32 – 36	15
36 – 40	20
40 – 44	14
44 – 48	3
48 – 52	1

SOLUTION:

We use the following table.

C.I	f	l.c.f	m.c.f
28 – 32	7	7	60
32 – 36	15	22	53
36 – 40	20	42	38
40 – 44	14	56	18
44 – 48	3	59	4
48 – 52	1	60	1
	$\sum f = 60$		

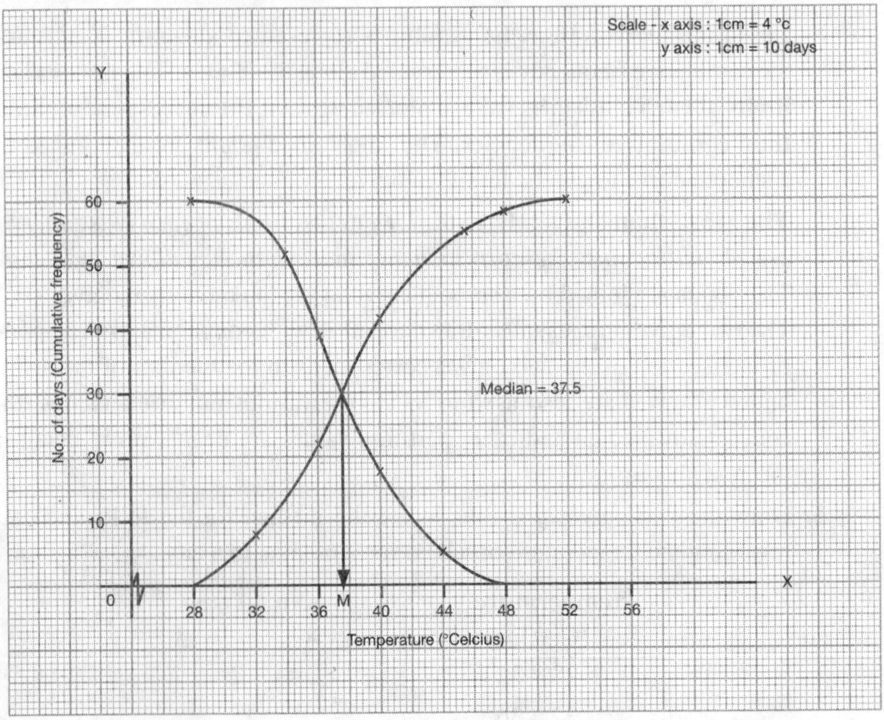

Fig. 8.5. Ogives representing the data regarding temperatures

IN A NUTSHELL

- In its plural sense the word 'statistics' means facts and figures and in its singular sense it is the science of collecting, analysing, presenting and interpreting numerical data which aid in decision making.
- Quantification of information is very important since it makes the information precise, objective, authentic and amenable to further analysis.
- Data can be presented using frequency distribution or graphs. Frequency distribution is a systematic presentation of the values taken by a variable and the corresponding frequencies.
- Data can be represented using graphs by constructing histogram, frequency polygon, frequency curve or ogives.

CHECK YOUR PROGRESS

1. What is quantitative data?
2. What is qualitative data?
3. Distinguish the various scales of measurement.

4. Write a short note on 'frequency distribution' as a method of presenting data.
5. Distinguish between variable and attribute.
6. Draw a histogram for the following data regarding monthly expenditure per household in a town.

Monthly expenditure	No. of households
1000 – 1400	15
1400 – 1800	22
1800 – 2200	30
2200 – 2600	38
2600 – 3000	28
3000 – 3400	16
3400 – 3800	12

7. Draw a histogram for the following data

C.I.	*f*
0 – 10	30
10 – 20	70
20 – 30	50
30 – 35	30
35 – 50	60

8. Represent the frequency distributions in exercise 8 and 9 using frequency polygon.
9. Mention the uses of cumulative frequency curves.
10. Define:

    (a) Relative frequency

    (b) Frequency density

    (c) Cumulative frequency

11. Prepare a histogram and a frequency curve for the following frequency distribution.

C.I.	*f*
0 – 6	4
6 – 12	8
12 – 18	15
18 – 24	20
24 – 30	12
30 – 36	6

12. Represent the following distribution using frequency curve.

Marks	No. of students
0 – 10	3
10 – 20	9
20 – 30	15
30 – 40	30
40 – 50	18
50 – 60	5

13. Draw the ogives and find the median for data given in exercise 11 and 12.
14. Find the median by drawing the ogives for the following.

Weekly wages	100 – 150	150 – 200	200 – 250	250 – 300	300 – 350	350 – 400	400 – 450
No. of workers	9	12	23	31	10	8	7

15. The following table shows age distribution of persons in a particular region. Draw the ogives and find the median age.

Age (years)	No. of persons ('000)
Below 10	2
Below 20	5
Below 30	9
Below 40	12
Below 50	14
Below 60	15
Below 70	16.5
70 and above	17.2

16. Draw a histogram and the two ogives for the following.

Height (in cm)	No. of persons
More than 140	65
More than 145	63
More than 150	50
More than 155	30
More than 160	18
More than 165	7

9

Measures of Central Tendency

Quantitative data collected from survey reports, interviews, etc., are often summarised and presented using: a) frequency tables or frequency distributions and b) graphs and diagrams. These would just be the first steps in reducing the bulk of data. The next logical step in reduction of data and better understanding of a frequency distribution is to effectively replace a data set by a few summary figures. Among these summary figures (which include measures of dispersion, skewness and kurtosis) measures of central tendency are the most important ones.

Also called **'measures of location'** or **'averages'** these values are intended to identify the point around which most of the data would lie. In other words, a 'measure of central tendency' locates the typical value of a frequency distribution around which the observations exhibit a tendency to cluster.

The purpose of finding averages is manifold.

(1) Averages give us a single representative value which has the characteristics of the entire data set.
(2) Averages facilitate easy comparison between two or more data sets.
(3) Averages offer a base for computing other measures such as dispersion, skewness and kurtosis.

Remarks: The peculiar property of observations in a data set by which they tend to cluster around a central value is called the property of central tendency. Among the various measures of central tendency we consider:

(1) Arithmetic mean (simple and weighted)
(2) Median
(3) Mode

REQUISITES OF AN IDEAL MEASURE OF CENTRAL TENDENCY

We make use of any of several averages depending on the purpose. According to Prof. Yule, the following are the characteristics to be satisfied by an ideal measure of central tendency.

(i) It should be rigidly defined.

(ii) It should be readily comprehensible and easy to calculate.

(iii) It should be based on all observations.

(iv) It should be suitable for further mathematical treatment. By this we mean that if we are given the averages and sizes of a number of series, we should be able to calculate the average of the composite series obtained on combining the given series.

(v) It should be affected as little as possible by fluctuations of sampling.

(vi) It should not be affected much by extreme values.

ARITHMETIC MEAN

Arithmetic mean (AM) or simply, mean is the most popular and widely used measure of central tendency. It is perhaps the most common type of averaging used to obtain a summary measure. It is usually denoted by $\bar{x}$ (read as x bar).

The AM of a set of observations is the quotient that results when the sum of these observations is divided by the number of observations

$$\text{i.e.,}\quad \bar{x} = \frac{\text{sum of observations}}{\text{number of observations}}$$

AM in raw data

When the original data is taken as it is (i.e., without classifying or grouping) we call it raw data. The AM of such a set of n ungrouped observations $x_1, x_2, \ldots, x_n$ is given by

$$\bar{x} = \frac{x_1 + x_2 + x_3 + \cdots + x_n}{n}$$

$$\bar{x} = \frac{\sum x}{n}$$

Steps

1. Add all the values of x and obtain $\sum x$.
2. Divide this sum by the total number of observations n.
3. Apply the formula $\bar{x} = \dfrac{\sum x}{n}$.

Remarks: The symbol $\sum$ is the capital letter sigma of the Greek alphabet and is used in mathematics and is used to denote 'the sum of values'.

SOLVED EXAMPLES

1. Calculate mean for the following data consisting of height of 10 individuals.

Sl. No	1	2	3	4	5	6	7	8	9	10
Height (in cm)	152	150	154	152	154	155	154	156	150	155

SOLUTION:

We know that

$$\bar{x} = \frac{\sum x}{n}$$

$$\therefore \quad \bar{x} = \frac{152+150+154+152+154+155+154+156+150+155}{10}$$

$$\therefore \quad \bar{x} = 153.2 \text{ cm.}$$

2. In a survey of 5 steel companies, the profit (in Rs. crores) earned during a year was 15, 20, 10, 35 and 32. Find the average profit earned.

SOLUTION:

We know that,

$$\bar{x} = \frac{\sum x}{n}$$

$$= \frac{15+20+10+35+32}{5}$$

$$= 22.4$$

Thus, the average profit earned by these companies during the year is Rs. 22.4 crores.

AM in grouped discrete data

If the raw data consists of too many observations, then calculation of AM using the above formula becomes time-consuming and cumbersome. The data could probably be grouped as a discrete frequency distribution. In a discrete frequency distribution there are 'k' distinct values of the variable $X - x_1, x_2, \ldots, x_k$ each having frequency $f_1, f_2, \ldots, f_k$ respectively.

In such a case, the AM is given by

$$\bar{x} = \frac{f_1x_1 + f_2x_2 + \cdots + f_kx_k}{f_1 + f_2 + \cdots + f_k}$$

$$\bar{x} = \frac{\sum fx}{\sum f}$$

Remarks: $\sum f = N$ is the total no. of observations in the data set.

Steps

(i) Multiply variable value (x) and frequency (f) in each row to get fx and note them down in the last column. Add them to get $\sum fx$.

(ii) Add all the frequencies to get $\sum f$.

(iii) Apply the formula $\bar{x} = \dfrac{\sum fx}{\sum f}$ to get AM.

3. The number of new contracts received by a legal firm over the last 25 working days were recorded as follows: 3, 1, 0, 4, 4, 2, 4, 5, 3, 6, 4, 1, 5, 2, 4, 0, 3, 0, 2, 5, 0, 4, 2, 1, 3, 3. Calculate the average number of contracts received by the legal firm on a typical day.

SOLUTION:

If the data given in the above problem is considered as it is, **i.e.**, raw or ungrouped, then we know that

$$\begin{aligned}\bar{x} &= \frac{\sum x}{n}\\ &= (3+1+0+4+4+2+4+5+3+6+4\\ &\quad +1+5+2+4+0+3+0+2+5+0+4\\ &\quad +2+1+3+3)/25\\ &= \frac{71}{25}\\ &= 2.84 \simeq 3\end{aligned}$$

Alternatively, if the above data were to be grouped as a discrete frequency distribution as follows, we can use the formula for AM for grouped data.

Number of contracts (x_i)	**Frequency (f_i)**	$f_i x_i$
0	13	10
1	13	13
2	14	18
3	15	15
4	16	24
5	13	15
6	1	6
	$\sum f = 25$	$\sum fx = 71$

We know that for grouped discrete distribution.

$$\bar{x} = \frac{\sum f_i x_i}{\sum f_i}$$

$$= \frac{71}{25}$$

$$= 2.8$$

$$\simeq 3 \text{ contracts}$$

Thus, the average number of contracts received by the legal firm is 3 per day.

4. A startup company employs 10 people with their monthly salaries as given below.

Calculate the average salary of an employee belonging to the Startup. Also find the total salary expenses incurred by the company for a month.

Monthly Salary (in Rs.)	5000	5200	5400	5500	5600
No. of employees	2	2	3	2	1

SOLUTION:

We know that for grouped discrete distribution, AM:

$$\bar{x} = \frac{\sum f_i x_i}{\sum f_i}$$

From the data

x_i	f_i	$f_i x_i$
5000	2	10000
5200	2	10400
5400	3	16200
5500	2	11000
5600	1	5600
	$\sum f_i = 10$	$\sum f_i x_i = 53200$

Substituting in the above formula we have,

$$\bar{x} = \frac{53200}{10}$$

$$= \underline{5320}$$

Thus, the average salary in the Startup company is Rs. 5320.

Also, the total salary expenses incurred by the company is given by

$$\sum f_i x_i = \text{Rs. } 53200$$

AM in grouped continuous data

When the data are presented in the form of frequency distribution with 'k' class intervals with corresponding frequencies $f_1, f_2, f_3, \ldots, f_k$, we have with us a grouped continuous data and AM in such a case is given by

$$\bar{x} = \frac{\sum f_i x_i}{\sum f_i}$$

where $\bar{x}$ = arithmetic mean

x_i = midpoint of ith C.I.

f_i = frequency of ith C.I.

Steps

1. Obtain the midpoint x_i, of each class interval.
2. Multiply the midpoint x_i, and the corresponding frequency f_i to get $f_i x_i$ for each row. Add them to get $\sum f_i x_i$
3. Add the frequencies f_i to get $\sum f_i$
4. Apply the formula $\bar{x} = \dfrac{\sum f_i x_i}{\sum f_i}$ to get AM.

5. One hundred students took up an examination and their results were tabulated as follows.

Find the average marks.

Marks	No. of students
0 – 10	12
10 – 20	18
20 – 30	27
30 – 40	20
40 – 50	17
50 – 60	6

SOLUTION:

C.I.	f	x	fx
0 – 10	12	5	60
10 – 20	18	15	270
20 – 30	27	25	675
30 – 40	20	35	700
40 – 50	17	45	765
50 – 60	6	55	330
	$\Sigma f = 100$		$\Sigma fx = 2800$

We know that AM,

$$\bar{x} = \frac{\Sigma fx}{\Sigma f} = \frac{2800}{100} = 28 \text{ marks.}$$

Change of Origin and Scale (The Short Cut Method)

If the values of the observations (x_i) or frequencies (f_i) are large, the calculation of the AM by the formulae discussed so far becomes quite time consuming and tedious. In such cases, the arithmetic is reduced to a great extent by taking deviations of the given values from any arbitrary point A. (In effect, we are actually changing the origin of the data set). The procedure is explained below:

$$\text{Let } d_i = x_i - A$$

$$\text{Then,} \quad f_i d_i = f_i(x_i - A) = f_i x_i - f_i A$$

Summing both sides over i from 1 to n, we get

$$\sum_{i=1}^{n} f_i d_i = \sum_{i=1}^{n} f_i x_i - A \sum_{i=1}^{n} f_i$$

$$\text{i.e.,} \quad \sum f_i d_i = \sum f_i x_i - A.N \quad \because \sum f_i = N$$

Dividing by N throughout, we get

$$\frac{\Sigma f_i d_i}{N} = \frac{\Sigma f_i x_i}{N} - \frac{A.N}{N}$$

$$\Rightarrow \quad \frac{\Sigma f_i d_i}{N} = \bar{x} - A$$

$$\Rightarrow \quad \bar{x} = A + \frac{\Sigma f_i d_i}{N}$$

This formula is much more convenient to apply.

Remarks: Any number can serve the purpose of the arbitrary point A but, usually a value in the middle of the distribution is chosen for the sake of convenience.

In case of grouped or continuous frequency distribution, the computations can be further reduced by 'changing the scale' as follows.

Let $d_i = \dfrac{x_i - A}{h}$

where $A =$ arbitrary point as seen earlier

and $h =$ common magnitude of the C.I. or common difference in the values x_i

Further, it implies,

$$hd_i = x_i - A$$

and proceeding as earlier we get

$$\boxed{\bar{x} = A + h\frac{\sum f_i d_i}{\sum f_i}}$$

Remarks:

1. The arbitrary value 'A' is also referred to as the assumed mean.
2. The change of scale method is also called the step deviation method.

6. In a one-day cricket match a bowler bowls 8 overs. He concedes 12, 8, 10, 7, 9, 13, 11 and 10 runs respectively in these overs. Find his economy rate.

SOLUTION:

Let us use the short-cut method to find the AM of the raw data given above. Let $A = 10$ be the assumed mean.

x	$d = x - A = x - 10$
12	2
8	−2
10	0
7	−3
9	−1
13	3
11	1
10	0
	$\sum d = 0$

We know that

$$\bar{x} = A + \frac{\sum d}{n}$$

$$= 10 + \frac{0}{10} = 10$$

Thus, the economy rate of the bowler is 10 runs/over.

7. The daily wages (in rupees) of labourers working for a contractor are.

Daily wages (Rs.)	100	120	140	160	180	200	220
No. of labourers	3	6	10	15	24	42	75

Calculate the average daily wages of the labourers. Also calculate the total wages per day paid by the contractor.

SOLUTION:

Daily wages (x_i)	**No. of labourers (f_i)**	$d = x_i - A = x_i - 160$	$f_i d_i$
100	3	−60	−180
120	6	−40	−240
140	10	−20	−200
160 ← A	15	0	0
180	24	20	480
200	42	40	1680
220	75	60	4500
	$\sum f_i = 175$		$\sum f_i d_i = 6040$

Note that in the above table $A = 160$ is taken as the assumed mean. The AM is given by

$$\bar{x} = A + \frac{\sum f_i d_i}{\sum f_i}$$

$$= 160 + \frac{6040}{175}$$

$$\text{i.e.,} \quad \bar{x} = \text{Rs } 194.51$$

Thus, the average daily wage is Rs. 194.51 per labourer.

Also, the total amount spent per day by the contractor as wages is given by

$$\begin{aligned}\sum f_i x_i &= N\bar{x} \\ &= 175(194.51) \\ &= \text{Rs. } 34{,}039.25\end{aligned}$$

Thus, the total amount spent by the contractor is Rs. 34,039.

Steps

1. Assume any arbitrary value as the mean and denote it by A. (Generally, a value in the middle of the distribution, or a value with highest frequency is chosen as A. This reduces calculations).
2. Take deviations of the observations (x_i) from the assumed mean and denote them by d_i i.e., $d_i = x_i - A$.
3. Multiply the deviations (d_i) with the corresponding frequencies (f_i) in each row and note them in the column $f_i d_i$. Add them up to get $\sum f_i d_i$. Add the frequencies (f_i) to get $\sum f_i$.
4. Apply the formula for AM,

$$\bar{x} = A + \frac{\sum fd}{\sum f}.$$

8. Calculate AM for the below mentioned data using the short-cut method.

Let the assumed mean $A = 5400$

x_i	f_i	$d_i = x - 5400$	$f_i d_i$
5000	2	−400	−800
5200	2	−200	−400
5400	3	0	0
5500	2	100	200
5600	1	200	200
	$\sum f_i = 10$		$\sum f_i d_i = -800$

We know that, AM by short-cut method is given by

$$\begin{aligned}\bar{x} &= A + \frac{\sum f_i d_i}{\sum f_i} \\ &= 5400 + \left\{\frac{-800}{10}\right\}\end{aligned}$$

i.e., $\bar{x} = 5320$

Thus, the average salary in the Startup company is Rs. 5320.

Remarks: Obviously, the answers by either methods ought to be the same.

Step deviation method for grouped data

Steps

1. Assume any arbitrary value as the mean and denote it by A (as noted earlier, a value in the middle of the distribution or the value with the highest frequency reduces calculations).

2. If the distribution is grouped discrete, then take deviations of the observations (x_i) from the assumed mean. If the distribution is grouped continuous, then take deviations of the midpoints of each class interval (x_i) from the assumed mean. Denote the deviations by d_i

$$\text{i.e.,}\quad d_i = x_i - A$$

3. Decide the scale factor 'c'. If the distribution is grouped discrete, probably the common difference between the values (x_i) could be 'c'. If the distribution is grouped continuous, with equal width class intervals, then 'c' could be the width of the class intervals.

4. Now find $d_i = \dfrac{x_i - A}{C}$

5. Multiply d_i by the corresponding frequencies (f_c) to get $f_i d_i$. Sum them up to get $\sum f_i d_i$.

6. Finally, to get the AM by the step deviation method apply the formula.

$$\bar{x} = A + \left\{\frac{\sum f_i d_i}{\sum f_i}\right\} \times C$$

9. Calculate AM by step deviation method for the data given below.

SOLUTION:

Let $A = 180$ and $C = 20$.

Daily Wages (x_i)	**No. of labourers (f_i)**	$d = \dfrac{x - A}{C} = \dfrac{x - 180}{20}$	$f_i d_i$
100	3	−4	−12
120	6	−3	−18
140	10	−2	−20
160	15	−1	−15
180 ← A	24	0	0
200	42	1	42
220	75	2	150
	$\sum f_i = 175$		$\sum f_i d_i = 127$

Now, AM by step deviation method is

$$\bar{x} = A + \left\{ \frac{\sum f_i d_i}{\sum f_i} \right\} \times C$$

$$= 180 + \left\{ \frac{127}{175} \right\} \times 20$$

$$= 180 + (0.72571) \times 20$$

$$\bar{x} = \text{Rs. } 194.51$$

10. Calculate the mean by using the step deviation method for the data given below.

SOLUTION:

Let $A = 25$ and $C = 10$ (the width of class intervals). Then,

C.I.	f_i	x_i	$d_i = \frac{x_i - A}{C} = \frac{x_i - 25}{10}$	$f_i d_i$
0–10	12	5	−2	−24
10–20	18	15	−1	−18
20–30	27	25 → A	0	0
30–40	20	35	1	20
40–50	17	45	2	34
50–60	6	55	3	18
	$\sum f_i = 100$			$\sum f_i d_i = 30$

We know that AM by step deviation method is given by

$$\bar{x} = A + \left\{ \frac{\sum f_i d_i}{\sum f_i} \right\} \times C$$

$$= 25 + \left\{ \frac{30}{100} \right\} \times 10$$

i.e., $\bar{x} = 28$

11. Calculate the AM for the following frequency distribution

C.I.	f
0–100	4
100–200	8
200–300	11
300–400	15
400–500	12
500–600	6
600–700	2

SOLUTION:

Let $A = 350 \quad C = 100$

C.I.	f_i	midpoint x_i	$d_i = \frac{x_i - A}{C} = \frac{x_i - 350}{100}$	$f_i d_i$
0–100	4	50	−3	−12
100–200	8	150	−2	−16
200–300	11	250	−1	−11
300–400	15	350 $\rightarrow A$	0	0
400–500	12	450	1	12
500–600	6	550	2	12
600–700	2	650	3	6
	$\Sigma f_i = 58$			$\Sigma f_i d_i = -9$

We know that AM by step deviation method is

$$\bar{x} = A + \left\{ \frac{\Sigma f_i d_i}{\Sigma f_i} \right\} \times C$$

$$= 350 + \left\{ \frac{-9}{58} \right\} \times 100$$

$$\bar{x} = 334.5$$

Thus, the AM of the frequency distribution is 334.5.

12. A survey of 80 households in a town gave the following data on expenditure towards food items. Calculate the average expenditure towards food of family in that town.

Monthly food expenditure	No. of households
800–1000	8
1000–1200	22
1200–1400	26
1400–1600	14
1600–1800	10

SOLUTION:

Let $A = 1300$ and $C = 200$

C.I.	f_i	x_i	$d_i = \frac{x_i - A}{C} = \frac{x_i - 1300}{200}$	$f_i d_i$
800–1000	8	900	−2	−16
1000–1200	22	1100	−1	−22
1200–1400	26	1300 → A	0	0
1400–1600	14	1500	1	14
1600–1800	10	1700	2	20
	$\sum f_i = 80$			$\sum f_i d_i = -4$

We know that AM using step deviation method is given by

$$\bar{x} = A + \left\{ \frac{\sum f_i d_i}{\sum f_i} \right\} \times C$$

$$= 1300 + \left\{ \frac{-4}{80} \right\} \times 200$$

$$\bar{x} = \text{Rs. } 1290$$

Thus, the average expenditure towards food for a household in that town is Rs. 1290.

SOME SPECIAL TYPES OF PROBLEMS AND THEIR SOLUTIONS

Type 1: Frequencies are given in cumulative form (i.e., either 'more than cf' or 'less than cf')

Recall that more than cumulative frequencies (mcf) are calculated by adding frequency from bottom to top, so that the first class interval has the highest cumulative frequency and it goes on decreasing in the subsequent classes. On the other hand, the cumulation in the case of 'less than cumulative frequency' (lcf) is done downwards so that the first class interval has the lowest cumulative frequency and it goes on increasing in the subsequent classes.

In both these cases, data are first converted to regular format with inclusive class intervals or exclusive class intervals. Then the calculations for AM are done in the usual manner.

13. In an examination of 675 candidates, the data regarding the marks obtained is as under.

Marks obtained (percentage)	No. of candidates
Less than 10	7
Less than 20	39
Less than 30	95
Less than 40	201
Less than 50	381
Less than 60	545
Less than 70	631
Less than 80	675

Find the average percentage of marks obtained using step deviation method.

SOLUTION:

Let us convert the given data into the regular format with exclusive type class intervals.

Table 9.1. Conversion to regular format

Marks obtained (percentage)	No. of candidates (more than *cf*)	C.I.	f_i
Less than 10	7	0–10	7
Less than 20	39	10–20	$(39 - 7) = 32$
Less than 30	95	20–30	$(95 - 39) = 56$
Less than 40	201	30–40	$(201 - 95) = 106$
Less than 50	381	40–50	$(381 - 201) = 180$
Less than 60	545	50–60	$(545 - 381) = 164$
Less than 70	631	60–70	$(631 - 545) = 86$
Less than 80	675	70–80	$(675 - 631) = 44$

We shall now proceed to find AM using the step deviation method in the usual manner.

Let $A = 35$ and $C = 10$

C.I.	f_i	x_i	$d_i = \frac{x_i - A}{c} = \frac{x_i - 35}{10}$	$f_i d_i$
0-10	7	5	−3	−21
10–20	32	15	−2	−64
20–30	56	25	−1	−56
30–40	106	(35) → A	0	0
40–50	180	45	1	180
50–60	164	55	2	328
60–70	86	65	3	258
70–80	44	75	4	176
	$\sum f_i = 675$			$\sum f_i d_i = 801$

Arithmetic mean,

$$\bar{x} = A + \left\{ \frac{\sum f_i d_i}{\sum f_i} \right\} \times C$$

$$= 35 + \left\{ \frac{801}{675} \right\} \times 10$$

i.e., $\bar{x} = 46.86$

Thus the average percentage of marks is 46.86

14. Following is the data regarding height of students in a class. Calculate the average height.

Height (in cm)	No. of students
> 120	45
> 130	42
> 140	35
> 150	24
> 160	10
> 170	4

SOLUTION:

Let us convert the given data into regular format with exclusive type class intervals.

Height (in cm) lower limits	No of students mcf	C.I.	Freq f_i	Mid pts x_i	$d = \frac{x_i - A}{c} = \frac{x_i - 155}{10}$	$f_i d$
> 120	45	120–130	3	25	−3	−9
> 130	42	130–140	7	35	−2	−14
> 140	35	140–150	11	45	−1	−11
> 150	24	150–160	14	(55) ← A	0	0
> 160	10	160–170	6	65	1	6
> 170	4	170–180	4	75	2	8
			$\Sigma f_i = 45$			$\Sigma f_i d_i = -20$

Here $A = 155$ and $C = 10$

We know that AM by short cut method is given by

$$\bar{x} = A + \left\{ \frac{\Sigma f_i d_i}{\Sigma f_i} \right\} \times C$$

$$= 155 + \left\{ \frac{-20}{45} \right\} \times 10$$

i.e., $\bar{x} = 150.56$ cm.

Type 2: Frequencies are missing but are to be calculated from the given data.

15. In the following distribution of marks, find the missing frequency if the average is known to be 52.

Marks	No. of students
0–20	8
20–40	–
40–60	19
60–80	14
80–100	9

SOLUTION:

Let F be the missing frequency

$$\text{Let} \quad A = 30 \text{ and } C = 20$$

$$\text{Given:} \quad \bar{x} = 52$$

C.I	f_i	x_i	$d_i = \frac{x_i - A}{C} = \frac{x_i - 30}{20}$	$f_i d_i$
0–20	8	10	−1	−8
20–40	F	30	0	0
40–60	19	50	1	19
60–80	14	70	2	28
80–100	9	90	3	27
	$\Sigma f_i = 50 + F$	–	–	66

Wkt, AM by step deviation method is given by

$$\bar{x} = A + \left\{ \frac{\Sigma f_i d_i}{\Sigma f_i} \right\} \times C$$

$$52 = 30 + \left\{ \frac{66}{50 + F} \right\} \times 20$$

$$\text{i.e.,} \quad 22 = \frac{1320}{50 + F}$$

$$\text{i.e.,} \quad 22(50 + F) = 1320$$

$$\text{i.e.,} \quad 1100 + 22F = 1320$$

$$\text{i.e.,} \quad 22F = 1320 - 1100$$

$$F = \frac{220}{22}$$

$$= \underline{10}$$

i.e., Thus, the missing frequency is 10.

16. Find the missing frequencies in the following frequency distribution if the AM is given to be 11.09.

C.I.	f_i
9.3–9.7	2
9.8–10.2	5
10.3–10.7	f_3
10.8–11.2	f_4
11.3–11.7	14
11.8–12.2	6
12.3–12.7	3
12.8–13.2	1
	60

SOLUTION:

Given : $\bar{x} = 11.09$

$$N = \sum f_i = 60$$

Let $A = 11.0$ and $C = 0.5$

C. I.	f_i	x_i	$d_i = \frac{x_i - A}{C} = \frac{x_i - 11}{0.5}$	$f_i d_i$
9.3 –9.7	2	9.5	−3	−6
9.8 –10.2	5	10.0	−2	−10
10.3–10.7	f_3	10.5	−1	$-f_3$
10.8–11.2	f_4	11.0→ A	0	0
11.3–11.7	14	11.5	1	14
11.8–12.2	6	12.0	2	12
12.3–12.7	3	12.5	3	9
12.8–13.2	1	13.0	4	4
	$\sum f_i = 60$			$\sum f_i d_i = 23 - f_3$

Wkt,

$$\bar{x} = A + \left\{ \frac{\sum f_i d_i}{\sum f_i} \right\} \times C$$

i.e., $$11.09 = 11 + \left\{ \frac{23 - f_3}{60} \right\} \times 0.5$$

$$0.09 = \frac{23 - f_3}{30}$$

$$2.7 = 23 - f_3$$

$$f_3 = 23 - 2.7$$

$$= 12.2$$

$$\underline{f_3 \simeq 12} \quad \text{[since } f_3 \text{ has to be an integer]}$$

Since $\sum f_i = 60$,

$$f_4 = 60 - (2+5+12+14+6+3+1)$$

i.e., $f_4 = 17$

Thus, the missing frequencies are 12 and 17.

Type 3: Frequency distributions have open-ended class intervals.

In case of open ended C.I. we cannot accurately calculate AM. We can only find an approximate value as shown in the following example

17. Compute the mean salary from the data regarding annual salaries.

Salary (Rs '000)	No. of employees
Below 10	4
10–20	6
20–30	10
30–40	20
40 and above	10

SOLUTION:

Note that both the first and the last class intervals are open ended. (The lower limit of first C.I. and upper limit of the last C.I. are not specified.) But since all the other class intervals are of uniform width we can assume the first and the last C.I's to be of the same width. Hence, we proceed to calculate AM in the usual manner with assumed mean $A = 25$ and scale factor $C = 10$ as follows.

Salary ('000 Rs) C. I	No. of employees f_i	Mid point x_i	$d_i = \frac{x_i - A}{C} = \frac{x_i - 25}{10}$	$f_i d_i$
0–10	4	5	−2	−8
10–20	6	15	−1	−6
20–30	10	25→ A	0	0
30–40	20	35	1	20
40–50	10	45	2	20
	50	–	–	$\sum f_i d_i = 26$

$$\text{Now } \bar{x} = A + \left\{\frac{\sum f_i d_i}{\sum f_i}\right\} \times C$$

$$= 25 + \left\{\frac{26}{50}\right\} \times 10$$

$$= 30.2 \text{ (Rs. '000)}$$

Thus, the mean salary is Rs. 30,200/-

Remarks: This mean is not accurate and is only an approximation.

Properties of Arithmetic Mean

The mean may be viewed as the 'centre of gravity' (i.e., a point of balance) of the frequency distribution. In other words, the sum of positive deviations from the mean is equal to the sum of negative deviations from it. This equivalence gives us the first property of the mean.

Property 1

The algebraic sum of the deviations of a set of values from their arithmetic mean is zero.

$$\text{i.e.,} \quad \sum (x_i - \bar{x}) = 0$$

The other important properties of AM are as follows.

Property 2

The sum of the squared deviations of a set of values is a minimum when deviations are from their arithmetic mean.

$$\text{i.e.,} \quad \sum (x_i - \bar{x})^2 \leq \sum (x_i - A)^2$$

where A is any value.

Property 3

(Mean of composite series or pooled mean)

If $\bar{x_i}(i = 1, 2, \ldots, k)$ are the means of k-component series of sizes $n_i(i = 1, 2, \ldots, k)$ respectively, then the mean of the composite series is given by

$$\bar{x_c} = \frac{n_1\bar{x_1} + n_2\bar{x_2} + \ldots n_k\bar{x_k}}{n_1 + n_2 + \ldots + n_k}$$

$$\text{i.e.,} \quad \boxed{\bar{x_c} = \frac{\sum n_i\bar{x_i}}{\sum n_i}}$$

In particular, if $\bar{x_1}$ is the AM of a set of n_1 values and $\bar{x_2}$ is the AM of another set of n_2 values, then the combined mean or the composite mean is given by

$$\bar{x} = \frac{n_1\bar{x_1} + n_2\bar{x_2}}{n_1 + n_2}$$

Property 4

If all the values in a series are increased (or decreased) by a constant number, then the arithmetic mean will also increase (or decrease) by the same constant.

$$\text{i.e.,} \quad \boxed{\frac{\sum(x_i + c)}{n} = \bar{x} + c}$$

18. There are one hundred students in a class with 30 of them obtaining a first class with an average of 72 marks; 40 of them have obtained a second class with an average of 55 marks, 20 of them have obtained third class with an average of 48 marks and the rest of them have failed with an average of 28 marks. What is the average of marks of the entire class.

SOLUTION:

$$\begin{aligned} \text{Given:} \quad n_1 &= 30 \qquad \bar{x_1} = 72 \\ n_2 &= 40 \qquad \bar{x_2} = 55 \\ n_3 &= 20 \qquad \bar{x_3} = 48 \\ \Rightarrow \quad n_4 &= 100 - (30 + 40 + 20) \\ &= 10 \qquad \bar{x_4} = 28 \end{aligned}$$

The average marks of the entire class (i.e., the composite mean) is given by,

$$\begin{aligned} \bar{x} &= \frac{n_1\bar{x_1} + n_2\bar{x_2} + n_3\bar{x_3} + n_4\bar{x_4}}{n_1 + n_2 + n_3 + n_4} \\ &= \frac{30(72) + 40(55) + 20(48) + 10(28)}{30 + 40 + 20 + 10} \\ &= \frac{5600}{100} \\ &= 56 \text{ marks.} \end{aligned}$$

Thus, the average marks of the entire class is 56

19. The average salary of an employee in an organisation of 50 employees is Rs. 6000. What is the total amount of money paid as salary per month by the firm? What will be the average salary and the total amount of money paid as salary per month if the management of the organisation decides to give a raise of Rs. 1000 to each and every employee.

SOLUTION:

$$\text{Given no. of employees}, n = 50$$
$$\text{and average salary} \bar{x} = \text{Rs. } 6000$$

Therefore, the total amount of money paid as salary,

$$\sum x = n\bar{x} \quad \left[\because \quad \bar{x} = \frac{\sum x}{n}\right]$$
$$= 50(6000)$$
$$= \text{Rs. } 3,00,000$$

The total amount on salary after a raise of Rs. 1000 to all the 50 employees is

$$\sum x = 3,00,000 + 50(1000)$$
$$= 3,50,000$$

$\therefore$ The average salary of an employee after the raise is,

$$\bar{x} = \frac{\sum x}{n} = \frac{3,50,000}{50} = \text{Rs. } 7,000$$

Alternatively, by property 4 of AM, we have

$$\frac{\sum(x_i + c)}{n} = \bar{x} + c$$

i.e., since every employee gets a raise of Rs. 1000/- the AM also increases by Rs. 1000 from Rs. 6000 to Rs. 7,000.

20. Ram quizzed his friend Shyam with the following riddle. "Eight years ago when my parents got married their average age was 22 years. Now, the average age of the three of us is also 22 years. How old am I?" Help Shyam solve the riddle.

SOLUTION:

8 years ago

$n = 2,\ \bar{x} = 22$

$$\therefore \quad \sum x = n\bar{x}$$
$$= 2(22)$$
$$= 44 \text{ years.}$$

i.e., the combined age of Ram's parents was 44 years eight years ago.

Now, let Ram's age be '*a*' years. Note that now

$$n = 3 \text{ and } \bar{x} = 22$$

$$\text{i.e.,} \quad \sum x = n\bar{x}$$

$$= 3(22)$$

$$\text{i.e.,} \quad \sum x = 66 \text{ years.} \qquad (1)$$

i.e., the combined age of Ram and his parents is 66 years.

Also

$$\sum x = \begin{Bmatrix} 44 + 8 \text{ years for Ram's father} \\ +8 \text{ years for Ram's mother } + a \end{Bmatrix}$$

$$= 44 + 16 + a$$

$$\sum x = (60 + a) \qquad (2)$$

i.e., the combined age of Ram *and* his parents is $(60 + a)$ years.

from (1) and (2), it is clear that

$$66 = 60 + a$$

$$\text{i.e.,} \quad a = 6 \text{ years.}$$

Thus Ram is 6 years old now.

21. The mean of 20 values was found to be 45. It was later discovered that one of the values was wrongly recorded as 64 instead of 46. What is the correct mean?

SOLUTION:

$$\text{Given:} \quad n = 20$$

$$\text{and incorrect} \quad \bar{x} = 45$$

$$\text{i.e., incorrect} \quad \sum x = n\,(\text{incorrect } \bar{x})$$

$$= 20(45)$$

$$\text{i.e., incorrect} \quad \sum x = 900$$

$$\text{Now correct} \quad \sum x = \text{ incorrect } \sum x - 64 + 46$$

$$= 900 - 64 + 46$$

$$= 882$$

$$\therefore \quad \text{correct} \quad \bar{x} = \frac{\text{correct} \sum x}{n}$$

$$= \frac{882}{20}$$

$$= 44.1$$

Thus, the correct mean is 44.1

22. The mean weight of 150 workers in a factory is 56 kg. If the mean weight of the men in the factory is 64 kg and the mean weight of the women is 48 kg, find the number of men and women in the factory.

SOLUTION:

Let n_1 be the number of men in the factory

n_2 be the number of women in the factory

$\bar{x}_1$ be the average weight of men

$\bar{x}_2$ be the average weight of women.

Given: $\bar{x}_1 = 64$ kg

$\bar{x}_2 = 48$ kg

and $n_1 + n_2 = 150$ (1)

Also given is the combined mean of the workers

$$\bar{x}_{12} = 56 \text{ kg}$$

$$\text{wkt,} \quad \bar{x}_{12} = \frac{n_1\bar{x}_1 + n_2\bar{x}_2}{n_1 + n_2}$$

$$\text{i.e.,} \quad 56 = \frac{n_1(64) + n_2(48)}{150}$$

$$\text{i.e.,} \quad 64n_1 + 48n_2 = 8400 \tag{2}$$

Solving (1) and (2) simultaneously, we have

$$64n_1 + 48n_2 = 8400$$

$$64n_1 + 64n_2 = 9600 \qquad [(1) \times 64]$$

$$\underline{- \quad - \quad -}$$

$$-16n_2 = -1200$$

$$n_2 = \frac{-1200}{-16}$$

$$\text{i.e.,} \quad n_2 = 75.$$

Substituting $n_2 = 75$ in (1), we get

$$n_1 + 75 = 150$$

$$\text{i.e.,} \quad n_1 = 75$$

Thus, the number of men in the factory is 75 while the number of women in the factory is also 75.

WEIGHTED ARITHMETIC MEAN

The AM, discussed so far, gives equal importance (or weight) to each observation in the data set. However, there are situations in which values of individual observations in the data set are not of equal importance. Some values may be more important than others.

Under these circumstances, we may attach to each observation a 'weight' $w_1, w_2, \ldots, w_n$ as an indicator of their importance. We may then proceed to find the **'weighted average'** or the **' weighted mean'** denoted by $\bar{x}_w$ as

$$\boxed{\bar{x}_w = \frac{\sum x_i w_i}{\sum w_i}}$$

Note that this formula is similar to the formula for simple AM with frequencies replaced by weights.

23. The Mathematics Society in a town was to decide the awarding of a scholarship. The marks obtained by 3 candidates and the weights for each subject as deemed by the Mathematics Society are given below. Calculate the weighted mean to award the scholarship.

Subject	**weight**	**Students**		
		A	***B***	***C***
Mathematics	4	60	57	62
Physics	3	62	61	67
Chemistry	2	55	53	60
English	1	67	77	49

SOLUTION:

The calculations of the weighted means for each of the student is given below.

Subject	**weight** (w_i)	**Students**					
		A		**B**		**C**	
		Marks		**Marks**		**Marks**	
		(x_i)	$x_i w_i$	(x_i)	$x_i w_i$	(x_i)	$x_i w_i$
Maths	4	60	240	57	228	62	248
Physics	3	62	186	61	183	67	201
Chemistry	2	55	110	53	106	60	120
English	1	67	67	77	77	49	49
	$\sum w_i = 10$	–	603	–	594		618

Applying the formula for weighted mean, we get

$$\text{For student A:} \quad \bar{x}_w = \frac{\sum x_i w_i}{\sum w_i} = \frac{603}{10} = 60.3$$

$$\text{For student B:} \quad \bar{x}_w = \frac{594}{10} = 59.4$$

$$\text{For student C:} \quad \bar{x}_w = \frac{618}{10} = 61.8$$

Since the weighted mean for student C is highest he / she deserves the scholarship.

Advantages and Disadvantages of Arithmetic Mean

Advantages

1. It is rigidly defined.
2. It is easy to understand and easy to calculate.
3. It is based on all the observations.
4. It is amenable to algebraic treatment (as seen in the mean of composite series in terms of means and sizes of component series).
5. Of all the averages, mean is the most stable as it is least affected by fluctuations of sampling.

Thus, it can be seen that AM satisfies almost all the requisites laid down by Prof. Yule for an ideal average.

Disadvantages

1. AM can neither be determined by inspection nor can it be located graphically. (Median and mode which are introduced next can be located graphically and sometimes can be determined by mere inspection.)
2. AM cannot be used in the case of qualitative data (median is the only average that can used in such a case).
3. AM cannot be calculated accurately for a frequency distribution with open ended classes.
4. AM cannot be calculated even if a single observation is missing (because it is based on all the observations).
5. It is highly affected by abnormal extreme values.
6. Sometimes, the AM may be a value which is not assumed by the variable.

In the context of the disadvantages of mean let us introduce ourselves to another average, viz., median.

MEDIAN

The **median** of a set of observations, M, is the **middlemost** value when they are arranged in either ascending or descending order of magnitude (such an arrangement is called an *array*).

In other words, median of a distribution is an observation in the data set which divides the distribution into two equal parts. It is the central value in the sense that it exceeds and is exceeded by an equal number of observations. Thus, median is a *positional average*. Also median could be thought of as a measure of *central location* such that one half of the observations in the data set are less than or equal to it.

Median in Ungrouped Data

Let $x_1, x_2, \ldots, x_n$ be n observations arranged in an array.

(i) If n is odd, the middle observation of the array is clearly defined and hence median, M is given by

$$M = \left\{n + \frac{1}{2}\right\}^{\text{th}} \text{observation}$$

i.e., when the number of observations is odd, i.e., the observation in $\left(\frac{n+1}{2}\right)^{\text{th}}$ position is the median.

(ii) If n is even, there are two middle values and we take the mean of these values as the median. Hence, median M in this case is given by.

$$M = \frac{a+b}{2} \text{ where } a = \left\{\frac{n}{2}\right\}^{\text{th}} \text{observation; } b = \left\{\frac{n}{2}+1\right\}^{th} \text{observation}$$

Remarks: In case of even number of observations, in fact any value lying between the two middle values can be taken as median. But conventionally, the mean of the middle two observations is taken as median.

To sum up, the steps to find median in ungrouped data are:

Step 1: Make an array of the raw data.
Step 2: Count the number of observations and denote it by n.
Step 3: (a) If n is odd,

$$M = \left\{\frac{n+1}{2}\right\}^{\text{th}} \text{observation}$$

(b) If n is even,

$$M = \frac{a+b}{2}$$

$$\text{where } a = \left(\frac{n}{2}\right)^{\text{th}} \text{observation; } b = \left\{\frac{n}{2}+1\right\}^{\text{th}} \text{observation}$$

Median in Grouped Discrete Data

In case of discrete frequency distribution, median is that observation for which the cumulative frequency is just greater than or equal to $\frac{N}{2}$, where $N = \Sigma f_i$, i.e., total no. of observations.

To find median for discrete frequency distribution

Step 1: Find the cumulative frequency for each observation.

Step 2: Find $N = \Sigma f$, the total no. of observations.

Step 3: Find the observation for which the cumulative frequency (cf) is just greater than or equal to $\frac{N}{2}$

This is the median

i.e., $M =$ 'x' for which cf is just $\geq \frac{N}{2}$.

Median in Grouped Continuous Data

In case of continuous frequency distribution, the class for which the cf is just greater than or equal to $\frac{N}{2}$ is called the median class and the value of median is obtained using the following formula.

$$M = 1 + \frac{h}{f}\left(\frac{N}{2} - c\right)$$

where $l =$ lower limit of the median class

$f =$ frequency of the median class

$h =$ width of the median class

$c = cf$ of the class preceeding the median class.

$N = \Sigma f$

The steps for finding median in grouped continuous data are

Step 1: Find the cf for each class.

Step 2: Find the median class. It is the C.I. For which cf is just $\geq \frac{N}{2}$

Step 3: Apply the formula for M given above.

24. Find the median height from the following data regarding height of members of a cricket team.

Member	1	2	3	4	5	6	7	8	9	10	11
Ht (in cm)	185	155	159	163	162	185	178	187	169	163	174

SOLUTION:

We first arrange the given data in an array as follows:

Array: 155, 159, 162, 163, 169, 178, 181, 185, 189

Here no. of observations, $n = 11$ (odd)

$$\text{Hence,} \quad M = \left\{\frac{n+1}{2}\right\}^{\text{th}} \text{observations}$$

$$= \left\{\frac{11+1}{2}\right\}^{\text{th}} \text{observation}$$

$$= \text{6th observation} = 169 \text{ cm.}$$

The median height of the cricket team is 169 cm.

25. Find the median wage from the following data regarding wages of 8 workers Wages (in Rs.): 140, 150, 135, 80, 250, 180, 120, 200.

SOLUTION:

We first arrange the given data in an array as follows.

Array: 80, 120, 135, 140, 150, 180, 200, 250

Here no. of observations $n = 8$ (even)

Hence,

$$M = \frac{a+b}{2}$$

$$\text{where} \quad a = \left(\frac{n}{2}\right)^{\text{th}} \text{observation}$$

$$b = \left(\frac{n}{2}+1\right)^{\text{th}} \text{observation}$$

$$\text{Here } a = \left(\frac{8}{2}\right) = \text{4th observation} = 140$$

$$b = \left(\frac{8}{2}+1\right) = \text{5th observation} = 150$$

$$M = \frac{140+150}{2} = \text{Rs. } 145$$

The median wage of the workers is Rs. 145.

26. Calculate the median marks from the following data regarding the marks of passed students.

Marks	5	6	7	8	9	10
No. of Students	3	4	5	8	4	1

SOLUTION:

We find the *cf* for each observation as follows:

	x	f	cf
	5	3	3
	6	4	$3+4=7$
	7	5	$7+5=12$
$M=$	8	8	20
	9	4	24
	10	1	25
		$\sum f=25$	

Here $N=\sum f=25$ and,

$$M = \text{observation for which } cf \text{ is just} \geq \frac{N}{2}$$

$$= \text{observation for which } cf \text{ is just} \geq \frac{25}{2} = 8$$

Hence, the median marks of the students who have passed is 8.

27. The management of a factory has decided to replace 50 per cent of its aged machines this year. The following is the data regarding the ages (in years) of the machines in the factory. Find the median age to help the management decide which of the machines have to be replaced.

Age (in yrs)	**No. of Machines**
0–3	9
3–6	17
6–9	30
9–12	44
12–15	31
15–18	19

SOLUTION:

We use the following table:

C.I.	f	cf
0 – 3	9	9
3 – 6	17	9 + 17 = 26
6 – 9	30	26 + 30 = 56*
9 – 12	44	100 Median Class
12 – 15	31	131
15 – 18	19	150
	$\Sigma f = 150$	

Here $\frac{N}{2} = \frac{150}{2} = 75$

The cf just $\geq$ 75 is 100 and the corresponding class, (9–12), is the median class.

Also, we know that,

$$M = 1 + \frac{h}{f}\left(\frac{N}{2} - c\right)$$

where l = lower limit of the median class = 9

h = width of the median class = $12 - 9 = 3$

f = frequency of the median class = 44

$N = \sum f = 150$

$c = cf$ of the class proceeding the median class = 56

Hence, $M = 9 + \frac{3}{44}\left(\frac{150}{2} - 56\right)$

= 10.3 years.

The management can replace all machines older than 10.3 years.

Merits and Demerits of Median

Merits

1. It is rigidly defined.
2. It is easily understood.
3. It is easy to calculate and in some cases can be located by mere inspection.
4. It is not at all affected by the extreme value.
5. It can be calculated even for distributions with open end classes.

Demerits

1. In case of even number of observations, median cannot be determined exactly. The mean of the middle two observations is only an estimate of the median.

2. It is not based on all the observations. This property referred to as the insensitivity of the median can be explained by the following example.

   The median of the data set 1001, 1002, 1003, 1004, 1005 is 1003. The value of the median is not at all affected even if all the other observations are changed as long as the first two observations are less than 1003 and the last two observations are greater than 1003.

3. It is not amenable to algebraic treatment.

4. It is affected by fluctuations of sampling.

PARTITION VALUES

Similar to the median, there are a few other positional measures called the **partition** values or **fractiles** or **quantiles**.

> **Definition:** Partition values are values in the data set which divide it into a desired number of equal parts.

Remarks: Partition values are *not* measures of central tendency but are positional measures.

While we have one median which divides the data set into two equal parts, there are three points, called the quartiles, which divide the data set into four equal parts. The first or the lower quartile, Q_1, is the value which exceeds 25% of the observations and is exceeded by 75% of the observations. The second quartile, Q_2 (which obviously coincides with the median) exceeds and is exceeded by 50% of the observations. The third or upper quartile Q_3, exceeds 75% of the observations and is exceeded by 25% of the observations.

The nine points which divide the series into ten equal parts are called the deciles and the ninety nine-points that divide the data into hundred equal parts are called percentiles.

For example, D_6, the sixth decile exceeds 60% of the observations and P_{72}, the seventy-second percentile exceeds 72% of the observations.

Remarks

1. It is very much evident that the median M, Q_2, D_5 and P_{50} all coincide and $Q_1 = P_{25}; Q_2 = P_{75}$.
2. The method of locating the various partition values using the ogives is explained in illustration 2.16.

   The methods for computing the partition values are the same as those of computing the median and can be summarised in the following formulae.

Raw Data

$$\text{Quartiles,} \quad Q_i = \left(\frac{in}{4}\right)^{\text{th}} \text{ observation } i = 1,2,3$$

$$\text{Deciles,} \quad D_i = \left(\frac{in}{10}\right)^{\text{th}} \text{ observation } i = 1,2,\ldots,9$$

$$\text{Percentiles,} \quad P_i = \left(\frac{in}{100}\right)^{\text{th}} \text{ observation } i = 1,2,\ldots,99$$

Grouped discrete Data

$$\text{Quartiles,} \quad Q_i = \text{ observation for which } cf \text{ is just } \geq \frac{iN}{4}; i = 1,2,3$$

$$\text{Deciles,} \quad D_i = \text{ observation for which } cf \text{ is just } \geq \frac{iN}{10}; i = 1,2,\ldots,9$$

$$\text{Percentiles,} \quad P_i = \text{ observation for which } cf \text{ is just } \geq \frac{iN}{100}; i = 1,2,\ldots,99$$

Grouped continuous data

$$\text{Quartiles,} \quad Q_i = 1 + \frac{h}{f}\left[\frac{iN}{4} - c\right]; i = 1,2,3,$$

$$\text{Deciles,} \quad D_i = 1 + \frac{h}{f}\left[\frac{iN}{10} - c\right]; i = 1,2,\ldots 9$$

$$\text{Percentiles,} \quad P_i = 1 + \frac{h}{f}\left[\frac{iN}{100} - c\right]; i = 1,2,\ldots 99$$

where $1 =$ lower limit of $Q_i{}^{\text{th}}/D_i{}^{\text{th}}/P_i{}^{\text{th}}$ class

$h =$ width of $Q_i{}^{\text{th}}/D_i{}^{\text{th}}/P_i{}^{\text{th}}$ class

$f =$ frequency of $Q_i{}^{\text{th}}/D_i{}^{\text{th}}/P_i{}^{\text{th}}$ class

$c =$ cf of class preceeding $Q_i{}^{\text{th}}/D_i{}^{\text{th}}/P_i{}^{\text{th}}$ class

28. Eight coins were tossed together and the resulting number of heads noted. The operation was repeated 256 times and the frequencies (f) that were obtained for different values of X: the number of heads, are shown in the following table. Calculate median, quartiles, the 8th decile and 32nd percentile.

x	0	1	2	3	4	5	6	7	8
f	1	9	26	59	72	52	29	7	1

SOLUTION:

We use the following table:

x	f	**cf**
0	1	1
1	9	10
2	26	36
3	59	95
4	72	167
5	52	219
6	29	248
7	7	258
8	1	256
	$N = \Sigma f = 256$	

Here $N = \Sigma f = 256$

Median,

$$M = \text{Observation for which } cf \text{ is just} \geq \frac{N}{2}$$

$$= \text{Observation for which } cf \text{ is just} \geq \frac{256}{2} = 128$$

$$= 4$$

Quartiles:

$$Q_i = \text{Observation for which } cf \text{ is just} \geq \frac{iN}{4};\ i = 1, 2, 3$$

$$\therefore \quad Q_1 = \text{Observation for which } cf \text{ is just} \geq \frac{N}{4}$$

$$= \text{Observation for which } cf \text{ is just} \geq \frac{256}{4} = 64$$

$$= 3$$

$$Q_2 = \text{Observation for which } cf \text{ is just} \geq \frac{2N}{4}$$

$$= 4$$

$$Q_3 = \text{Observation for which } cf \text{ is just} \geq \frac{3N}{4}$$

$$= \text{Observation for which } cf \text{ is just} \geq \frac{3(256)}{4} = 192$$

$$= 5$$

Deciles:

$$D_i = \text{Observation for which } cf \text{ is just} \geq \frac{iN}{10}; i = 1, 2, \ldots, 9$$

$$\therefore \quad D_8 = \text{Observation for which } cf \text{ is just} \geq \frac{8(N)}{10}$$

$$= \text{Observation for which } cf \text{ is just} \geq \frac{8(256)}{10} = 204.8$$

$$= 5$$

Percentiles:

$$P_i = \text{Observation for which } cf \text{ is just} \geq \frac{iN}{100}$$

$$\therefore \quad P_{32} = \text{Observation for which } cf \text{ is just} \geq \frac{32(N)}{100}$$

$$= \text{Observation for which } cf \text{ is just} \geq \frac{32(256)}{100} = 81.92$$

$$= 3$$

29. Data regarding the life of eighty condensors obtained in a life testing experiment has been given below. Draw a less than ogive and verify using formulae the values of the median, the upper quartile, the 4th decile and 64th percentile.

Life of condensers. (in '000 hrs)	No. of condensers
Less than 1	3
Less than 2	12
Less than 3	14
Less than 4	22
Less than 5	33
Less than 6	46
Less than 7	58
Less than 8	66
Less than 9	75
Less than 10	8

SOLUTION:

The given distribution can be written in the regular format as follows:

	C.I.	f	cf
	0 – 1	3	3
	1 – 2	9	12
	2 – 3	2	14
	3 – 4	8	22
D_4 Class →	4 – 5	11	33
Median Class →	5 – 6	13	46
P_{64} Class →	6 – 7	12	58
Q_3 Class →	7 – 8	8	66
	8 – 9	9	75
	9 – 10	5	80
		$\Sigma f = 80$	

Here $N = \Sigma f = 80$

Median class is the C.I. for which cf is just $\geq \frac{N}{2} = 40$ i.e., median class is (5 – 6)

Median,

$$M = 1 + \frac{h}{f}\left(\frac{N}{2} - C\right)$$

$$= 5 + \frac{1}{13}\left[\frac{80}{2} - 33\right]$$

$$= 5.54(\text{'000 hrs })$$

Q_3 class is the C.I. for which *cf* is just $\geq \frac{3N}{4} = 60$. i.e., Q_3 class is $(7-8)$

$$\therefore \quad Q_3 = 1 + \frac{h}{f}\left(\frac{3N}{4} - C\right)$$

$$= 7 + \frac{1}{8}[60-58] = 7.25(\text{'000 hrs })$$

D_4 class is that C.I. for which cf is just $\geq \frac{4N}{10} = 32$, i.e., D_4 class is $(4-5)$

$$\therefore \quad D_4 = 1 + \frac{h}{f}\left(\frac{4N}{10} - C\right)$$

$$= 4 + \frac{1}{11}[32-22]$$

$$= 4.909(\text{'000 hrs})$$

P_{64} class is that C.I. for which cf is just $\geq \frac{64N}{100} = 51.2.$, i.e., P_{64} class is $(6-7)$

$$\therefore \quad P_{64} = 1 + \frac{h}{f}\left(\frac{64N}{100} - C\right)$$

$$= 6 + \frac{1}{12}[51.2-46]$$

$$= 6.433(\text{'000 hrs})$$

To locate graphically the value of median, mark the point corresponding to $\frac{N}{2}$ on the Y-axis. At this point draw a line parallel to X-axis meeting the ogive at the point '*A*' (say). From '*A*' draw a line perpendicular to X-axis meeting it at *M*. Then, the absicca of '*M*' gives the value of median.

To locate the values of Q_i, we mark the points along Y-axis corresponding to $\frac{iN}{4}$ and proceed similarly.

To locate the values of D_i (or P_i), we mark the points along Y-axis corresponding to $\frac{iN}{10}\left(\text{or } \frac{iN}{100}\right)$ and proceed as earlier.

MODE

The word 'mode' originates from the French word '*la mode*' meaning '*in fashion*'. Fashion of the day, as we know, is something that is followed by most people. This concept of the most frequently occurring value, when formalised, leads to the definition of a mode.

Definition: The value in the data set that has the highest frequency is called the mode.

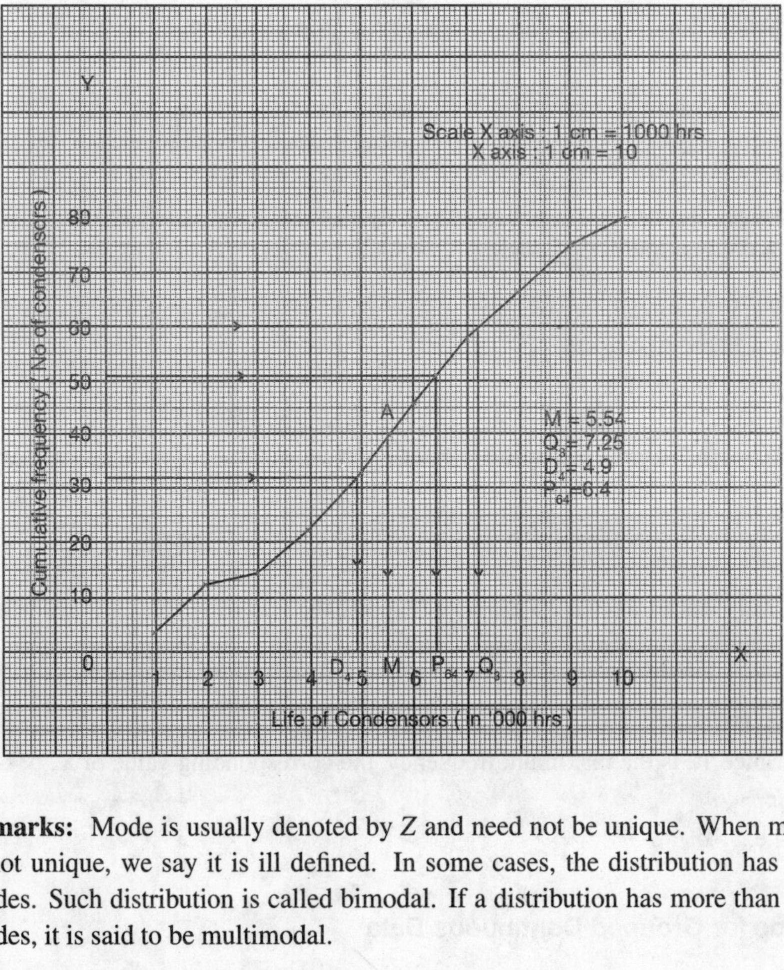

Remarks: Mode is usually denoted by Z and need not be unique. When mode is not unique, we say it is ill defined. In some cases, the distribution has two modes. Such distribution is called bimodal. If a distribution has more than two modes, it is said to be multimodal.

30. (Quantitative data): The sizes of garments sold in a shop during a day were as follows:

Size (in inches): 28, 32, 30, 34, 30, 32, 30, 32

What is the modal size of the garments sold?

SOLUTION:

Since the observation 32 occurs most frequently the modal size of the garment sold is 32 inches.

$$\text{i.e.,} \quad Z = 32 \text{ inches}$$

31. (Qualitative data): It was noticed that among the customers visiting a restaurant, most of them ordered for Masala Dosas. Hence, the modal choice of the cusomters is Masala Dosa.

Mode for Grouped Discrete Data

In the case of discrete frequency distribution, mode is the value of X corresponding to the maximum frequency.

32. Find the modal shoe size from the following data regarding shoes sold in a shop during in a week

Shoe size (x)	No of pairs sold (f)
4	3
5	8
$Z = 6$	12 Maximum frequency
7	9
8	4
9	1

SOLUTION:

Since 12 is the maximum frequency, the corresponding value of X, 6, is the mode

i.e., $Z = 6$

Mode for Grouped Continuous Data

In the case of grouped continuous distribution the class which has the maximum frequency is called the modal class and the value of the mode is obtained using the formula:

$$Z = 1 + \left(\frac{\Delta_1}{\Delta_1 + \Delta_2}\right) h$$

where $1 =$ lower limit of modal class

$h =$ width of modal class

$\Delta_1 = f_1 - f_0$

$\Delta_2 = f_1 - f_2$

$f_0 =$ frequency of premodal class

$f_1 =$ frequency of modal class

$f_2 =$ frequency of post-modal class

33. Construct a histrogram and locate mode. Also verify your result using the formula

Daily earnings (in Rs.)	No. of persons
40 - 50	15
50 - 60	$35 \rightarrow f_0$
60 - 70	$50 \rightarrow f_1$
70 - 80	$30 \rightarrow f_2$
80 - 90	10
90 - 100	5

SOLUTION:

Here the maximum frequency is 50. Hence, the class interval corresponding to it, i.e., $(60-70)$ is the modal class.

$$Z = l + \left(\frac{\Delta_1}{\Delta_1 + \Delta_2}\right) h$$

$$\Delta_1 = f_1 - f_0 = 50 - 35 = 15$$

$$\Delta_2 = f_1 - f_2 = 50 - 30 = 20$$

$$l = \text{lower limit of modal class} = 60$$

$$h = \text{width of modal class} = 70 - 60 = 10$$

$$\therefore \quad Z = 60 + \left[\frac{15}{15+20}\right] 10 = Rs.\ 64.28$$

Hence, the modal daily earning is Rs. 64.28

Identification of Mode Using Graph

Identify the tallest rectangle and mark the points A, B, C and D as shown in the graph. Joint AC and BD and from the point of intersection, P, draw a line perpendicular to meet the X axis at Z. The abscissa of Z is the value of mode, i.e., $Z \simeq 64$.

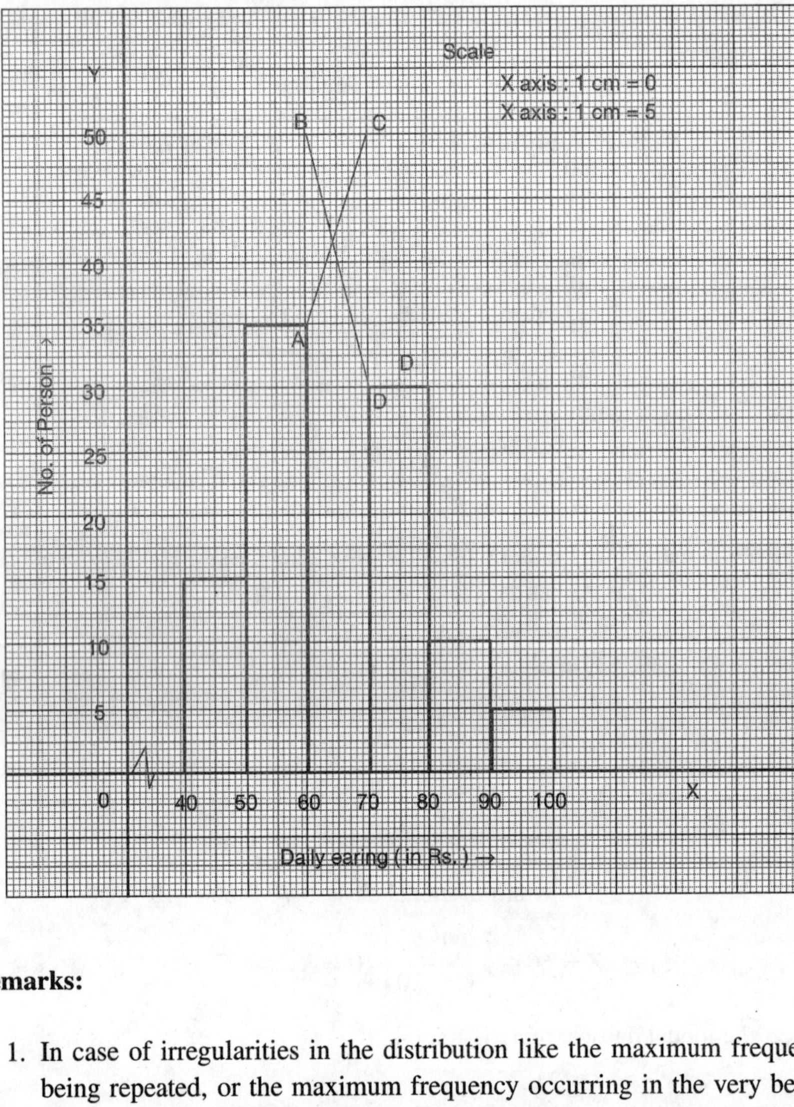

Remarks:

1. In case of irregularities in the distribution like the maximum frequency being repeated, or the maximum frequency occurring in the very beginning or at the end of the distribution, the modal class is determined by the method of grouping (the discussion about which is omitted).

2. In case of moderately skewed distributions, (the concept of skewness is dealt with in the next chapter), the mode is determined by the following empirical relationship.

$$\text{Mode} = 3\ \text{Median} - 2\ \text{Mean}$$

$$\text{i.e.,}\quad Z = 3M - 2\bar{x}$$

34. If the mean and median of a moderately skewed distribution are known to be 30 and 28 respectively. Find the mode.

SOLUTION:

By the empirical relationship between the averages, we have

$$\begin{aligned} Z &= 3M - 2\bar{x} \\ &= 3(28) - 2(30) \\ &= 24 \end{aligned}$$

Merits and Demerits of Mode

Merits

1. Mode is easily understood and easy to calculate. Like median, in some cases, mode can be located merely by inspection.
2. It is not at all affected by extreme values.
3. It can be calculated even for data with open end classes.

Demerits

1. It is not rigidly defined and is sometimes not unique.
2. It is not based on all the observations.
3. It is not amenable to further mathematical treatment.
4. It is affected by sampling fluctuations.

SOLVED EXAMPLES

1. Out of 100 numbers, 20 were fours, 40 were fives, 30 were 6's and the remainder were 7's. Find the arithmetic mean of number.

SOLUTION:

Given:

Number	4	5	6	7	total
frequency	20	40	30	10	100

The number of sevens is $\{100 - (20 + 40 + 30)\} = 10$

Now,

We know that for grouped discrete

x	f	fx
4	20	80
5	40	200
6	30	180
7	10	70
	$\Sigma f = 100$	$\Sigma f_x = 530$

Frequency distribution,

$$\bar{x} = \frac{\Sigma fx}{\Sigma f}$$

$$= \frac{530}{100}$$

$$= 53$$

Hence, the average of the numbers is 5.3.

2. A company wants to pay bonus to its employee. The bonus is to be paid as under:

Monthly Salary not exceeding (Rs.)	Bouns
120	50
140	60
160	70
180	80
200	90
220 and over	110

Actual salary of the members of the staff is given under:

Rs. 200, 180, 195, 218, 187, 160, 250, 168, 190, 168, 170, 178, 175, 140, 120, 148, 165, 155, 145, 125, 110, 162, 130, 150, 185.

What is the bonus paid? And, what is the average bonus paid to the employees?

SOLUTION:

To find the average bonus paid, we first need to find the frequency distribution of the bonus paid. Let us find the number of employees for each bonus amount using the information on salary.

Bonus	Salary	No. of employees (*f*) tally bars
50	100 – 120	1 = 1
60	120 – 140	111 = 3
70	140 – 160	~~1111~~ = 5
80	160 – 180	~~1111~~111 = 8
90	180 – 200	~~1111~~ = 5
100	200 – 220	11 = 2
110	220 & above	1 1

Thus, the frequency distribution of bonus paid is

Bonus (*x*)	No. of employees (*f*)	*fx*
50	1	50
60	3	180
70	5	350
80	8	640
90	5	450
100	2	200
110	1	220
	$\Sigma f = 25$	$\Sigma fx = 1980$

We know that for grouped discrete frequency distribution,

$$\bar{x} = \frac{\Sigma fx}{\Sigma f}$$

$$= \frac{1980}{25}$$

$$\bar{x} = \text{Rs. } 79.2$$

Thus, the average bonus paid per employee is Rs. 79.2. Also, the total bonus paid is $\sum fx =$ Rs. 1980

3. In a class the numbers of books issued to the students from the library were as follows.

No. of books issued	0	1	2	3	4	5	6	7
No. of students	7	12	10	7	6	4	3	1

Find the average number of books issued to a student of the class.

SOLUTION:

From the given data the frequency distribution of the numbers of books issued is:

No. of books issued x	**No. of students** f	fx
0	7	0
1	12	12
2	10	20
3	7	21
4	6	24
5	4	20
6	3	15
7	1	7
	$\sum f = 500$	$\sum fx = 122$

The above is a grouped discrete frequency distribution and its mean is given by

$$\bar{x} = \frac{\sum fx}{\sum f}$$

$$= \frac{122}{50}$$

$$= 2.44. \simeq 2$$

Thus, the average numbers of books issued to a student of the class is 2.

4. You are given the following distribution with a missing value. Find the missing value of the mean is known to be 115.86.

Height (in cm)	110	112	113	117	?	125	128	130
No. of students	25	17	13	15	14	8	6	2

SOLUTION:

Let us assume the missing value to be A

Height (in cm) (x)	**No. of students** (f)	fx
110	25	2750
112	17	1904
113	13	1469
117	15	1755
A	14	$14A$
125	8	1000
128	6	768
130	2	260
	$\Sigma f = 100$	$\Sigma fx = 9906 + 14A$

We know that for a grouped discrete frequency distribution

$$\bar{x} = \frac{\Sigma fx}{\Sigma f}$$

$$\text{i.e.,} \quad 115.86 = \frac{9906 + 14A}{100}$$

$$\text{i.e.,} \quad 115.86 = 9906 + 14A$$

$$\text{i.e.,} \quad A = \frac{115.86 - 9906}{14}$$

$$= 120$$

Hence, the missing value is 120.

5. Find the missing frequency from the following distribution is its mean is 15.25.

x	10	12	14	16	18	20
f	3	7	?	20	8	5

SOLUTION:

Let the missing frequency be a

x	f	fx
10	3	30
12	7	84
14	a	$14a$
16	20	320
18	8	144
20	5	100
	$\Sigma f = 43 + a$	$678 + 14a$

$$\text{Wkt,} \quad \bar{x} = \frac{\Sigma fx}{\Sigma f}$$

$$11.25 = \frac{678 + 14a}{43 + a}$$

$$655.75 + 15.25a = 678 + 14a$$

$$(15.25 - 14)a = 678 - 655.75$$

$$a = \frac{22.25}{1.25}$$

$$= 17.8$$

$$\simeq 18 \quad [\because \quad \text{frequency has to be an integer}]$$

Hence, the missing frequency is 18.

6. The following is the data regarding 60 children in a nursery school. Find the missing frequencies in the frequency distribution. The average height is known to be distribution 111.09.

Height (in cm)	**No. of children**
109.3 – 109.7	2
109.8 – 110.2	5
110.3 – 110.7	f_3
110.8 – 111.2	f_4
111.3 – 111.7	14
111.8 – 112.2	6
112.3 – 112,7	3
112.8 – 113.2	1

SOLUTION:

Let us use the step deviation method to find the mean of this grouped continuous frequency distribution.

Let $A = 111.0$ and $c = 0.5$

C.I.	f	Mid value x_i	$d = \frac{x_i - A}{C}$	fd
109.3 – 109.7	2	109.5	−3	−6
109.8 – 110.2	5	110.0	−2	−10
110.3 – 110.7	f_3	110.5	−1	$-f_3$
110.8 – 111.2	f_4	111.0 A	0	0
111.3 – 111.7	14	111.5	1	14
111.8 – 112.2	6	112.0	2	12
112.3 – 112.7	3	112.5	3	9
112.8 – 113.2	1	113.0	4	4
	$\sum f_i = 60$			$23 - f_3$

$$\text{Wkt,} \quad \bar{x} = A + \left\{\frac{\sum f_i d_i}{\sum f_i}\right\} \times C$$

$$\text{i.e.,} \quad 111.09 = 111.0 + \left\{\frac{23 - f_3}{60}\right\} \times 0.05$$

$$0.09 = \frac{23 - f_3}{30}$$

$$2.7 = 23 - f_3$$

$$f_3 = 23 - 2.7$$

$$= 12.2$$

$$f_3 \simeq 12 \qquad \text{[Since } f_3 \text{ has to be an integer]}$$

To find f_4, Wkt

$$\sum f = 60$$

$$\text{i.e.,} \quad f_4 = 60 - \{2 + 5 + 12 + 14 + 6 + 3 + 1\}$$

$$\text{i.e.,} \quad f_4 = 17$$

Hence, the missing frequencies are 12 and 17.

7. Find the missing frequencies for the following frequency distribution of the AM is given to be 33.

Marks	0 – 10	10 – 20	20 – 30	30 – 40	40 – 50	50 – 60	Total
No. of Students	5	?	25	30	?	10	100

SOLUTION:

Let the missing frequencies be f_2 and f_5

C.I.	f	x	fx
0 – 10	5	5	25
10 – 20	f_2	15	$15f_2$
20 – 30	25	25	625
30 – 40	30	35	1050
40 – 50	f_5	45	$45f_5$
50 – 60	10	55	550
	$\sum f = 100$		$2.250 + 15f_2 + 45f_5$

$$\text{Now, given} \quad \bar{x} = 33 \qquad (1)$$

$$\text{and} \quad \sum f = 100 \qquad (2)$$

(1) →

$$33 = \frac{2250 + 15f_2 + 45f_5}{100}$$

$$\text{i.e.,} \quad 3300 = 2250 + 15f_2 + 45f_5$$

$$\text{i.e.,} \quad 15f_2 + 45f_5 = 1050 \qquad (3)$$

(2) →

$$5 + f_2 + 25 + 30 + f_5 + 10 = 100$$

$$\text{i.e.,} \quad f_2 + f_5 = 30 \qquad (4)$$

Solving (3) and (4) simultaneously, we have

$$15f_2 + 45f_5 = 1050$$

$$f_2 + f_5 = 30 \times 15$$

$$\text{i.e.,} \quad 15f_2 + 45f_5 = 1050$$

$$15f_2 + 15f_5 = 450$$

$$- \quad - \quad -$$

$$30f_5 = 600$$

$$f_5 = \frac{600}{30}$$

$$\text{i.e.,} \quad f_5 = 20$$

Substituting a $f_5 = 20$ in (2), we have

$$f_2 + 20 = 30$$
$$\text{i.e.,} \quad f_2 = 10$$

i.e., the missing frequencies are 10 and 20.

8. Comment as the performance of the students of three different universities from the hypothetical data using simple and weighted averages:

Course	Bangalore		Mysore		Dharwar	
	Pass (%)	**No. of students (in 100s)**	**Pass(%)**	**No. of students (in 100s)**	**Pass(%)**	**No. of students (in 100s)**
M.Sc	71	3	82	2	81	2
M.B.A	83	4	76	3	76	3.5
M.C.A	73	5	73	6	74	4.5
M.A	74	2	76	7	58	2
M.Com	65	3	65	3	70	7
M.T.A	66	3	60	7	73	2

SOLUTION:

Calculation of simple and weighted arithmetic mean

University Course	Bangalore			Mysore			Dharwar		
	Pass(%)	**No. of students**		**Pass(%)**	**No. of students**		**Pass(%)**	**No. of students**	
	X	W	WX	X	W	WX	X	W	WX
M.Sc.	71	3	213	82	2	164	81	2.0	162
M.B.A.	83	4	332	76	3	228	76	3.5	226
M.C.A.	73	5	365	73	6	438	74	4.5	333
M.A.	74	2	148	76	7	532	58	2.0	116
M.Com.	65	3	195	65	3	195	70	7.0	490
M.T.A.	66	3	198	60	7	420	73	2.0	146
	$\Sigma X = 432$	$\Sigma W = 20$	$\Sigma WX = 1451$	$\Sigma X = 432$	$\Sigma W = 28$	$\Sigma WX = 1,977$	$\Sigma X = 432$	$\Sigma W = 21$	$\Sigma WX = 15$

Simple and weighted arithmetic mean.

Bangalore: $$\overline{X} = \frac{\Sigma X}{n} = \frac{432}{6} = 72$$

$$\overline{X}_w = \frac{\Sigma wx}{\Sigma w} = \frac{1{,}451}{20} = 72.55$$

Mysore: $$\overline{X} = \frac{\Sigma X}{n} = \frac{432}{6} = 72$$

$$\overline{X}_w = \frac{\Sigma wx}{\Sigma x} = \frac{1{,}977}{28} = 70.61$$

Dharwar: $$\overline{X} = \frac{\Sigma X}{n} = \frac{432}{6} = 72$$

$$\overline{X}_w = \frac{\Sigma wX}{\Sigma w} = \frac{1{,}513}{21} = 72.05$$

The arithmetic mean is the same for all the universities, i.e., 72, and hence it may be concluded that the performance of students is similar. But, since the number of students in each of the universities is different, we should compare the weighted arithmetic means. In that case, the weighted arithmetic mean of Bangalore University is the highest. Hence, it can be concluded that the performance of the Bangalore University is the best.

9. In a class of 15, 5 students failed in a test. The marks of 10 students who have passed were 9, 6, 7, 8, 9, 6, 5, 4, 7 and 8. What is the median marks of all the students.

SOLUTION:

Let the marks of the 5 students who have failed be x_1, x_2, x_3, x_4, and x_5. We now arrange the data in an array.

Array: $x_{(1)}, x_{(2)}, x_{(3)}, x_{(4)}, x_{(5)}, 4, 5, \boxed{6}, 6, 7, 7, 8, 8, 9, 9$

Since the total number of observations in $n = 19$, an odd number, the median is given by

$$M = \left\{\frac{n+1}{2}\right\}^{\text{th}} \text{ observation in the array}$$

$$= \left\{\frac{15+1}{2}\right\}^{\text{th}} \text{ observation in the array}$$

$$= 8^{\text{th}} \text{ observation in the array}$$

$$\boxed{M = 6}$$

10. Calculate the median from the following data.

Weight (in gm)	No. of apples
410–419	14
420–429	20
430–439	42
440–449	54
450–459	45
460–469	18
470–479	7

SOLUTION:

Since the class intervals in the given data are inclusive type class intervals, we convert them to exclusive type class intervals and proceed to find the median.

C.I.	f	cf
409.5–419.5	14	14
419.5–429.5	20	34
429.5–439.5	42	76
439.5–449.5	54	130
449.5–459.5	45	175
459.5–469.5	18	193
469.5–479.5	7	200
	$\Sigma f = 200$	

$$\Sigma f = N = 200$$

$$\therefore \quad \text{Median is } \frac{N}{2} = \frac{200}{2}^{\text{th}} \text{ observation} = 100^{\text{th}} \text{ observation}$$

Now, the 100th observation lies in the C.I. (439.5–449.5). This is because the cf just greater than 100 is 130 and the corresponding C.I. is (439.5–449.5).

We know that,

$$M = l + \left\{ \frac{N/2 - m}{f} \right\} \times c$$

where

M = Median

l = lower limit of median class

$N = \Sigma f$ = total number of observations

$m = cf$ of the class proceeding the median class
$c =$ width of the median class
$f =$ frequency of the median class

Thus,

$$M = 439.5 + \left\{ \frac{100 - 76}{54} \right\} \times 10$$

$$M = 443.94$$

11. Calculate median from the following data

Marks	100–110	110–130	130–160	160–180	180–190
No. of students	5	15	30	8	2

SOLUTION:

Note that the C.I. are of unequal width. But, we can use the same formula. Only, care should be taken, while noting the width of the median class.

C.I.	***f***	***cf***
100–110	5	5
110–130	15	20
130–160	30	50
160–180	8	58
180–190	2	60
	$\Sigma f = N = 60$	

Since $N = 60$, the median class is the C.I. which has the $\frac{60}{2} = 30^{\text{th}}$ observation. The C.I. which has the cf just $\geqslant \frac{N}{2} = 30$ is (130–160). Its width is $(160 - 130) = 30$.

We know that median is given by

$$M = l + \left\{ \frac{N/2 - c}{f} \right\} \times c$$

$$= 130 + \left\{ \frac{30 - 20}{30} \right\} \times 30$$

$$M = 140$$

12. In a group of 1000 wage earners, the daily wages of 4% are below Rs. 60 and 15% are below 62.50. 15% earned more than Rs. 95 while 5% earned Rs. 100 of more. Find the median daily wage and the modal daily wage.

SOLUTION:

With the given information, let us form a frequency distribution

Daily wages (in Rs.)	No. of wage earners
Less than 60	4%
Less than 62.5	15%
62.5–95	(Difference)
More than 95	15%
100 and over	5%

The frequency distribution table can be written as

C.I.	Percentage of wage earners	No.of wage earners (f)	cf	
0–60	4	$4/100 \times 1000 = 40$	4	
60–62.5	11	$11/100 \times 1000 = 110$	150*	
62.5–95	70	700	850	→median class
95–100	10	100	950	
100 and over	5	50	1000	
		$\Sigma f = 1000$		

$$\text{Now,} \quad N = \Sigma f = 1000$$

$$\text{i.e.,} \quad N/2 = 500.$$

The cf just $\geqslant 500$ is 850. The corresponding class interval (62.5–95) is the median class.

We know that

$$M = l + \left\{ \frac{N/2 - m}{f} \right\} \times c$$

$$= 62.5 + \left\{ \frac{500 - 150}{100} \right\} \times 32.5$$

$$= 78.75$$

The modal daily wage is found as follows:

C.I.	f	
0–60	40	
60–62.5	110	$\rightarrow f_0$
62.5–95	700	$\rightarrow f_1 \rightarrow$ modal class
95–100	100	$\rightarrow f_2$
100 and above	50	

$$\text{Now,}\quad \Delta_1 = f_1 - f_0 = 700 - 110 = 590$$
$$\Delta_2 = f_1 - f_2 = 700 - 100 = 600$$

We know that mode is given by

$$Z = l + \left\{\frac{\Delta_1}{\Delta_1 + \Delta_2}\right\} \times C$$
$$= 62.5 + \left\{\frac{590}{590 + 600}\right\} \times 32.5$$
$$Z = 78.61$$

13. Find the median and mode of the following distribution:

Marks	5–15	15–25	25–35	35–45	45–55	55–65	65–75
Students	7	12	17	29	31	16	3

SOLUTION:

C.I.	f	cf	
5–15	7	7	
15–25	12	19	
25–35	17	36*	
35–45	29 $\rightarrow f_0$	65	$\rightarrow$ median class.
45–55	31 $\rightarrow f_1$	96	$\rightarrow$ modal class.
55–65	16 $\rightarrow f_2$	112	
65–75	3	115	
	$\Sigma f = 115$		

To find median

$$\text{Now,}\quad N = \Sigma f = 115$$
$$\text{i.e.,}\quad N/2 = 115/2 = 57.5$$

The cf just $\geqslant 57.5$ is 65 and the corresponding C.I. (35–45) is the median class.

We know that

$$M = l + \left\{\frac{N/2 - m}{f}\right\} \times c$$
$$= 35 + \left\{\frac{57.5 - 36}{29}\right\} \times 10$$
$$\text{i.e.,}\quad M = 42.4137$$

To find the mode

The highest frequency (f_1) in the frequency distribution is 31 and the corresponding C.I. (45–55) is the modal class.

We know that mode is given by

$$Z = l + \left\{\frac{\Delta_1}{\Delta_1 + \Delta_2}\right\} \times c$$
$$\text{Here,}\quad \Delta_1 = f_1 - f_0 = 31 - 29 = 2$$
$$\Delta_2 = f_1 - f_2 = 31 - 16 = 15$$
$$\therefore\quad Z = 45 + \left\{\frac{2}{2 + 15}\right\} \times 10$$
$$Z = 46.1764$$

Hence, the median and mode are 42.4137 and 46.1764 respectively.

14. Find the modal value from the following data:

C.I.	12–18	18–14	24–30	30–36	36–42
f	5	12	22	10	3

SOLUTION:

C.I	f	
12–18	5	
18–14	$12 \rightarrow f_0$	
24–30	$22 \rightarrow f_1$	$\rightarrow$ modal class
30–36	$10 \rightarrow f_2$	
36–42	3	

Here the maximum frequency is 22 and the corresponding C.I. (24–30) is the modal class.

We know that,

$$Z = l + \left\{\frac{\Delta_1}{\Delta_1 + \Delta_2}\right\} \times c$$

Now, $\Delta_1 = f_1 - f_0 = 22 - 12 = 10$

$\Delta_2 = f_1 - f_2 = 22 - 10 = 12$

$$\therefore \quad Z = 24 + \left\{\frac{10}{10+12}\right\} \times 6$$

$$Z = 26.727$$

Hence, the mode of the distribution is 26.727.

15. The monthly profits (in rupees) of 100 shops are distributed as follows:

Profit/shop	0–100	100–200	200–300	300–400	400–500	500–600
No. of shop	12	18	27	20	17	06

Determine mode.

SOLUTION:

C.I	f	
0–100	12	
100–200	$18 \rightarrow f_0$	
200–300	$27 \rightarrow f_1$	$\rightarrow$ modal class
300–400	$20 \rightarrow f_2$	
400–500	17	
500–600	06	

Here, the maximum frequency is 27 and the corresponding class (200–300) is the modal class.

We know that,

$$Z = l + \left\{ \frac{\Delta_1}{\Delta_1 + \Delta_2} \right\} \times c$$

where $Z =$ mode

$l =$ lower limit of the modal class $= 200$

$\Delta_1 = f_1 - f_0 = 27 - 18 = 9$

$\Delta_2 = f_1 - f_2 = 27 - 20 = 7$

$c =$ width of modal class

$= (300 - 200) = 100$

Hence, $$Z = 200 + \left\{ \frac{9}{9+7} \right\} \times 100$$

$$= 256.25$$

Thus, the modal value is Rs. 256.25

16. You are given the following data:

Expenditure (Rs.)	No. of families
0-20	14
20-40	?
40-60	27
60-80	21
80-100	15

The value of the median is 50. Calculate the missing frequency.

SOLUTION:

Let the missing frequency be denoted by 'a'. The median is given to be 50 and it lies in the C.I. (40–60). Hence (40–60) is the median class.

C.I	f	$c.f$	
0-20	14	14	
20-40	a	$14 + a$	
40-60	27	$41 + a$	→ median class
60-80	21	$62 + a$	
80-100	15	$77 + a$	
	$N = \Sigma f = 77 + a$		

We know that

$$M = l + \left\{\frac{N/2 - m}{f}\right\} \times c$$

where M = median $= 50$

l = lower limit of median class $= 40$

$N = \sum f = 77 + a$

$m = cf$ of the class proceeding median class $= 14 + a$

f = frequency of median class $= 27$

c = width of median class $= (60 - 40) = 20$

i.e., $$50 = 40 + \left\{\frac{\frac{77+a}{2} - (14+a)}{27}\right\} \times 20$$

$$50 = 40 + \left\{\frac{77 + a - 28 - 2a}{2 \times 27}\right\} \times 20$$

$$= 40 + \left\{\frac{49 - a}{54}\right\} \times 20$$

$$27 = 49 - a$$

i.e., $$a = 49 - 27$$

$$= 22$$

Thus, the missing frequency is 22.

17. If the mode = 33 find the missing frequencies.

C.I.	10–20	20–30	30–40	40–50	50–60	Total
f	12	?	40	?	10	122

SOLUTION:

Since the mode is given to be 33 and it lies in the class (30–40), (30–40) is the modal class. Let 'a' and 'b' be the missing frequencies.

Then

$$b = 122 - [12 + a + 40 + 10]$$
$$= 60 - a$$

C.I.	f
10–20	12
20–30	$a \rightarrow f_0$
30–40	$40 \rightarrow f_1$ → modal class
40–50	$(60 - a) \rightarrow f_2$
50–60	10

We know that

$$Z = l + \left\{ \frac{\Delta_1}{\Delta_1 + \Delta_2} \right\} \times c$$

where $Z = \text{mode} = 33$

$l = \text{lower limit of modal class} = 30$

$\Delta_1 = f_1 - f_0 = 40 - a$

$\Delta_2 = f_1 - f_2 = 40 - (60 - a) = a - 20$

$h = \text{width of modal class} = (40 - 30) = 10$

Now, $$33 = 30 + \left\{ \frac{40 - a}{(40 - a) + (a - 20)} \right\} \times 10$$

$$3 = \frac{40 - a}{20} \times 10$$

$$6 = 40 - a$$

$$a = 40 - 6 = 34$$

Now $b = 60 - a = 60 - 34 = 26$

Thus, the missing frequencies are 34 and 26 respectively.

18. The following is the data regarding the absenteeism of employees in a factory. Find the median and mode.

No. of days absent	No. of employees
Less than 5	29
Less than 10	224
Less than 15	465
Less than 20	582
Less than 25	634
Less than 30	644
Less than 35	650
Less than 40	653
Less than 45	655

SOLUTION:

In the data above, upper limits of each class interval and the corresponding cumulative frequencies are given. We now have to convert the above information into a regular frequency distribution.

No. of days absent C.I	No. of employees f	Cf.
0 – 5	29	29
5 – 10	$224 - 229 = 195 \rightarrow f_0$	$224^* \rightarrow$ m
10 – 15	$241 \rightarrow f_1$	465 $\rightarrow$ medianclass
15 – 20	$117 \rightarrow f_2$	582 $\rightarrow$ medianclass
20 – 25	52	634
30 – 35	6	650
35 – 40	3	653
40 – 45	2	655
	$\sum f = 655$	

To find median

$$\text{Now,} \quad N = \sum f = 655$$
$$N/2 = 327.5$$

The cumulative frequency just ≥ 327.5 is 465 and the corresponding C.I. (10-15) is the median class.

We know that, the median is given by

$$M = l + \left\{ \frac{N/2 - m}{f} \right\} \times c$$

where $\quad l =$ lower limit of median class $= 10$

$$N = \sum f = 655 \Rightarrow N/2 = 327.5$$

$m = cf$ of the class preceeding median class $= 224$

$f =$ frequency of the median class $= 241$

$c =$ width of the median class $= 15 - 10 = 5$

Now, $$M = 10 + \left\{ \frac{327.5 - 224}{241} \right\} \times 5$$

$$M = 12.1473 \text{ days}$$

To find mode

The highest frequency is 241 and the corresponding class (10-15) is the modal class.

We know that

$$Z = l + \left\{ \frac{\Delta_1}{\Delta_1 + \Delta_2} \right\} \times c$$

where $l =$ lower limit of modal class $= 10$

$$\Delta_1 = f_1 - f_0 = 241 - 195 = 46$$

$$\Delta_2 = f_1 - f_2 = 241 - 117 = 124$$

$c =$ width of modal class $= 15 - 10 = 5$

i.e., $$Z = 10 + \left\{ \frac{46}{46 + 124} \right\} \times 5$$

$$Z = 11.3529 \text{ days}$$

Thus, the median and the mode of the given distribution are 12.1473 and 11.3529 days respectively.

19. Find median and mode for the following data.

Height (in cm)	No. of persons
More than 140	65
More than 145	63
More than 150	50
More than 155	30
More than 160	18
More than 165	7

SOLUTION:

The lower limits of class intervals and the corresponding more than cumulative frequencies are given in the above data. Let us convert the given data into a regular frequency distribution.

Height (in cm) C.I	No. of persons f	Cf.
140 – 145	65 – 63 = 2	2
145 – 150	63 – 50 = 13 → f_0	15 → m
150 – 155	20 → f_1	35
155 – 160	12 → f_2	47
160 – 165	11	58
165 – 170	7	65
	65	

SOLUTION:

To find the median

$$\text{Here,} \quad N = \sum f = 65$$
$$\therefore \quad N/2 = 65/2 = 32.5$$

The $cf.$ just $\geq N/2(32.5)$ is 35. The corresponding C.I. (150-155) in the median class.

We know that median is given by

$$M = l + \left\{ \frac{N/2 - m}{f} \right\} \times c$$

where l = lower limit of median class = 150

$N = \sum f = 65$

$M = cf.$ of the class preceeding the median class = 15

f = frequency of median class = 20

c = width of median class (155150) = 5

$$\text{i.e.,} \quad M = 150 + \left\{ \frac{65/2 - 15}{20} \right\} \times 5$$

$M = 154.375$ cm

To find the mode

The maximum frequency is 20 and hence, the corresponding C.I. (150–155) is the modal class.

We know that mode is given by

$$Z = l + \left\{ \frac{\Delta_1}{\Delta_1 + \Delta_2} \right\} \times c$$

where l = lower limit of modal class = 150

$\Delta_1 = f_1 - f_0 = 20 - 13 = 7$

$$\Delta_2 = f_1 - f_2 = 20 - 12 = 8$$

$$c = \text{width of modal class} = (155 - 150) = 5$$

$$\text{i.e.,} \quad Z = 150 + \left\{ \frac{7}{778} \right\} \times 5$$

$$Z = 152.33 \text{ cm}$$

Thus, the median and the mode of the given distribution are 154.375 and 152.33 cm respectively.

20. In a moderately asymmetrical distribution, the mode and mean are 32.1 and 35.4 respectively. Find the value of the median.

SOLUTION:

The empirical relation between mean, median and mode is given by

$$\text{Mode} = 3 \text{ Median} - 2 \text{ Mean}$$

$$\text{i.e.,} \quad Z = 3M - 2\bar{x}$$

Given:

$$\bar{x} = 35.4$$

$$Z = 32.1$$

$$\text{i.e.,} \quad 32.1 = 3M - 2(35.4)$$

$$\text{i.e.,} \quad M = \frac{2(35.4) + 32.1}{3}$$

$$= 34.3$$

21. Find the mean, if the median and mode of a distribution are known to be 20.6 and 26 respectively.

SOLUTION:

$$\text{Given:} \quad M = 20.6$$

$$Z = 26$$

By empirical relation between mean median and mode, we know that

$$Z = 3M - 2\bar{x}$$

$$\text{i.e.,} \quad 26 = 3(20.6) - 2\bar{x}$$

$$\text{i.e.,} \quad \bar{x} = \frac{3(20.6) - 26}{2}$$

$$\text{i.e.,} \quad \bar{x} = 17.9$$

22. For a distribution the value of mode is 28 and the median is 30. What will be the value of arithmetic mean

SOLUTION:

$$\text{Given:} \quad Z = 28$$
$$M = 30$$

By the empirical relation between mean, median and mode, we have

$$Z = 3M - 2\bar{x}$$
$$\text{i.e.,} \quad 28 = 3(30) - 2\bar{x}$$
$$\text{i.e.,} \quad \bar{x} = \frac{3(30) - 28}{2}$$
$$\text{i.e.,} \quad \bar{x} = \frac{90 - 28}{2} = 31$$

23. Find median if *AM* =12 and *Z* = 13

SOLUTION:

Given: $\bar{x} = 12$, $Z = 13$

We know that,

$$Z = 3M - 2\bar{x}$$
$$\text{i.e.,} \quad 13 = 3M - 2(12)$$
$$\text{i.e.,} \quad M = \frac{13 + 2(12)}{3}$$
$$\therefore \quad M = 12.33$$

IN A NUTSHELL

- Measures of central tendency are summary statistics which help in replacing a data set effectively.
- A measure of central tendency or average indicates the point around which most of the observations in the data set cluster around.
  - (i) Arithmetic mean $(\bar{x})$ is the quotient resulting when the total of the observations is divided by the number of observations.
  - (ii) Median, *M* is the middlemost observation in the arrayed data set.
  - (iii) Mode, *Z*, is the most frequent observation in data set.
- Partition values which are measures of location include median, quartiles, deciles and percentiles. They help us divide the data into the desired number parts.

CHECK YOUR PROGRESS

1. What is central tendency?
2. What are the objectives of averaging?
3. List the requisites of an ideal measure of central tendency
4. What are the functions of an average?
5. List the types of averages.
6. What is arithmetic mean? Define
7. What are the merits and demerits of mean?
8. Write a note on the properties of arithmetic mean.
9. Define median.
10. Under what circumstances would it be appropriate to use median.
11. What are the merits and demerits of median.
12. What is an array? How is it useful in finding median?
13. Define mode.
14. Write a note on multimodal distributions.
15. What are the merits and demerits of mode.
16. Write a note on empirical relation between mean, median and mode.
17. Define weighted arithmetic mean.
18. Write a note on weights in the context of averages.

PROBLEMS

1. The following table gives the monthly income of 10 employees in an office

Income (**Rs.**):	3780	3760	3690	3750	3840
	3920	3100	3050	3810	3950

Calculate the average monthly income.

[Ans. Rs. 3,665]

2. Calculate average marks from the following.

Marks	50	60	40	70	85
No. of students	5	7	3	12	3

[Ans. 62.83]

3. Find the arithmetic mean of the following frequency distribution.

Value	11	12	13	14	15	16	17
Frequency	5	9	12	17	14	10	6

[**Ans.** 14.09]

4. The data regarding pocket money/week given to students of a class by their parents was collected and tabulated as follows. Find the average pocket money/week.

Pocket money (in Rs.)	**No. of students**
0 – 100	5
100 – 200	18
200 – 300	27
300 – 400	20
400 – 500	17
500 – 600	6
	100

[**Ans.** Rs. 128]

5. Calculate the mean for the following distribution.

C.I.	**Frequency**
0 – 80	8
80 – 160	7
160 – 240	16
240 – 320	24
320 – 400	15
400 – 480	7

[**Ans.** 254.04]

6. Calculate AM for the following data.

C.I	19 – 21	22 – 24	25 – 27	28 – 30	31 – 33	34 – 36	37 – 39
f	6	13	19	23	18	12	9

[**Ans.** 29.11]

7. Find the AM of the following data regarding profit/week of shops in a locality.

Profit/week (in Rs)	No. of shops
Below 100	15
Below 200	35
Below 300	60
Below 400	84
Below 500	96
Below 600	127
Below 700	198
Below 800	250

[**Ans.** Rs. 504]

8. The arithmetic mean of 98 items is 50. Two items 60 and 70 were left out at the time of calculations. What is the correct mean.

[**Ans.** Correct AM = 50.3]

9. The mean marks of 25 boys in a class is 61 and the mean marks of 35 girls in the same class is 58. Find the continued mean marks of 60 students in the class.

10. The mean annual salary of employees of a company is Rs. 30,000. The mean annual salaries of male and female employees are Rs. 35,000 and Rs. 23,000 respectively. Find out the percentage of male and female employees working in the company.

[**Ans.** Male = 71.43%
Female = 28.57%]

11. The mean weight of the students of a class is 53 kg. The mean weight of the girls is 50 kg and the mean weight of the boys is 55 kg. What is the percentage of girls?

[**Ans.** 40%]

12. A set of 20 values have mean 54. Another set of values have mean. If the combined mean is 56, how many values are there in the latter set.

[**Ans.** 10]

13. The average marks of 60 students in a class is 75%. If 5% grace marks is given to everybody what would be the average marks.

[**Ans.** 80%]

14. The average marks of 50 students in a class is 60%. Suppose a grace of 5% is given to everybody except two students who have scored 100%. What would be the average?

[**Ans.** 64.8%]

15. The mean weight of 12 mangoes in a box is 150 gm. Two mangoes who were weighing 100 gm are replaced by mangoes weighing 140 and 160 gm. What would be the new average.

[**Ans.** 158.33%]

16. Following is the data regarding sugarcane yield in 216 plots of similar size. Find the average yield.

Yield (in tons)	No. of plots
Over 0	216
Over 60	210
Over 120	156
Over 180	98
Over 240	57
Over 300	31
Over 360	13
Over 420	7
Over 480	2
Upto 540	216

[Ans. 189.444 tons]

17. Obtain the value of the median from the following data.

1391, 1384, 1591, 1407, 1672,
1522, 1777, 1753, 3488, 2490,

[Ans. M = 1631.5]

18. Find the median annual income from the following data.

Annual Income (in Rs)	No. of persons
10000	24
15000	26
8000	16
20000	20
25000	6
18000	30

(Hint: average values in ascending order)

[Ans. M = Rs. 15000]

19. Draw the two ogives for the following data and locate the median.

Marks	No. of students
Less than 5	29
Less than 10	224
Less than 15	465
Less than 20	582
Less than 25	634
Less than 30	644
Less than 35	650
Less than 40	653
Less than 40	655

Also verify using the formula.

[**Ans.** 14.29]

20. An incomplete distribution is given below.

Variable	Frequency
0 – 10	10
10 – 20	20
20 – 30	?
30 – 40	40
40 – 50	?
50 – 60	25
60 – 70	15
	Total 170

(i) You are given that the median value is 35. Find out the missing frequencies.

(ii) Calculate the AM of the completed distribution.

[**Ans.** $f_1 = 35$
$f_2 = 25$
$\text{AM} = 35.882$]

21. Calculate the missing frequency given that the median is 317.5

C.I.	f
100 – 200	8
200 – 300	?
300 – 350	20
350 – 400	12
400 – 500	5

[**Ans.** $f_1 = 15$]

22. Compute median, upper quartile and lower quartile for the following.

Size of shoes	Frequencies
4.0	20
4.5	36
5.0	44
5.5	50
6.0	80
6.5	30
7.0	30
7.5	16
8.0	14

[**Ans.** $M = 6$, $Q_1 = 5$, $Q_3 = 6.5$]

23. Locate the quartiles and the median on a graph using the less-than ogive for the following data. Also verify algebraically.

C.I.	f
0 – 10	5
10 – 20	8
20 – 30	7
30 – 40	12
40 – 50	28
50 – 60	20
60 – 70	10
70 – 80	10

[**Ans.** $Q_1 = 34.16$, $M = 46.42$, $Q_3 = 57.50$]

24. Calculate the lower and upper quartile, the third decile and the 20th percentile for the following

Central value	Frequency
2.5	7
7.5	18
12.5	25
17.5	30
22.5	20

$$\left[\textbf{Ans.}\quad \begin{aligned} Q_1 &= 10 \\ Q_2 &= 19.17 \\ D_3 &= 11 \\ P_{20} &= 8.61 \end{aligned}\right]$$

25. Calculate the median wage from the following data. Also find the number of workers who earned wages between Rs. 1365 and Rs. 1430 using the ogive.

Wages less than (in Rs)	No of workers
1100	6
1200	16
1300	38
1400	68
1500	84
1600	98
1700	110

[**Ans.** M = Rs. 1356.67]

No. of workers whose wages are between Rs. 1365 and Rs. 1430 = 16.

26. Compute the median height from the following.

Height more than (in cm)	No. of people
100	390
120	384
130	359
140	311
150	239
160	123
170	63
180	25
190	3

[**Ans.** $M = 153.79$]

27. Calculate the mode from the following data of the marks obtained by 10 students

Sl. No.	1	2	3	4	5	6	7	8	9	10
Marks obtained	10	27	24	12	27	27	20	18	15	30

[**Ans.** $Z = 27$]

28. Calculate mode from the following data.

Value	30	32	34	36	38	40	42
Frequency	7	18	30	25	20	10	5

[**Ans.** $Z = 34$]

29. Calculate mode from the following data.

Marks	No. of students	Marks	Above
Above 0	80	Above 60	28
Above 10	77	Above 70	16
Above 20	72	Above 80	10
Above 30	65	Above 90	8
Above 40	55	Above 100	0

30. Draw a histogram for the following distribution and find the modal wage. Also check the value by direct calculation.

Wages	10 – 15	15 – 20	20 – 25	25 – 30	30 – 35	35 – 40	40 – 45
No. of workers	60	140	110	150	120	100	90

[**Ans.** $Z = 27.86$]

31. Calculate arithmetic mean, median and mode from the following distribution.

Variable	**Frequency**
10 – 13	8
13 – 16	15
16 – 19	27
19 – 22	51
22 – 25	75
25 – 28	54
28 – 31	36
31 – 34	18
34 – 37	9

[**Ans.** $M = 24.19$
$Z = 23.96$
$AM = 23.6$]

32. Calculate median and mode of the data given below. Using them find the AM.

Marks (less than):	10	20	30	40	50	60
No of students:	8	23	45	65	75	80

[**Ans.** $M = 27.73$
$Z = 27.78$
$AM = 27.705$]

10

MEASURES OF DISPERSION

Averages or measures of central tendency give us information as to where exactly the distribution is located. But to increase our understanding of the pattern of the data, we must look into another important characteristics, i.e., its dispersion, spread or variability and its measurement.

The above concept can be clearly understood with the help of the following example.

Consider the following three data sets of equal size; all having mean, 10

Data Set A:	8	9	10	11	12
Data Set B:	−5	8	10	12	25
Data Set C:	10	10	10	10	10

Though the three data sets have the same mean and even the median, viz., 10, it is obvious that the sets are not identical. While data set C exhibits no scatter the other two sets exhibit different degrees of scatters. Set B is "more variable" than set A.

Thus, to analyse and compare the variability in data sets we need a '*measure of dispersion*'. It should be a number that effectively summarises the scatter in the set or the distribution of the values. The measure should indicate the extent to which observations tend to spread over an interval rather than to cluster around a central value.

An ideal measure of variation, too, has to satisfy all the requisites laid down for an ideal measure of location listed in the earlier chapter.

MEASURES OF VARIATION

We consider the following measures of variation.

(i) Range (R)
(ii) Quartile deviation (QD)
(iii) Variance (V) and Standard Deviation (SD)
(iv) Co-efficient of range (co-efficient of R)
(v) Co-efficient of quartile deviation (co-efficient of QD)
(vi) Co-efficient of variation (CV)

Remark: The first three are absolute measures of variation in the sense that they have the same unit of measurement as the original observations. Unlike these, the latter three are relative measures, being numbers free from the units of measurement.

RANGE (R)

The Range R, is the simplest and the crudest measure of dispersion. It is merely the difference between the largest (L) and the smallest (S) values in a set. Thus,

$$R = L - S,$$

where $L =$ largest observation

$S =$ smallest observation

Remark: For grouped continuous distributions the lower class limit of the first class may be taken as 'S' and the upper class limit of the last class as 'L'.

Co-efficient of Range

This relative measure of dispersion associated with range is given by,

$$\text{Co-efficient of range} = \frac{L - S'}{L + S'}$$

Remark: Note that the co-efficient of range like all relative measures is a pure number devoid of any unit of measurement Range, on the other hand, will have the same unit of measurement as those of the observations.

Merits and Demerits of Range

Merits

1. It is the simplest measure of dispersion.
2. It is rigidly defined and the earliest measure of dispersion to compute.
3. It is readily comprehensible and requires very little calculations.

Demerits

1. Unfortunately, range is not a stable measure of dispersion because it is affected by the extreme values only.
2. It is not a suitable measure of dispersion when the distribution has open ended class Intervals.
3. It is not suitable for mathematical treatment.
4. It is completely dependent on the two extreme values only and is not based on all the values in the data set.
5. It is very sensitive to the fluctuations in the sample size.
6. It cannot tell us anything about the character of distribution within the two extreme observations.

Remark: Inspite of its demerits, range is widely used to study the variations in the prices of stocks and shares and the quality control charts.

It is also used for studying weather conditions where minimum and maximum temperatures are noted.

SOLVED EXAMPLES

1. Find the range for each of the following data sets. Also calculate co-efficient of range

Set A:	0	2	4	5	6	8	10
Set B:	−7	−3	0	5	8	10	22
Set C:	5	5	5	5	5	5	5

SOLUTION:

For Set A: Largest value, $L = 10$; Smallest value, $S = 0$

Hence, $R = L - S$

$= 10 - 0 = 10$

Similarly, for Set B: Largest value, $L = 22$; Smallest value, $S' = (-7)$

$$\therefore \quad R = L - S$$
$$= 22 - (-7) = 29$$

and for Set C: Largest value $L = 5$; Smallest value $S' = 5$

$$\therefore \quad R = L - S$$
$$= 5 - 5 = 0$$

Remark: Notice that for the above three data sets mean and also the median are the same, viz., 5.

To calculate the co-efficient of range

For set A, co-efficient of range $= \dfrac{L-S}{L+S} = \dfrac{10-0}{10+0} = 1$

For Set B, co-efficient of range $= \dfrac{L-S'}{L+S} = \dfrac{22-(-7)}{22+(-7)} = 1.93$

For Set C co-efficient of range $= \dfrac{L-S}{L+S} = \dfrac{5-5}{5+5} = 0$

Remark: It means that the variation in set C is nil.

QUARTILE DEVIATION (QD)

Quartile deviation or semi inter-quartile range, QD, is simply half of the difference between upper and lower quartiles. Thus,

$$QD = \frac{Q_3 - Q_1}{2}$$

$$\text{where } Q_3 = \text{ upper quartile}$$

$$Q_1 = \text{ lower quartile}$$

Remark: Range depends on only two extreme values and is consequently unstable. QD is obviously a better measure. It makes use of 50% of the data.

CO-EFFICIENT OF QD

The co-efficient of QD is given by

$$\text{co-efficient of QD} = \frac{Q_3 - Q_1}{Q_3 + Q_1}$$

2. Calculate range, semi inter-quartile range and their co-efficients for the following data

Age (in yrs)	20	30	40	50	60	70	80
No. of persons	3	61	132	153	140	51	3

SOLUTION:

$$R = L - S$$

$$= 80 - 20 = 60 \text{ years}$$

$$\text{Co-efficients of range} = \frac{L-S}{L+S} = \frac{80-20}{80+20} = 0.6$$

Semi inter-quartile range,

$$QD = \frac{Q_3 - Q_1}{2}$$

$$\text{Co-efficient of QD} = \frac{60-40}{60+40} = 0.2$$

It can be verified that
$Q_3 = 60$ yrs; $Q_1 = 40$ years

$$\therefore \quad QD = \frac{60-40}{2} = 10\text{years}$$

3. Calculate the range and semi inter-quartile range of the weekly wages of 86 labourers from the distributions given below.

Wages (in Rs.)	30 – 32	32 – 34	34 – 36	36 – 38	38 – 40	40 – 42	42 – 44
No. of labourers	12	18	16	14	12	8	6

SOLUTION:

$$R = L - S$$

$$= 44 - 30 = \text{Rs.}14$$

$$\text{Co-efficient of range} = \frac{L-S}{L+S} = \frac{44-30}{44+30} = 0.1891$$

It can be verified that for the above distribution
$Q_1 =$ Rs. 33.06; $Q_3 =$ Rs. 38.75

$$QD = \frac{Q_3 - Q_1}{2}$$

$$= \frac{38.75 - 33.06}{2} = \text{Rs. } 2.85$$

$$\text{Co-efficient of QD} = \frac{Q_3 - Q_1}{Q_3 + Q_1} = \frac{38.75 - 33.06}{38.75 + 33.06}$$

$$= 0.03969$$

Merits and demerits of QD

Merits

1. It can be used even when the distribution has open ended classes.
2. It is not affected by extreme values.

Demerits

1. It is not amenable to mathematical manipulation.
2. It is affected by sampling fluctuations.
3. It is not based on all values. It uses only 50% of the values.

STANDARD DEVIATION

Variance and Standard Deviation are popular measures of dispersion. The standard deviation, usually denoted by the Greek letter 'σ' (sigma), is the *positive square root of the arithmetic mean of the squares of the deviations of the observations from their arithmetic mean.* Thus,

(a) For raw data with observations $x_1, x_2, \ldots, x_n$

$$\sigma = \sqrt{\sum_{i=1}^{n} \frac{(x_i - \bar{x})}{n}}$$

where $\bar{x} =$ arithmetic mean

$n =$ no. of observations

(b) For frequency distribution $x_i/f_i\ i = 1, 2, \ldots, n$

$$\sigma = \sqrt{\frac{\sum f_i(x_i - \bar{x})}{\sum f_i}}$$

where $\bar{x} =$ arithmetic mean

$\sum f_i = N =$ total no. of observations

VARIANCE

The square of the standard deviation is called variance and is denoted by σ^2 or V

i.e., $\boxed{V = \sigma^2}$

where $\sigma =$ Standard deviation

Alternative formula (or short-cut method): When $\bar{x}$ is not a whole number, the calculation of σ^2 by the formula given earlier is very cumbersome and time consuming. To reduce the arithmetic calculations and, for the sake of convenience we use the following alternative formulae.

(a) For raw data with n observations $x_i,\ i = 1, 2, \ldots, n$

$$\sigma = \sqrt{\frac{\sum x_i^2}{n} - \left(\frac{\sum x_i}{n}\right)^2}$$

(b) For a frequency distribution $x_i/f_i,\ i = 1, 2, \ldots n$,

$$\sigma = \sqrt{\frac{\sum f_i x_i^2}{N} - \left(\frac{\sum f_i x_i}{N}\right)^2}$$

where $N = \sum f_i$

(c) For raw data with n observations $\ldots x_i,\ i = 1, 2, \ldots n,$

$$\sigma = h\sqrt{\frac{\sum d_i^2}{n} - \left(\frac{\sum d_i}{n}\right)^2}$$

where $d_i = (x_i - A)/h$

$A =$ any arbitrary number

$h =$ common factor

(d) For a frequency distribution $x_i/f_i\ i = 1, 2, \ldots n,$

$$\sigma^2 = h\sqrt{\frac{\sum fd^2}{\sum f} - \left(\frac{\sum fd}{\sum f}\right)^2},$$

where $d_i = \dfrac{x_i - A}{c}$

$A =$ any arbitrary number

$C =$ common factor.

Remark: The above formulae show that variance and hence standard deviation are independent of the change in the orgin of reference but are dependent on the change in the scale of measurement.

4. Calculate the standard deviation for the following data

14, 22, 9, 15, 20, 17, 12, 11

SOLUTION:

We use the following table where $\overline{x} = \dfrac{\sum x}{n} = \dfrac{120}{8} = 15$

x	$x - \overline{x} = x - 15$	$(x - \overline{x})^2$
14	−1	1
22	7	49
9	−6	36
15	0	0
20	5	25
17	2	4
12	−3	9
11	−4	16
$\sum x = 120$		$\sum(x - \overline{x})^2 = 140$

Standard deviation,

$$\sigma = \sqrt{\frac{\Sigma(x-\bar{x})^2}{n}}$$

$$\text{where } \bar{x} = \text{ arithmetic mean } = \frac{\Sigma x}{n} = \frac{120}{8} = 15$$

$$n = \text{no. of observations} = 8$$

$$\therefore \quad \sigma = \sqrt{\frac{140}{8}} = 4.18$$

Aliter:

x	x^2
14	196
22	484
9	81
15	225
20	400
17	289
12	144
11	121
$\Sigma x = 120$	$\Sigma x^2 = 1940$

$$\sigma = \sqrt{\frac{\Sigma x^2}{n} - \left(\frac{\Sigma x}{n}\right)^2}$$

$$= \sqrt{\frac{1940}{8} - \left(\frac{120}{8}\right)^2}$$

$$= 4.18$$

5. Calculate the standard deviation for the following

Marks	No. of students
10	8
20	12
30	20
40	10
50	7
60	3

SOLUTION:

We use the following table where $d = \frac{x-A}{C} = \frac{x-30}{10}$

x	f	$d = \frac{x-30}{10}$	fd	fd^2
10	8	−2	−16	32
20	12	−1	−12	12
30	20	0	0	0
40	10	1	10	10
50	7	2	14	28
60	3	3	9	27
	$N = 60$		$\Sigma fd = 5$	$\Sigma fd^2 = 109$

Standard deviation,

$$\sigma = h\sqrt{\frac{\Sigma fd^2}{\Sigma f} - \left(\frac{\Sigma fd}{\Sigma f}\right)^2}$$

$$= 10.\sqrt{\frac{109}{60} - \left(\frac{5}{60}\right)^2}$$

$$\sigma = 1.3452$$

6. The daily temperatures recorded in a city in Russia in a year are as follows. Calculate the mean and standard deviation.

Temperature °C	No. of days
−40 to −30	10
−30 to −20	28
−20 to −10	30
−10 to −0	42
0 to 10	65
10 to 20	180
20 to 30	10
	365

Solution:

We make use of the following table where $d = \frac{x-A}{h} = \frac{x-0}{5}$

CI	f	Mid Pt. x	$d=\frac{x-0}{5}$	fd	fd^2
$(-40)-(-30)$	10	−35	−7	−70	490
$(-30)-(-20)$	28	−25	−5	−140	700
$(-20)-(-10)$	30	−15	−3	−90	270
$(-10)-0$	42	−5	−1	−42	42
$0-10$	65	5	1	65	65
$10-20$	180	15	3	540	1620
$20-30$	10	25	5	50	250
	$N=365$			$\Sigma fd=313$	$\Sigma fd^2=3437$

$$\text{Mean,}\quad \bar{x}=A+\frac{h(\Sigma fd)}{N}$$

$$=0+\frac{5(313)}{365}=4.3°\text{C}$$

$$\sigma=h\sqrt{\frac{\Sigma fd^2}{N}-\left(\frac{\Sigma fd}{N}\right)^2}$$

$$=5\sqrt{\frac{3437}{365}-\left(\frac{313}{365}\right)^2}=14.73°\text{C}$$

Co-efficient of Variation (CV)

When comparing two or more data sets expressed in different units of measurement or with means which differ considerably we use a **relative measure** of dispersion. The relative measure of dispersion based on the standard deviation 'σ' is called co-efficient of variation, CV, and is given by

$$\text{CV}=\frac{\sigma}{\bar{x}}\times 100$$

where $\sigma=$ Standard deviation

$\bar{x}=$ Arithmetic mean

Remark:

1. CV is simply a number without any units of measurement.
2. The data set having lesser CV is said to be more consistent or more uniform than the other. The data set having greater CV is said to be more variable than the others.
3. $\bar{x}$ can be taken as a measure of efficiency while CV can be used to measure consistency.

7. The hypothetical data relating to weight of 100 adults and 100 children are summarised below.

Group	Mean Weight (in kg)	S.D. (in kg)
Adults	65	14
Children	16	8

Comment on the consistency of weights in the two groups.

SOLUTION:

Co-efficient of variation

$$CV = \frac{\sigma}{\bar{x}} \times 100$$

$$CV \text{ (for adults)} = \frac{14}{65} \times 100$$

$$= 21.53$$

$$\text{and } CV \text{ (for children)} = \frac{8}{16} \times 100$$

$$= 50$$

Since CV (adults)< CV (children), the weights of the adults are more consistent.

8. Two workers on the same job show the following results over a period of time.

	Worker *A*	Worker *B*
Mean time of completion of work (in min.)	30	25
S.D. of time of completion (in min.)	5	6

(i) Which worker is efficient?

(ii) Which worker is consistent?

SOLUTION:

(i) Since mean time of completion of work is lesser for worker *B*, he is more efficient.

(ii) Co-efficient of variance,

$$CV = \frac{\sigma}{\bar{x}} \times 100$$

$$CV(A) = \frac{5}{30} \times 100 = 16.7$$

$$CV(B) = \frac{6}{25} \times 100 = 24$$

Since CV(A)<CV(B), worker *A* is more consistent.

9. Price of a particular commodity in five years in two cities are given below.

(i) In which city are the prices higher?

(ii) In which city are prices more stable

Price in city (A) (in Rs.)	Price in city (B) (in Rs.)
20	10
22	20
19	18
23	12
16	15

SOLUTION:

It can be verified that for,

City A:

$\sigma = \text{Rs. } 2.45;\ \bar{x} = \text{Rs. } 20$

$$\text{Hence,}\quad \text{CV}(A) = \frac{\sigma}{\bar{x}} \times 100$$

$$= 12.25$$

City B

$\sigma = \text{Rs. } 3.69;\ \bar{x} = \text{Rs. } 15;\ \text{CV}(B) = 24.6$

(i) Since A.M. for city *A* is more than A.M. for city *B*, the prices in city *A* are higher

(ii) Since $CV(A) < CV(B)$, prices in city *A* are more stable.

Merits and Demerits of Standard Deviation

Merits

1. It is rigidly defined.
2. It is based on all the observations in the data set.
3. It is amenable to further algebra treatment.
4. It is not unduly affected by fluctuations in sampling.
5. In comparing the variability of two or more distributions, *CV* which is based mean and standard deviation is considered to be most appropriate.

Demerits

1. It is difficult to compute.
2. It is affected by extreme values.

Remark: With many merits to its credit, standard deviation is considered by far the best measure of dispersion:

Solved Examples

1. Compute the range and the co-efficient of range from the following distribution:

C.I.	1100-1120	1120-1140	1140-1160	1160-1180	1180-1200
f	2	7	10	8	3

Solution:

We know that range is given by

$$R = L - S'$$

where $L =$ largest value in the data set $= 200$

$S' =$ smallest value in the data set $= 100$

$$\therefore \quad R = L - S' = 1200 - 1100 = 100$$

Also,

$$\text{Co-efficient of range} = \frac{L - S'}{L + S'} = \frac{1200 - 1100}{1200 + 1100} = \frac{100}{2300} = 0.04348$$

2. Compute the range and co-efficient of range of the series and state which are/is more dispersed and which are is move stable.

Series	Values of the variable
A	20, 21, 22, 23, 24
B	80.0, 80.1, 82.8, 83.5, 83.75, 84.0
C	1000.00, 1001.82, 1002.62, 1003.54, 1003.9, 1003.98, 1004.00

SOLUTION:

We know that range

$$R = L - S'$$

$$\text{and co-efficient of range } = \frac{L - S'}{L + S'}$$

For series A

$$R = 24 - 20 = 4$$

$$\text{co-efficient of } R = \frac{24 - 20}{24 + 20} = 0.09091$$

For series B

$$R = 84.0 - 80.0 = 4$$

$$\text{co-efficient of } R = \frac{84.0 - 80.0}{84.0 + 80.0} = \frac{4}{164.0} = 0.02$$

For series C

$$R = 1004.0 - 1000.0 = 4$$

$$\text{and co-efficient of range} = \frac{1004.0 - 1000.0}{1004.0 + 1000.0} = 0.002$$

Conclusion: Although the range is same (i.e., 4) for all the three sets, the co-efficient of range indicate that serves C is the most uniform (least co-efficient) while serves A is the most dispersed (highest co-efficient).

3. Compute quartile deviation and its co-efficient from the following marks of 12 students

55, 57, 37, 78, 86, 91, 93, 94, 35, 42, 44, 53

SOLUTION:

To find the quartiles we arrange the observations in ascending order. Hence,

array: 35, 37, 42, 44, 53, 55, 57, 78, 86, 91, 93, 94

Hence, $n = 12$.

$$\text{Now, } Q_1 = \left(\frac{n+1}{4}\right)^{\text{th}} \text{ observation in the array.}$$

$$\text{i.e., } Q_1 = \left(\frac{12+1}{4}\right)^{\text{th}} \text{ observation in the array.}$$

$$= (3.25)^{\text{th}} \text{ observation in the array.}$$

$$= 3^{\text{rd}} \text{ observation} + 0.25(4^{\text{th}} \text{ observation} - 3^{\text{rd}} \text{ observation})$$

$$= 42 + 0.25\,(44 - 42)$$

$$= 42.5$$

$$\text{Similarly, } Q_3 = \left(\frac{3(n+1)}{4}\right)^{\text{th}} \text{ observation in the array.}$$

$$= \left(\frac{3(12+1)}{4}\right)^{\text{th}} \text{ observation in the array.}$$

$$= 9.75^{\text{th}} \text{ observation in the array.}$$

$$= 9^{\text{th}} \text{ observation } + 0.75(10^{\text{th}} \text{ observation} - 9^{\text{th}} \text{ observation})$$

$$= 86 + 0.75(91 - 86)$$

$$Q_3 = 89.75$$

We know that quartile deviation,

$$\text{QD} = \frac{Q_3 - Q_1}{2}$$

$$= \frac{89.75 - 42.5}{2}$$

$$= 23.625$$

And, the co-efficient of quartile deviation,

$$\text{Co-efficient of QD} = \frac{Q_3 - Q_1}{Q_3 + 1}$$

$$= \frac{89.75 - 42.5}{89.75 + 42.5}$$

$$= \frac{47.25}{132.25}$$

$$\text{Co-efficient of QD} = 0.35728$$

4. Find the quartile deviation and co-efficient of quartile deviation for the following data.

No. of fruits per tree:	36	43	30	37	38	29	35
	38	32	35	36	44	50	

SOLUTION:

We arrange the given data in array to find the quartiles

Array: 29, 30, 32, 35, 35, 36, 36, 37
38, 38, 43, 44, 50

Here $n = 14$

The lower quartile Q is given by

$$Q_1 = \left(\frac{n+1}{4}\right)^{\text{th}} \text{ observation in the array.}$$
$$= \left(\frac{14+1}{4}\right)^{\text{th}} \text{ observation in the array.}$$
$$= 3.75^{\text{th}} \text{ observation in the array.}$$
$$= 3^{\text{rd}} \text{ observation} + 0.75(4^{\text{th}} \text{ observation} - 3^{\text{rd}} \text{ observation})$$
$$= 32 + 0.75\,(35 - 32)$$
$$= 34.25$$

The upper quartile Q_3 is given by

$$Q_3 = \left(\frac{3(n+1)}{4}\right)^{\text{th}} \text{ observation in the array.}$$
$$= \left(\frac{3(14+1)}{4}\right)^{\text{th}} \text{ observation in the array.}$$
$$= 11.25^{\text{th}} \text{ observation in the array.}$$
$$= 11^{\text{th}} \text{ observation} + 0.25\,(12^{\text{th}} \text{ observation} - 11^{\text{th}} \text{ observation})$$
$$= 43 + 0.25\,(44 - 43)$$
$$Q_3 = 43.25$$

Now, quartile deviation is given by

$$\text{Q.D} = \frac{Q_3 - Q_1}{2}$$
$$= \frac{43.25 - 34.25}{2}$$
$$\text{Q.D} = 4.5 \text{ fruits}$$

And, the co-efficient of quartile deviation is given by

$$\text{co-efficient of Q.D} = \frac{Q_3 - Q_1}{Q_3 + Q_1}$$

$$= \frac{43.25 - 34.25}{43.25 + 34.25}$$

$$\text{co-efficient of QD} = 0.11613$$

5. Calculate QD and its co-efficient for the following data.

Value	10	20	30	40	50	60
Frequency	28	36	24	32	40	16

SOLUTION:

	x	f	cf
	10	28	28
$Q_1 \leftarrow$	20	36	64
	30	24	88
	40	32	120
$Q_3 \leftarrow$	50	40	160
	60	16	176
		$\Sigma f = 176$	

Now $N = \Sigma f = 176$

For grouped discrete data, $Q_1 = \frac{N}{4}^{\text{th}}$ value $= \frac{176}{4}^{\text{th}}$ value $= 44^{\text{th}}$ value

The cf just ≥ 44 is 64 and the corresponding value 20 is Q_1

i.e., $Q_1 = 20$

And, $Q_3 = \left\{\frac{3N}{4}\right\}^{\text{th}}$ value

Now $\frac{3N}{4} = \frac{3 \times 176}{4} = 132$

The cf just ≥ 132 is 160 and the corresponding value in 50.

Hence, $Q_3 = 50$.

Now, quartile deviation is given by

$$\text{Q.D} = \frac{Q_3 - Q_1}{2}$$

$$= \frac{50 - 20}{2}$$

$$= 15$$

The co-efficient of quartile deviation is given by

$$\text{co-efficient of QD} = \frac{Q_3 - Q_1}{Q_3 + Q_1}$$

$$= \frac{50 - 20}{50 + 20}$$

$$= 0.4287$$

6. Calculate the semi-interquartile range and its co-efficient from the following data.

x	58	59	60	61	62	63	64	65	66
f	15	20	32	35	33	22	20	10	8

SOLUTION:

	x	f	cf
	58	15	15
	59	20	35
$Q_1 \leftarrow$	60	32	67
	61	35	102
	62	33	135
$Q_3 \leftarrow$	63	22	157
	64	20	177
	65	10	187
	66	8	195
		$N = \Sigma f = 195$	

The semi-interquartile range or quartile deviation is given by

$$\text{QD} = \frac{Q_3 - Q_1}{2}$$

Now Q_1 for a grouped discrete data is $\left(\frac{N}{4}\right)^{\text{th}}$ value.

Here, $N = \Sigma f = 195$

Now, $\frac{N}{4} = \frac{195}{4} = 48.75$

The cf just ≥ 48.75 is 60

$\therefore \quad Q_1 = 60$

And $Q_3 = \left\{\frac{3N}{4}\right\}^{\text{th}}$ value

$\frac{3N}{4} = 146.25$

The *cf* just ≥ 146.25 is 157

$\therefore \quad Q_3 = 63$

Therefore,

$$\text{QD} = \frac{Q_3 - Q_1}{2}$$
$$= \frac{63 - 60}{2}$$
$$= 1.5$$

and co-efficient of QD $= \frac{Q_3 - Q_1}{Q_3 + Q_1}$
$$= 0.02439$$

7. Calculate the quartile deviation and its co-efficient

C.I.	15 – 25	25 – 35	35 – 45	45 – 55	55 – 65	65 – 75	75 – 85	85 – 95
f	32	38	45	98	122	80	50	25

SOLUTION:

C.I	*f*	*cf*	
15 – 25	32	32	
25 – 35	38	70	
35 – 45	45	115	
45 – 55	98	213	→ Q_1 Class
55 – 65	122	335	
65 – 75	80	415	→ Q_3 Class
75 – 85	50	465	
85 – 95	25	490	
	$\Sigma f = 490$		

We know that quartile deviation is given by

$$\text{QD} = \frac{Q_3 - Q_1}{2}$$

Now,

$Q_1 = \{N/4\}^{\text{th}}$ value

$$N/4 = \frac{490}{4} = 122.5$$

The cumulative frequency just $\geqslant N/4 (= 122.5)$ is 213 the corresponding CI is the Q_1 class i.e. $(45 - 55)$ is the Q_1 class

Now,

$$Q_1 = l + \left\{\frac{N/4 - m}{f}\right\} \times C$$

where l = lower limit of the Q_1 class = 45

$N = \sum f = 490$

m = cumulative frequency of the class preceding Q_1 class $= 115$

f = frequency of Q_1 class $= 98$

C = width of Q_1 class $= (55 - 45) = 10$

$$\therefore \quad Q_1 = 45 + \left\{\frac{\frac{490}{4} - 115}{98}\right\} \times 10$$

$$\boxed{Q_1 = 45.765}$$

Similarly, $Q_3 = \{3N/4\}^{\text{th}}$ value $= 367.5^{\text{th}}$ value

The *cf* just $\geqslant 3N/4 (= 367.5)$ in 415 and the corresponding C.I. $(65 - 75)$ in the Q_3 class.

Now,

$$Q_3 = l + \left\{\frac{3N/4 - m}{f}\right\} \times C$$

where l = lower limit of Q_3 class $= 65$

$N = \sum f = 490$

$m = cf$ of the class preceeding Q_3 class $= 335$

f = frequency of Q_3 class $= 80$

C = width of Q_3 class $= (75 - 65) = 10$

$$\therefore \quad Q_3 = 65 + \left\{\frac{\frac{3(490)}{4} - 335}{80}\right\} \times 10$$

$$= 69.0625$$

Therefore,

$$QD = \frac{Q_3 - Q_1}{2}$$
$$= \frac{69.0625 - 45.765}{2}$$
$$= 11.64875$$

$$\text{Co-effcient of QD} = \frac{Q_3 - Q_1}{Q_3 + Q_1}$$
$$= \frac{69.0625 - 45.765}{69.0625 + 45.765}$$
$$= \frac{23.2975}{114.8275}$$
$$= 0.20289$$

8. Calculate quartile deviation and its co-efficient

C.I.	5 – 7	8 – 10	11 – 13	14 – 16	17 – 19	Total
f	14	24	38	20	4	100

SOLUTION:

Since the class intervals are inclusive type, we convert them to exclusive type as follows

C.I.	f	cf	
4.5 – 7.5	14	14	
7.5 – 10.5	24	38	→ Q_1 Class
10.5 – 13.5	38	76	→ Q_3 Class
13.5 – 16.5	20	96	
16.5 – 19.5	4	100	
	$\sum f = 100$		

We know that

$$Q.D = \frac{Q_3 - Q_1}{2}$$

Now $Q_1 = \{N/4\}^{\text{th}}$ value where $N = \sum f = 100$.

i.e., $Q_1 = \left\{\frac{100}{4}\right\}^{\text{th}}$ value $= 25^{\text{th}}$ value

The cumulative frequency just $\geqslant N/4(=25)$ is 38 and the corresponding C.I. $(7.5 - 10.5)$ is the Q_1 class.

$$Q_1 = lt\left\{\frac{N/4 - m}{f}\right\} \times C$$

where $l =$ lower limit of Q_1 class $= 7.5$

$N = \sum f = 100$

$m =$ cumulative frequency of the class preceeding Q_1 class $= 14$

$f =$ frequency of Q_1 class $= 24$

$C =$ width of Q_1 class $= (10.5 - 7.5) = 3$

$$\therefore \quad Q_1 = 7.5 + \left\{\frac{\frac{100}{4} - 14}{24}\right\} \times 3$$

$$Q_1 = 8.875$$

Similarly, $Q_3 = \{3N/4\}^{\text{th}}$ value

i.e., $Q_3 = \left\{\frac{3 \times 100}{4}\right\}^{\text{th}}$ value

i.e., $Q_3 = 75^{\text{th}}$ value

The cumulative frequency just $\geqslant 3N/4(=75)$ is 76 and the corresponding C.I. $(10.5 - 13.5)$ is the Q_3 class.

$$Q_3 = l + \left\{\frac{3N/4 - m}{f}\right\} \times C$$

where $l =$ lower limit of Q_3 class $= 10.5$

$N = \sum f = 100$

$m =$ cumulative frequency of the class preceeding Q_3 class $= 38$

$f =$ frequency of Q_3 class $= 38$

$C =$ width of Q_3 class $= (13.5 - 10.5) = 3$

$$\therefore \quad Q_3 = 10.5 + \left\{\frac{\frac{3 \times 100}{4} - 38}{38}\right\} \times 3$$

$$Q_3 = 13.4210.$$

Therefore,

$$QD = \frac{Q_3 - Q_1}{2}$$

$$= \frac{13.421 - 8.875}{2}$$

$$QD = 2.273$$

$$\text{and co-eff. of QD} = \frac{Q_3 - Q_1}{Q_3 + Q_1}$$

$$= \frac{13.421 - 8.875}{13.421 + 8.875}$$

$$= 0.2038$$

9. Following are the runs scored by two batsmen *A* and *B* in ten innings:

A	101	0	27	82	36	45	13	7	65	14
B	98	40	12	13	96	8	8	85	56	15

Who is the better run getter? who is the more consistent batsman.

SOLUTION:

Let *X* denote runs of batsman *A*

and *Y* denote runs of batsman *B*

X	$d_x = x - A = x - 39$	d_x^2	Y	$d_y = y - A = y - 43$	d_y^2
101	62	3844	97	54	2916
0	−39	1521	40	−3	9
27	−12	144	12	−31	96
82	43	1849	13	−30	901
36	−3	9	96	53	280
45	6	36	8	−35	122
13	−26	676	8	−35	122
7	−32	1024	85	42	176
65	26	676	56	13	textcut
14	−25	625	15	−28	textcut
$\Sigma x = 390$	$\Sigma d = 0$	10404	$\Sigma y = 430$	$\Sigma d = 0$	textcut

Now, the average of batsman A is given by

$$\bar{x} = \frac{\sum x}{n} = \frac{390}{10} = 39$$

and, the average of batsman B is

$$\bar{y} = \frac{\sum y}{n} = \frac{430}{10} = 43$$

The S.D. for batsman A is

$$\sigma_x = \sqrt{\frac{\sum d_{x^2}}{n} - \left(\frac{\sum d_x}{n}\right)^2} = \sqrt{\frac{10404}{10} - \left(\frac{0}{10}\right)^2} = 32.255$$

and the co-efficient of variance is

$$CV_A = \frac{\sigma_x}{\bar{x}} \times 100 = \frac{32.255}{39} \times 100 = 82.705\%$$

The standard deviation for batsman B is

$$\sigma_y = \sqrt{\frac{\sum d_{y^2}}{n} - \left(\frac{\sum d_y}{n}\right)^2} = \sqrt{\frac{12762}{10} - \left(\frac{0}{10}\right)^2} = 35.7239$$

and the co-efficient of variation is given by

$$CV_B = \frac{\sigma_y}{\bar{y}} \times 100 = \frac{35.7239}{43} \times 100 = 83.079\%$$

The results can be summarised as follows.

Batsman	Mean	Std. dev.	CV
A	39	32.255	82.705
B	43	35.7239	83.079

Since batsman *B*'s average is more than batsmen *A*'s average, batsman *B* is a better batsman. But since the CV for batsman *A* is less than CV for batsman *B*, batsman *A* is more consistent.

10. Following are the marks obtained by two students *A* and *B* in 10 tests of 100 marks each.

Tests	1	2	3	4	5	6	7	8	9	10
A	44	80	76	48	52	72	72	51	60	54
B	48	75	54	60	63	69	72	51	57	66

Find out who is better in studies and if co-efficient in the criteria for awarding a prize who should get the prize.

SOLUTION:

Let *X* denote marks of student *A* and *Y* denote marks of student *B*.

Let us assume the mean for student *A* as $A = 60$ and that of *B* as $B = 60$

X	$d_x = x - A = x - 60$	d_x^2	Y	$d_y = y - B = y - 60$	d_y^2
44	−16	256	48	−12	144
80	20	400	75	15	225
76	16	256	54	−6	36
48	−12	144	60	0	0
52	−8	64	63	3	9
72	12	144	69	9	81
72	12	144	72	12	144
51	−9	81	51	−9	81
60	0	0	57	−3	9
54	6	36	66	6	36
	$\sum d = 9$	1525		$\sum d = 15$	765

$$\overline{X} = A + \overline{d} = A + \frac{\sum d}{n} = 60 + \frac{9}{10} = 60.9$$

$$\overline{Y} = B + \overline{d} = 60 + \frac{\sum d}{n} = 60 + \frac{15}{10} = 61.5$$

$$\sigma_x = \sqrt{\frac{\sum d_{x^2}}{n} - \left(\frac{\sum d_x}{n}\right)^2} \qquad \sigma_y = \sqrt{\frac{\sum d_{y^2}}{n} - \left(\frac{\sum d_y}{n}\right)^2}$$

$$= \sqrt{\frac{1525}{10} - \left(\frac{9}{10}\right)^2} \qquad = \sqrt{\frac{765}{10} - \left(\frac{15}{10}\right)^2}$$

$$= 12.316 \qquad = 8.617$$

$$\text{CV}_x = \frac{\sigma_x}{\bar{x}} \times 100 \qquad \text{CV}_y = \frac{\sigma_y}{\bar{y}} \times 100$$

$$= \frac{12.316}{60.9} \times 100 \qquad = \frac{8.617}{61.5} \times 100$$

$$= 20.23\% \qquad = 14.01\%$$

B is a better student since his average is higher. Also, if consistency is the criteria, B gets the prize because he is more consistent (his CV is less).

11. The following gives the age distribution of boys and girls in a school. Find which of the two groups is more variable in age

Age :	10	11	12	13	14	15
No. of boys :	11	14	14	10	8	5
No. of girls :	13	15	12	9	5	3

SOLUTION:

Let us assume the mean age of boys and girls to be $A = 12$.

BOYS					GIRLS				
x	f_b	$d = x - 12$	$f_b d$	$f_b d^2$	x	f_g	$d = x - 12$	$f_g d$	$f_g d^2$
10	11	−2	−22	44	10	13	−2	−26	52
11	14	−1	−14	14	11	15	−1	−15	15
12	14	0	0	0	12	12	0	0	0
13	10	1	10	10	13	9	1	9	9
14	8	2	16	32	14	5	2	10	20
15	5	3	15	30	15	3	3	9	27
	$\sum f_b = 62$	$\sum d = 3$	5	130		$\sum f_g = 57$	$\sum d = 3$	−13	123

Now

$$\overline{X} = A + \frac{\sum d}{\sum f_b} \qquad \overline{X}_g = A + \frac{\sum d}{\sum f_g}$$

$$= 12 + \frac{3}{62} \qquad = 12 - \frac{3}{57}$$

$$= 12.048 \qquad = 11.947$$

$$\sigma_b = \sqrt{\frac{\sum f_b d^2}{\sum f_b} - \left(\frac{\sum f_b d}{\sum f_b}\right)^2} \qquad \sigma_g = \sqrt{\frac{\sum f_g d^2}{\sum f_g} - \left(\frac{\sum f_g d}{\sum f_g}\right)^2}$$

$$= \sqrt{\frac{130}{62} - \left(\frac{3}{62}\right)^2} \qquad = \sqrt{\frac{123}{57} - \left(\frac{-13}{62}\right)}$$

$$= 1.447 \qquad = 1.5386$$

$$CV_b = \frac{\sigma_b}{\bar{x}_b} \times 100 \qquad CV_g = \frac{\sigma_g}{\bar{x}_g} \times 100$$

$$= \frac{1.447}{12.048} \times 100 \qquad = \frac{1.5386}{11.947} \times 100$$

$$= 12.01\% \qquad = 12.87\%$$

Girls are more variable in age since their co-efficient of variance is higher.

12. The table below gives the distribution of companies by the size of work-force

No. of workmen	No. of companies
0 – 50	13
50 – 100	9
100 – 150	0
150 – 200	7
200 – 250	4
250 – 300	5
300 & above	2

Calculate: (a) the standard deviation

(b) coefficient of variation

SOLUTION:

We use the following table where $A = 175$ and $C = 50$.

C.I.	V	x	$d = \frac{x-A}{C} = \frac{x-175}{50}$	d^2	fd	fd^2
0 – 50	13	25	−3	9	−39	117
50 – 100	9	75	−2	4	−18	36
100 – 150	0	125	−1	1	0	0
150 – 200	7	175	0	0	0	0
200 – 250	4	225	1	1	4	4
250 – 300	5	275	2	4	10	20
300 – 350	2	325	3	9	6	18
	$\sum n = 40$		$\sum d = 0$	$\sum d^2 = 28$	$\sum fd = -37$	$\sum fd^2 = 195$

We know that AM by short-cut method is

$$\bar{x} = A + \frac{\sum fd}{\sum f} \times C$$
$$= 175 + \left(\frac{-37}{40}\right) \times 50$$
$$= 128.75$$

and, the standard deviation is given by

$$\sigma = \sqrt{\frac{\sum fd^2}{\sum f} - \left(\frac{\sum fd}{\sum f}\right)^2}$$
$$= \sqrt{\frac{195}{40} - \left(\frac{-37}{40}\right)^2}$$
$$= 2.004.$$

And the co-efficient of variance is given by

$$CV = \frac{\sigma}{\bar{x}} \times 100$$
$$= \frac{2.004}{128.75} \times 100$$
$$= 1.56\%$$

13. The following information is related to the marks scored in a test by girls section and boys section in a school. From this you are required to find out.

(i) Which section scores more marks on an average?

(ii) Which section is more consistent in scoring?

Marks	0 – 10	10 – 20	20 – 30	30 – 40	40 – 50
Boys' sections	9	13	20	10	8
Girls' section	5	12	24	12	7

Let f_b denote the frequencies in the boys' section and f_g denote the frequencies in the girls' section.

We use the following table mean where we assume the mean to be $A = 25$, and the common difference $c = 10$

C.I.	x (mid pt)	$d=\frac{x-A}{c}=\frac{x-25}{10}$	Boys			Girls		
			f_b	$f_b d$	$f_b d^2$	f_g	$f_g d$	$f_g d^2$
0–10	5	–2	9	–18	36	5	–10	20
10–20	15	–1	13	–13	13	12	–12	12
20–30	25	0	20	0	0	24	0	0
30–40	35	1	10	10	10	12	12	12
40–50	45	2	8	16	32	7	14	28
			$\sum f_b = 60$	$\sum f_b d = -5$	$\sum f_b d^2 = 91$	$\sum f_g = 60$	$\sum f_g d = 4$	$\sum f_g d^2 = 72$

BOYS

$$\overline{X}_B = A + \left\{\frac{\sum f_b d}{\sum f_b} \times c\right\}$$

$$= 25 + \left\{\left(\frac{-5}{60}\right) \times 10\right\}$$

$$\therefore \quad \overline{X}_B = 24.17$$

GIRLS

$$\overline{X}_G = A + \left\{\frac{\sum f_g d}{\sum f_g} \times c\right\}$$

$$= 25 + \left\{\frac{4}{60} \times 10\right\}$$

$$\therefore \quad \overline{X}_G = 25.67$$

$$\sigma_B = \sqrt{\frac{\sum f_b d^2}{\sum f_b} - \left(\frac{\sum f_b d}{\sum f_b}\right)^2} \times c$$

$$= \sqrt{\frac{91}{60} - \left(\frac{-5}{60}\right)^2} \times 10$$

$$\sigma_B = 12.23$$

$$\sigma_G = \sqrt{\frac{\sum f_g d^2}{\sum f_g} - \left(\frac{\sum f_g d}{\sum f_g}\right)^2} \times 10$$

$$= \sqrt{\frac{72}{60} - \left(\frac{4}{60}\right)^2} \times 10$$

$$\sigma_G = 10.93$$

$$CV_B = \frac{\sigma_B}{\overline{X}_B} \times 100$$

$$= \frac{12.3}{24.17} \times 100$$

$$CV_B = 50.89\%$$

$$CV_G = \frac{\sigma_G}{\overline{X}_A} \times 100$$

$$= \frac{10.93}{25.67} \times 100$$

$$CV_G = 42.57$$

(i) On an average, girls' section scales more than the boys' section.

(ii) Also, the girls' section is more consistent (because the CV is lesser for girls).

14. The CV of a series is 80% and SD = 16. Calculate the arithmetic mean.

SOLUTION:

$$\text{Given} \quad CV = 80\%$$

$$SD = 16$$

$$\text{Wkt} \quad CV = \frac{\sigma}{\bar{x}} \times 100$$

$$80 = \frac{16}{\bar{x}} \times 100$$

$$\text{i.e.,} \quad \bar{x} = \frac{16}{80} \times 100$$

$$= 20$$

15. Co-efficient of variation of a series is 58% and its standard deviation is 212. Find mean.

SOLUTION:

$$\text{Given} \quad CV = 58\%$$
$$SD = 21.2$$

We know that

$$CV = \frac{\sigma}{\overline{x}} \times 100$$

$$58 = \frac{21.2}{\overline{x}} \times 100$$

$$\text{ie} \quad \overline{x} = \frac{21.2}{58} \times 100$$

$$= 36.5517$$

IN A NUTSHELL

- Measures of dispersion indicate the 'extent of spread' of observed values over an interval.
- Range, quartile deviation and standard deviation are the common measures of absolute measures of dispersion.
- Associated with each of the above, we have co-efficient of range, co-efficient of quartile deviation and co-efficient of variance which are relative measures of dispersion. Relative measures of dispersion are pure numbers devoid of any unit of measurement.
- The square of standard deviation is the variance.
- SD is by far the most popular and best measure of dispersion.
- When comparing two or more distributions for consistency (uniformity) we use co-efficient of variation (CV).

CHECK YOUR PROGRESS

1. What is dispersion? Mention any two methods of measuring dispersion.
2. Define 'range'.
3. What do you mean by 'Interquartile range'?
4. What is quartile deviation?
5. State any two merits of quartile deviation.

6. What do you mean by standard deviation?
7. Define variance.
8. What are absolute measures of dispersion? How are they different from relative measures of dispersion?
9. What are the merits and demerits of range?
10. List the merits and demerits of quartile deviation.
11. What are the merits and demerits of SD?
12. What is co-efficient of variance? How is it useful?
13. Why is SD considered the best measure of dispersion?

PROBLEMS

1. Find the range and co-efficient of range for the following distribution regards the heights of plants in a nursery

   Ht of plant (in cm): 32, 48, 60, 53, 58, 59, 35, 38, 45, 54, 52, 33

   [**Ans.** $R = 28$ cm. co-eff. of $R = 0.3043$]

2. For a distribution regarding the ages of a group of students it is known that the range is 8 years and the co-efficient of range is 0.2. Find the maximum age and the minimum age of the group.

   [**Ans.** Minimum age = 16 Maximum age = 24]

3. Calculate the range and co-efficient of range for the following.

Salary (in Rs.)	No. of employees
8000	7
9000	12
10000	25
11000	14
12000	10
13000	3

[**Ans.** $R =$ Rs. 5000/– co-eff. of $R = 0.2321$]

4. Calculate range and co-efficient of range for the following.

Height (in inches)	No. of students
60 – 62	4
62 – 64	12
64 – 66	18
66 – 68	8
68 – 70	6

[**Ans.** $R = 10$ inches
co-eff. of $R = 0.076$]

5. Find out the value of the quartile deviation and its co-efficient from the following.

Register No	Marks
001	60
002	28
003	20
004	15
005	40
006	30
007	50

[**Ans.** QD = 12.5
co-eff. of QD = 0.455]

6. Calculate quartile deviation from the following data.

Size	2	4	6	8	10	12	14	16	18	20
Frequency	2	9	11	14	20	24	20	16	5	2

[**Ans.** QD = 3
co-eff. of QD = 0.27273]

7. Compute co-efficient of quartile deviation from the following data.

[**Ans.** co-eff. of QD = 0.333]

Marks	10	20	30	40	50	60
No. of students	4	7	15	8	7	2

8. Calculate quartile deviation and the co-efficient of QD from the following data.

Wages is Rs/week	less than 35	35–37	38–40	41–43	over 43
No. of wage earners	14	62	99	18	7

[**Ans.** QD = 1.67
co-eff. of QD = 0.044]

9. From the following compute QD and the co-efficient of QD.

Weekly wages	4–8	8–12	12–16	16–20	20–24
No. of workers	6	10	18	30	15
Weekly wages	24–28	28–32	32–36	36–40	
No. of workers	12	10	6	2	

[**Ans.** co-eff. of QD = 0.2642]

10. Calculate quartile deviation and its co-efficient.

X	0–19	20–39	40–49	50–59	60–69	70–79	80–89
f	15	31	19	15	8	7	7

[**Ans.** QD = 15.4465
co-eff. of QD = 0.3702]

11. The sum of upper and lower quartiles is 90 and their difference 2. Find:

   (a) Q_1 and Q_3

   (b) QD.

   (c) Co-efficient of QD

[**Ans.** a) $Q_1 = 44$ $Q_3 = 46$
b) QD = 1
c) co-eff. of QD = $0.0\dot{2}2$]

12. Calculate QD from the following data.

Class:	10–20	20–30	30–40	40–50	50–60	60–70
Frequency:	3	5	15	10	3	4

[**Ans.** QD = 7.835]

13. The annual salaries of a group of employees are given in the following table.

Salaries (in Rs '000)	45	50	55	60	65	70	75	80
Number of persons	3	5	8	7	9	7	4	7

Calculate the standard deviation of the salaries.

[**Ans.** SD = 10.35 (Rs in '000)]

14. Calculate the standard deviation from the following observations.

240.12	240.13	240.15	240.12	240.17
240.15	240.17	240.16	240.22	240.21

[**Ans.** SD = 0.033]

15. Calculate standard deviation for the following data.

Mid pt	1	2	3	4	5	6	7	8	9
Frequency	6	45	103	147	205	160	80	40	4

[**Ans.** SD = 1.575]

16. Calculate standard deviation from the data given below.

C.I.	**Frequency**
0 – 10	5
10 – 20	8
20 – 30	12
30 – 40	15
40 – 50	14
50 – 60	12
60 – 70	6

[**Ans.** SD = 18.74]

17. Calculate SD from the following data.

Age under (in years)	10	20	30	40	50	60	70	80
No of persons dying	10	40	85	125	160	200	220	280

[**Ans.** SD = 2.63 years]

18. The arithmetic mean of runs scored by three batsmen A, B and C in a series of 10 innings are 50, 48 and 12 respectively. The standard deviation of their runs are 15, 12 and 2 respectively. Find out who is the most consistent batsman.

$$\left[\begin{array}{l}\textbf{Ans.}\quad CV_A = 30\% \\ CV_B = 25\% \\ CV_C = 16.66\% \\ \therefore \quad \text{Batsman } C \text{ is most consistent}\end{array}\right]$$

19. From the prices of shares of X and Y for 10 days given below, state which share prices are more stable.

X (Rs):	55	53	53	54	68	56	49	51	50	52
Y (Rs):	101	104	103	104	107	106	105	105	107	108

$$\left[\begin{array}{l}\textbf{Ans.}\quad CV_{(X)} = 9.369\% \\ CV_{(Y)} = 1.905\% \\ \text{share } Y \text{ is more stable}\end{array}\right]$$

20. Find out by calculating co-efficient of variantion which of the following two series has more variation?

Age	0–10	10–20	20–30	30–40	40–50	50–60	60–70
Population in thousands City A	18	16	15	12	10	5	2
City B	10	12	14	32	29	11	3

$$\left[\begin{array}{l}\textbf{Ans.}\quad CV_{(A)} = 65.64\% \\ CV_{(B)} = 43.75\% \\ \therefore \quad \text{City } A \text{ has more variation}\end{array}\right]$$

21. Compute the co-efficient of variation for the following data.

Monthly Profit/loss (in ’00Rs)	No. of shops
(−4)−(−3)	4
(−3)−(−2)	10
(−2)−(−1)	22
(−1)−0	28
0−1	38
1−2	56
2−3	46
3−4	24
4−5	18
5−6	10

[**Ans.** $CV = 152.75\%$]

11

Index Numbers

INTRODUCTION

Index numbers are commonly used statistical indicators for measuring the combined fluctuations in a group of related variables. Generally used to indicate the state of the economy, index numbers are aptly called 'barometers of economic activity'. Index numbers are used in comparing prices, production, sales, exports or imports over a certain period of time. For example, consumer price index (CPI) is a commonly quoted index, which measures price fluctuations. The CPI is a single numbers representing the general level of prices that affects consumers. Similarly, we have SENSEX (also called BSE 30), a stock market index that reflects current market conditions.

INDEX NUMBER – MEANING

An index number is a statistical measure designed to show changes in a variable or a group of related variables with respect to time.

It could be defined as a relative measure describing the average changes in any quantity over time. In other words, an index number measures the changing value of price, quantity or values over a period of time in relation to its value at some fixed point in time, called the base period. This resulting ratio of the current value to a base value is multiplied by 100 to express the index as a percentage.

$$\text{i.e.,}\quad \text{Index number} = \frac{\text{Current period value}}{\text{Base period value}} \times 100$$

Note that since an index number is a ratio of a measure taken during one time period (current period) to the same measure taken during another time period (base period) it has no units of measurement and is always expressed as a percentage.

Example

If the index number of wholesale prices of food articles in 2012 as compared to 2001 is 160, the implication is that overall level of wholesale prices of food articles in 2012 is 160% of the level in 2001. Here, 2012 is the current year while

2001 is the base year. In other words, there is an increase of 160% on an average in the prices of food articles from 2001 to 2012.

Index numbers can also be calculated for individual variables. For example, if the price of wheat is Rs. 40 in 2012 while it was Rs. 20 in 2001, the index number of the price for year 2012 with respect to the base 2001 is $P = \frac{40}{20} \times 100 = 200$. That is, the price of wheat in 2012 is 200% of its price in 2001. Here, since only a single variable is considered, the index is called 'relative'. In this particular case, it is 'Price Relative'.

Indices may be based at any convenient period and are published at frequent intervals.

Period	Index (Example)
Daily	Stock Market Prices (SENSEX)
Monthly	Index of Industrial Production (IIP)
Yearly	Gross National Product (GNP)

INDEX NUMBER DEFINED

Definitions of index numbers can be classified into the following three broad categories:

1. A Measure of Change

- It is a numerical value characterizing the change in complex economic phenomena over a period of time or space. —Maslow
- An index number is a quantity which, by reference to a base period, shows by its variations—the changes in the magnitude over a period of time. In general, index numbers are used to measure changes over time in magnitudes which are not capable of direct measurement. —John I. Raffin
- An index number is a statistical measure designed to show changes in variables or a group of related variables with respect to time, geographic location or other characteristics. —Speigel
- Index number is a single ratio (usually in percentages) which measures the combined (i.e., averaged change of several variables between two different times, places or situations. —A. M. Tuttle

2. A device to measure change

- Index numbers are devices for measuring differences in the magnitude of a group of related variables. —Corxton and Cowden
- An index number is a device which shows by its variation the changes in a magnitude which is not capable of accurate measurement in itself or of direct valuation in practice. —Wheldom

3. A series representing the process of change

- Index numbers are series of numbers by which changes in the magnitude of a phenomenon are measured from time to time or place to place. —Horace Secris
- A series of index numbers reflects in its trend and fluctuations the movements of some quantity of which it is related. —B. L. Bowley
- An index number is a statistical measure of fluctuations in a variable arranged in the form of a series, and using a base period for making comparisons. —L. J. Kaplan

To summarize from the above definitions–index numbers (or simply, indices) have the following characteristics.

- They are expressed as percentages.
- They are specialised averages.
- They measure changes that are not directly measurable.

USES OF INDEX NUMBERS

According to a Simpson and F. Kafka index numbers are one of the most widely used statistical tools. They are used to feel the pulse of the economy and they have come to be used as indicators of inflatory or deflatory tendencies:

Following is a list of users of the index numbers.

1. **Index numbers help in establishing trends**

   Indexes, when analyzed reveal a general trend of the phenomenon under study. For example, index number of industrial production of the country not only reflects the trends in the phenomenon but are actually useful in determining factors leading to industrial production.

2. **Index numbers help in policy making**

   Index number help the policy makers in a government or an organisation in crafting new policies. For example, it is widely known that the dearness allowance, (a major component of the salary of an employee) is linked to the cost of living index, usually the consumer price index. Whenever the government of the management of an organisation announces its wage policy the basis will be the cost of living index. Thus, indices guide policy making.

3. **Index numbers help determine the purchasing power of the rupee**

   Indices are used to determine the purchasing power of the rupee. The consumer price index for industrial workers–CPI(IW) increased from 100 in 2001 to 198 in January 2012. The real purchasing power of the rupee is found out as follows.

   $$\frac{100}{198} = 0.505$$

   It indicates that if the rupee was worth 100 paise in 2001 its purchasing power is 50.5 paise in 2012.

4. **Index numbers help deflate time series data**

   Indexes play an important role in adjusting the original data to reflect the reality. For example, nominal income (income at current prices) can be transformed into real income (reflecting the actual purchasing power) by using income deflators. Similarly, suppose that the industrial production is represented in value terms (i.e., product of volume of production and price). If the subsequent years value industrial production were to increase by 25%, this increase may not be a result of increase in the volume of production as one would assume. It could be because of the increase in the price. This inflation which has caused the increase in the series can be eliminated by the usage of an appropriate price index and thus making the series real.

5. **Index numbers act as economic barometers**

   Just as barometers indicate the atmospheric pressure, many indices are used to indicate the pressure of the economic and business behaviour. They are also used to measure ups and downs in the general economic condition of a country. For example, SENSEX is often seen as a leading indicator of India's economic strength and market sentiment.

STEPS IN CONSTRUCTING INDEX NUMBERS

The various steps involved in constructing a index number are as follows:

Step 1: Defining (Stating) the Purpose of the Index Number

An index number which is designed keeping specific objective in mind is a very powerful tool. Hence, a clear definition of the purpose will help in selection of the right index number. The subsequent steps involving the selection of items, base period, weights, etc., depend mainly on the purpose. Absence of clear definition of purpose leads often leads to construction of an unsuitable index number.

For example, an index whose purpose is to measure consumer price index should not include wholesale rates of items while the index number meant for slum colonies should not include luxury items like cars air-conditioners, etc.

Step 2: Selecting the Base Period

Base period, as we have seen earlier in the chapter, is the time period that serves as a basics for comparison in the index number. Hence, while constructing the index, an appropriate base period should be selected. It must be kept in mind that this base year must be a normal year and an economically stable year. In other words, the year should be free of wars, floods, famines, etc., with no abnormal variations. Also, the base year should not be too distant in the past and the consumption patterns during the two periods should not differ much. Note that, depending on the situation, fixed base index number or chain base index number can be prepared.

Step 3: Selecting the Items

The purpose of constructing an index number will usually help us in selecting the items for it. For example, a wholesale price index number requires items which are transacted at the wholesale market. Similarly, a consumer price index for a group of people requires items which are consumed by that particular group of people. The items for a CPI for another group would differ with the habits, customs and standard of living. Generally, there are many items that could be included in the index number. But, the list can be reduced by selecting the representative items only.

Step 4: Obtaining Price Quotations

After the items are selected for constructing the index number, price quotations for these items should be obtained from authentic sources. If different places or agencies are involved, then the prices should be averaged.

Step 5: Selecting the Appropriate System of Weight

The items considered in constructing index do not always have equal weights. Weights are attached to these items according to their importance. For example, it is universally argued that wheat is the most important cereal as against other cereals for the North Indians. Hence, highest weight should be attached to this item while constructing an index number which includes wheat.

Mostly, the weights are quantities in the base period, current period or any other period. Sometimes, a combination of quantities in different periods may be considered weights.

Step 6: Selecting the Appropriate Formula

The selection of formula is based mainly as the availability of data. Depending on the availability of data regarding quantities Laspeyre's Paasche's, Fisher's or any other index number is calculated (All these index numbers are introduced in the subsequent sections.) While selecting the formula, care should be taken to see that maximum use of available data is made.

TYPES OF INDEX NUMBERS

There are three types of principal indexes.

1. Price index
2. Quantity index
3. Value index

Price Index

The price index is the most frequently used form of index numbers. *Price index numbers indicate* the general level of prices of articles in the current period as compared to that of the base period. For example, a price index for edible oils would compare changes in the price of edible oils. If we are trying to compare the price of edible oils this year to the prices of edible oils last year, it involves.

(i) a comparison of two price situations over time, and
(ii) the heterogeneity of the edible oils given the various varieties of oil.

By constructing a price index number, we are summarizing the price movements of each type of oil in this group of edible oils into a single number. The wholesale price index (WPI), consumer price index (CPI), and retail price index (RPI) are some popularly used price indices.

Quantity Index

A quantity index measures the changes in quantity from one period to another. If in the above example, we are interested in the quantum of production of edible oils, instead of the price of edible oils, then we are comparing quantities in two different years or over a period of time. It is the quantity index that needs to be constructed here. Index of industrial production (IIP)and index of agricultural production are some popularly used quantity indices.

Value Index

The value index is a combination index. It combines price and quantity changes to present a more spatial comparison. Value index numbers as such measure changes in net monetary worth. Usually value index is used in sales, inventories, foreign trade, etc. Though it enables comparison of value of a commodity in a year to the value of that commodity in a base year, it has limited use. Its limited use is owing to its inability to distinguish the effects of price and quantity separately.

Export value index and import value index are popular value index numbers.

Remarks: Special purpose index numbers: A few index numbers such as consumer price index, industrial production, etc., are constructed for specific purposes depending on the nature and degree of relationship between groups and items.

Note:

1. Index number for the base year is always 100.
2. Price index is 130 means price level in the current year is 130% of the price level in the base year.
3. Index number for 2012 with base 2001 is 275 means average price level has increased by 175% from 2001 to 2012.
4. Average price level in 2012 is double the average price level of 2001 means index of prices for 2012 with base 2001 in 2012.

NOTATIONS AND SYMBOLS USED IN INDEX NUMBERS

It is customory to denote the base year by '0' and the current year by 1 in index numbers.

Thus,

P_{01} = Price index number for the current year with respect to the base year.

Q_{01} = Quantity index number for the current year with respect to the base year.

V_{01} = Value index number for the current year with respect to the base year.

P = Price relative

Q = Quality relative

p_0 = Price in the base year

p_1 = Price in the current year

q_0 = Quantity in the base year

q_1 = Quantity in the current year

$$P = \frac{p_1}{p_0} \times 100$$

$$Q = \frac{q_1}{q_0} \times 100$$

W = Weight

$\sum$ = Summation

METHODS OF CONSTRUCTING INDEX NUMBERS

There are two approaches for constructing an index number, namely:

(i) The aggregates method.

(ii) The average of relatives method.

Note that the index constructed in either of these methods could be:

(a) An unweighted index: An unweighted index is an index where equal weights are assigned implicitly.

(b) A weighted index: A weighted index is an index where weights are assigned to the various items according to their importance.

To sum up, the methods of constructing of indexes can be classified into categories as shown below.

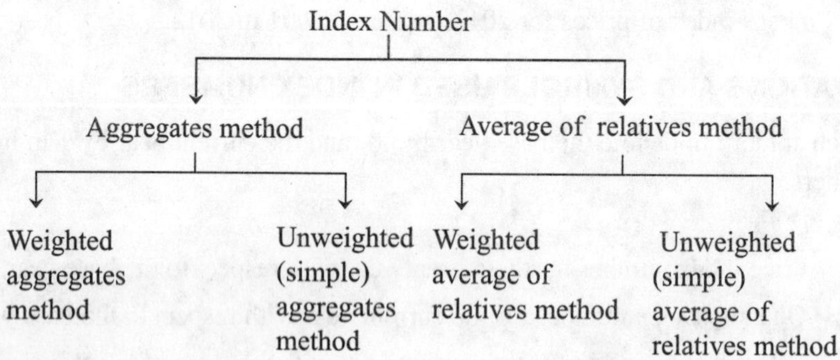

Now, if we are constructing price index numbers we could have

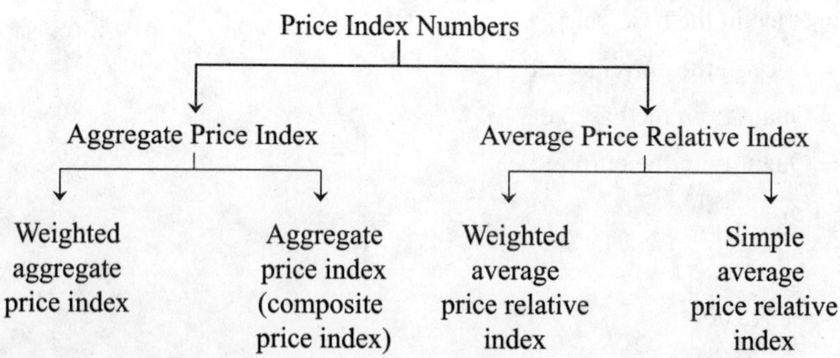

Quality index number can also be constructed in a similar fashion.

Let us discuss each method in detail.

A. The Aggregates Method

Simple Aggregative Price Index (Composite Price Index)

This is the simplest method of constructing an index. An ***aggregate price index*** or ***composite price index*** measures the average price change for a basket of related items from the base period to the current period. When this method is used to construct a price index, the total of the current year prices of the various commodities is divided by the total of the base year prices and this quotient is multiplied by 100.

$$\text{i.e.,}\quad P_{01} = \frac{\sum p_1}{\sum p_0} \times 100$$

where $\sum p_1$ = Sum of prices of all items in the current year.

$\sum p_0$ = Sum of prices of all items in the base year.

P_{01} = Price index

Steps:

1. Add the current year prices of all the items i.e., obtain $\sum p_1$.
2. Add the base year prices of the items ($\sum p_0$)
3. Divide $\sum p_1$ by $\sum p_0$ and multiply the quotient by 100 to get the price index P_{01}.

SOLVED EXAMPLES

1. From the following data construct an index for 2011 taking 2010 as base.

Commodity	Price in 2011 (Rs.)	Price in 2010 (Rs.)
A	170	150
B	160	140
C	190	180
D	220	110
E	120	120

SOLUTION:

We know that

$$P_{01} = \frac{\sum p_1}{\sum p_0} \times 100$$

We use the following table.

Commodity	Price in 2011 p_1	Price in 2010 p_0
A	170	150
B	160	140
C	190	180
D	220	110
E	120	120
	$\sum p_1 = 860$	$\sum p_0 = 700$

Now,

$$P_{01} = \frac{\sum p_1}{\sum p_0} \times 100$$

$$= \frac{860}{700} \times 100$$

$$\boxed{P_{01} = 122.86}$$

Interpretation

This means that as compared to 2010, in 2011 there is an increase in the prices of commodities included in the index to the extent of 22.86% on an average.

2. Find the price index number, using simple aggregate method, from the following information.

Commodity	Unit	Prices (Rs.)	
		2005	2010
Wheat	Quintal	3000	3800
Rice	Quintal	3500	4200
Milk	Litre	20	30
Pulses	Kilogram	80	95
Clothing	Metre	25	30
Meat	Kilogram	80	120

SOLUTION:

We know that the price index number

$$P_{01} = \frac{\sum p_1}{\sum p_0} \times 100$$

Representing the prices of 2005 (base year) as p_0 and those of 2010 (current year) as p_1, we construct the table as under.

Commodity	p_0	p_1
Wheat	3000	3800
Rice	3500	4200
Milk	20	30
Pulses	80	95
Clothing	25	30
Meat	80	120
	$\sum p_0 = 6705$	$\sum p_1 = 8275$

$$P_{01} = \frac{\sum p_1}{\sum p_0} \times 100$$

$$= \frac{8275}{6705} \times 100$$

$$\boxed{P_{01} = 123.42}$$

Interpretation: There is an increase in the price levels by $123.42 - 100 =$ 23.42%

3. The prices of there commodities A, B and C increased from Rs. 60, 10 and 15 in 2008 to Rs. 75, 15 and 20 respectively in 2010. Using the simple aggregate method, find by much on an average the prices have increased?

SOLUTION:

Let p_0 represent the prices in base year (2008) and p_1 represent the prices in the current year (2010).

We know that

$$P_{01} = \frac{\sum p_1}{\sum p_0} \times 100$$

Using the data given, a table is constructed as under:

Commodity	Price in 2008 P_0	Price in 2010 P_1
A	60	75
B	10	15
C	15	20
	$\Sigma p_0 = 85$	$\Sigma p_1 = 110$

$$\text{Now,}\quad P_{01} = \frac{\Sigma p_1}{\Sigma p_0} \times 100$$
$$= \frac{110}{85} \times 100$$
$$= 129.41$$

Thus, there is an increase of $(129.41 - 100) = 29.41\%$ in prices on an average increase.

Merits and Demerits of Simple Aggregates Method

Merits

1. This is the simplest method of constructing index numbers.
2. This is an intuitively easy method to understand.

Demerits

1. It does not consider the relative importance of the various commodities involved.
2. The units used in the price or quantity quotations can exert a big influence on the value of the index.

The index is based on the assumption that for the various items the units of measurement (both quantity and price) are the same. If the unit of measurement is different for different items, the index will produce vastly divergent results. For example, refer to Solved Example 2. Notice that the units of measurement for the quantity of wheat and rice is 'quintal' while it is 'kilogram' for pulses and meat. If we were to change the units to 'kilogram' for wheat and rice, we can rewrite the table as under.

Commodity	Unit	Prices (Rs.)	
		2005 (p_0)	2010 (p_1)
Wheat	Kilogram	30	38
Rice	Kilogram	35	42
Milk	Litre	20	30
Pulses	Kilogram	80	95
Clothing	Metre	25	30
Meat	Kilogram	80	120
		$\sum p_0 = 270$	$\sum p_1 = 355$

We know that

$$P_{01} = \frac{\sum p_1}{\sum p_0} \times 100$$

$$= \frac{355}{270} \times 100$$

$$\boxed{P_{01} = 131.48}$$

Notice that this is vastly different from the index number calculated with quintal as unit of measurement. It has increased from 123.42 to 131.48. Manipulations are thus possible to suit one's requirements by quoting favourable units of measurements. Any index whose value can be manipulated in this manner can be hardly used as an objective measure.

Since equal weights are attached to all the items, this hardly reflects, the reality where some items are more essential than others.

It is for these reasons that the simple aggregative index has never gained any great degree of acceptance.

WEIGHTED AGGREGATES METHOD

We noted in the earlier section that a major limitation (demerit) of the simple aggregates method was the equal importance attached to all the items in the index. In weighted aggregatesmethod, weights are assigned to items based on their importance. Different statisticians have suggested different weights and consequently a large number of formulae for constructing index numbers have been devised. Some of the important ones are:

Method	Weights used	Formula	Remark
(1) Laspeyre's	base year quantity q_0	$P_{01} = \frac{\sum p_1 q_0}{\sum p_0 q_0} \times 100$	
(2) Paasche's	current year quantity q_1	$P_{01} = \frac{\sum p_1 q_1}{\sum p_0 q_1} \times 100$	
(3) Dorbish and Bowley	both q_0 and q_1	$P_{01} = \left[\sum \frac{p_1 q_0}{\sum p_0 q_0} + \frac{\sum p_1 q_1}{\sum p_0 q_1}\right]$	Arithmatic mean of Laspeyre's and Paasche's
(4) Fisher's Ideal Method	both q_0 and q_1	$q_{01} = \sqrt{\frac{\sum p_1 q_0}{\sum p_0 q_0} \times \frac{\sum p_1 q_1}{\sum p_0 q_1}} \times 100$	Geometric mean of Laspeyre's
(5) Masshall-Edgeworth	both q_0 and q_1	$P_{01} = \frac{\sum (q_0 + q_1) p_1}{\sum (q_0 + q_1) p_0} \times 100$	$P_{01} = \frac{\sum p_1 q_0 + \sum p_1 q_1}{\sum p_0 q_0 + \sum p_0 q_1} \times 100$

All these methods are named after the persons who have suggested them. Note that in the above table, the Fishiers ideal index number is the geometric mean of the Laspeyre's and Paasche's indices. Fishes index number formula is considered 'ideal' because of the following reasons:

(i) It is based on the geometric mean which is considered to be the best average for constructing index numbers theoretically.

(ii) The formula takes into account both the current as well as the base period.

(iii) The formula is free from bias.

(iv) The formula satisfies both the time reversal test (TRT) as well as the factor reversal test (FRT). (These two tests are dealt its detail in later sections of their chapter.)

4. Construct price index numbers from the following data by applying:

1. Laspeyre's method
2. Paasche method
3. Bowley's method
4. Fisher's ideal method
5. Marshall-Edgeworth method

Commodity	2010		2011	
	Price	**Quantity**	**Price**	**Quantity**
L	2	8	4	6
M	5	10	6	5
N	4	14	5	10
O	2	19	2	13

SOLUTION:

Let us denote the price and quantity for year 2010 as p_0 and q_0 respectively. Similarly, the price and quantity for year 2011 are denoted as p_1 and q_1 respectively. We use the following table to construct the various price indexes.

Commodity	p_0	q_0	p_1	q_1	$p_0 q_0$	$p_1 q_0$	$p_0 q_1$	$p_1 q_1$
L	2	8	4	6	16	32	12	24
M	5	10	6	5	50	60	25	30
N	4	14	5	10	56	70	40	50
O	2	19	2	13	38	38	26	26
					$\sum p_0q_0 = 160$	$\sum p_1q_0 = 200$	$\sum p_0q_1 = 103$	$\sum p_1q_1 = 130$

Substituting the above values we get the price index as under:

1. Laspeyre's Method

$$P_{01} = \frac{\sum p_1 q_0}{\sum p_0 q_0} \times 100$$

$$= \frac{200}{160} \times 100$$

$$\boxed{P_{01} = 125}$$

2. Paasche's Method

$$P_{01} = \frac{\sum p_1 q_1}{\sum p_0 q_1} \times 100$$

$$= \frac{130}{103} \times 100$$

$$\boxed{P_{01} = 126.21}$$

3. Bowley's Method

$$P_{01} = \left[\frac{\left(\frac{\sum p_1 q_0}{\sum p_0 q_0} + \frac{\sum p_1 q_1}{\sum p_0 q_1}\right)}{2}\right] \times 100$$

$$= \left[\frac{\frac{200}{160} + \frac{130}{103}}{2}\right] \times 100$$

$$= \left(\frac{1.25 + 1.262}{2}\right) \times 100$$

$$= \frac{2.512}{2} \times 100$$

$$\boxed{P_{01} = 125.6}$$

Aliter: Remember that the Bowley's method is the arithmetic mean of Laspeyre's method and Paasche's method. Hence,

$$P_{01} = \frac{L+P}{2}$$

$$= \frac{125 + 126.2}{2}$$

$$\boxed{P_{01} = 125.6}$$

4. Fisher's Ideal Method

$$P_{01} = \sqrt{\frac{\sum p_1 q_0}{\sum p_0 q_0} \times \frac{\sum p_1 q_1}{\sum p_0 q_1}} \times 100$$

$$= \sqrt{\frac{200}{160} \times \frac{130}{102}} \times 100$$

$$\boxed{P_{01} = 126.6}$$

Aliter: Remember that the Fisher's index no. is the geometric mean of Laspeyre's and Paasche's index number, i.e., Fisher's index number

$$P_{01} = \sqrt{L \times P}$$

$$= \sqrt{125 \times 126.21}$$

$$\boxed{P_{01} = 125.6}$$

5. Marshall-Edgeworth Method

$$P_{01} = \frac{\Sigma(q_0 + q_1)p_1}{\Sigma(q_0 + q_1)p_0} \times 100$$

$$= \frac{\Sigma q_0\, p_1 + \Sigma q_1\, p_1}{\Sigma q_0\, p_0 + \Sigma q_1\, p_0} \times 100$$

$$= \frac{200 + 130}{160 + 103} \times 100 \quad \Rightarrow \quad \boxed{P_{01} = 125.47}$$

5. From the following data, construct a price index number of the group of four commodities by using appropriate formula.

Commodity	Base Year		Current year	
	Price for unit	Expenditure (Rs.)	Price per unit	Expenditure (Rs.)
A	2	40	5	75
B	4	16	8	40
C	1	10	2	24
D	5	25	10	60

SOLUTION:

Note that we are given both the base year as well as current year prices. Also the quantities in both the years can be deduced by using the relationship

$$\text{Expenditure} = \text{Price} \times \text{Quantity}$$

$$\text{i.e., quantity} = \frac{\text{Expenditure}}{\text{Price}}$$

We use the following table to calculate the Fisher's index number given by

$$P_{01} = \sqrt{\frac{\Sigma p_1\, q_0}{\Sigma p_0\, q_0} \times \frac{\Sigma p_1\, q_1}{\Sigma p_0\, q_1}} \times 100$$

Commodity	p_0	$p_0 q_0$	p_1	$p_1 q_1$	q_0	q_1	$p_0 q_1$	$p_1 q_0$
A	2	40	5	75	20	15	30	100
B	4	16	8	40	4	5	20	32
C	1	10	2	24	10	12	12	20
D	5	15	10	60	5	6	30	50
		$\sum p_0 q_0 = 91$		$\sum p_1 q_1 = 199$			$\sum p_0 q_1 = 92$	$\sum p_1 q_0 = 202$

$$P_{01} = \sqrt{\frac{\sum p_1 q_0}{\sum p_0 q_0} \times \frac{\sum p_1 q_1}{\sum' p_0 q_1}} \times 100$$

$$= \sqrt{\frac{202}{91} \times \frac{199}{92}} \times 100$$

$$\boxed{P_{01} = 219.12}$$

B. The Average of Price Relatives Method

We must at this point understand the meaning of the term 'price relative'. A price relative is the ratio of the price of a single commodity in a given period to its price in another period called the base period (or reference period). If p_0 and p_1 denote the prices of the commodity in the base period and the current period respectively, them by definition, price relative

$$\boxed{P = \frac{p_1}{p_0} \times 100}$$

As noted earlier, under the average of price relatives approach, there are two methods to construct an index.

(i) Simple average of price relatives method

(ii) Weighted average of price relatives method.

Simple Average of Price Relatives Method

In this method, an average of the price relatives is calculated. Theoretically, any of the measures of central tendency can be used to obtain the index. But, conventionally, the price relatives are averaged either by the arithmetic mean or the geometric mean. When arithmetic mean is used for averaging the relatives, the formula for computing the index is

$$P_{01} \frac{\sum P}{n}$$

$$\text{where} \quad P = \frac{p_1}{p_0} \times 100$$

when geometric mean is used for averaging the relatives, the formula for computing the index is

$$\log P_{01} = \frac{\sum \log P}{N}$$

$$\text{or} \quad P_{01} = \text{Antilog}\left\{\frac{\sum \log p}{N}\right\} \text{where} \quad P = \frac{p_1}{p_0} \times 100$$

6. Compute the price index number for the following data using simple average of price relatives by arithmetic mean.

Commodity	**Price in 2010 (Rs.)**	**Price in 2011 (Rs.)**
L	10	16
M	20	21
N	5	6
O	2	3
P	7	14

SOLUTION:

Denoting prices in 2010 as p_0 and the prices in 2011 p_1 as we construct the following table:

Commodity	p_0	p_1	$P = \frac{p_1}{p_0} \times 100$
L	10	16	160
M	20	21	105
N	5	6	300
O	2	3	150
P	7	14	200
			$\sum P = 735$

We know that price index using the average of price relatives by arithmetic mean is

$$P_{01} = \frac{\Sigma P}{n}$$

$$P_{01} = \frac{735}{5} = 147$$

$$\text{i.e.,} \quad \boxed{P_{01} = \text{Rs.}147}$$

7. From the following data, construct an index for 2010 taking 2009 as base by the average of relatives method using.

(i) arithmetic mean and

(ii) geometric mean

for the averaged relatives.

Commodity	Price in 2009 (Rs.)	Price in 2010 (Rs.)
L	20	20
M	110	120
N	80	90
O	40	60
P	50	70

SOLUTION:

(i) Average of price relatives when arithmetic mean is used for averaging (i.e., index number using arithmetic mean of price relatives).

Commodity	Price in 2009 (Rs.) p_0	Price in 2010 (Rs.) p_0	Price relations $P = \frac{p_1}{p_0} \times 100$
L	20	20	100.0
M	110	120	109.1
N	80	90	112.5
O	40	60	150.0
P	50	70	140.0
			$\Sigma P = 611.6$

Now,

$$P_{01} = \frac{\Sigma P}{n}$$

$$= \frac{611.6}{5}$$

$$\boxed{P_{01} = 122.32}$$

(ii) Average of price relatives when geometric mean is used for averaging (i.e., number using geometric mean of price relative).

Commodity	Price in 2009 p_0	Price in 2010 p_1	Price relative $P = \frac{p_1}{p_0} \times 100$	log P
L	20	20	100.0	2.0000
M	110	120	109.1	2.0378
N	80	90	112.5	2.0512
O	40	120	150.0	2.1761
P	50	20	140.0	2.1461
				$\Sigma \log P = 10.4112$

Now,

$$P_{01} = \text{Antilog}\left[\frac{\Sigma \log P}{n}\right]$$

$$= \text{Anitlog}\left[\frac{10.4112}{5}\right]$$

$$= \text{Antilog } 2.0822$$

$$\boxed{P_{01} = 120.9}$$

Merits and Demerits of Simple Average of Price Relatives

Merits

1. Extreme items do not influence the index. Equal importance is given to all the items.
2. This index is not influenced by the units of measurement of prices. Relatives are pure numbers and are, therefore, independent of the original units. Consequently, index numbers computed by this method would be the same regardless of the way in which prices are quoted. Thus, simple average of price relatives are said to meet what is called the 'units test'.

Demerits

1. While constructing this index number difficulties are faced with regard to the selection of an appropriate average. Arithmetic mean is not always a justified method of averaging as it causes an upward bias. The use of geometric mean involves computational difficulties. Other averages are hardly ever used.
2. The relatives are all assigned equal importance when in reality this hardly is the case. Some relatives are more important than others economically.

WEIGHTED AVERAGE OF PRICE RELATIVES

In this method, appropriate weights (w), are assigned to various terms and a weighted average of the price relatives is calculated. As earlier, either arithmetic mean or geometric mean is used for averaging to obtain the index.

When arithmetic mean is used for averaging, the weighted average of price relative is

$$P_{01} = \frac{\sum wP}{\sum w}$$

$$\text{where} \quad P = \frac{p_1}{p_0} \times 100 \text{ is the price relative.}$$

When geometric mean is used for averaging, the weighted average of price relatives is

$$P_{01} = \text{antilog}\left[\frac{\sum w \log P}{\sum w}\right]$$

$$\text{where} \quad p = \frac{p_1}{p_0} \times 100 \text{ is the price realtive}$$

Remarks:

1. The weights generally used are the values of the items at the base year

$$w = p_0 q_0$$

2. Sometimes current year values are also used as weights. In such cases

$$w = p_1 q_1$$

3. Note that when base year values are used as weights to calculate the weighted arithmetic mean of price relatives, the result is identical to the index number as calculated by Laspeyre's formula.

8. From the following data computer price index by the weighted average of relatives using:

(a) arithmetic mean

(b) geometric mean

Commodity	Price in base year (Rs.)	Price in current year (Rs.)	Quantity used
Sugar	3.00	4.00	20 kg
Flour	1.50	1.60	40 kg
Milk	1.00	1.50	10 lt

SOLUTION:

(i) Calculation of the weighted arithmetic mean of price relatives

Commodity	Price in base year p_0	Price in current year p_1	Quantity in base year q_0	Price relative $P = \frac{p_1}{p_0} \times 100$	Weights $w = p_0\, q_0$	wP
Sugar	3.00	4.00	20	133.333	60	8000
Flour	1.50	1.60	40	106.667	60	6400
Milk	1.00	1.50	10	150.000	10	1500
					$\sum w = 130$	$\sum wP = 15900$

$$\text{Now,} \quad P_{01} = \frac{\sum wp}{\sum w}$$

$$= \frac{15900}{130}$$

$$\text{i.e.,} \quad \boxed{P_{01} = 122.3077}$$

(ii) Calculation of weighted geometric mean price relatives

Commodities	p_0	p_1	q_0	$P = \frac{p_1}{p_0} \times 100$	$\log P$	$w = p_0\, q_0$	$w\log P$
Sugar	3.00	4.00	20	133.333	2.1249	60	127.4914
Flour	1.50	1.60	40	106.667	2.0282	60	121.692
Milk	1.00	1.50	10	150.000	2.1761	10	21.761
						$\sum w = 130$	$\sum w\log P = 270.947$

$$\text{Now} \quad P_{01} = \text{Antilog}\left[\frac{\sum w \log P}{\sum w}\right]$$

$$= \text{Antilog}\left[\frac{270.947}{130}\right]$$

$$= \text{Antilog } 2.084$$

$$\boxed{P_{01} = 120.9}$$

Check!

Price Index by Laspeyre's method

Commodity	p_0	p_1	q_0	$p_0 q_0$	$p_1 q_0$
Sugar	3.00	4.00	20	60	80
Flour	1.50	1.60	40	60	64
Milk	1.00	1.50	10	10	15
				$\sum p_0 q_0 = 130$	$\sum p_1 q_0 = 159$

$$P_{01} = \frac{\sum p_1 q_0}{\sum p_0 q_0} \times 100$$

$$= \frac{159}{130} \times 100$$

$$\boxed{P_{01} = 122.3077}$$

9. A large manufacturer purchases a particular component from three different vendors that differ in unit price and quantity supplied. The relevant data for 2009 and 2010 are given below:

Supplier	Quantity in 2009	Unit Prices (Rs.)	
		2009	2010
A	10	15	16
B	40	12	14
C	20	18	20

Calculate the weighted average of price relative index by using: (a) arithmetic mean and (b) geometric mean.

SOLUTION:

(i) Calculation of weight arithmetic mean of twice relatives

Supplier	quantity q_0	Price in 2009 p_0	Price in 2010 p_1	Price relative $P = \frac{p_1}{p_0} \times 100$	Weights $w = p_0 q_0$	wP
A	10	15	16	106.67	150	39,999.60
B	40	12	14	116.67	480	56,0001.60
C	20	18	20	111.11	360	16,000.50
					$\sum w = 990$	$\sum w\ P =$ 1, 12, 001.70

$$\text{Now,} \quad P_{01} = \frac{\sum wp}{\sum wP}$$

$$= \frac{1,12,001.70}{990}$$

$$\boxed{P_{01} = 113.13}$$

(ii) Calculation of weighted geometric mean of price relatives

Supplier	q_0	p_0	p_1	$w = p_0\, q_0$	$P = \frac{p_1}{p_0} \times 100$	$\log P$	$w \log P$
A	10	18	16	150	106.67	2.028	304.20
B	40	12	14	480	116.67	2.067	992.16
C	20	18	20	360	111.11	2.046	736.56
				$\sum w = 990$			$\sum w \log P$ = 2032.92

$$\text{Now} \quad P_{01} = \text{Antilog}\left[\frac{\sum w \log P}{\sum w}\right]$$

$$= \text{Antilog}\left[\frac{2032.92}{990}\right] = \text{antilog } 2.0535$$

$$\boxed{P_{01} = 113.11}$$

TESTS OF ADEQUACY FOR INDEX NUMBER FORMULAE

Among the various index number formulae, it is difficult to select the most appropriate one. Various adequacy tests have been suggested. A few of them are:

(i) Unit test

(ii) Time reversal test (TRT)

(iii) Factor reversal test (FRT)

(iv) Circular test.

1. Unit Test

The unit test requires that the formula for construction an index should be independent of the units in which prices and quantities are quoted. All index number formulae except the simple aggregative index satisfy this test.

2. Time Reversal Test (TRT)

According to Prof. Irving Fisher, who proposed this test, an index number should be such that when the base year and current year are reversed (interchanged), the resulting index number should be reciprocal of the original index number.

The time reversal test requires that the index number computed backwards should be the reciprocal of the index number computed forwards, except for the constant of proportionality.
Symbolically,

$$\boxed{P_{0n} \times P_{no} = 1}$$

where P_{0n} = Index number for period n with base period 0

P_{n0} = index number for period 0 with base period n.

The following five index number formulae satisfy time reversal test:

(a) The Fisher's ideal index number

(b) Simple geometric mean of place relatives

(c) Aggregative indices with fixed weights

(d) The weighted geometric mean of price relatives if we use fixed weights

(e) Marshall-Edgeworth index formula.

3. Factor Reversal Test (FRT)

According to this test, also proposed by Prof. Irving Fisher, the index number formula should be such that the price index and quantity index computed accordingly to the formula should be equally effective in indicating changes.

Factor reversal test requires that the product of the index number of prices (with quantities as weights) and the index number of quantity (with prices as weights) should indicate net change in value taking place in between the two periods.

Symbolically

$$P_{01} \times Q_{01} = \frac{\sum p_1 q_1}{\sum p_0 q_0}$$

where P_{01} and Q_{01} are price and quantity index numbers. Note that here P_{01} and Q_{01} are mere ratio — they should not be expressed as percentages.

Fisher's ideal index number formula is the only one to satisfy this test.

4. Circular Test

This test is an extension of the time reversal test. The test requires that if an index is constructed for the year '*a*' with base year '*b*' and for the year '*b*' with base year '*c*', we ought to get the same result

Symbolically

$$P_{01} \times P_{12} = P_{02}$$

$$\text{or} \quad P_{01} \times P_{12} \times P_{20} = 1 \quad \left(\text{notice that } P_{20} = \frac{1}{P_{02}}\right)$$

where P_{01}, P_{12}, P_{02} and P_{20} are price indices with three periods 0, 1 and 2.

Index number formulae that satisfy the circularity test are:

(i) Simple aggregative index number

(ii) Fixed weight aggregative index number.

10. Show that.

(i) Laspeyre's index number does not satisfy time reversal test.

(ii) Paasche's index number does not satisfy factor reversal test.

(iii) Fisher's index number satisfies both time reversal and factor reversal test.

SOLUTION:

Laspeyre's index number for period 1 with respect to base period 0 is

$$P_{01} = \frac{\sum p_1 q_0}{\sum p_0 q_0} \tag{1}$$

Laspeyre's index number for period 0 with respect to base period 1 is

$$P_{10} = \frac{\sum p_0 q_1}{\sum p_1 q_1} \tag{2}$$

Note that the factor 100 is left out in both cases. Now, the time reversal test requires that

$$P_{01} \times P_{10} = 1$$

Substituting (1) and (2) in the above we get

$$\frac{\sum p_1 q_0}{\sum p_0 q_0} \times \frac{\sum p_0 q_1}{\sum p_1 q_1} \neq 1$$

Hence, Laspeyre's index number does not satisfy time reversal test.

(ii) Paasche's price index number is

$$P_{01} = \frac{\sum p_1 q_1}{\sum p_0 q_1}$$

Paasche's quantity index number is

$$Q_{01} = \frac{\sum q_1 p_1}{\sum q_0 p_1}$$

The factor reversal test requires that

$$P_{01} \times Q_{01} = \frac{\sum p_1 q_1}{\sum p_0 q_0}$$

Here

$$P_{01} \times Q_{01} = \frac{\sum p_1 q_1}{\sum p_0 q_1} \times \frac{\sum p_1 q_1}{\sum q_0 p_1} \neq \frac{\sum p_1 q_1}{\sum p_0 q_0}$$

Hence, Paasche's index number does not satisfy factor reversal test.

(iii) TRT for Fisher's index number

The Fisher's index number is

$$P_{01} = \sqrt{\frac{\sum p_1 q_0}{\sum p_0 q_0} \times \frac{\sum p_1 q_1}{\sum p_0 q_1}}$$

Fisher's index number with time reversed is

$$P_{10} = \sqrt{\frac{\sum p_0 q_1}{\sum p_1 q_1} \times \frac{\sum p_0 q_0}{\sum p_1 q_0}}$$

Now, the time reversal test requires that

$$P_{01} \times P_{10} = 1$$

i.e., $$\sqrt{\frac{\Sigma p_1 q_0}{\Sigma p_0 q_0} \times \frac{\Sigma p_1 q_1}{\Sigma p_0 q_1}} \times \sqrt{\frac{\Sigma p_0 q_1}{\Sigma p_1 q_1} \times \frac{\Sigma p_0 q_0}{\Sigma p_1 q_0}} = 1$$

Thus, Fisher's index number satisfies time reversal test.

FRT for Fishers Index Number

Fisher's price index no. is

$$P_{01} = \sqrt{\frac{\Sigma p_1 q_0}{\Sigma p_0 q_0} \times \frac{\Sigma p_1 q_1}{\Sigma p_0 q_1}}$$

Fisher's quantity index no. is

$$Q_{01} = \sqrt{\frac{\Sigma q_1 p_0}{\Sigma q_0 p_0} \times \frac{\Sigma q_1 p_1}{\Sigma q_0 q_1}}$$

Now, the FRT requires that

$$P_{01} \times Q_{01} = \frac{\Sigma p_1 q_1}{\Sigma p_0 q_0}$$

$$\sqrt{\frac{\Sigma p_1 q_0}{\Sigma p_1 q_0} \times \frac{\Sigma p_1 q_1}{\Sigma p_0 q_1}} \times \sqrt{\frac{\Sigma q_1 p_0}{\Sigma q_0 p_0} \times \frac{\Sigma q_1 p_1}{\Sigma q_0 p_1}} = \frac{\Sigma p_1 q_1}{\Sigma p_0 q_0}$$

Thus, Fisher's index number satisfy FRT.

CONSUMER PRICE INDEX

Cost of Living Index Numbers Retail Price Index

Consumer price index numbers are special purpose index numbers that are intended to represent the average change over time in the prices paid by the ultimate consumer of a specified basket of goods and services.

The need for constructing consumer price index arrives because the general price indexes fail to explain the effects of rise or fall in prices of various commodities consumed by different classes of people on their cost of living. This is because different classes of people consume different types of commodities, that too in varying proportions. For example, the consumption pattern of a household belonging to the rich class will be different from a household belonging to the middle class. Also the consumption pattern of a middle class household from say, Delhi would be different from the consumption pattern of a middle class household in Bangalore.

Clearly one single cost of living index (CLI) cannot be constructed for the entire nation. Hence, cost of living indices (CLI) are constructed separately for different classes of people.

USES OF CONSUMER PRICE INDEX NUMBERS

The importance of CPI is due to its many uses as listed below:

(i) The CPI is used to formulate economic policies regarding control of prices, taxation, imports and export of commodities.

(ii) The CPI is used to measure the purchasing power of consumers in rupees. The purchasing power of the rupee is the value of one rupee in a given year as compared to a base year. It is calculated using the formula,

$$\text{Purchasing power} = \frac{1}{CPI} \times 100$$

(iii) CPI is used to deflate timeseries of values expressed in rupees such as retail sales amounts, wages rates, etc. For example, to deflate a time series on wage rates, we would use the following formula

$$\text{Real wage} = \frac{\text{Money value}}{\text{Consumer price index}} \times 100$$

(iv) CPI is commonly used in wage negotiations and wage contracts. Automatic adjustments or increments of wages or dearness allowance components of wages are governed in many countries by these indices.

CONSTRUCTION OF A CONSUMER PRICE INDEX

Remember that CPI is a weighted aggregate price index with fixed weights. The percentage of expenditure on different commodities by an average family constitutes the individual weights. The percentage of expenditure is considered for the five well-accepted groups of commodities or services, namely,

- Food
- Clothing
- Fuel and lighting
- House rent
- Miscellaneous

The weight applied to each commodity in the market basket is derived from the usage survey of families throughout the country. The consumer price index (or cost of living index) numbers are constructed by the following two methods.

(a) Aggregate expenditure method or weighted aggregate method.

(b) Family budget method or method of weighted average of prices relatives.

AGGREGATE EXPENDITURE METHOD OR WEIGHTED AGGREGATE METHOD

This method is similar to Laspeyre's method of constructing a weighted aggregate price index. The weights used are the base year quantities of various commodities used by that particular class of people. The formula is

$$\text{Consumer price index} = \frac{\text{Total expenditure in the current period}}{\text{Total expenditure in the base period}} \times 100$$

$$\text{i.e.,} \quad \boxed{\text{CPI} = \frac{\sum p_1 q_0}{\sum p_0 q_0} \times 100}$$

where p_1 and p_0 = prices in the current and base period respectively

and q_0 = quantities used in the base period

FAMILY BUDGET METHOD OR METHOD OF WEIGHTED AVERAGE OF PRICE RELATIVES

When this method is applied, family budgets of a large number of people for whom the index is meant are collected and carefully studied. The aggregate expenditure of an average family on various commodities are then estimated. These constitute the weights. Note that these weights would be values $(p_o q_o)$ of various commodities. Then,the CPI is calculated by using the weighted average of price relatives. Symbolically,

$$\text{Consumer price index} = \frac{\sum PV}{\sum V}$$

where $P = \frac{p_1}{p_0} \times 10$ the price relative for each commodity

and $V = p_0 q_0$ = weights for each commodity

Remarks: The CPI would be the same when either of the methods is used.

11. Construct the cost of living index number for 2002 taking 2000 as base year using:

(a) Aggregate expenditure method

(b) Family budget method.

Commodity	Qty consume	unit	Price in 2000 (Rs.)	Price in 2002 (Rs.)
Wheat	20	kg	12.50	15.00
Rice	6	kg	15.00	19.00
Gram	5	kg	30.00	32.00
Pulses	8	kg	25.00	30.00
Ghee	2	kg	40.00	60.00
Sugar	10	kg	15.00	12.00
House rent	1	House	500.00	600.00

SOLUTION:

(a) CPI by aggregate expenditure method

$$\text{CPI} = \frac{\sum p_1 q_0}{\sum p_0 q_0} \times 100$$

Commodity	q_0 (qty consumed)	p_0 price in 2000	p_1 price in 2002	$p_0 q_0$	$p_1 q_0$
Wheat	20	12.50	15.00	250	300
Rice	6	15.00	19.00	90	114
Gram	5	30.00	32.00	150	160
Pulses	8	25.00	30.00	200	240
Ghee	2	40.00	60.00	80	120
Sugar	10	15.00	12.00	150	120
House rent	1	500.00	600.00	500	600
				$\sum p_0 q_0 = 1420$	$\sum p_1 q_0 = 1650$

$$\text{CPI} = \frac{\sum p_1 q_0}{\sum p_0 q_0} \times 100$$

$$= \frac{1650}{1420} \times 100$$

$$\boxed{\text{CPI} = 116.4789}$$

(b) CPI by family budget method

$$\text{CPI} = \frac{\sum PV}{\sum V}$$

$$\text{where} \quad P = \frac{p_1}{p_0} \times 100$$

$$V = p_0 q_0$$

Commodity	q_0	p_0	p_1	$V = p_0 q_0$	$p = \frac{p_1}{p_0} \times 100$	PV
Wheat	20	12.50	15.00	250	120.00	30000
Rice	6	15.00	19.00	90	126.667	11400
Gram	5	30.00	32.00	150	106.667	16000
Pulses	8	25.00	30.00	200	120.00	24000
Ghee	2	40.00	60.00	80	150.00	12000
Sugar	10	15.00	12.00	150	80.00	12000
House rent	1	500.00	600.00	500	120.00	60000
				$\Sigma V = 1420$		$\Sigma PV = 165400$

$$\text{CPI} = \frac{\Sigma PV}{\Sigma V}$$

$$= \frac{165400}{1420}$$

$$\therefore \quad \text{CPI} = 116.4789$$

(Note that the answer by either of the methods is the same.)

12. An enquiry into the budget of middle class families in Mumbai gave the following information:

Expenses on	**Food 35%**	**Rent 15%**	**Clothing 20%**	**Fuel 10%**	**Miscellaneous 20%**
Price in 2000 (Rs.)	150	50	100	20	60
Price in 2003 (Rs.)	174	60	125	25	90

What changes have taken place in the CPI for 2003 as compared to 2002?

SOLUTION:

Since weightages of various items are given, let us use the family budget method to construct CPI.

$$\text{CPI} = \frac{\sum PV}{\sum V}$$

$$\text{where} \quad P = \frac{p_1}{p_0} \times 100$$

$$\text{and} \quad V = \text{Weightages given.}$$

Item	p_0	p_1	V = Weightages	$P = \frac{p_1}{p_0} \times 100$	PV
Food	150	174	35	116	4060
Rent	50	60	15	120	1800
Clothing	100	125	20	125	2500
Fuel	20	25	10	125	1250
Misc	60	90	20	150	3000
			$\sum V = 100$		$\sum PV = 12610$

$$\text{CPI} = \frac{\sum PV}{\sum V}$$

$$= \frac{12160}{100}$$

$$\boxed{\text{CPI} = 126.1}$$

Hence, there is an increase of 26.1% in the cost of living in 2003 as compared to 2002.

13. The annual wages (Rs.) of workers are given along with consumer price indices. Find:

(i) The real wages

(ii) The real wage indices.

Year	2006	2007	2008	2009
Wages	1,800	2,200	3,400	3,600
CPI	100	170	300	320

SOLUTION:

Year	**Wages**	**CPI**	**Real wages** $= \frac{\textbf{Wages}}{\textbf{CPI}} \times 100$	**Real wage Indices 2006 = 100**
2006	1800	100	$\frac{1800}{100} \times 100 = 1800$	100
2007	2200	170	$\frac{2200}{170} \times 100 = 1294.1$	$\frac{1294.1}{1800} \times 100 = 71.89$
2008	3400	300	1,133.3	94.44
2009	3600	320	1,125.0	62.50

14. Construct consumer price index number for the following data by

(i) Aggregate expenditure method

(ii) Family budget method

Commodities	**Unit**	**Qty consumed in 2000**	**Price per unit**	
			2000	**2010**
L	Quintal	5 quintals	1200	1800
M	kg	25 kg	20	25
N	litre	20 litre	20	30
O	meter	25 meter	50	45
P	Unit	20 unit	100	200

SOLUTION:

CPI using aggregate expenditure method.

Commodity	q_0	p_0	p_1	p_0q_0	p_1q_0
L	5	1200	1800	6000	9000
M	25	20	25	500	625
N	20	20	30	400	600
O	25	50	45	1250	1125
P	20	100	200	2000	4000
				$\Sigma p_0q_0 = 10150$	$\Sigma p_1q_0 = 15350$

$$\text{CPI} = \frac{\sum p_1 q_0}{\sum p_0 q_0} \times 100$$

$$= \frac{15350}{10150} \times 100 = 151.23$$

(b) CPI using family budget method.

Commodity	q_0	p_0	p_1	$V = p_0 q_0$	$P = \frac{p_1}{p_0} \times 100$	PV
L	5	1200	1800	6000	133.33	900000
M	25	20	25	500	125.00	62500
N	20	20	30	400	133.33	60000
O	25	50	45	1250	90.00	112500
P	20	100	200	2000	200.00	400000
				$\sum V = 10150$		$\sum PV = 1535000$

$$\text{CPI} = \frac{\sum PV}{\sum V}$$

$$= \frac{1535000}{10150}$$

$$\boxed{\text{CPI} = 151.23}$$

15. A textile worker earns Rs. 350 per month.The cost of living index for that particular month is 136. Using the following data find the amount spent by him on house rent and clothing.

Group	Expenditure	Group index
Food	140	180
Clothing	x	150
House rent	y	100
Fuel	56	110
Miscellaneous	63	80

SOLUTION:

Note that expenditure = value = p_0q_0 and group index is the price relative $P = \frac{p_1}{p_0} \times 100$.

Hence, the above data can be written as

Group	V	P	PV
Food	140	180	25200
Clothing	x	150	$150x$
House rent	y	100	$100y$
Fuel	56	110	6160
Misc	63	80	5040
	$\sum V = 259 + x + y$		$\sum PV = 36400 + 150x + 100y$

$$\text{Given} \quad \text{CPI} = 136$$

$$\text{Wkt} \quad \text{CPI} = \frac{\sum PV}{\sum V}$$

$$\text{i.e.,} \quad 136 = \frac{36400 + 150x + 100y}{259 + x + y}$$

Also, the textile worker earns Rs. 350.

$$\text{i.e.,} \quad \sum V = 350$$

$$\text{i.e.,} \quad 259 + x + y = 350$$

$$\text{i.e.,} \quad x + y = 91 \qquad (1)$$

$$\text{Also,} \quad 136 = \frac{36400 + 150x + 100y}{350}$$

$$\text{i.e.,} \quad 47600 = 36400 + 150x + 100y$$

$$\text{i.e.,} \quad 150x + 100y = 11200 \qquad (2)$$

Solving (1) and (2) simultaneously, we get

$$150x + 100y = 11200$$

$$100x + 100y = 9100$$

$$- \quad - \quad -$$

$$50x = 2100$$

$$x = \frac{2100}{50} = 42$$

Substituting $x = 42$ in 1 we get

$$x + y = 91$$

$$\text{i.e.,} \quad 42 + y = 91$$

$$y = 91 - 42 = 49$$

Thus, the worker spends Rs. 42 on clothing and Rs. 49 on house rent.

IN A NUTSHELL

- An index number is a percentage ratio of prices, quantities or values comparing two time periods or two points in time.
- There are four different types of index numbers. (i) price (ii) quantity (iii) value and (iv) special purpose index numbers.
- Index numbers act as economic barometers, help policy making, help establish trends, determine purchasing power and help deflate time series data.
- There are two approaches for constructing an index number:

  (i) The aggregate method (simple and weighted)

  (ii) The average of relatives (simple and weighted).
- Different weights used by different statisticians have given rise to different formulae in weighted aggregates method (like Marshall Edgeworth, Laspeyrie's, Paasche's, Fisher's etc).
- Unity test, time reversal test, factor reversal test and circularity test are a few adequacy tests for an index number.
- Consumer price index (CPI) or cost of living index are special purpose indices used to measure the average change over time in the prices paid by the ultimate consumer of specified basket of goods and services. They are constructed by either.

  (i) Aggregate expenditure method or

  (ii) Family budget method.

CHECK YOUR PROGRESS

1. What are index numbers?
2. What are the uses of index numbers?
3. Why are index numbers called the economic barometers?
4. Which are the different types of index numbers?
5. Explain the steps involved in the construction of index numbers.
6. How are index numbers constructed? Explain the different methods.
7. Mention some tests of adequacy for index numbers.
8. Why is Fisher's index number called the ideal index number?
9. Explain time reversal test (TRT).
10. Explain factor reversal test (FRT).
11. What are consumer price indices? Explain why there is a need for them?
12. What are base and current periods in the context of index numbers?
13. Explain circular test. Why is it used?
14. What is unit test?
15. Mention the methods of constructing cost of living index number.
16. What are the uses of CPI?

PROBLEMS

1. From the following data construct an index for 2005 taking 2004 as base:

Commodity	Price in 2004	Price in 2005
Rice	90	105
Wheat	70	85
Tea	40	55
Coffee	20	60
Sugar	60	70

[Ans. 133.92]

2. Compute price index number for the following data using simple average of price relatives by:

Arithmetic mean	*A*	*B*	*C*	*D*	*E*
Prices in 2001	10	20	5	2	7
Prices in 2002	16	21	6	3	14

[Ans. $P_{01} = 147$]

3. From the following data calculate index number using price relatives method:

Commodity	Price in 2009	Price in 2010
L	100	140
M	80	120
N	160	180
O	220	240
P	40	40

[**Ans.** $P_{01} = 122.3$]

4. From the data given below compute quantity index number:

Commodity	Quantity		Price in 2010
	2009	2010	
L	30	25	30
M	20	30	40
N	10	15	20

[**Ans.** $Q_{01} = 118.42$]

5. Compute by Fisher's index formula the quantity index from the data given below:

	2009		2010	
Commodity	Price	Total value	Price	Total value
A	10	100	8	96
B	16	96	14	98
C	12	36	10	40

[**Ans.** $Q_{01} = 120.65$]

6. For the following data, construct:

   (i) Laspeyre's index

   (ii) Paasche's index

   (iii) Durbish-Bowky's index

   (iv) Fisher's index

   (v) Marshall-Edgeworth

Commodity	2009		2010	
	Price	Quantity	Price	Quantity
A	5	100	6	150
B	4	80	5	100
C	2.5	60	5	72
D	12.0	30	9	33

$$\left[\begin{array}{ll}\textbf{Ans.} & P_L = 118.05 \\ & P_P = 119.18 \\ & P_{PB} = 118.61 \\ & P_F = 118.61 \\ & P_{ME} = 118.68\end{array}\right]$$

7. From the following data compute price index by using weighted average of price relatives. Use. (i) Arithmetic mean and (ii) Geometric mean to show the difference between them.

Commodity	Base year price	Base year quantity	Current year price
Wheat	2 per kg	5 kg	3 per kg
Milk	1 per litre	2 litres	2 per liter
Eggs	3 per dozen	1 dozen	4 per dozen

$$\left[\begin{array}{ll}\textbf{Ans.} & \text{By A.M } P_{01} = 153.33 \\ & \text{By G.M } P_{01} = 152.1\end{array}\right]$$

8. Calculate Fisher's index from the following data and show that it satisfies both TRT and FRT tests.

Commodity	Base year price	Base year value	Current year value	Current year quantity
A	35	280	300	25
B	18	114	220	22
C	20	160	250	10
D	8	108	140	7
E	10	200	300	10

$$\left[\begin{array}{ll}\textbf{Ans.} & P_{01} = 109.552 \\ & P_{01} \times Q_{01} = \dfrac{\sum p_1q_1}{\sum p_0q_0} = \dfrac{1210}{892}\end{array}\right]$$

9. Construct Fisher's index and show that it satisfies both time and factor reversibility tests.

Commodity	Base year		Current year	
	Price	Quantity	Price	Quantity
A	8	5	20	26
B	2	15	6	10
C	1	20	2	25
D	2	10	5	8
E	1	40	3	30

$$\left[\textbf{Ans.}\quad P_{01} = 260.34 \quad \frac{\sum p_1 q_1}{\sum p_0 q_0} = \frac{760}{150}\right]$$

10. Construct cost of living indices for 2002 and 2003 from the following indices, the weights being food 55, clothing 15, Rent 20, fuel and lighting 15 and miscellaneous 5.

Year	Food	Rent	Clothing	*F & L*	Misc
2000	100	100	100	100	100
2001	105	104	98	100	110
2002	110	112	102	101	115
2003	112	115	105	103	120

$$\left[\begin{array}{ll}\textbf{Ans.}\quad CPI\ (2002) & = 108.27 \\ \quad\quad CPI\ (2003) & = 110.73\end{array}\right]$$

11. It is stated that Marshall-Edgeworth's index is a good approximation to the Fisher's ideal index number. Verify using the following data:

Commodity	2009		2010	
	Price	Qty	Price	Qty
A	2	74	3	82
B	5	125	4	140
C	7	40	6	33

$$\left[\begin{array}{ll}\textbf{Ans.}\quad P_{01\ (ME)} & = 91.53 \\ \quad\quad P_{01\ (F)} & = 91.523\end{array}\right]$$

12

Time Series Analysis

INTRODUCTION

It is very important for any business organisation to predict the key decision variables in today's increasingly competitive world. Generally, planning of economic and business activities of an organisation are based on predictions of production, demand, sales, etc. This is usually done by a detailed study of the historical data. Thus, for example, future demand for a particular product can be predicted fairly by studying the variations in the demand for that product for the last few years. Now, such a series of observations of demand for that product recorded, say, every month is called time series.

A series of observations of a phenomenon recorded at successive points in time is called time series. In other words, time series is a *chronological* arrangement of statistical data regarding the phenomenon.

DEFINITIONS OF TIME SERIES

1. "A time series is a set of statistical observations arranged in chronological order."

   —*Morris Hamburg*

2. "A time series consists of statistical data which are collected, recorded and observed over successive increments of time."

   —*Patterson*

3. "A time series may be defined as a collection of magnitudes belonging to different time periods, of some variable or composite of variables, such as production of steel, per capita income, gross national product, price of tobacco, or index of industrial production."

   —*Ya-Lun-Chou*

4. "When quantitative data are arranged in the order of their occurrence, the resulting statistical series is called a time series."

—*Wessel & Wellet*

5. "A time series is a set of observations taken at specified times, usually at 'equal intervals'. Mathematically, a time series is defined by the values $Y_1, Y_2, \ldots$ of a variable Y (temperature, closing price of a share, etc.) at times $t_1, t_2, \ldots$. Thus Y is a function of t symbolised by $Y = F(t)$."

—*Spiegel*

Usually, in a line series equidistant points of time are considered. These time points may vary from as little as per second to as big as every millenium

Time points	Phenomenon observed
Century	Migration
Decade	Population
Year	Production
Quarterly	Bank deposits
Monthly	Exports
Daily	Stock price

A graphical presentation of a time series is called historigram (not to be confused with **histogram**).

The problem of time series analysis can be best appreciated with the help of the following example. The following are the figures of sales of air-conditioners of a company in thousand units.

Year	2000	2001	2002	2003	2004	2005	2006	2007	2008
Sales ('000)	80	82	87	81	83	88	105	90	94

If we observe the above series we find that generally sales have increased, but for one year a decline is also noticed. A time series analysis, therefore tries to analyse the effect of various forces under four broad heads.

(i) *Secular movements (trend):* Changes that have occurred as a result of general tendency of the data to increase or decrease.

(ii) *Seasonal variation:* Changes that have taken place during a period of 12 months as a result of change in climate, weather conditions, festivals, etc.

(iii) *Cyclical variation:* Changes that have taken place as a result of boom and depression of the general economy.

(iv) *Irregular variation:* Changes that have taken place as a result of one-off incidents that cannot be predicted like war, floods, famine, etc.

The above are called the components of time series. An analytical study of different components of a time series, the effects of these components, etc., is called analysis of time series.

MEASUREMENT OF TREND

Given any long term time series, a basic question arises as whether it is increasing, decreasing or remaining constant. For this, we have various methods of measuring trend, that include:

(i) Free hand or graphic method

(ii) Semi average method

(iii) Moving average method

(iv) The least squares method

Free Hand or Graphic Method

This is the simplest of the method to determine trend. This method consists of the following steps.

1. Plot the historigram (i.e., plot the time series with time points along X-axis and variable values on the Y axis)
2. Draw a straight line which will best fit the plotted points according to your personal judgement.

The line now shows the direction of the trend.

SOLVED EXAMPLES

1. Determine the trend using the free hand method for the following time series.

Year	2000	2001	2002	2003	2004	2005
Sales (in ’000)	40	42	44	41	43	45
Year	2006	2007	2008	2009	2010	
Sales (in ’000)	43	46	45	48	46	

SOLUTION:

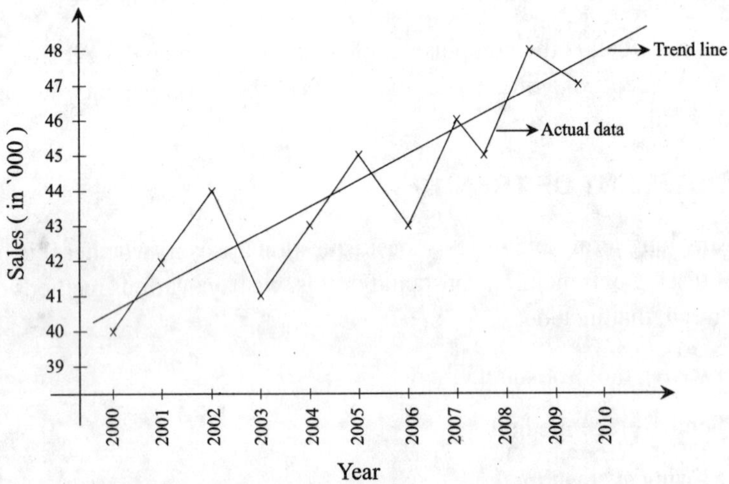

It is clear from the graph that there is an *upward* trend.

Merits and demerits of graphical method (Free hand method)

Merits

1. This is the simplest method of measuring trend.
2. This method is very flexible. It can be used for both linear and non-linear trends.
3. This is a very useful method for seasoned and experienced statisticians.

Demerits

1. This method is highly subjective because the trend line depends on the judgment of the investigator.
2. Since the method is subjective, it cannot be used for predictions.

Method of Semi Averages

In this method, the given time series in divided into two parts. Averages (arithmetic means) are found for both parts. These two averages are then plotted against the middle time points of the respective time period groups. These two points are then joined by a straight line to determine trend.

Remark: When we have even number of time points it is straight forward to divide them into two halves, In case of odd number of time points, two equal parts can be made by simply omitting the middle time point.

2. Fit a trend line by the method of semi-averages.

Year	2004	2005	2006	2007	2008	2009
Production (in '000 units)	82	85	94	90	98	100

SOLUTION:

Year	Production	Semi-Average
2004	82	
2005	85	$\frac{82+85+94}{3}=87$
2006	94	
2007	90	
2008	98	$\frac{90+98+100}{3}=96$
2009	100	

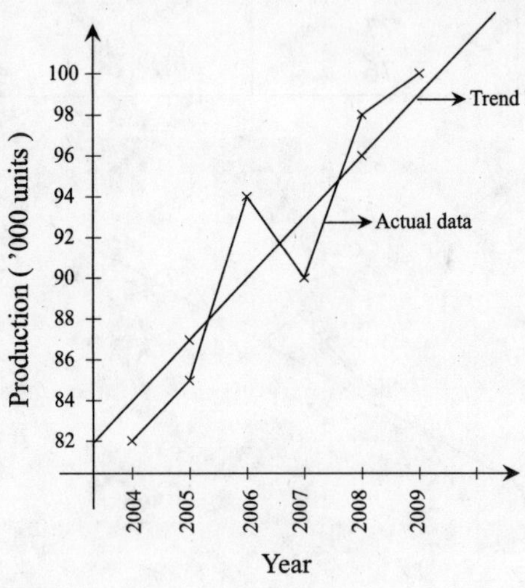

Remark: Note that the average of the first group 87 is plotted against the middle time period 2005. And the average of the second group 96 is plotted against the middle time period of the second group 2008. From the graph there is an upward trend.

3. Fit a straight line trend using the method of semi averages for the following data.

Year	2001	2002	2003	2004	2005	2006	2007	2008	2009
Advertising expenditure (in lakhs of Rs.)	62	68	65	70	72	75	73	77	76

SOLUTION:

Year	Ad. expenditure	Semi-average
2001	62	
2002	68	
	→	$\frac{62+68+65+70}{4} = 66.28$
2003	65	
2004	70	
2005	72	
2006	75	
2007	73	
	→	$\frac{75+73+77+76}{4} = 75.25$
2008	77	
2009	76	

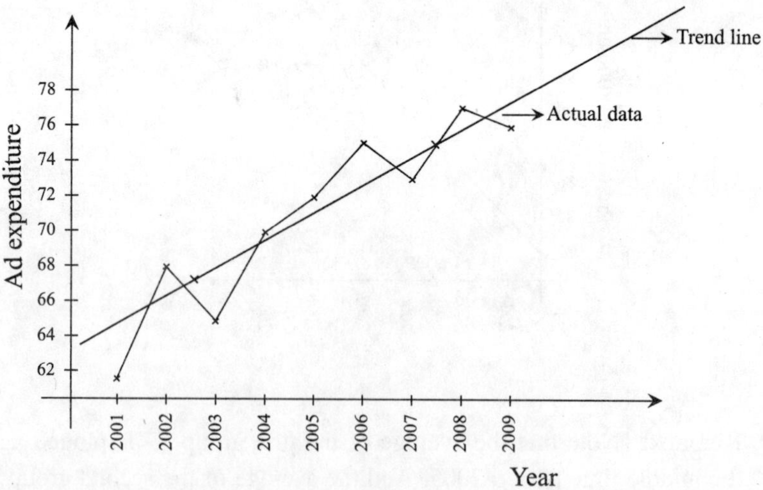

There is an upward trend

Merits and demerits of Methods of Semi-averages

Merits

(1) The method is simple as compared to the methods of moving averages and least squares.

(2) This is an objective method.

Demerits

(i) This method assumes a straight line trend regardless of the fact that a non-linear trend might exist.

(ii) The limitations of arithmetic mean are automatically transferred to this method. For example, if there is extreme value in either half of the time series, the tread is miscalculated.

Method of Moving Averages

In this method, moving averages are used to eliminate the short time variations. If the time series shows variations with period '*m*' (it could be seasonal or cyclical variation), moving averages with period *m* are obtained. These moving averages indicate the trend.

If $y_1, y_2, y_3, \ldots, y_n$ are the observations and if '*m*' is the period, the successive moving average are

$$\frac{y_1 + y_2 + \cdots y_m}{m}, \quad \frac{y_2 + y_3 + \cdots + y_{m+1}}{m}, \quad \frac{y_3 + y_4 + \cdots + y_{m+2}}{m}, \text{ etc.}$$

Note that *m* could be either odd or even.

When m is odd

Here the first moving average is the average of the first *m* observations. It is written against the middlemost time point of the first *m* time points. For example, if $m = 3$ the first moving average is the average of the first three observations. It is written against the second time point (the middle most of the first, second and the third time points).

The second moving average is found by deleting the first observation and including the $(m+1)^{\text{th}}$ observation and so on.

When m is even

Here a procedure called 'centring' is used. The first part of finding the moving average remains the same as in the case of odd period. But since the problem of writing it against which time point arises, centring of averages is done. This is done by finding the average of two *m* period moving averages. This procedure is illustrated in the solved example 6.5.

4. Compute the trend values by finding three yearly moving average of the following time series.

Year	2003	2004	2005	2006	2007	2008	2009
Population (in millions)	512	538	546	554	570	583	590

SOLUTION:

Here $m = 3$ is an odd number. We find the moving averages by first finding the moving totals and then dividing these moving totals by $m = 3$ as shown in the following table.

Year	**Population (in million)**	**3-yearly moving sums**	**3-yearly moving averages or trend values (in millions)**
2003	512	—	
2004	538	1596	532.00
2005	546	1638	546.00
2006	554	1670	556.67
2007	570	1707	569.00
2008	583	1743	581.00
2009	590	—	

Clearly, there is an upward trend.

5. Compute the trend values by taking a four yearly moving average.

Year	**Value**	**Year**	**Value**
1990	12	1997	100
1991	25	1998	82
1992	39	1999	65
1993	54	2000	49
1994	70	2001	34
1995	87	2002	20
1996	105	2003	7

[M.Com. Madras Univ.]

SOLUTION:

Here $m = 4$ is even. Hence, we use the procedure of centring as follows.

Year	Values	4-Year moving total	4-Year moving average	4-Year centred moving average or trend values
1990	12	—	—	—
1991	25	—	—	—
		← 130	32.5	
1992	39			← 39.75
		← 188	47.0	
1993	54			← 54.75
		← 250	62.5	
1994	70			← 70.75
		← 316	79.0	
1995	87			← 84.75
		← 362	90.5	
1996	105			← 92.00
		← 374	93.5	
1997	100			← 90.75
		← 352	88.0	
1998	82			← 81.00
		← 296	74.0	
1999	65			← 65.75
		← 230	57.5	
2000	49			← 49.75
		← 168	42.0	
2001	34			← 34.75
		← 110	27.5	
2002	20	—	—	—
2003	7	—	—	—

Clearly, the time series shows a downward trend.

6. Calculate 5-yearly moving averages for the following data regarding sales (in lakh rupees).

Year	Sales
2000	1100
2001	1040
2002	980
2003	1050
2004	1090
2005	1200
2006	1150
2007	1100
2008	1140
2009	1220
2010	1300
2011	1270

SOLUTION:

Year	Values	5-Year moving total	5-Year moving average or trend values
2000	1100	—	—
2001	1040	—	—
2002	980	5260	1052
2003	1050	5360	1072
2004	1090	5470	1094
2005	1200	5590	1118
2006	1150	5680	1136
2007	1100	5810	1162
2008	1140	5910	1182
2009	1220	6070	1214
2010	1300	—	—
2011	1270	—	—

Clearly there is an upward trend.

7. Use 2-yearly moving averages to find the trend.

Year	Value
1	142
2	137
3	128
4	133
5	134
6	133
7	130

SOLUTION:
Here $M = 2$, an even number.

Year	Value	2-Year moving total	2-Year moving average	Centred 2-Year moving average or trend value
1	142	-		
	←	279	139.5	
2	137		←	136
	←	265	132.5	
3	128		←	131.5
	←	261	130.5	
4	133		←	132
	←	267	133.5	
5	134		←	133.5
	←	267	133.5	
6	133		←	132.5
	←	263	131.5	
7	130			

Clearly there is a downward trend.

Merits and Demerits of Method of Moving Averages

Merits

1. The method is simple to use and understand.
2. If the time series shows periodic variations, this method is highly effective in detecting the trend.

Demerits

1. This method cannot be used for forecasting since a mathematical relationship is not established.
2. The method does not provide the trend values at the beginning and at the end of the time series.
3. The method is not effective if the period of cyclical or seasonal variation is unknown or is not definite.

The Method of Least Squares

In this method, a mathematical relation of the type

$$y = a + bx$$

is fitted to the time series. Here y denotes the variable values, x denotes the time points. The constants 'a' and 'b' are obtained by solving the following equations.

$$na + b\sum x = \sum y$$
$$a\sum x + b\sum x^2 = \sum xy$$

The above equations are called the **normal equations**. Here, y denotes the observed values, x denotes time points and n denotes the number of time points. If x is chosen such that $\sum x = 0$, the above normal equations reduce to

$$a = \frac{\sum y}{n}$$

$$\text{and} \quad b = \frac{\sum xy}{\sum x^2}$$

Note:

If n is *odd*, then the middlemost time point is designated the origin $(x = 0)$. Then the time points after the origin are designated 1, 2, 3,... while the time points before the origin are designated −1, −2, −3 etc., are the time scale.

If n is *even*, the time series is divided into two halves. The upper half of the time series are designated −1, −3, −5 etc., while in the lower half time points are designated 1, 3, 5 etc.

In both the cases, changing the time scale so makes $\sum x = 0$ and we can easily use the formulae

$$a = \frac{\sum y}{n} \quad \text{and} \quad b = \frac{\sum xy}{\sum x^2}$$

to get 'a' and 'b'.

8. The following table relates to profits (in million rupees) of a company. Fit a straight line trend and estimate the profit for the year 2010.

Year	Profit
2000	18
2001	20
2002	23
2003	25
2004	24
2005	28
2006	30

SOLUTION:

Let the straight line trend be $y = a + bx$. Note that the number of time points 7 (odd).

Year	Time scale x	Value y	xy	x^2
2000	−3	18	−54	9
2001	−2	20	−40	4
2002	−1	23	−23	1
2003	0	25	0	0
2004	1	24	24	1
2005	2	28	56	4
2006	3	30	90	9
	$\sum x = 0$	$\sum y = 168$	$\sum xy = 53$	$\sum x^2 = 28$

In the method of least squares, we know that if $\sum x = 0$,

$$a = \frac{\sum y}{n} \quad \text{and} \quad b = \frac{\sum xy}{\sum x^2}$$

$$a = \frac{168}{7} \quad \text{and} \quad b = \frac{53}{28}$$

$$\text{i.e.,} \quad \boxed{a = 24} \quad \text{and} \quad \boxed{b = 1.893}$$

Hence, the straight line trend is

$$y = 24 + 1.893x$$

Now, to estimate the profits for the year 2010, $(x = 7)$

Substituting $x = 7$ in the above equation, we have

$$y = 24 + 1.893(7)$$

$$\boxed{y = 37.251}$$

i.e., the estimated profit for the year 2010 is 37.251 million rupees.

9. Fit a straight line by the method of least squares to the following data.

Year	1994	1995	1996	1997	1998	1999
Value	300	700	600	800	900	1000

SOLUTION:

Note that the no. of time points is 6—an even number. Hence, we use the following time scale, such that $\sum x = 0$

Year	**Time scale *x***	**Value *y***	***xy***	x^2	**Trend values** $y = a + bx$
1994	−5	300	−1500	25	409.57
1995	−3	700	−2100	9	532.41
1996	−1	600	−600	1	655.25
1997	+1	800	800	1	778.07
1998	+3	900	2700	9	900.93
1999	+5	1000	5000	25	1023.77
	$\sum x = 0$	$\sum y = 4300$	$\sum xy = 4300$	$\sum x^2 = 70$	

We are to fit a straight line of the form

$$Y = a + bx$$

Here since $\sum x = 0$; we have

$$a = \frac{\sum' y}{n} \quad \text{and} \quad b = \frac{\sum' xy}{\sum' x^2}$$

$$a = \frac{4300}{6} \quad \text{and} \quad b = \frac{4300}{70}$$

$$\text{i.e.,} \quad \boxed{a = 716.67} \quad \text{and} \quad \boxed{b = 61.42}$$

Hence, the trend line is given by

$$y = 716.67 + 61.42x$$

The trend values are found as follows.

For year 1994, $x = -5$

$$\text{Hence, } y = 716.67 + 61.42(-5) = 409.57$$

For year 1995, $x = -3$

$$\text{and hence, } y = 716.67 + 61.42(-3) = 532.41$$

and so on.

Merits and Demerits of Least Squares Method

Merits

1. This method is mathematical and hence is highly efficient.
2. It is useful in predicting future trend values.

Demerits

1. The procedure of calculation is difficult.
2. The general form of the relationship, has to be ascertained priorly by judgement.
3. If fresh data is available, the entire procedure has to be repeated.

IN A NUTSHELL

- Time series is a chronological arrangement of statistical data regarding a phenomenon.
- The components of a time series are: (a) secular trend (b) cyclical variational (c) seasonal variation and (d) irregular variation
- Secular trend is upward, downward or constant movement of the observations in the long run.
- Trend is measured using method of moving averages, method of least squares, free hand method and semi-averages method.
- The method of least squares is the most robust of them all. It involves fitting of a mathematical relation of the type $y = a + bx$. The constants '*a*' and '*b*' are found by solving the normal equations.

CHECK YOUR PROGRESS

1. Define time series?
2. What are the components of the time series?
3. What do you mean by analysis of time series?

4. What is secular trend?
5. What is seasonal variation? Give examples.
6. What is cyclical variation?
7. How is seasonal variation measured?
8. What is irregular variation?
9. How is secular trend measured? Discuss the various methods.
10. What are the merits and demerits of method of moving averages?
11. How is the method of semi averages an improvement over the free hand method? What are its demerits?
12. What are the uses of times series analysis?
13. Explain the centering procedure in the method of moving averages.

PROBLEMS

1. Find the trend by the method of free hand and method of semi averages for the following.

Year	1	2	3	4	5	6	7	8
Value	25	26	24	27	26	29	28	30

2. Find the trend by the free hand and method of semi average for the following.

Year	2000	2001	2002	2003	2004	2005	2006
Profit (in Cr. Rs.)	7	9	8	12	10	14	13

3. Calculate the trend values by moving averages (5-yearly) method and plot the actual and trend values on a graph from the following data:

Year	1986	87	88	89	90	91	92	93	94	95	96	97
Consumption units	20	28	36	48	44	40	52	68	76	56	52	48

4. Calculate trend values for the above data using 3-yearly moving averages.

5. Using a 3-yearly moving averages determine the trend values.

Year	Production (in '00 units)
1995	210
1996	220
1997	230
1998	240
1999	250
2000	260
2001	270
2002	280

6. Determine trend values using 4-year moving averages. Plot the historigram and the trend values.

Year	Value	Year	Value
1994	75	2000	96
1995	62	2001	128
1996	76	2002	116
1997	78	2003	76
1998	94	2004	102
1999	84	2005	168

7. Find the trend values using 6-yearly moving averages for the above data.
8. Fit a straight line trend by the method of least squares and obtain the trend value for the following data.

Year	Sales (in crores)
2000	24
2001	20
2002	28
2003	22
2004	26
2005	30
2006	32

$$\begin{bmatrix} a = 26 \\ b = 1.5 \end{bmatrix}$$

9. Fit a straight line trend by the method of least squares.

Year	Profit (in lakhs of Rs.)
2000	60
2001	72
2002	65
2003	75
2004	85
2005	80
2006	95

$$\left[\begin{array}{l} a = 76 \\ b = 5.035 \end{array}\right]$$

10. From the data given below, calculate the trend values by least squares method and estimate sales for the year 2005.

Year	Sales (000 units)
1996	100
1997	105
1998	109
1999	96
2000	102
2001	108

$$\left[\begin{array}{l} a = 103.3 \\ b = 0.26 \\ y_{2005} = 106.68 \end{array}\right]$$

13

Correlation and Regression

In the first five units, we analysed univariate distributions, i.e., data relating to a single variable. In the unit 'time series', we analysed two variables, one of which was necessarily 'time'. In this unit, we consider the simultaneous variation in any two or more variables. For example, if we measure 'heights' and 'weights' of students in a class, we get what is known as a bivariate distribution.

It is easy and simple to give many examples of inherently related variables as shown in the Table below.

Variable 1	Variable 2	Type of relation
Annual profit	Annual sale	Direct
Marks	Hours of study	Direct
Sales	Expenditure on advertising	Direct
Demand for a commodity	Price of the commodity	Indirect
Yield of crops	Amount of rainfall	Direct
Volume of perfect gas	Volume of a perfect gas	Indirect

Almost always, the variables listed under Variable-2 can be measured with negligible error and indeed are often controlled in the experiments or observed phenomena. The variables listed under Variable-1 are the responses and are dependent on the Variable-2. Thus, we may call them **'dependent'** and **'independent variables'** respectively.

In the language of physics, they have an **'effect'** and **'cause'** relation. The type of relation between them may be **direct** or **positive** in the sense that an increase (or decrease) in one variable results in corresponding increase (or decrease) in the other or it may be **indirect** or **inverse** when an increase (or decrease) in one variable results in corresponding decrease (or increase) in the other. The methods of expressing the relation between two variables were first developed by British biometricians Sir Francis Galton (1822–1911) and Karl Pearson (1857–1936)

Under the bivariate setup, let X and Y denote the two variables of interest. For example, X: yield of paddy, and Y: amount of fertilizers used. Mainly, there are two problems. The first is to find a measure of *intensity* or *degree of interdependence*, or **correlation** as it is called, between the two variables. The second problem is to find the most suitable form of equation for use in predicting the **average value** of the dependent variable, given the value of the independent variable and to estimate the error in the predicted value. This is called the problem of **regression**. It is obvious that the two problems are closely connected.

To sum up: Regression and correlation analyses show us how to determine both the **nature** and **strength** of a relationship between two variables.

CORRELATION

Two variables X and Y are said to be correlated when a change in one results in a corresponding change in the other. In particular, the variables are said to be **positively** or **directly** correlated if an increase (or decrease) results in a corresponding increase (or decrease) in the other. And, they are said to be **negatively** or **indirectly correlated** if an increase (or decrease) in one results in a corresponding decrease (or increase) in the other.

Correlation can be linear or curlinear **and** simple, partial or multiple. We shall discuss the case of simple linear correlation. A detailed discussion on the other types is beyond the scope of this book.

MEASURING CORRELATION

Correlation analysis attempts to measure the *strength, intensity* or *degree* of relationships between two variables by means of a single number called a **correlation co-efficient**. Correlation co-efficient between two variables X and Y is denoted by 'r_{xy}' or simply 'r'. Broadly speaking, there are two methods of finding the correlation co-efficient 'r'.

(a) Graphical method – the Scatter diagram
(b) Algebraic method – the Karl Pearson's formula and the Spearman's formula for rank correlation.

Scatter Diagram

Data on related variables X and Y can be represented graphically as a set of 'n' points, i.e., $\{(x_i, y_i); i = 1, 2, \ldots, n\}$ on a graph. The two variables are taken along one each of the two axes on the xy-plane and the data on the 'n' pairs of observations are plotted as 'n' points on the graph paper. This gives us **a dot diagram** or a **scatter diagram** which provides us an initial tool for analysis of related variables. It helps us to judge the nature and the type of relation between the variables.

If in the scatter diagram, the plotted points:

(i) cluster around a line with a positive slope, the two variables X and Y are positively correlated. Here $r > 0$ [as in Fig. 13.1(a)]

(ii) cluster around a line with a negative slope, the two variables are negatively or inversely correlated. Here $r < 0$ as in Fig. 13.1 (b)]

(iii) fall exactly on a line with positive slope, there exists a positively perfect correlation between the variable. Here $r = +1$ [as in Fig. 13.1 (c)]

(iv) fall exactly on a line with negative slope, the two variables are perfectly inversely correlated. Here $r = -1$ [as in Fig. 13.1 (d)]

(v) are spread all over the graph with no particular pattern the variables are uncorrelated and $r = 0$ [as in Fig. 13.1 (e)]

(vi) follow any other pattern (other than a straight line) there exists a **curvilinear** correlation. Since 'r' is measure of linear correlation, no statement regarding 'r' is made [as in Fig. 13.1 (f)]

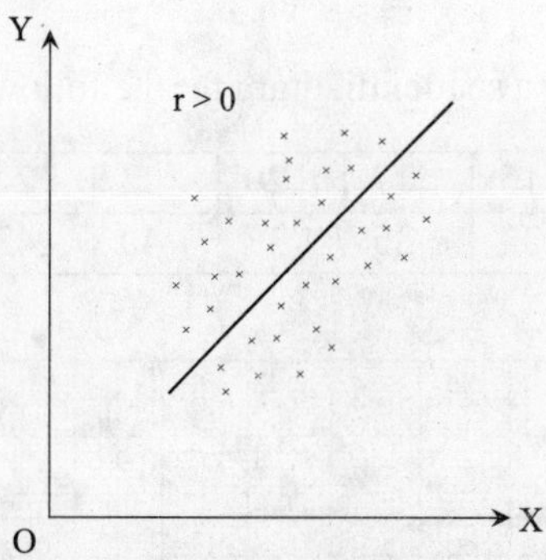

(a) Positive correlation

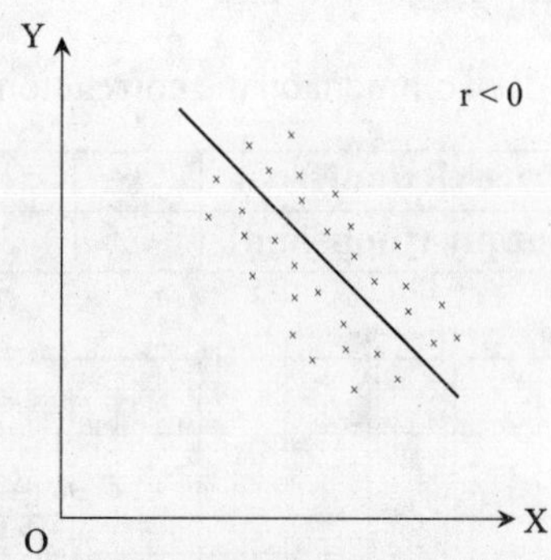

(b) Negative correlation

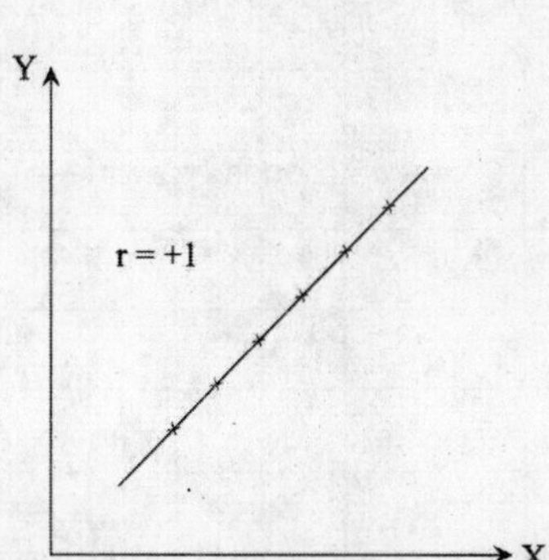

(c) Perfect Positive correlation

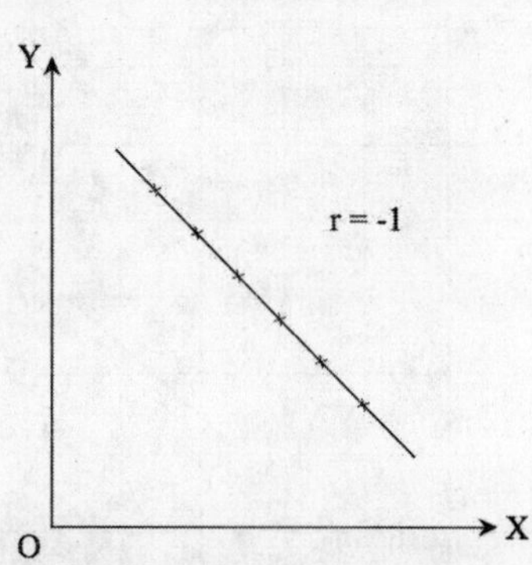

(d) Perfect Negative correlation

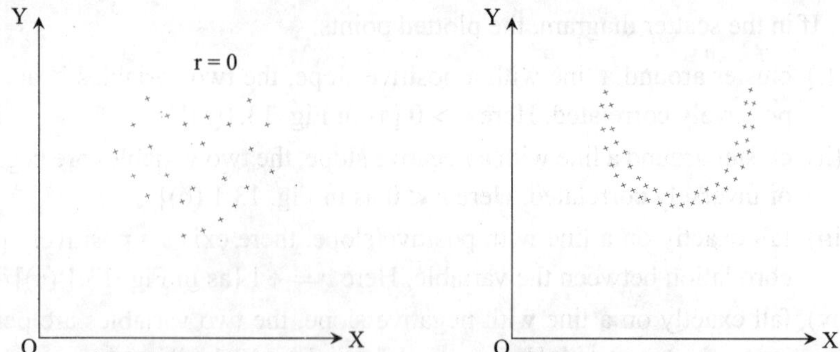

(e) No correlation (f) Curvilinear correlation

Fig. 13.1. Types of correlation

Remark: Scatter diagram only gives a vague idea about the extent of correlation between X and Y. Hence, the need for a more precise algebraic method.

SOLVED EXAMPLES

1. Comment on the correlation using a scatter diagram for the following data:

Price (Rs/unit)	8	10	15	17	20	22	24	25
Supply (thousand)	25	30	32	35	37	40	42	45

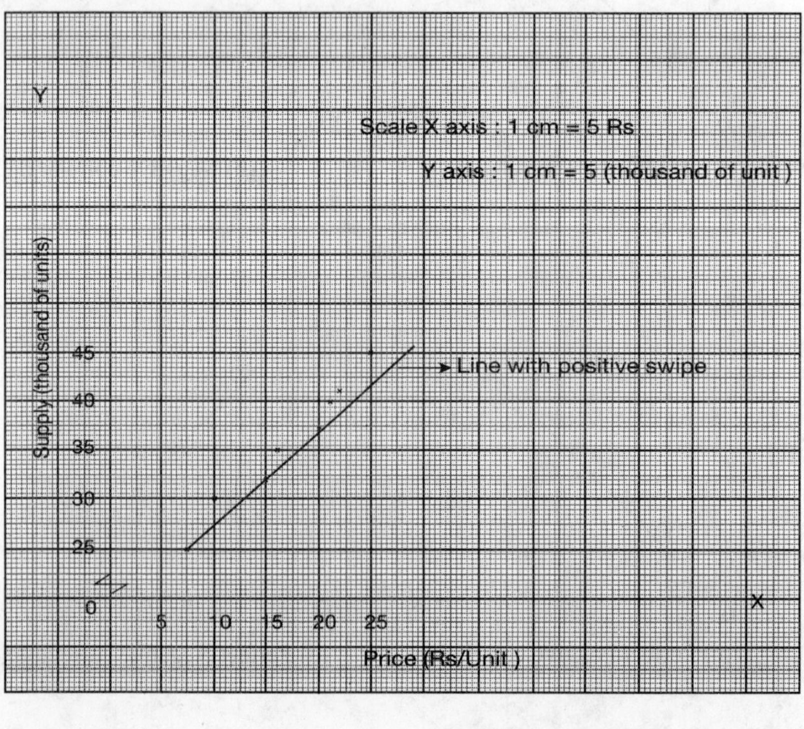

Comment: Since the plotted points cluster around a line with a positive slope, 'price' and 'supply' are positively correlated.

KARL PEARSON'S CO-EFFICIENT OF CORRELATION (PRODUCT MOMENT CORRELATION CO-EFFICIENT)

By far, the most commonly used measure of degree of linear relationship between two variables, X and Y, is due to Karl Pearson and is defined for a sample of 'n' observations by

$$r_{xy} = \frac{\text{Cov}\,(X,Y)}{SD(X)\;SD(Y)}$$

$$= \frac{\frac{1}{n}\Sigma(x-\bar{x})(y-\bar{y})}{\sqrt{\frac{1}{n}\Sigma(x-\bar{x})^2 \cdot \frac{1}{n}\Sigma(y-\bar{y})^2}}$$

$$= \frac{\Sigma(x-\bar{x})(y-\bar{y})}{\sqrt{\Sigma(x-\bar{x})^2 \cdot \Sigma(y-\bar{y})^2}}$$

For computation purpose, we use the following simplified formula.

$$r = \frac{n\sum xy - \sum x \sum y}{\sqrt{[n\sum x^2 - (\sum x)^2][n\sum y^2 - (\sum y)^2]}} \quad \text{for raw data}$$

Interpretation of r

1. If r is a positive value, it indicates a positive correlation between X and Y
2. If r is a negative value, it indicates a negative correlation
3. If $r = 0$, then the two variables are uncorrelated
4. Closer the value of r to ± 1, stronger the correlation.

Remark: 'r' is only a measure of linear association and practically nothing about non-linear associations is conveyed. Thus, if $r = 0$, we merely say X and Y are uncorrelated. This does not necessarily imply that they are independent. i.e., it does not rule out other kinds of functional associations.

Properties of r

1. It is a number free from the units of measurement.
2. It lies between -1 and $+1$. That is, $r^2 \leq 1$
3. It is independent of the origin of reference and scale of measurement.

Thus, if

$$u = \frac{x - A}{h} \quad \text{and} \quad v = \frac{y - B}{k}$$

where A, B, h, k are specified constants, $r_{uv} = r_{xy}$

Remark: An important practical implication of this property of 'r' is that the computational arithmetic is reduced to a great extent by a suitable change in origin and scale.

2. Calculate the product moment co-efficient of correlation between marks in statistics (X) and marks in computer science (Y)

x	65	66	67	67	68	69	70	72
y	67	68	65	68	72	72	69	71

SOLUTION:

x	y	x^2	y^2	xy
65	67	4225	4489	4355
66	68	4356	4624	4488
67	65	4489	4225	4355
67	68	4489	4625	4556
68	72	4624	5184	4896
69	72	4761	5184	4968
70	69	4900	4761	4830
72	71	5184	5041	5112
$\Sigma x = 544$	$\Sigma y = 552$	$\Sigma x^2 = 37028$	$\Sigma y^2 = 38132$	$\Sigma xy = 37560$

Here $n = 8$

$$r = \frac{n\Sigma xy - \Sigma x \Sigma y}{\sqrt{[n\Sigma x^2 - (\Sigma x)^2][n\Sigma y^2 - (\Sigma y)^2]}}$$

$$= \frac{8(37560) - (544)(552)}{\sqrt{[(8)(37028) - (544)^2][(8)(38132) - (552)^2]}} = \mathbf{0.603}$$

There is positive correlation between marks in Statistics and marks in Computer Science.

3. Calculate Karl Pearson's co-efficient between X and Y from the following:

x	1640	1760	1780	1840	1750	1670	1730	1800
y	1680	1740	1750	1810	1730	1660	1730	1790

SOLUTION:

We use the following table, where $u = \frac{x-A}{h} = \frac{x-1700}{10}$ and $v = \frac{y-B}{h} = \frac{y-1700}{10}$

x	y	$u = \frac{X-1700}{10}$	$v = \frac{Y-1700}{10}$	u^2	v^2	uv
1640	1680	−6	−2	36	4	12
1760	1740	+6	4	36	16	24
1780	1750	8	5	64	25	40
1840	1810	14	11	196	121	154
1750	1730	5	3	25	9	15
1670	1660	−3	−4	9	16	12
1730	1730	3	3	9	9	9
1800	1790	10	9	100	81	90
		$\sum u = 37$	$\sum v = 29$	$\sum u^2 = 475$	$\sum v^2 = 281$	$\sum uv = 356$

Here $n = 8$

Since 'r' is independent of the origin and scale of measurement.

We have

$$r_{xy} = r_{uv} = \frac{n\sum uv - \sum u \sum v}{\sqrt{[n\sum u^2 - (\sum u)^2][n\sum v^2 - (\sum v)^2]}}$$

$$= \frac{8(356) - (37)(29)}{\sqrt{[8(475) - (37)^2][8(281) - (29)^2]}}$$

$$= \mathbf{0.9598}$$

There is a high degree of positive correlation between X and Y.

SPEARMAN'S CO-EFFICIENT OF RANK CORRELATION

When the data is qualitative in nature or if it is possible to assign ranks to the given quantitative data, we use rank correlation co-efficient, ρ (rho).

(a) Case of no Ties

Let us first assume that no two units, are ranked equal. Thus if there are 'n' pairs of observations let $R(x)$ and $R(y)$ denote the ranks in the respective series—both $R(x)$ and $R(y)$ assume natural numbers $1, 2 \ldots, n$ though possibly in different orders. Then, the co-efficient of correlation is given by

$$\rho = 1 - \left[\frac{6\sum d_i^2}{n(n^2-1)}\right]$$

$$\text{where} \quad d_i = R(x) - R(y)$$

'ρ' possesses all the properties of '*r*' and the interpreations are the same. This is because the above formula for 'ρ' is simply the Karl Pearson's correlation co-efficient with ranks treated as variables and noting the facts that

$$\sum x = \sum y = \frac{n(n+1)}{2}$$

$$\text{and} \quad \sum x^2 = \sum y^2 = \frac{n(n+1)(2n+1)}{6}$$

Remark: Note that

$$\begin{aligned}\sum d_i &= \sum[R(x) - R(y)]\\ &= \sum[R(x) - R(y)]\\ &= \sum x - \sum y\\ &= \frac{n(n+1)}{2} - \frac{n(n+1)}{2} = 0\end{aligned}$$

This serves as a check while solving problems.

4. In a singing competition 6 candidates were ranked by two judges as follows. Compute co-efficient of rank correlation and interpret.

Candidate	1	2	3	4	5	6
Rank by Judge A	3	4	5	6	1	2
Rank by Judge B	4	3	5	6	2	1

SOLUTION:

Candidate	$R(x)$	$R(y)$	$d = R(x) - R(y)$	d^2
1	3	4	−1	1
2	4	3	1	1
3	5	5	0	0
4	6	6	0	0
5	1	2	−1	1
6	2	1	1	1
$n = 6$			$\sum d = 0$ (check)	$\sum d^2 = 4$

The co-efficient of rank correlation,

$$\rho = 1 - \left[\frac{6\sum d^2}{n(n^2-1)}\right]$$

$$= 1 - \left[\frac{6(4)}{6(6^2-1)}\right]$$

$$= \mathbf{0.886}$$

This indicates a close agreement in the opinions of Judges *A* and *B* w.r.t singing abilities.

5. The following are the marks of 8 students in Computer Science and Statistics. Find the co-efficient of rank correlation and interpret.

Marks in C.S.	65	54	86	75	90	68	70	81
Marks in Statistics	55	60	82	80	94	72	69	75

SOLUTION:

We use the following table and note that $n = 8$

x	y	$R(x)$	$R(y)$	$d = R(x) - R(y)$	d^2
65	55	2	1	1	1
54	60	1	2	–1	1
86	82	7	7	0	0
75	80	5	6	–1	1
90	94	8	8	0	0
68	72	3	3	0	0
70	69	4	4	0	0
81	75	6	5	1	1
				$\sum d = 0$ (check)	$\sum d^2 = 4$

Spearman's rank correlation co-efficient,

$$\rho = 1 - \left[\frac{6\sum d^2}{n(n^2-1)}\right]$$

$$= 1 - \left[\frac{6(4)}{8(8^2-1)}\right]$$

$$= \mathbf{0.9523}$$

This indicates a high degree of linear dependence of between marks in C.S. and marks in statistics.

(b) Case of Ties

If, while assigning ranks to the observations, we find that they are repeated, there arises a case of ties among ranks. Hence, we cannot use the Spearman's rank correlation directly. In this case a common rank, which is the arithmetic means of the ranks the items would have got had they been slightly different from each other, is assigned to the repeated observations. However, the next item will get the rank next to the ranks already assumed. This necessitates a correction factor $\frac{m(m^2-1)}{12}$ to be added to $\sum d^2$ in the formula for 'ρ', where m is the number of times an item has repeated. Note that this correction is to be applied for each repeated value.

Hence, in case of ties.

$$\rho = 1 - \frac{6(\sum d^2 + CF)}{n(n^2-1)}$$

where $d = R(x) - R(y)$

$n =$ No. of pairs of observations

$CF = \frac{m(m^2-1)}{12}$ for each repeated observation

$m =$ no. of times an observation repeats.

6. Calculate rank correlation co-efficient for the following:

x	48	33	40	9	16	16	65	24	16	57
y	13	13	24	6	15	4	20	9	6	19

SOLUTION:

We use the following table:

x	y	$R(x)$	$R(y)$	$d = R(x) - R(y)$	d^2
48	13	8	5.5	2.5	6.25
33	13	6	5.5	0.5	0.25
40	24	7	10	−3	9.00
9	6	1	2.5	−1.5	2.25
16	15	3	7	4	16.00
16	4	3	1	2	4.00
65	20	10	9	1	1.00
24	9	5	4	1	1.00
16	6	3	2.5	0.5	0.25
57	19	9	8	1	1.00
				$\sum d = 0$ (check)	$\sum d^2 = 41$

Assignment of rank: Notice that '16' is repeated thrice in the X series and the ranks they would have got had they been slightly different from each other are 2, 3 and 4. Hence, the A.M. of 2,3 and 4, viz., 3 is assigned to all the three 16's. Similarly, rank 2.5 is assigned to the two 6's and rank 5.5 to the two 13's in Y series.

Also $m = 3$ for 16; $m = 2$ for 6 and $m = 2$ for 13

$$\rho = \left[1 - \frac{6(\sum d^2 + CF)}{n(n^2 - 1)}\right]$$

$$= 1 - \frac{6\left[\sum d^2 + \frac{m(m^2-1)}{12} + \frac{m(m^2-1)}{12} + \frac{m(m^2-1)}{12}\right]}{n(n^2-1)}$$

$$= 1 - \frac{6\left[41 + \frac{3(3^2-1)}{12} + \frac{2(2^2-1)}{12} + \frac{2(2^2-1)}{12}\right]}{10(10^2-1)} = \mathbf{0.7333}$$

Hence, X and Y are positively correlated variables.

Co-efficient of Determination

The quantity $100\ r^2$, where 'r' is Karl Pearsons correlation co-efficient, is called the co-efficient of determination. It represents the percentage of variation in the dependent variable explained by its linear association with the independent variable. For example, let Y be a dependent variable on the independent variable X and let $r_{xy} = 0.7$. Then $100r^2 = 49$ and we conclude that the linear association with X is responsible for 49% of the variation in Y. The remaining 51% of the variation is to be attributed to other factors.

Probable Error of Correlation Co-efficient

If r is the correlation co-efficient between two variable X and Y in a sample of n pairs of observations, then the probable error is given by

$$\text{P.E.}(r) = 0.6745\frac{(1-r^2)}{\sqrt{n}}$$

Probable error is a measure used for testing the reliability of observed correlation co-efficient.

If $r \leq 6$ PE(r) then correlation is said to be insignificant.

If $r > 6$ PE(r) then correlation is said to be significant.

Probable error also enables us to find the limits within which the correlation co-efficient can be expected to vary. The limits are $r \pm \text{PE}(r)$.

Correlation, Causation and Spurious Correlation

The interpretation of 'r' as a measure of linear association between two variables is purely a mathematical one and is completely devoid of any cause and effect implication. Correlation only establishes *covariation*. In other words, all by itself, correlation does not manifest **causation** or functional relationship. In order to establish causation and functional relationships, we have to go beyond the confines of statistical analysis to other fields of knowledge. For example, there is a high degree of positive correlation between the hardness of a metal and its tensile strength. But this does not establish that hardness **causes** tensile strength. The cause may lie elsewhere.

Correlation in the absence of a 'cause and effect' relationship is called **'spurious correlation'** or 'nonsense correlation'. To illustrate this concept, we consider the possible correlation between the following pairs of variables.

1. The number of crows and crime rate in a city
2. The height and IQ of students
3. No. of inmates in the institution for the insane and teacher's salary.

REGRESSION ANALYSIS

Regression analysis deals with the methods of estimating the unknown value of one variable with the help of known values of a correlated variables. The estimated value obtained may not exactly be equal to the observed value, but it will be close to the actual value. This property of the tendency of the actual value to lie close to the estimated values is called **'regression'**.

There is one important distinction between regression and correlation. Regression assumes a 'cause and effect' relation between the variables. For instance let X: amount of fertilizers used and Y: the yield of paddy, be two variables. Clearly Y depends on X. Change in the value of X causes a change in value of Y. Thus Y is the **explained variable** and X is the **explanatory** variable. In the terminology of regression analysis, Y is called the regress and X is the regressor.

Unlike this, we have noted earlier, correlation analysis does not assume any cause and effect relation, i.e., in correlation, it is immaterial as to which of the variables is dependent and which is independent (note that $r_{xy} = r_{yx}$)

The Regression Lines

Give two correlated variables, X and Y, the mathematical relation, called the regression equation, we get by assuming that X is dependent on Y is called the regression of X on Y and is given by,

$$(X-\bar{x}) = b_{xy}(Y-\bar{y}) \tag{1}$$

The regression equation we get by assuming that Y is dependent on X is called the regression of Y on X and is given by,

$$(Y-\bar{y}) = b_{xy}(X-\bar{x}) \tag{2}$$

The two equations are obtained using the principle of least squares discussed in the chapter. Curve fitting. The constants b_{xy} and b_{yx} are called regression co-efficients and are given by,

$$b_{xy} = r\cdot\frac{\sigma_x}{\sigma_y} \quad \text{and} \quad b_{yx} = r\cdot\frac{\sigma_y}{\sigma_x} \tag{3}$$

where $\sigma_x =$ standard deviation of series x

$\sigma_y =$ standard deviation of series y

$r =$ correlation co-efficient

For computation purpose, we use the following formulae,

$$b_{xy} = \frac{n\sum xy - \sum x\sum y}{n\sum y^2 - (\sum y)^2} \tag{4}$$

and $$b_{yx} = \frac{n\sum xy - \sum x\sum y}{n\sum x^2 - (\sum x)^2} \tag{5}$$

Remark: The graph of the regression equations are called the **regression lines.**

Properties of Regression Lines

There are two regression lines — the regression line of X on Y and the regression line of Y and X. They possess the following properties.

1. The two lines intersect at $(\bar{x}, \bar{y})$.
2. The two regression lines have a positive slope if the two variables are positively correlated. They have a negative slope if there exists a negative correlation between the variables.
3. The two regression lines coincide if there is perfect correlation and they are perpendicular to each other if the two variables are uncorrelated.

Properties of Regression Co-efficients

The regression co-efficients b_{xy} and b_{yx} have the following properties:

1. They are independent of the change in the origin of reference but are dependent on the scale of measurement.
2. The geometric mean of the two regression co-efficients is numerically equal to correlation co-efficient

   $$\text{i.e.,} \quad \sqrt{b_{xy}\, b_{yx}} = |r|$$

3. Two regression co-efficient b_{yx} and b_{xy}, and the correlation co-efficient r, are all positive, zero or negative together.
   i.e., if r is positive, then b_{xy} and b_{yx} are positive.
   if r is zero, then b_{yx} and b_{xy} are zero.
   if r is negative, then b_{yx} and b_{xy} are negative.
4. Since $r^2 \leq 1$, then $b_{yx} \cdot b_{xy} \leq 1$, i.e., the product of two regression co-efficients cannot be greater than 1.
5. The regression co-efficient b_{xy} is the change occurring is X for a unit change in $Y \cdot b_{yx}$ is the change occurring in Y for unit change in X.

7. The following table gives the age of cars of a certain make and annual maintenance costs. (i) Obtain the two regression equations, (ii) What would be the cost of maintenance given that the car is 5 years old.

Age of cars (in years)	2	4	6	8
Maintenance cost (in hundreds of Rs.)	10	20	25	30

SOLUTION:

(i) Let X: age of cars in years and, Y: maintenance cost

We use the following table

x	y	x^2	y^2	xy
2	10	4	100	20
4	20	16	400	80
6	25	36	625	150
8	30	64	900	240
$\Sigma x = 20$	$\Sigma y = 85$	$\Sigma x^2 = 120$	2025	490

Here $n = 4$

$$\bar{x} = \frac{\sum x}{n} = \frac{20}{4} = 5 \text{ years}$$

$$\bar{y} = \frac{\sum y}{n} = \frac{85}{4} = 21.25 \text{ (hundred Rs.)}$$

The co-efficient of regression,

$$b_{xy} = \frac{n\sum xy - \sum x \sum y}{n\sum y^2 - (\sum y)^2}$$

$$= \frac{4(490) - (20)(85)}{4(2025) - (85)^2} = 0.297$$

and

$$b_{yx} = \frac{n\sum xy - \sum x \sum y}{n\sum x^2 - (\sum x)^2}$$

$$= \frac{4(490) - (20)(85)}{4(120) - (20)^2} = 3.25$$

Hence, the regression line of X on Y is

$$(X - \bar{x}) = b_{xy}(Y - \bar{y})$$

i.e.,

$$(X - 5) = 0.297 + (Y - 21.25)$$

$\Rightarrow$

$$\mathbf{X = 0.297Y - 1.31}$$

and the regression line of Y on X is

$$(Y - \bar{y}) = b_{yx}(X - \bar{x})$$

$$(Y - 21.25) = 3.25(X - 5)$$

$\Rightarrow$

$$\mathbf{Y = 3.25X + 5}$$

(ii) To calculate the cost of maintenance when the age of case is 5 years (i.e., given $X = 5$, $Y = ?$). We use the regression of Y on X

$$Y = 3.25X + 5$$

Substituting $X = 5$, we get

$$Y = 3.25(5) + 5$$

$$= \mathbf{21.25 \text{ (in hundred Rs.)}}$$

8. Find the lines of regression using the following. Hence, estimate the value of Y when $X = 30$ and of X when $Y = 16$.

x	21	23	24	28	29	31	34
y	11	12	14	15	17	18	19

SOLUTION:

We use the following table where $A = 28$ and $B = 15$

x	y	$u = x - A$	$v = Y - B$	u^2	v^2	uv
21	11	−7	−4	49	16	28
23	12	−5	−3	25	9	15
24	14	−4	−1	16	1	4
28	15	0	0	0	0	0
29	17	1	2	4	4	2
31	18	3	3	9	9	9
34	19	6	4	6	16	24
		$\sum u = -6$	$\sum v = 1$	$\sum u^2 = 136$	$\sum v^2 = 55$	$\sum uv = 82$

Here $n = 4$

$$\bar{x} = A + \frac{\sum u}{n}$$

$$= 28 + \frac{(-6)}{7} = 27.14$$

$$\bar{y} = B + \frac{\sum v}{n}$$

$$= 15 + \frac{1}{7} = 15.14$$

$$b_{xy} = b_{uv} = \frac{n\sum uv - \sum u \cdot \sum v}{n\sum v^2 - (\sum v)^2}$$

$$= \frac{7(82) - (-6)(1)}{7(136) - (-6)^2} = 0.6332$$

Hence, the regression of X and Y is

$$(X - \bar{x}) = b_{xy}(Y - \bar{y})$$

i.e., $$(X - 27.14) = 1.5104(Y - 15.14)$$

i.e., $$\mathbf{X = 1.5104Y + 4.2725}$$

and the regression of Y on X is

$$(Y - \bar{y}) = b_{yx}(X - \bar{x})$$

$$(Y-15.14)=0.6332(X-27.14)$$

i.e., $\mathbf{Y=0.6332X-2.045}$

To estimate the value of Y when $X=30$, we use the regression of Y on X, i.e.,

$$Y=0.6332X-2.045$$

Substituting $X=30$, we get

$$Y=0.6332(30)-2.045$$

$$=\mathbf{16.951}$$

To estimate the value of X when $Y=16$, we use the regression of X on Y i.e.,

$$X=1.5104Y+4.2725$$

$$=1.5104(16)+4.2725$$

$$=\mathbf{28.4389}$$

9. In a partially destroyed record, only the following results are available. Regression equations: $8x-11y=6$; $40x-18y=214$, variance of $X=9$. Find out:

(i) the mean values of X and Y

(ii) the correlation between X and Y

(iii) the standard deviation of Y

SOLUTION:

(i) Since the two regression lines intersects at $(\overline{x},\overline{y})$ the mean values of X and Y are obtained by simultaneously solving the regression equations for x and y.

The equations are

$$8x-11y=6 \quad (1)$$

$$40x-18y=214 \quad (2)$$

Multiplying (1) by 5 and subtracting (2) from it, we get

$$40x-55y=30$$

$$40x-18y=214$$

$$-\quad+\quad-$$

$$-37Y=-184$$

$\Rightarrow$ $y=\mathbf{4.973}$

Substituting the value of y in (1), we get

$$8x - 11(4.973) = 6$$

$$\Rightarrow \qquad \mathbf{x = 7.589}$$

Hence, the mean values of X and Y are $\bar{x} = 7.589$ and $\bar{y} = 4.973$

(ii) To find the correlation between X and Y:

$$\text{we know that } |r| = \sqrt{b_{xy} \cdot b_{yx}}$$

Hence, we need to find b_{xy} and b_{yx} from the regression equation. But we do not know which of the regression equations is the regression of X on Y and which of them is the regression of Y on X. Let us assume (1) to be the regression of X on Y. Then it must be of the form,

$$X = b_{xy}\, Y + c \tag{3}$$

i.e.,

$$8X - 11Y = 6$$

$$X = \frac{11}{8}Y + \frac{6}{8} \tag{4}$$

Comparing (3) and (4), we get

$$b_{xy} = \frac{11}{8} = 1.375$$

If (2) is the regression of y on x

$$Y = b_{yx}\, X + c_2 \tag{5}$$

i.e.,

$$40X - 18Y = 214$$

$$Y = \frac{40}{18}x - \frac{214}{40} \tag{6}$$

Comparing (5) and (6), we get

$$b_{yx} = \frac{40}{18} = 2.22$$

Now,

$$|r| = \sqrt{b_{xy} \cdot b_{yx}}$$

$$= \sqrt{(1.375)(2.22)}$$

$$= \mathbf{1.74}$$

Since $r^2 > 1$, our assumptions regarding the regression equations should be changed as follows: (1) is the regression of Y on X. It must be of the form of (5)

Consider

$$8X - 11Y = 6$$

i.e.,

$$Y = \frac{8x}{11} - \frac{6}{11} \tag{7}$$

Comparing (5) and (7), we get

$$b_{yx} = \frac{8}{11} = 0.727$$

If (2) is the regression of X on Y, it must be from (3)

i.e., $$40X - 18Y = 214$$

$$x = \frac{18}{40}y + \frac{214}{40} \quad (8)$$

Comparing (3) and (8), we get

$$b_{xy} = \frac{18}{40} = 0.45$$

$$|r| = \sqrt{b_{xy}.b_{yx}}$$

$$= \sqrt{(0.45)(0.727)}$$

$$= \mathbf{0.572}$$

Since b_{xy} and b_{yx} are positive,

$$r = 0.572$$

(iii) To find standard deviation of Y:

Given $V(X) = 9$

$\Rightarrow$ $$\sigma_x = \sqrt{v(x)} = \sqrt{9} = 3$$

Also $$b_{yx} = r\frac{\sigma_y}{\sigma_x}$$

$\Rightarrow$ $$\sigma_y = \frac{b_{yx}\sigma_x}{r}$$

$$= \frac{(0.727)(3)}{0.572}$$

$$= \mathbf{3.812}$$

10. In a bivariate data, the regression co-efficients are -0.333 and -0.75. Find the co-efficient of correlation.

SOLUTION:

The numerical value of r is

$$|r| = \sqrt{b_{xy} \cdot b_{yx}}$$

$$= \sqrt{(-0.33)(-0.75)}$$

$$= \mathbf{0.5}$$

Since the regression co-efficients are negative, the correlation co-efficient also has to be negative. Hence, $r = -0.5$.

11. In a bivariate data, $\bar{x} = 20$, $\bar{y} = 15$, $\sigma_x = 4$, $\sigma_y = 3$ and $r = 0.7$. Obtain the two regression lines and estimate Y when $X = 24$.

SOLUTION:

The regression co-efficients

$$b_{xy} = r\frac{\sigma_x}{\sigma_y}$$

$$= \frac{0.7(4)}{3} = 0.933$$

and,

$$b_{yx} = r\frac{\sigma_y}{\sigma_x}$$

$$= (0.7) \times \left(\frac{3}{4}\right) = 0.525$$

The regression line of X on Y is

$$(X - \bar{x}) = b_{xy}(Y - \bar{y})$$

$$(X - 20) = 0.933(Y - 15)$$

i.e.,

$$\mathbf{X = 0.933Y + 6.005}$$

The regression line of Y on X is

$$(Y - \bar{y}) = b_{yx}(X - \bar{x})$$

$$(Y - 15) = 0.525(X - 20)$$

$$\mathbf{Y = 0.525x + 4.5}$$

To estimate the value of Y when $X = 24$, we use the regression of Y on X

i.e.,

$$Y = 0.525X + 4.5$$

$$= 0.525(24) + 4.5$$

$$= \mathbf{17.1}$$

IN A NUTSHELL

- Correlation analysis deals with the association between two or more variables. Correlation may be simple, multiple or partial and linear or curvilinear.
- Regression analysis is concerned with predicting the average value of the dependent variable, given the value of the independent variable.
- Statistical measures of correlation are proof only of a covariation between series, not of functional or casual relationship. Correlation in the absence of a cause and effect relation is called **spurious correlation**.

- The co-efficient of correlation, 'r' is a measure of linear association only. It is a value between -1 and $+1$. It is independent of the origin and scale of measurement.
- The scatter diagram is a simple visual aid and a basic tool in the analysis of bivariate data. It plots Y against X on the graph.
- The Karl Pearson's co-efficient 'r' is given by

$$r = \frac{n\sum xy - \sum x \sum y}{\sqrt{[n\sum x^2 - (\sum x)^2][n\sum y^2 - (\sum y)^2]}}$$

- The quantity $100r^2$, called the **co-efficient of determination**, represents the proportion of variation in dependent variable explained by the independent variable.
- The Spearman's rank correlation co-efficient is used in the qualtitiative characteristics or ranked data. It is just a modification of Karl Pearson's correlation co-efficient.
- The regression co-efficient of X on Y, b_{xy} is the rate of change in X for a unit change in Y.
- There are two regression lines and they intersect at $(\overline{x}, \overline{y})$.
- We use the regression of X on Y to estimate the value of X given a value of Y.

CHECK YOUR PROGRESS

1. What is correlation?
2. Explain briefly the various types of correlation.
3. What are scatter diagrams? What is their use in correlation analysis?
4. Give examples for related variables. Explain the regression and correlation problems. How do they differ from each other?
5. What are regressor and regressand variables? What is the relation between them?
6. List the various methods of measuring correlation.
7. Define Karl Pearson's co-efficient of correlation? What are its properties?
8. Define the rank correlation. When and how is it useful? How will you deal with the case of ties?
9. Define co-efficient of determination. What does it measure?
10. Write a note on probable error.
11. Explain the terms 'regression equations' and 'regression co-efficients'.
12. List the properties of regression co-efficients and regression lines.

13. In a bivariate data, $V(X) = 49$, $V(Y) = 81$ and Cov $(X,Y) = 12$. Find the co-efficient of correlation.

14. In a bivariate data, $\sum x = 30$, $\sum y = 400$, $\sum x^2 = 196, \sum y^2 = 46500$ and $n = 10$. Find the co-efficient of correlation.

15. In a bivariate data, $\sum(x-\bar{x})^2 = 412, \sum(y-\bar{y})^2 = 53$ and $\sum(x-\bar{x})(y-\bar{y}) = 47$. Find the co-efficient of correlation.

16. Calculate the co-efficient of correlation between X and Y.

x	30	32	34	35	36	37	38	40
y	11	12	14	12	18	22	29	31

17. Calculate the co-efficient of correlation between X and Y

x	15	16	14	19	20	22	24
y	32	33	30	31	29	25	32

18. The following data relates to the ages of wives and husbands. Calculate co-efficient of correlation.

Ages of wives	20	25	30	32	34	35	36	38
Ages of husbands	24	30	34	39	38	37	40	42

19. The following are the percentage marks scored by 7 students in computer science and statistics

Marks in computer science	36	43	47	28	35	50	40
Marks in statistics	73	44	35	30	20	36	40

(a) Calculate the product moment co-efficient of correlation.

(b) Calculate the co-efficient of rank correlation.

20. Calculate Spearman's rank correlation for the following data.

Student	1	2	3	4	5	6	7	8
Rank in sports	2	4	8	5	7	1	6	3
Rank in studies	1	3	5	7	3	4	8	2

21. Find the rank correlation co-efficient for the following:

(a)

x	2	5	7	6	8	1	3	4	9	10
y	4	6	8	5	9	2	1	3	7	10

(b)

X	1	2	3	4	5	6
y	2	1	5	3	4	6

22. The following are the marks of 10 B.C.A. Students in computer science (X) and mathematics(Y). Find the co-efficient of rank correlation:

x	43	96	74	38	35	43	22	56	35	80
y	30	94	84	38	30	18	30	41	48	95

23. Find the co-efficient of rank correlation for the following:

(a)

x	35	56	50	65	44	38	44	50	15	26
y	50	35	70	25	35	58	75	60	55	35

(b)

x	124	100	105	112	102	93	99	115	123	104	99	113	121	103	101
y	80	100	102	91	100	111	109	100	89	104	111	102	98	111	123

24. In a bivariate data, the regression co-efficients are 8.3 and 0.01. Find the co-efficient of correlation.

25. Following are the marks of 10 students in Mathematics (X) and Statistics(Y)

x	40	45	52	39	46	52	75	80	25	32
y	50	55	38	61	50	58	80	85	32	34

(i) Find the two regression equations.

(ii) Find the probable marks in Statistics of a person who has scored 84 in Mathematics.

(iii) Find the probable marks in Mathematics of a person who has scored 59 in Statistics.

26. Find the regression lines for the following data:

x	1	2	3	4	5
y	2	5	3	8	7

Estimate x when $y = 8$ and y when $x = 6$.

27. The regression lines between height(X) in inches and weight(Y) in lb of male students are $4y - 15x + 530 = 0$ and $20x - 3y - 975 = 0$

(i) Find the mean height and weight of weights of students.

(ii) Find the co-efficient of correlation.

(iii) Estimate the weight of a student when he is 60 inches tall.

28. In a bivariate data, the regression lines are $3x + 5y - 5 = 0$ and $4x + 3y - 4 = 0$. Find $\bar{x}$, $\bar{y}$ and 'r'.

29. The following data relates to the ages of husbands and wives.

	Husbands	Wives
Mean	26	24
S.D.	3	2

The co-efficient of correlation is $r = 0.91$. Find the age of a lady whose husband is 24 years old.

30. The following data relates to the prices of onions and potatoes per kg.

	Onions	Potatoes
Mean	6	8
S.D.	3	2

The co-efficient of correlation $r = 0.92$. Find the price of potatoes when the price of onion is Rs. 8/kg.

Index